FUJIMORI'S PERU:

THE POLITICAL ECONOMY

Edited by

John Crabtree
and
Jim Thomas

Institute of Latin American Studies
31 Tavistock Square, London WC1H 9HA

In memory of Sylvia (1909-98)

Institute of Latin American Studies
School of Advanced Study
University of London

British Library Cataloguing-in-Publication Data
A catalogue record for this book is available
from the British Library

ISBN   1 900039 25 7

Institute of Latin American Studies
University of London, 1998

CONTENTS

CONCLUSIONS

Acknowledgements

Special thanks need to go to the Director and staff of the Institute of Latin American Studies, for their role in organising the original conference and their encouragement and enthusiasm in converting the original proceedings into published form. The editors would also like to thank the following for the financial and other help they were able to provide: ING Barings, BBV-LatInvest, the Foreign and Commonwealth Office, the Peruvian Embassy in London and the British Embassy in Lima. Thanks also are due Felipe Portocarrero at the Universidad del Pacifico in Lima for his many useful suggestions, and to Tony Bell and Anna Hayes for their help in preparation of the final text. Apart from all the contributors, the editors would also like to thank those who acted as discussants in the various sessions. These included Valpy Fitzgerald, Chris Scott, Lewis Taylor, Maxine Molyneux, Rachel Sieder and Victor Bulmer-Thomas.

CHAPTER II

List of Contributors

Luis Abugattas Majluf is Executive Director of the Instituto de Estudios Económicos y Sociales of the Sociedad Nacional de Industrias. He has acted as consultant to many international organisations as well as the private sector. He has been advisor to a number of Peruvian government departments, and has written extensively on aspects of the Peruvian economy in academic and official publications.

Elena Alvarez is Professor in the Department of Latin American Studies and the Caribbean at the State University of New York at Albany. She is also an Adjunct Senior Research Associate with the University of Miami's North-South Center in Coral Gables, Florida. She has written extensively on agricultural economics issues as well as on illicit drugs, including *Política Económica y Agricultura en el Perú, 1969-1979* (Lima, 1983), *La economía ilegal de la coca en el Perú* (Lima, 1991).

Javier de Belaúnde is a practising lawyer and Professor in the Faculty of Law at the Pontificia Universidad Católica del Perú. He was a member of the first Advisory Council of the Academia de la Magistratura (1994-96), and has been a member of various commissions on the administration of justice. He has also been Executive Secretary of the *Consejo Latinoamericano de Derecho y Desarrollo*. He has published work on constitutional law, human rights, civil law and the administration of justice.

José Coronel is Professor of Anthropology at the Universidad Nacional de San Cristóbal de Huamanga and President of the Instituto para la Paz (IPAZ). His publications include *Las rondas campesinas y la derrota de Sendero Luminoso* (Lima, 1996), with Carlos Iván Degregori and Ponciano del Pino.

John Crabtree is Latin America editor at Oxford Analytica and a Visiting Research Fellow of the Institute of Latin American Studies, University of London (1997-98). He has been a Senior Associate Member of Saint Antony's College, Oxford (1993-95) and visiting professor at the Universidade de São Paulo (1990) and the Universidad del Pacífico, Lima (1995 and 1996). He is the author of *Peru Under Garcia: An Opportunity Lost* (Basingstoke, 1992).

Carlos Iván Degregori is Professor of Anthropology at the Universidad Nacional Mayor de San Marcos and Principal Researcher at the Instituto de Estudios Peruanos. His most recent book is *Las rondas campesinas y la derrota de Sendero Luminoso* (Lima, 1996), with José Coronel and Ponciano del Pino. He is coeditor of *The Peru Reader* (Durham, N.C., 1996), with Orin Starn and Robin Kirk.

Francisco Durand is Associate Professor of Political Science at the University of Texas, San Antonio. He is a former Director of the Tax Administration Institute of Peru. His publications include *Business and Politics in Peru* (Boulder, 1994). He has published numerous articles in Latin American and European journals. He is currently doing research on business associations in Latin America and politics in Peru under Fujimori.

Adolfo Figueroa is Professor of Economics at the Universidad Católica del Perú. He has been Visiting Professor at the Universities of Oxford, Illinois at Urbana-Champaign, Notre Dame, Texas at Austin. He is an international consultant to the World Bank, FAO, IFAD, IADB, and ILO. His recent publications include *Social Exclusion and Inequality in Peru* (Geneva, 1996).

Raúl Hopkins lectures at Queen Mary and Westfield College, University of London. He has carried out extensive research and consultancy work on the agricultural sector of developing countries. Other areas of interest include the study of macroeconomic performance and capital flows in Latin America, and the economics of development organisations.

Javier Iguíñiz is Professor of Economics at the Pontificia Universidad Católica del Perú, and Director of the Andean academic multidisciplinary magazine *Allpanchis*. His recent publications include *Aplanar los andes y otras propuestas* (Lima, 1998), and *Buscando salidas: ensayos sobre la pobreza* (Lima, 1994). He has published numerous articles on the Peruvian economy in international journals and edited books, including 'The difficult moments of the Fujimori Economic Strategy', in E. Gonzales de Olarte (ed.) *The Peruvian Economy and Structural Adjustment: Past, Present and Future* (Miami, 1996).

Drago Kisic is Director of the Grupo Macro, and the founder and president of the Centro Peruano de Estudios Internacionales (CEPEI). He is a member of the Comisión Consultiva de Relaciones Exteriores and has acted as Advisor to the Executive Director of the World Bank in Washington D.C. He has been Chairman of the board of directors of CONASEV, Peru's business and securities supervisory commission; Vice-president of the Lima Stock Exchange; Head of the Economic Advisory Office of the Banco Central.

Enrique Obando is currently President of the Institute of Political and Strategic Studies at the Universidad Católica del Perú. He was Coordinator of the Area of Security at the Peruvian Center of International Studies (CEPEI) (1989-95), Adviser to the Peruvian Secretary of Defence (1984-89), and Director of International Affairs at the Peruvian National Planning Institute (1977-84). He is the author of *Industrias militares en América del Sur* (Lima, 1991) and editor of *Nuevas amenazas a la seguridad y relaciones civiles-militares en un mundo en desorden* (Lima, 1994).

Ponciano del Pino is Professor of Anthropology at the Universidad Nacional de San Cristóbal de Huamanga. His publications include *Las rondas campesinas y la derrota de Sendero Luminoso* (Lima, 1996), with Carlos Iván Degregori and

José Coronel.

Martín Tanaka is a researcher at the Instituto de Estudios Peruanos and Professor in Economics at the Universidad Católica del Perú. He is author of *Los espejos y espejismos de la democracia y el colapso de un sistema de partidos. Perú, 1980-1995, en perspectiva comparada* (Lima, 1998).

Jim Thomas is Senior Lecturer in Economics at the London School of Economics. His publications include (with R.G. Rossini and the Equipo Económico del ILD) *Los fundamentos estadísticos de 'El otro sendero': debate sobre el sector informal en el Perú* (Lima, 1988), *Surviving in the City: The Urban Informal Sector in Latin America* (Boulder, 1995).

Rosemary Thorp is Reader in the Economics of Latin America and Director of the Latin American Centre at the University of Oxford. She is a Fellow of St Antony's College, and a member of Queen Elizabeth House. Her publications include *Peru, 1890-1977: Growth and Policy in an Open Economy* (London, 1978), written with Geoffrey Bertram, and *Economic Management and Economic Development in Peru and Colombia* (London, 1991). She has just completed *Progress, Poverty and Exclusion: An Economic History of Latin America in the XXth Century*, published by the Inter-American Development Bank.

PREFACE

The chapters in this book are revised versions of papers presented at an international conference entitled 'Fujimori's Peru: is it sustainable?'. Organised by the Institute of Latin American Studies of the University of London, the conference was held on 19-20 June 1997 and involved leading *Peruanistas* from the United Kingdom, the United States and Peru itself. All those who agreed to take part did so with great enthusiasm and in the belief that the conference provided a useful opportunity, albeit from afar, to exchange ideas and to reflect on the significance of the changes that have taken place in Peru in recent years.

The starting point for the conference was that, by 1997, Peru had experienced seven years of government by President Alberto Fujimori, and that although it remained unclear how long he would remain as president, this timespan was sufficiently long to reach some conclusions as to the nature of the regime and its support-base, the factors influencing decision-making and the effect of policies on politics, the economy and society. One of the purposes of the conference was to adopt a multidisciplinary approach to the topic in hand, in order better to understand the inter-relationship between these various facets.

In the design of both the conference and this book, we have opted for a thematic rather than a purely chronological approach. A sequential account would no doubt have revealed the many major political, economic and institutional changes which took place in these seven years, such as the collapse of traditional political parties, the vanquishing of the guerrilla threat posed by Sendero Luminoso, the successful stabilisation of the economy and the radical process of economic liberalisation that began in 1990. However, such an account needs to be placed in an appropriate context. This raises a number of questions. Are all these changes only attributable to the Fujimori government, or are there continuities with the past which need to be taken into account? Do they represent changes which will prove sustainable over the medium and long term, or will they themselves revert when political conditions change? What sort of lasting effects will they have? Will they serve to solve the deep structural problems which have afflicted Peru this century?

These are questions for which it is possible to provide only tentative replies. Those who contributed to the conference were asked to bear some of these questions in mind in analysing specific problems, actors or policies. They were not required to provide crystal balls, but rather to consider the influence of the past in shaping the present, and to use this analysis to provide some clues as to possible future outcomes. No attempt was made to force the papers into a rigid mould, rather a diversity of approaches and insights was considered essential as a nutrient of discussion. Nevertheless, despite differences of opinion and emphasis, there was considerable underlying congruence amongst the views expressed, a meeting of minds which the editors hope comes through in the text of this book.

The conference also benefited enormously from the presence of Richard Webb, our guest speaker. As one of the main authorities on income distribution in Peru, as president of the central bank (1980-85), as co-founder of Lima's foremost statistical consultancy agency and the official historian of the World Bank, Richard Webb brought with him that rare combination of eminent academic, policy-maker and statistician which helped orient and inform our discussions. In his keynote speech, he touched on four key elements that underpinned our various preoccupations, all raising the issue of 'sustainability': the problem of poverty; the nature of informality; some strengths and weaknesses in the economy; and some ways in which politics had become more democratic.

The problems of poverty, inequality and social exclusion underlay much of the discussion in the conference, in terms of its distorting effects on the economy, and on society and political development. Classification of 'poverty', 'extreme poverty' and 'non-poverty' represents obvious problems of definition and measurement, and is complicated by the movement of people between these various categories over time. Also such measurement frequently ignores the effect of public goods such as healthcare or education. The question of inequality presents even more difficulties, but most people seem to believe that the gap between the poor and the rich has increased over the 1990s, not necessarily because the poor have become poorer but because the rich have become richer. If true, this is a worrying development for a country with deep historical divisions, accentuated by class, ethnicity and geography. In his chapter on poverty and exclusion, Adolfo Figueroa – who worked with Webb on income distribution in the 1970s – reminds us of the need for a theoretical explanation of why it is that inequality has remained so pervasive for so long.

Informality is a concept which, partly through the writings of Hernando de Soto, has become associated with Peru. It has also proved a contentious term. Whilst for some the informal sector is a reservoir for potential entrepreuneurs, for others it is synonymous with poverty and exclusion. Again, as Webb reminded us, problems of definition and measurement abound. There are many ways of defining both 'formality' and 'informality'. It is not simply a question of who pays taxes and contributions to the social security system, who has title to the land they occupy or work on, or who is eligible to receive credit in one form or another. The frontiers between informality and formality are fluid, with people crossing from one side to another and having one foot in each camp. Whilst not necessarily synonymous with poverty, it is fairly clear that informal labour is closely associated with activities of very low productivity and remuneration. The structure of the labour market is such that poverty is usually a corollary of inadequate employment and that, while this remains the case, the majority of the population will remain poor.

As Javier Iguíñiz and Drago Kisic argue in their respective chapters, both in terms of policy and performance, the Peruvian economy has undergone a signal transformation since 1990: export-led growth has effectively supplanted all vestiges of import-substituting industrialisation. The turnaround has been at least as dramatic as anywhere in Latin America. However, in his comments, Webb highlighted a number of dangers and stressed that Peru remains extremely vulnerable to exogenous shocks. The first of these was Peru's perilous dependence on the inflow of foreign savings, with most domestic saving being used to finance consumption. A second problem was the exchange rate and the tendency towards sustained overvaluation, arising in part from the 'Dutch disease' associated with capital inflows of one sort or another. A third problem was the size of the current account deficit and the speed at which international reserves (mostly in the hands of the private sector) could diminish in response to any crisis of confidence. A fourth problem was the continued dependence of fiscal income on trade, mainly imports.

Peru's political system, as it has developed since 1990, has given rise to considerable international comment for peculiar hybrid features (neither fully democratic nor fully authoritarian) and for the way in which traditional patterns of political mediation have been supplanted by a 'direct democracy' between people and president. One of the remarkable things about the Fujimori phenomenon has been its ability to perceive and articulate the views of 'the man in the street'. Although by 1997-98, Fujimori's popularity had waned somewhat, he has enjoyed consistently high opinion poll ratings over a protracted period in which most Peruvians have probably gained little in purely economic terms. This raises the question of whether academics and politicians (who tend to belong to a privileged minority) really understand what people want and what they value. Whilst corruption has the capacity rapidly to corrode legitimacy, Fujimori appears to have avoided the sort of 'cronyism' which developed in a number of east Asian countries where presidents have perpetuated themselves in office over protracted periods of time. Nevertheless, the incestuous relationships between government and business only tend to become clearer once a regime is no longer in power. Meanwhile, in the longer run, support for a regime must surely bear some relation to its ability to benefit a sufficiently large number of citizens to keep its legitimacy intact.

This book does not attempt to predict in any detail what may happen in Peru after the year 2000. Rather, it is intended that the contributions from authors from a variety of branches of the social sciences will provide a preliminary evaluation of both the successes and failures of the first seven years of the *Fujimorato* and highlight some of the problems and constraints to which it has been subject and which may continue to constrain policy-makers in the future. It is hoped, at the very least, that we offer the reader a useful framework in which to comprehend the events of the 1990-97 period.

John Crabtree
Jim Thomas
May 1998

PART I

OVERVIEW

CHAPTER 1

Neo-populism and the Fujimori Phenomenon

John Crabtree

Change and continuity

Following a lengthy period out of fashion, the concept of populism has returned to the fore once again. The appearance in Latin America of political leaders like Carlos Menem in Argentina, Fernando Collor in Brazil, Abdala Bucaram in Ecuador, Alberto Fujimori in Peru and even Rafael Caldera in Venezuela, not to mention variants in other parts of the world, has caused writers to go back to some of the methods of analysis common in the 1950s and 1960s used to categorise earlier bouts of more classic populism.

The main definition of populism used here is a style of government, characterised by an appeal by strong, sometimes charismatic, leaders to the people, over the heads of existing parties and politicians and therefore 'unmediated by institutions'.[1] We return to the notion of an identity between a leader or a political movement with the 'populus', even though the popularity of some so-called populists may prove fleeting and unsustainable. Once again we see the emergence of politicians who seek to override existing institutions in their desire to challenge the status quo and who seek to legitimise themselves through a direct appeal to 'the people' through what O'Donnell has termed 'delegative democracies' (O'Donnell, 1994). Often the norms of liberal democracy are eschewed, representative institutions sidelined and political mediation becomes a question of 'top down' mobilisation rather that any articulation upwards of grass-roots demands. Such forms tend to prosper in countries where representative institutions which 'bridge' the gap between state and civil society are weak or ineffectual.

The nature of the discourse of these 'new' populists is clearly different to that of the earlier variety. In economic terms, they usually seek the very opposite of their forebears, by spearheading a neo-liberal transformation which reduces the power of the state to intervene and which not only draws a veil over the earlier phase of import-substituting industrialisation (ISI) but seeks to reverse it. However, in political terms the continuities are more evident and the coining of the term 'neo-populism' responds to a need to understand such phenomena.

The utility of the notion of populism has often been called into question

---

[1]   This was a definition introduced by the conference on 'New and old Populism in Latin America', held at the Institute of Latin American Studies, University of London, November 1995, at which a precursor of this paper was presented.

(Conniff, 1982; Conovan, 1981). The term has been seen as analytically vague and imprecise, lacking in rigour. Indeed, it has never lent itself to the same kind of theorisation as other concepts in political science. Often, it has developed a notably pejorative connotation, further accentuating the distrust of 'rigorous' political scientists. It is not my purpose here to return to this debate, but simply to assert that the concept has sufficient content to facilitate useful comparisons between types of political movements and/or regimes in different places and at different times. Certainly, the history of Latin America provides no shortage of regimes which can be recognised as 'populist' or exhibiting populist traits. This chapter will argue that the Fujimori government in Peru since 1990 is one such regime.

It is axiomatic that there are never any totally new starts in politics, even when the breaks appear as strong reactions against what went before. Though they may wish to stress the way in which they seek to depart from the status quo, politicians are themselves a product of a prevailing political culture from which they cannot entirely disentangle themselves. This chapter seeks to identify some continuities in Peruvian politics that need to be borne in mind in discussing the 'new' Peru under President Alberto Fujimori.

For many observers, the elections of 1990 and the victory of Fujimori represent a watershed dividing the chaos and disorder of the García years from a 'new era' of stability and recovery. Fujimori and his supporters have naturally sought to maximise this contrast, seeking to legitimise themselves by highlighting the 'bad old days' under the preceding García administration, when Peru seemingly came close to the brink of the abyss. While of course Fujimori's policies in the economic sphere have been a far cry from those of Alan García, this should not blind us to a number of telling continuities that bind him to the past. These suggest that the style of his government is not just a consequence of his own personal attributes or the exigencies of a particular conjuncture, but rather are a response to more deep-rooted problems. To be sure, García and Fujimori exhibit some common characteristics. Both governments were presided over by leaders of an authoritarian bent, disposed towards abruptly changing the existing rules of the game when it suited them to do so. Both shunned the sharing of power with others, preferring to bypass institutions and intermediaries and to legitimise themselves through a direct appeal to the 'people'. Both were *personalista* in inclination, highly preoccupied with their own popularity and disdainful towards formal systems of accountability.

This chapter thus seeks to place the Fujimori government within an historical setting. It argues that some of its characteristics reflect long-lasting structural features of Peru's political development. Therefore, while primarily concerned with the contemporary scene, we cannot divorce it from the past. For this reason, we begin with a brief résumé of the populist tradition in Peru and the circumstances that helped generate it.

A populist tradition

In the 40 years between 1930 and 1970, Peru stands out in contrast to the larger countries of Latin America, where populist-type governments helped prompt a new model of national state-led development. Overall, this period in Peru was characterised by the continuance of a non-interventionist state, reliance on a liberal export-oriented model of growth and a relatively weak pattern of industrial development (Thorp and Bertram, 1978). The new social forces which in other parts of the region provided both the driving force of and the constituency for ISI were weaker, and the political parties with which they were associated failed to build up sufficient strength to overturn the status quo.

More than most of the other larger countries of the region, Peru remained largely rural, poorly integrated (both physically and socially) and with a relatively small middle and working class. Although the period saw urban migration beginning to accelerate, the majority of the population still lived in the rural sector, where political involvement was curtailed by the predominant *hacienda* system and the limited horizons of the peasant community. It was the progressive breakdown of such patterns, accelerated by the agrarian reform of the 1970s, which brought with it the emergence of the mass into politics.[2] Julio Cotler has insistently stressed the importance of this lack of integration and its endurance right up to the present, with patterns of clientelistic and patrimonial behaviour obstructing repeated attempts at reorganisation (Cotler, 1978; 1994; and 1995).

The failure of mass-based popular political parties to consolidate themselves delayed the moment at which the power of the oligarchy was finally broken and new structures created to channel popular pressures. Although new parties evolved during this period, they did not constitute a stable party system through which the interests of emerging social groups could be articulated at the level of government. Instead, the emerging popular sectors began to participate as political actors at the margins of formally-constituted politics. Elements of popular mobilisation are to be found during this period, as are attempts on the part of the still dominant elite to direct or co-opt incipient popular pressures, caused by – amongst other things – urbanisation, industrialisation and the spread of education. However, these were only weakly represented at the national level.

There were periods (some of them brief) in which popular movements helped shape state policy. Such was the case, for instance, during the post-war government of José Luis Bustamente y Rivero (1945-48), supported by APRA, which embarked on policies (subsequently abandoned) of incipient interventionism. The government of Manuel Odria (1948-56), which saw the return to orthodox policies in the economic sphere, also saw the country's political leadership trying to develop a personalist relationship with the urban

---

[2] The strength of APRA was concentrated in the more 'developed' parts of the country, especially in the north.

poor (Collier, 1976). After 1963, Fernando Belaúnde sought to mobilise popular support around a semi-nationalist ideology (*'Perú como doctrina'*), a programme of moderate social reform mixed in with a strong dose of *personalismo*. There was therefore a history of mobilisation from above, often with politicians posing as 'saviours'. Moreover, there was no real tradition of liberal democracy or the emergence of solidly-based representative institutions. This reflected, in part, the organisational weakness and lack of integration in Peruvian society.

It is to APRA that we must look for the clearest expression of Peruvian populism. Founded in 1924 by Víctor Raúl Haya de la Torre, APRA embodied many classic populist traits. Like other populist-type movements elsewhere, APRA burst on the scene in a context of political and economic collapse: the political breakdown was made evident by the exhaustion of the autocratic Leguía regime, the so-called *oncenio*; the economic breakdown was caused by the 1929 crash and its effects on a vulnerable economy. The APRA programme bore many of the classic hallmarks of populism.[3] Mobilising from above, it involved a strong *'invocación al pueblo'*, interpreting the needs and aspirations of the people, seeing in *lo popular* the roots of political legitimacy. It sought to establish itself as a multi-class movement, bringing together the middle classes, the working class and sectors of the peasantry, in pursuit of a progressive, reformist agenda. It aimed to mobilise large sectors of the population, both urban and rural, excluded from the established political system. Its ideology was strongly nationalist, with the interests of the nation (with which it identified itself) standing up against foreign 'imperialisms' of all sorts. In its internal structure, it evolved into a strongly hierarchical, clientelistic and authoritarian movement, with little internal democracy, and a marked cult of leadership. Haya's *personalista* style – indeed his posture as a quasi-saviour figure – was a source of both strength and weakness; strength in that he had extraordinary powers of leadership and commanded strong personal loyalties; weakness in that the movement was excessively dependent on one man.

In the Peruvian case, it was not so much populist leaders like Haya, capable of mobilising popular dissatisfaction with the status quo, which ended the old oligarchy; rather it was the military that took the initiative, concerned that lack of reform would otherwise spark a Cuban-style revolutionary upsurge. The Velasco government, which ousted Belaúnde in 1968, sought to institute a break with the past, imposing from above the same sort of changes as more successful populist experiences had done elsewhere earlier on. Although the Velasco government never sought electoral validation and did not involve the same degree of *personalismo* as did, for example, Peronism in Argentina, it formed part of a populist tradition, replacing existing forms of political mediation and imposing new institutional channels for controlled participation. It justified its legitimacy through an *invocación al pueblo*. However, its relationship with the

---

[3]   In his classic typology of Latin American populism, Torcuato di Tella sees Aprismo as a specific variant (Di Tella, 1965).

social movements it sought to direct was always ambiguous, and ultimately it failed in its bid to maintain control over them.

The return to constitutional government in 1980 brought with it a more propitious context for the development of democratic institutions and the institutionalisation of procedures for popular participation in political life. Grass-roots organisations, linked to a variety of political parties, sought to participate more actively in decision making, both at the national and local levels. Frustration with the shortcomings of military rule, both during its left-wing phase (1968-75) and its more conservative *dénouement* (1975-80), generated a wide political consensus about the desirability of democratic transition. Democratic transition was a trend mirrored in many other countries of the region and encouraged from outside.

At the outset at least, there was considerable optimism that democracy could be made to work, in spite of the social demands placed upon it by a more politically articulate and demanding public. The 1979 constitution created a new institutional framework with rules of the game that commanded wide acceptance. Among other things, it established universal franchise for the first time. In the period after 1980, elections took place regularly, on time, reasonably fairly and with high degrees of public participation (Tuesta, 1994). Even more important, the 1980s saw the establishment – arguably also for the first time – of a party system with representative parties, covering a wide ideological spectrum and vying with one another for political office in keenly-fought electoral contests. It also saw the development of an increasingly organised civil society which helped articulate popular demands through new channels of representation.

However, the initial confidence soon proved misplaced. While the 1982 debt crisis heightened problems of macroeconomic management, two successive governments – those of Fernando Belaúnde (1980-85) and Alan García (1985-90) – proved woefully incapable of providing even a minimal level of political and economic security for the mass of the population. Moreover, the political parties retained many of the authoritarian, top-down, clientelistic, *personalista* characteristics of their forebears. Such traits made it more difficult for parties faithfully to carry out their representative role.[4] They also often jarred with the proliferation of grass-roots organisations at this time, both in the rural and urban spheres, some of them highly politicised.

---

[4]   Arguably, the electoral system adopted in the 1979 Constitution limited the ways in which politicians could represent specific constituencies. The Senate was elected on the basis of party lists for a national constituency. The Chamber of Deputies was elected from party lists at the departmental level. Either way, there was little by way of direct accountability of an elected politician to a specific constituency. The 1993 Constitution, while doing away with the Senate, did not change the way in which deputies were elected. Prior to 1979, congressmen had enjoyed the rights of *iniciativa del gasto* which enabled them to channel resources to those constituencies that had elected them. Whilst this led to clientelism and sometimes irrational forms of state spending, it helped form bonds that tightened the links between a politician and his electorate.

These were years in which democratic institutions found themselves having to withstand two major 'cyclones': the onset of rapid inflation and its degeneration into uncontrollable hyperinflation in 1988-90, bringing with it a collapse in real incomes and formal-sector employment; and the wave of guerrilla violence, which had begun in 1980 and by the late 1980s had enveloped most of the country. Although formal democratic institutions managed to weather these strains, together these pressures helped create a 'psychosis' of insecurity which undermined their credibility (Crabtree, 1995a). Political parties found themselves poorly placed to respond to people's needs, while organised civil society was weakened by the ravages of both economic crisis and political violence. As the volatility of voting behaviour between 1980 and 1990 suggests, party loyalties were not solidly established or deeply rooted among the voting public (Tuesta, 1994).[5] Grass-roots organisations became primarily concerned in helping people survive and those organisations which had previously relayed their concerns at the national level found themselves critically weakened. Meanwhile, as the period went on, the effective power of elected authorities was increasingly circumscribed by states of exception and military control of many parts of the country, reducing the space in which democratic politics could be conducted.

The Belaúnde government was something of a hybrid: while its economic policy had a clear neoliberal stamp, seeking to reverse the statism of the preceding military period, the government was also driven by more populist impulses. The latter came to the fore in the last two years of the administration, when it became clear that economic liberalisation, however timid, was not providing a route towards restored growth and prosperity. The populist streak was, in large part, represented by Belaúnde himself, always mindful of the way in which economic problems could threaten the legitimacy of a fledgling constitutional government and prompt yet another military coup.[6] Its moral authority sapped by poor economic performance and its failure to deal successfully with the guerrilla challenge, Belaúnde's party received a humiliating drubbing at the polls in 1985.

On the back of Belaúnde's failure to deal with these problems, voters turned to APRA's Alan García in 1985. García, whose youth and energy stood in contrast to his predecessor's paternalistic style, sought to adapt the old APRA message to new circumstances.[7] This is not the place to enter into a detailed description of the García government (see Crabtree, 1992), but simply to highlight some of its characteristics. In many ways, it reaffirmed the postulates

---

[5]   Acción Popular won the 1980 elections with 45.4% of the valid vote, while in 1985 its vote fell to 7.3%. APRA won the 1985 elections with 53.1%, but in 1990 saw its vote reduced to 22.6%.

[6]   Belaúnde had been unceremoniously removed from the presidency in 1968. Elected president again in 1980, he remained highly sensitive in his second administration to the demands of the military.

[7]   García was strongly influenced both by the experiences of the Velasco regime and by the legacy of Haya de la Torre. APRA was always a party for which the past loomed large over the present. The influence of Haya's legacy over Alan García should not be underestimated.

of the populist tradition; some indeed have seen it as the 'last gasp' of traditional Latin American populism. It once again raised the banner of economic nationalism and reaffirmed the virtues of state intervention over free market economics, arguing that the market exacerbates rather than reduces the country's inequalities and social divides. On the basis of a nationalistic ideology and expansionary economic policies, García sought to appeal to a wide community of interests, especially the least organised like the informal sector. In so doing, he sought to override political parties (including his own), bring to bear a strong dose of personalist and authoritarian leadership, and seek (as Haya had before him) to stand head and shoulders above all others and to develop a direct rapport with 'the people'. Borrowing O'Donnell's phrase, he wanted to be 'the alpha and omega' of politics (O'Donnell, 1994).

His critics liked to portray García as a megalomaniac, obsessed by opinion polls and carried away by the trappings of power. Whatever his psychological state, García's approach was shaped by the conviction that Peru was a potential social volcano, and that strong leadership, an active state with redistributive policies, and controlled participation were essential to prevent that volcano from erupting. In 1985, at least, there were good grounds for such a view. Not only did the country have one of the highest rates of poverty in Latin America, exacerbated by high inflation, but it faced challenges both from the implacable Sendero Luminoso guerrilla organisation and a Marxist left capable of attracting the support of over one-quarter of the voting population, mainly the poor. Such circumstances, it seemed, called for a different approach. García's cult of personality was guided, at least in part, by the conviction that popularity was his most important political asset, an asset which provided him with the authority to govern.

As is well known, the García government ended up creating worse problems than those it sought to remedy. By the end of the 1980s, the country found itself facing its most profound crisis since the late 1920s, one which (in the minds of some writers at least) threatened to destroy the very existence of the Peruvian state (Rospigliosi, 1988). The debate continues over whether or not the alternative policies espoused by García were doomed from the start or whether the problem was primarily one of mismanagement. Nevertheless, the García experience came to encapsulate many of the evils supposedly associated with populism, and it is hard to avoid the conclusion that Peru loomed large in the minds of such writers as Dornbusch and Edwards in their critique of what they call 'the macroeconomics of populism' (Dornbusch and Edwards, 1991). It was a powerful 'health warning' to those who might be tempted to follow García's example and buck the global trend towards economic liberalisation.

Arguably, 'old style' policies of the ISI type were particularly inappropriate at a moment when most other Latin American countries (either willingly or because they had no alternative) were moving in the opposite direction and when the exigencies of the debt crisis exacerbated the fiscal weaknesses and distributive capabilities of the state. Populism of the old sort went out of fashion in the 1980s partly because there was little for governments to redistribute. Moreover, García's overbearing *personalista* style of government revealed a critical problem: when things went wrong, there was no-one else to blame. However, at the same time, the García experience also highlighted the need to devise economic policies which took into account the political realities in which they are framed. Explanation of such populist impulses, whether doomed or not, has to involve serious consideration of the political logic driving them. As Paul Drake has argued, they were not the result simply of an irrational set of self-destructive ambitions (Drake, 1991). Analysis demands serious consideration of the dilemmas faced (perceived or real) and the alternatives on offer in a given set of circumstances. Although in retrospect it seems doubtful that the social 'volcano' was going to explode in the way García feared, it was not an entirely unreasonable hypothesis at the time.

In spite of the different economic policy orientations of successive governments – free market or interventionist – Peru's political development for much of the 20th century was characterised by the persistence of an authoritarian tradition and 'top-down' style of governance. The country lacked strong democratic traditions, institutions or culture, and the weakness of representative institutions provided fertile ground for the emergence of populist styles of government. The failure of APRA in the 1930s postponed the moment at which the mass was integrated into the political system, a process which took place in a disorganised and incomplete fashion in the 1970s and 1980s. Up until the early 1980s, periods of more open and representative government had been few and far between, and limited by restrictions on the franchise. The formal institutions of republican democracy had had an intermittent existence, representing the interests of a small fraction of society. The mass of the population remained largely excluded, although influencing the course of politics from outside as demographic and social change raised its profile. Weak political parties sought to tap discontent, but largely failed to direct it. During the 1980s, more democratic institutions took hold and with them an incipient party system emerged, based on norms of open competition. A wider concept of citizenship came into being as many of those previously excluded from the political system began to be incorporated within it. However, the roots put down by democratic institutions in civil society did not penetrate deep, and the crisis of the late 1980s created a highly unpropitious climate for their development. Once again, it became apparent how wide the gap was between the state and society, between the rulers and the ruled, a chasm that fragile parties found it very difficult to bridge.

Fujimori and 'neo-populism'

In the circumstances surrounding Peru's descent into economic chaos at the end of the 1980s and the extraordinary emergence of Fujimori during the 1990 election campaign, three connected aspects stand out with particular clarity.

The first was the crisis of confidence in the ability of the political elite to manage the country's problems. The twin 'cyclones' of hyperinflation and a generalised breakdown in law and order created a crisis of insecurity that variously affected all classes, both rich and poor, urban and rural. It was in this conjuncture of extreme political and economic instability that the figure of Fujimori emerged, a complete outsider, detected by the 'radar' of political pollsters only two or three weeks before the first round of presidential elections (Degregori and Grompone, 1991). It was not as if Fujimori played the populist in the election campaign – he promised the electorate little in a campaign of nuances and ambiguities – then to turn tail on what he did promise thereafter. Rather, Fujimori was the product of a desperate situation in which the alternatives appeared so much less attractive. His emergence as an alternative to the other candidates in the first round of elections was primarily a consequence of unprecedented tactical voting, the most remarkable feature of which was how he was first perceived as a viable alternative in his own right; in the second round he could count on support from all those who wished to block the way for Mario Vargas Llosa of the right-wing Fredemo coalition, the victor in the first round. One of Fujimori's strengths was that he was not a professional politician with a well-mapped out plan of government. Nor did he have a huge war chest to buy people's votes or the resulting need to repay political debts to vested interests.

The second aspect was the changing nature of the relationship between government and the people. The 1970s and 1980s saw a proliferation of popular organisations, both in the rural and urban spheres, often closely linked to political parties and highly politicised in themselves. They were a challenge to democratic consolidation, and at the same time they also represented a coming together of the state and society, with representative institutions of various sorts playing an influential role in decision-making at the national level. As we have seen, the crisis years of the late 1980s reduced the salience of such institutions, creating a representational vacuum, of which Fujimori's surprising victory in 1990 was but a symptom. Whilst popular organisation persisted at the grass-roots level, often in very precarious forms, it lost much of its overtly political influence and became concerned with more immediate and practical needs. This opened the way for new sorts of social and political intermediation to emerge.[8]

The third aspect was that it was abundantly clear from the experience of the preceding years that the statist model of development had run out of steam, that a new model was required. Although Fujimori flirted with some heterodox ideas at the beginning of his administration, he quickly appreciated that there was no alternative to a return to orthodoxy with a vengeance. The struggle between the state and the market had been fought out during the 1970s and 1980s, the emphasis falling one way or the other according to the political circumstances. As we have seen, in 1985 when García came to power, political conditions were

---

[8]   The changing orientation of popular organisation in the urban and rural spheres is taken up in Chapters 12 and 13 by Martín Tanaka and Carlos Iván Degregori.

not conducive to the implementation of the neoliberal agenda. By 1990, there was little by way of a constituency left to argue for statism, since the García experience had laid it bare, while erstwhile supporters (such as the unions or local manufacturers) were greatly weakened. Also, as Martín Tanaka argues in Chapter 12, the state became less important as an arena through which to contest popular demands. Ironically, then, it was the experience of the García regime that removed the main political obstacles to the implementation of the neoliberal agenda; the 1990s saw its rapid adoption, without anaesthesia, something inconceivable only a few years before. Although Fujimori realised what he had to do – it was a classic case of 'TINA' (There Is No Alternative) – he inherited a situation which made it politically possible since the obstacles to its implementation had been largely removed.

Compared with most other countries in Latin America, the process of liberalisation in Peru under Fujimori was very rapid. Between 1991 and 1995, as we see elsewhere in this volume, a substantial part of the public sector was privatised; prices in the economy were left to market forces; most forms of tariff protection were abandoned; an accommodation was sought with foreign creditors and priority was given to attracting foreign investors. In terms of economic policy, then, the contrast with the preceding García government could not have been more stark. Fujimori could not have been less 'populist' in the economic sense of buying support through a programme of fiscal and monetary profligacy. However, adhering to the political definition delineated above, it is clear that he inherited and developed a number of longstanding characteristics of government in Peru, albeit channelling them to different ends (Roberts, 1995).

The initial problem that faced Fujimori was that he was a political orphan; whilst being an outsider had its advantages in the peculiar electoral climate of 1990, it made the task of government much more difficult. Not only did he lack a majority in the two houses of Congress, but he lacked a political party to provide him with organised backing in society as a whole.[9] As its name suggests, his Cambio-90 grouping had been an electoral label arising from a specific conjuncture; it lacked national organisation either in the capital or elsewhere. Those who had joined it at the beginning of the campaign had not dreamt that it would form a government, anticipating at most that it might pick up one or two seats in Congress. The problem of this lack of organised support was made more acute by the unpopular nature of its economic strategy. Even if successful in bringing inflation under control, the social cost of the programme was extremely high. In such circumstances, it became necessary for Fujimori – like some of his predecessors – to seek to establish the legitimacy of his government by building up a close rapport between president and people, unmediated by other groups or parties. The low ebb to which the party system had fallen in 1990, of course, made this possible. Just as García had sought to forge unity around the 'external'

---

[9]   Although the political parties had polled poorly in 1990, there was no guarantee that they would not regain their lost popularity as Fujimori's policies encountered opposition. The main threat, it seemed, came from the possibility of García leading a resurgent APRA. It is possible that the 1992 *autogolpe* may have been motivated, in part, by an attempt to prevent this outcome.

issue of the debt, Fujimori tried to build consensus around a vilification of the political parties, at whose door Peru's problems were repeatedly laid.[10]

As it developed from 1990 onwards, the Fujimori government revealed a number of distinct and consistent features, all one way or another arising from the circumstances of his election but also representing continuities with preceding governments. Five of these, all inter-related, stand out.

The first was the personalisation of political power. Fujimori emerged as another leader who sought to be the 'alpha and omega' of politics, frequently likening himself to the chief executive of a corporate enterprise, the head of a hierarchical chain of command. Like Alan García before him, Fujimori saw himself as the mainspring of decision-making in government, insisting on the absolute loyalty and subordination of cabinet members and unwilling to delegate power and authority to lower echelons of government. Such an approach was justified in the name of 'efficiency', a potent term in Fujimori's lexicon in view of the traditional inefficiencies and corruption associated with the Peruvian state. Cabinet government bore more the hallmarks of a mechanism for the validation of decisions already made than the collective elaboration of policy.[11] Fujimori's grip on the reins of power was also reinforced by his appointment to key positions of persons of proven loyalty, many of them members of his own family or, like himself, members of the 'nisei' community of second-generation Japanese immigrants. In his policy of appointments, Fujimori conspicuously avoided alliance-building with other forces with the inclusion of 'big names' in the cabinet. Consistent with his 'anti-party' rhetoric, almost all of his appointments from 1991 onwards were of people from outside the world of formal politics.[12]

The second feature was the reaffirmation of executive power over other functions of the state. A strong executive branch was a feature of the 1979 constitution, and under Belaúnde and García (both of whom had the support of majorities in Congress) the legislature and judiciary proved pliant to the will of the executive. During his first two years, Fujimori's Cambio 90 lacked a majority in Congress. Nevertheless, the right-wing Fredemo grouping, the largest single bloc in Congress, supported most of his economic policies, which were broadly speaking consistent with their own outlook. An area where there was less harmony was the government's relationship with the military, looked upon with some suspicion in Congress. In late 1991 and early 1992, parliament

---

[10]   The attack on the so-called 'partidocracia' was a constant motif of Fujimori's speeches, especially in the period immediately before and after the April 1992 autogolpe. It appears that Fujimori was well aware of the potency of such attacks, which had an immediate and positive effect on his popularity ratings, as measured by the various Lima polling organisations. For an analysis of the role played by pollsters, see Conaghan (1995).

[11]   Interview with former agriculture minister, Carlos Amat y León, May 1995.

[12]   With the exception of some members of his first cabinet (none of whom lasted long), almost all cabinet appointments went to independents. One exception was the appointment of Javier Valle Riestra, formerly an Aprista senator, as Prime Minister in June 1998.

showed signs of resisting the government's desire to grant far-reaching new powers to the military, ostensibly to fight the war against guerrilla subversion. Fujimori's *autogolpe* (palace coup) of April 1992, when he arbitrarily closed down Congress and sacked the Supreme Court, has to be seen against this background. The 1993 Constitution, approved by a new Congress with a pro-Fujimori majority, reinforced executive powers vis-à-vis both the legislature and judiciary. As well as allowing for immediate presidential re-election, the new constitution reduced the powers of Congress to hold the government or senior military officers to account and increased those of the police and military in the judicial process (García Belaúnde and Planas, 1993). The new single-chamber Congress showed little disposition to question the legislation set before it by the government, and on several occasions voted to obstruct moves which were considered problematic or embarrassing for the government (Crabtree, 1995b).[13] The dominance of the executive over the Supreme Court has also been made clear on a number of occasions (see Javier de Belaúnde, Chapter 9). However, in justifying the position of the government on such matters, Fujimori, in 1992 and thereafter, was able to tap a deep-rooted dissatisfaction about these institutions and the corruption and *politiquería* with which they were widely associated in the public mind.

Thirdly, Fujimori proved capable of forging a new rapport with the mass of the people. During most of his first administration, and the first years of his second, he maintained extremely high popularity ratings. His was not a charisma born of bombastic oratory, rather an appeal derived from an unpretentious demeanour and a reputation for those 'Japanese' qualities of honesty, hard work and efficiency. Of course, his popularity was also bound up with his achievements, first in curbing inflation and, subsequently, in 1992 and thereafter, in subduing Sendero Luminoso. Like García before him, Fujimori seems to have seen his popularity as a key political asset, which it was easy for him to portray as evidence of legitimacy. It provided him with leeway to act in a more autonomous manner. His preoccupation with opinion poll ratings and focus groups is suggestive of his concern for legitimacy (Conaghan, 1995). Indeed, the 1992 *autogolpe* appears to have been carefully calibrated to boost his popularity at the expense of the political parties and their leaders. It was, however, a very personal popularity, which did not necessarily translate into support for his protégés or other members of his Cambio-90 grouping. While in the general election of 1995 his coat-tails were long enough to secure the election of Cambio 90 followers to Congress, this was not the case in the municipal elections of 1993 and 1995 when he was unable to ensure the election of key associates to the mayoralty of Lima. In building his rapport with the public, Fujimori was greatly helped by the diminished standing of the main political parties, since he was not obliged to enter into alliances with them to garner support. The rejection of what he called the *partidocracia* formed an

---

[13]   A classic instance was the government's response to the July 1992 La Cantuta murders, when politically embarrassing accusations about the involvement of the military command were side-stepped by the Congress and the Supreme Court (See also Javier de Belaúnde, Chapter 9 in this volume).

important part of his political offensive. As he put it in a neat exposition of a typically populist point of view: 'En el Perú no existen partidos ... El poder soy yo. Pero es un poder que me fue dado por el pueblo. Yo lo represento'[14] (quoted in Panfichi and Sanborn, 1995).

A fourth characteristic of Fujimori's style of government, intimately bound up with the last, was the use of the resources at his disposal to build up his own standing, especially among the poorest and most marginalised sectors of society. This became very clear following the 1993 referendum on the new constitution, which showed that – personal popularity apart – public opinion did not necessarily validate the policies of the government. Between 1993 and 1995, and even beyond, Fujimori concentrated on mobilising resources into carefully targeted social spending, and travelling constantly around the country to maximise the personal political benefits derived. Such spending (which accounted for as much as 40% of total government outlays in the 1996 budget) was channelled not through the traditional ministries, but through the ministry of the presidency, an office over which Fujimori maintained tight personal control. Through his spending policies, Fujimori, like García, was able to reach out to sectors which were relatively weakly organised, notably the urban poor and the Andean peasantry. Unlike García, though, he was able to make this a sustained effort and was less at the mercy of macroeconomic volatility.

The fifth and final characteristic was the tight relationship that came to bind the Fujimori government with the armed forces, a theme developed further in Chapter 10. Once again, this was partly a product of the peculiar circumstances surrounding Fujimori's election in 1990 and the new government's lack of an organised backing in society. In the context of the generalised crisis of the time, the army was one of the few functioning institutions at a national level. In this respect, the situation was somewhat different from what it had been under Belaúnde and García, when the armed forces adopted a more institutional posture. Under Fujimori, the military became a crucial element in the coalition of interests which helped sustain the government. Among his first actions in government was to purge the police force and replace key military commanders. The granting to the military of new powers to conduct counter-insurgency operations took place at the same time that a much closer relationship developed between the president and the military commander-in-chief, General Nicolás Hermoza. This was also paralleled by the upgrading of intelligence operations and the similarly close relationship that developed between Fujimori and his intelligence 'advisor', Vladimiro Montesinos. In spite of accusations about their involvement in human rights violations and drug trafficking and despite frictions between them, Montesinos and Hermoza both maintained their power and influence as linchpins of the new security system. In the case of Hermoza, his permanence in post involved an abandoning of established systems of military promotion and a shift from institutional autonomy towards a more overtly

---

[14] 'In Peru, there are no political parties ... I am the power in the land. But it is a power conferred on me by the people. I represent it.'

politicised role (Mauceri, 1996).

These characteristics of government were frequently criticised for contributing to a thinly-disguised personal dictatorship, lacking effective checks and balances to offset presidential power and ultimately accountable to no-one. A number of adjectives have been applied to describe this sort of regime. As well as 'neo-populism', terms like *'movimientismo'*, *'democradura'*, Bonapartism, 'delegative democracy', plebiscitarian democracy etc. have been used. Whatever the most appropriate, it is clear that, as it developed, the regime was personalist, clientelist, anti-institutional and less than sympathetic to the development of the institutions of representative democracy. In short, it brought about a concentration of power, a process facilitated by the lack of an effective opposition force.

This is not to decry the achievements of the Fujimori government in restructuring the economy and restoring some of the public order which had been so notably absent from the scene during the late 1980s. These achievements were, as we have seen, of critical importance in sustaining public support. Indeed, it is arguable that the concentration of power was a necessary prerequisite for the achievements of the Fujimori government in these fields. The subordinate role played by the Congress and the courts made it easier for the government to enact and implement policy. However, even if this was the case, it was not without costs. The Fujimori government was widely criticised, both within Peru and outside, for further weakening the institutional base of Peruvian democracy and making it more difficult, in the longer run, to pursue that elusive goal of bridging the gap between state and society.

Concentration of power also raised the more immediate problem of succession and sustainability. The main problem for a regime of this type is how to ensure continuity over time. Indeed, the creation of an inverted power pyramid makes the whole political system vulnerable to the fate of one individual.[15] Moreover, longer-term sustainability is placed in jeopardy if means are not found to distribute widely the benefits of economic reform. The logic of the neoliberal order, unless mitigated by the state, is to concentrate economic power and resources rather than distribute them more broadly. Fujimori's policies of distributing largesse to targeted populations was an attempt to build political support among the poorest and most excluded, yet it was hardly one geared to redressing the problem of social inequality, still less to 'empowering' those sectors. One of the potential dangers of a government like Fujimori's is that it encourages a widening of disparities, largely because a relatively small elite appears to gain handsomely from policies of liberalisation and privatisation. While price stabilisation in Peru no doubt benefited the majority of the population, its political effects over time were likely to become diluted, and new distributive policies would be required.

---

[15] Fujimori's selection for vice-presidential running mates (notably in 1995) of persons who could not act as political rivals potentially heightened this problem.

Sustainability was clearly one of the major preoccupations that lay behind the 1992 *autogolpe,* which cemented the relationship between the armed forces and the civilian government.[16] Lacking either an obvious successor within the ranks of his own entourage (something Fujimori was not keen to encourage) or among the parties of the opposition (still less so), a mechanism had to be found to obviate the constitutional ban on immediate presidential re-election. Amongst other things, the *autogolpe* achieved this objective, opening the way for Fujimori to stand once again in 1995 and defeat the opposition candidate, Javier Pérez de Cuéllar. Less than two years into his second term, the issue of re-election for a further five-year term (2000-2005) re-emerged. Fujimori's partisans argued that if he stood for re-election in 2000, it would be the first re-election under the new 1993 constitution, and would therefore be valid without further changes to the constitution. Many others, including the National Electoral Commission (JNE), disagreed with this interpretation. At the time of writing, the issue had yet to be finally resolved one way or another and a referendum on the issue seemed possible,[17] but few doubted that Fujimori would not take 'no' for an answer.

It was on the point of re-election that the issue of sustainability clashed most directly with established constitutional norms. In view of the lack of other obvious successors, continuity involved re-election. Furthermore, there is contradiction (often seen in the past both in Peru and elsewhere in Latin America) between the concentration and personalisation of political power and the creation of rules to ensure a smooth transfer of power and authority to others. In other countries and at other times, those who have held on to power for lengthy periods have not only contributed to their own eventual downfall but also to that of the system with which they were associated. For this reason, most Latin American constitutions forbid immediate re-election, and in some cases – Mexico for instance – impose a lifelong ban on former presidents standing again.

Whilst the transfer of power may prove troublesome and disruptive, arguably it is an essential component of regime regeneration. There is, therefore, a danger that the longer Fujimori tried to stay in office, the more disrputive his eventual downfall could be, especially if there are no functioning representative institutions to provide an alternative. Moreover, in the shorter term – as the García government also showed – popularity is a volatile commodity which, in certain circumstances, can be dissipated remarkably quickly. It is possible that,

---

[16]   The so-called 'Green Book' dated from the last years of the García government. It argued the need for a strong government that would last 20 years if necessary. It represented the view that necessary liberalising economic reforms would take years to implement and that a civil-military government, with backing from the business sector, was required to ensure successful implementation (see also Chapter 10 of this volume)

[17]   In early 1997, the Constitutional Tribunal upheld the constitutionality of re-election, but not by the majority required for its decision to be valid. Those who voted against were later dismissed from the tribunal. To achieve a referendum on the issue, opponents of re-election had to muster at least 1.2 million signatures to achieve this objective. In July 1998, 1.4 million signatures were handed to the electoral authorities, but it was still uncertain whether a referendum would in fact be held. It was also unclear whether, if one were held, the opposition would prevail.

as his victories over hyperinflation and Sendero Luminoso fade in the public mind and as new political controversies come to the fore, Fujimori will need to tap new sources of popularity to ensure his continued primacy. One of the paradoxes of Fujimori's first five years – explained in part by his resort to the populism we have described – was that support for the regime remained so high at a time when objectively the material living standards of most Peruvians were deteriorating and income distribution was becoming ever more skewed.[18] While Fujimori managed to generate extraordinary optimism among common people that belt-tightening would pay off in due course, the moment would arrive when positive expectations had to be met. The advent of disillusion threatened to bring with it disruptive consequences.

Conclusions

One of the arguments of this chapter is that while periods of economic and political breakdown may lead to the emergence of populist styles of government, countries like Peru provide particularly fertile soil for such types of regime to take root. Populism is more than just a response to periodic breakdown (though these have been frequent enough in Peru this century), rather it infuses Peruvian political culture. In part, this is because the size of the gap between state and society is such as to make the traditional functions of political parties particularly difficult to perform. Furthermore, the mass of the population have only been imperfectly integrated into the political system. Although the picture is not static, populist styles of government are a constant theme that underlies regimes of both statist and more liberal make-up. The propensity towards populism is therefore closely related to the absence of a functioning and embedded system of representative government which, ultimately, renders the rulers accountable to the ruled.

In spite of its pursuit of new policies in the economic sphere, the Fujimori government has resorted to many time-honoured 'populist' practices in the political sphere. An authoritarian tradition has been reaffirmed, based on a personalist style of government which shunned representative institutions and formal systems of accountability. A new rapport has been forged with the military, whilst political parties have been consigned further to the margins of the political system. Because of the new policies pursued in the economic sphere and their impact on distribution and inequality, a new system of political control has been established, based not on inclusion and participation but on new forms of patronage and clientelism. In this sense, then, it seems appropriate to talk of 'neo-populism' as a traditional type of response to new conditions. However, it remains to be seen the extent to which this sort of regime will prove durable in the long term. The Fujimori experience raises serious questions with regard to sustainability, not just in terms of an eventual succession and regime

---

[18] According to one commentator, 'populist policies may be an imperative for political survival in a neo-liberal age' (Kay, 1997).

regeneration but, in the longer-run, in terms of the absence of robust representative organisations to channel demands from below. When Fujimori falls, what sort of regime will follow?

CHAPTER 2

The Economic Strategy of the Fujimori Government

Javier Iguíñiz

The economy is always unstable and unsustainable. In one sense, instability is inherent in the physical state of things, but, in a rather more prosaic sense, unsustainability relates to the constant disequilibrium of traditional variables. Disequilibrium is the basis for economic growth (Hirschman, 1958) and is necessary to produce the motives, actors and resources needed for further change. However, it seems that the nature of change depends on the history that precedes it. If this change is the consequence of a failure of preceding growth in the sense that it lacked the durability to generate new actors with the capacity to provide alternative leadership, the extent of any novelty will be very limited and the pendulum will swing back (Gonzales de Olarte and Samamé, 1991). The old analytical models will return to the fore. If, on the other hand, the change is caused by barriers to a prolonged period of growth, it is likely that the change will be sufficiently novel to leave behind old problems and old analytical models.

In 1998 it is difficult to say categorically what sort of change has been achieved in Peru as a consequence of a decade of neoliberal reforms. Whilst the increased importance of the primary sector and the reduced profile of the productive state are obvious features, the importance of and the role played by different classes are not so obvious, nor the resulting structure of social institutionality. Nor can the longer-term stability of what has been achieved be taken for granted. On the one hand, some have argued that national capital lacks either the strength or the purpose to spearhead a process of change in Peruvian society over the medium to long term (Seminario, 1995; Hunt, 1995).[1] Others have argued that 'the main power groups in Peru have managed to adapt themselves well to the period of adjustment in the 1990s', placing themselves strategically as suppliers of long-term finance (Durand, 1996, p. 165). Among medium and small-scale or popular-based groups, there is little evidence of any new forms of emergent organisation capable of generating new disequilibria or forging a new order.

If this initial approach is valid, continued economic expansion is a prerequisite for the emergence and development of new forces. The potential for the economy to expand has been and remains an issue of debate. No-one seems to doubt the advent of an export boom in the first decade of the 21st century. Up

---

[1] Hunt points out that in Peru 'there is no dominant class. There was one, perhaps 50 or 80 years ago, but it lost its strength as a consequence of a series of political developments over the 20th century'.

to now, the forms of analysis used for forecasting are based on fairly traditional criteria. Indeed, recent writers who have forecast difficulties in the medium-to-long term point to an aspect that has been ignored and which now appears to have more relevance than before: the problems that may arise in the balance of payments as a result of profit remission and other expenses abroad by foreign companies (Schydlowsky and Schuldt, 1996; Iguíñiz, 1996; and Jiménez, 1997). The old concern about 'returned value' thus makes its reappearance (Thorp and Bertram, 1978). At the same time, there are those who connect this to the problem of productive disarticulation and sectoral imbalance that arises from a model centred on the export of primary commodities and the consequent tendency to generate large trade deficits (Jiménez, 1997). Nevertheless, the predominant tone among economic forecasters is one of caution, even amongst those who adopt a critical stance (Schuldt, 1995; Jiménez, 1997). The foreseeable problems in the primary export model will be delayed because of differential profits (Schuldt, 1995).

Doubts about the short term focus primarily on the transition towards a primary export model. Numerous writers have stressed concern about the viability of the economic programme in the period before new investment projects come on stream.[2] There have been many forecasts, which vary mainly in the financial variables they introduce – a relatively unimportant phenomenon until recent years. Faced with evident difficulties in the trade and current accounts in the 1990-95 period, confidence about stable growth over the short term has depended primarily on how the entry of capital inflows is projected, although the quality of imports with respect to growth is another consideration (Schuldt, 1994).

In my opinion, events have justified both points of view. The economic 'cooling' that took place in 1996 (when growth was reduced to 2.8%) showed the non-viability of rapid short-term growth. However, international circumstances and the process of economic opening to foreign capital made a full recession unnecessary, despite the inefficient way in which the 'brake' was applied (Dancourt and Mendoza, 1997). In 1997 the economy grew by 7.4%. Still, the problem has not been entirely resolved and there are good reasons to be cautious about the short-term future. The new factor is financial; never before have there been such large trade and current account deficits at a time when international reserves were on such a sustained upward growth path.[3] A facet of this situation was the coexistence of relative exchange rate stability with an overvalued currency. A number of evaluations have recommended some sort of devaluation, putting the exchange rate at the very centre of the analysis (Schydlowsky and Schuldt, 1996, pp. 52 and 76-8).

---

[2]   A great deal of discussion has been devoted to this point within the Consorcio de Investigación Económica which groups together a number of Lima research institutes. Moreover, the effects of the El Niño phenomenon on exports in 1998 – principally fishing and agricultural goods – seemed to emphasise the vulnerability of the economy to short-term exogenous factors.

[3]   The current acount deficit in 1997 was 5.3% of GDP and promised to increase substantially in 1998.

Objectives of the Peruvian growth strategy

In this section, I seek to define the economic strategy of the Fujimori government and to summarise some of the conditions necessary for its continuity.

The implicit strategy

There is considerable consensus about the Fujimori government's lack of an explicit long-term development plan (Sagasti and Guerra-García, 1997). We therefore have to seek to identify the implicit strategy. To do so, we need to pick up on some of the policy attributes which the government itself consistently defended from 1990 onwards and those advocated by the various international agencies which influenced policy-making. Among the various aspects of the government's strategy, we highlight the problems of growth and growth stability in the longer term.

A key notion was that the growth potential of the Peruvian economy in the medium and longer term was sustained by two mutually-supporting processes: capital inflows and an increase in primary exports – especially mining, but also agroindustry and fishing – coupled with the substitution of some imports (mainly fuel) (Promperú, 1996).

The official view supposed that the increase in exports would reduce country-risk and sustain a fairly lengthy period of current account deficits and heavy debt repayment. Regular debt payment would help generate financial confidence in Peru's creditworthiness which, alongside the maintenance of high domestic interest rates and non-interference in profit remission (which includes an important element of differential rents), would stimulate steady and growing direct investment in export-oriented enterprises.

The supposition here appears to be that domestic capital is neither sufficiently plentiful nor prepared to finance projects of this calibre. The external deficits, in turn, make it easier for the Fujimori government to maintain the internal political autonomy it has sought to establish since 1990 and to insulate the policies of international financial reinsertion from domestic political pressures.

The government's confidence in foreign capital and its dependence on it became manifest in 1990. The first indication of this was in the last quarter of 1990 when it took the unilateral decision to start repaying the foreign debt. Over this period, multilateral institutions, like the IMF, the World Bank and the Inter-American Development Bank (IDB), played a key role in the strategies adopted to stabilise and liberalise the economy. The speed at which incentives were authorised to promote foreign investment was but another indication of the importance of international economic support in underpinning the government and its policies.

However, the stability of the process depended on four variables: (i) the ability to achieve sufficient levels of domestic savings to provide protection from volatility in international financial markets; (ii) a macroeconomic policy based on a fiscal surplus and which provided incentives for the entry of foreign capital; (iii) sufficient flexibility to respond to external volatility and to problems arising from the way in which macro policy affected economic agents and the public sector; and (iv) a concentration of decision-making power and resource allocation in the office of the president with a view to ensuring his continuance in office.

The method for achieving the first of these objectives, and to buttress the stability of the financial system, was the establishment of a privatised system of pensions. By 1996, financial savings in private pension plans (AFPs) were equivalent to 1.5% of GDP, with pension funds reaching 3.2 billion soles. By 2000, it was believed that there would be a total of 3 billion dollars in the AFPs and a further 1.5 billion in the schemes for time service compensation (CTSs). Together they were expected to account for 8% of GDP by the end of the century (Seminario, 1997). With regard to the second objective, the letters of intent signed with the IMF indicated the government's intention to maintain a fairly tight control over the rhythm of economic activity and to avoid the introduction of controls over the inflow of short-term capital (Rojas, 1994, p. 153). Labour market liberalisation (Garavito, 1996) and the ending of protection for manufacturing industry and agriculture were conducive to the third objective. Meanwhile, the palace coup (the *autogolpe*) of April 1992, the system used to control public sector spending, the size of the budget afforded to the ministry of the presidency and Fujimori's use of housing funds (Fonavi) were all of critical importance in contributing to the fourth.[4]

The peculiarities of the Peruvian adjustment

One of the features of structural adjustment in Peru after 1990 was its radical nature, especially compared with other countries of Latin America. In trying to explain the radical nature of the adjustment, a number of points need to be stressed. First and foremost, the government sought to bury once and for all the business model introduced in the late 1960s and early 1970s by General Juan Velasco. In the minds of business leaders, the pendulum had to swing as far as possible in the opposite direction, especially vis-à-vis labour relations and state ownership. Secondly, it is also important to bear in mind the exceptionally long duration of adjustment prior to the Fujimori government. From the late 1970s, real living standards had been in decline, but without resolving the problem of inflation. The debt crisis exposed the reliance of state companies on foreign capital, and without that support they had to contend with an erratic policy of subsidies that varied with each successive adjustment package. The process of adjustment that began in 1988 and the economic crisis that lasted until 1990 brought a dramatic fall in fiscal income, and with it a sharp reduction in the

---

[4]   Between 1992 and 1996, Fonavi raised 4.57 billion soles. In the first quarter of 1997, for instance, it accounted for 6.2% of all state income.

incomes   of public employees and a suspension of most forms of public investment. The state found itself in virtual collapse. In many respects, the reforms that followed from 1990 were a response to this situation.

Thirdly, public disillusionment in the record of the García government (1985-90), especially in its last two years, made it easier politically to pursue a new agenda. The ending of the García administration brought with it a collapse in national self-confidence which had been the hallmark of its first two years in office. The experience heightened the belief that foreign capital was crucial for investment, brought better management practice and led to financial stability. The crisis of the García years proved profoundly demoralising.

A fourth feature was the way in which, in Peru, economic issues became enmeshed with the problem of public security in the minds of people from all social backgrounds, in response to the political violence unleashed by the conflict between the armed forces and Sendero Luminoso.

A fifth characteristic was the almost fundamentalist liberalising zeal of Carlos Boloña – who became economy minister in early 1991 – and his team. The speed and radical nature of the institutional changes which were introduced took even the multilateral institutions by surprise. The decision to lower tariffs drastically at a time of considerable currency overvaluation showed a determination amongst those in government to deal forcefully with firms they accused of being 'mercantilist'. An additional factor that helps explain the reformers' persistence was the extent of the leverage exercised over economic policy-making by the multilateral institutions after 1990.

Finally, the extreme weakness of the political parties, which had shown themselves wanting in their ability to stabilise the economy, meant that there was little organised political opposition. The 1992 *autogolpe* was the final *coup de grâce* for the political parties, which had in many respects shown themselves in Congress to have been pliant to the wishes of the executive on economic policy.

However, in spite of the radical nature of the Peruvian adjustment process, it was not conducted without certain pragmatism. A particularly interesting hallmark was the use of the flexible exchange rate. In view of Peru's history of inflation, it would not have been absurd to have tried to eliminate the exchange rate altogether as a policy variable by creating a sort of Argentine-style currency board. One reason why this was not adopted is to be found in the political positions adopted by the main parties in the 1989-90 election campaign. Most of the parties coincided on the sort of economic measures to be taken (although they differed in their emphasis), including the need to reduce and simplify tariffs, to reduce subsidies, to rationalise the tax system and take other measures similar in kind to those eventually applied. Where they differed was in the policy eventually applied by the Fujimori government with respect to a devaluation. APRA, Fredemo and Izquierda Unida all included the need for a devaluation, although Izquierda Unida was more reticent.

However, this near consensus probably had less influence in practice than studies conducted by the World Bank which ruled out a devaluation and the subsequent establishment of an exchange rate anchor (Iguíñiz, 1997, p. 108). The thinking of the World Bank influenced the recommendations made by the IMF to the Fujimori government which, also fearful for the possible public reaction, opted for the unusual course of seeking to stabilise the economy in the short run through dollarisation and the use of a flexible exchange rate.

The achievement of a primary fiscal surplus

Peru has followed a course similar to that of other Latin American countries in the area of public finance. Three main aspects of policy stand out: (i) the reduction of very high inflation rates since 1990; (ii) the emergency measures that were taken; and (iii) the reforms to the tax administration system.

With regard to the first, stabilisation was of critical importance, since the initial increase in tax income took place at the very moment that the inflation rate fell. Emergency measures were taken over the first few months – between the beginning of August and the end of November 1990 – and then once again in the middle of 1991 when it became clearer that the initial reforms taken at the end of 1990 had had disappointing results. The reforms to the tax system involved tax simplification; the key point for this was November 1990 when eleven decrees were issued to this end (Gómez, Urrunaga and Bel, 1997, pp. 61-7).

A crucial moment in the improvement of the tax yield was August 1990. Between them, the effects of the increase in fuel taxes (fuel prices rose by several hundred percent) and the reverse application of the 'Olivera-Tanzi' effect (whereby inflation erodes fiscal revenue), meant that tax income rose rapidly. Fiscal revenue on an annual basis increased from 4.75% of GDP in August 1990 to 9.04% in September, 10.06% in October, reaching 12.28% in November, the month when the fiscal reforms were decreed. From November 1990 onwards, the tax take stabilised at roughly this level. In 1992, it was 9.4% of GDP, 9.78% in 1993 and 11.1% in 1994 (Gómez, Urrunaga and Bel, 1997, p. 41). The main reason for the increase in 1994 was the reactivation of the economy.

During all this time, public spending was kept under tight control. The centralisation of the system for allocating public spending, the weakness of social organisation among the sectors most likely to demand higher spending, and the inability of the public administration to spend were all factors that helped. The consequence was a series of primary surpluses in the fiscal accounts (excluding capital income) that lasted several years. It is perhaps unsurprising that the return to growth (starting in 1993) coincided with a fall in these primary surpluses. Nevertheless, the primary surplus in 1997 was stil around 1.3% of GDP.

Stability in the financial system

During these years, Peru successfully weathered two potential exogenous upsets to financial stability: the 1992 *autogolpe* and the 'tequila effect' that followed the Mexican peso crisis and which coincided with the brief border conflict with Ecuador in January 1995. This apparent solidity was not unconnected with the relatively weak development of Peruvian capital markets. Furthermore, the prominence of the privatisation programme meant that short-term capital movements were less important than elsewhere as a component of the balance of payments. In 1994, for instance, at a rough tally, short-term inflows of capital were 1.7 billion dollars, or 37% of the annual total for capital inflows of all types (Dancourt and Mendoza, 1997, p. 38).[5] Furthermore, the almost complete lack of public or private bond issues in this period is also suggestive of the relative lack of financial sophistication in the Peruvian market. The public sector was thus virtually independent of short-term capital for its financial needs.

The exchange rate risk, of course, was not inconsiderable in a country like Peru. There had been years in which, despite an overall pattern of currency depreciation over the longer term, periods of sudden devaluation were interspersed with bouts of revaluation. Also, exchange rate risk was further enhanced by the size of the current account deficits and the burden of debt repayment. The system of a 'dirty float' provided a certain scope for manoeuvre, whilst at the same time the fiscal surplus helped ensure future debt repayment and push the dollar up. In this context, the interest rate on deposits in soles was scant inducement, reaching only 10.5% per annum at the end of 1996. Nevertheless, a large proportion of the foreign capital entering the country, lent to the banks and on-lent in dollars, bore no exchange-rate risk whatsoever. The interest rate in dollars at the end of 1996 for borrowers was 16.8%, whilst the rate for lenders was 5.7% and 3-months Libor was 5.5%. Moreover, these inflows were not subject to the 44% reserve requirement on dollar deposits. One of the main reasons for the relatively low impact of short-term capital on economic volatility in Peru had to do with the nature of these flows. In large part, it seems, they consisted of capital repatriated by Peruvians from abroad for the purposes of financing their domestic businesses. Also, the remission of dollars from Peruvians living abroad played an important role.

In spite of having a relatively under-developed capital market, Peru was a country receiving relatively heavy inflows (Held and Szalachman, 1996), in view of the importance of privatisation and other forms of foreign direct investment. At the same time, short-term borrowing by Peruvian banks increased: the international liabilities of commercial banks (*banca múltiple*) increased from 660 million dollars at the end of 1994 to 1.9 billion in December 1996, equivalent to 20% of the total dollar loans of the commercial banks (Dancourt and Mendoza, 1997, p. 8).[6]

---

[5]   The figure includes net income from official loans, which was fairly low and (on some reckonings) slightly negative.

[6]   According to the Banking Superintendency, the figure for 'debts and other financial

Therefore, Peru passed through the process of stabilisation without suffering the sort of banking crisis which erupted in several other countries in Latin America. There was a crisis in the financial system in 1992, but its effect was reduced substantially by the elimination of the development banks and some smaller financial intermediaries like savings and loans associations (*mutuales*), finance companies (*financieras*) and credit cooperatives (Rojas, 1994). The lack of intermediation in the period immediately following stabilisation was problematic, but the situation was eased by the reduction in the number of financial agents. In 1991, private commercial banks accounted for 52.4% of total liquidity; in 1993 this had risen to 78.7%. Only after the period of financial reforms did the figure begin to fall slightly, reducing to 75.4% in 1995.[7] The percentage of credit of the *banca múltiple* to the private sector was 71% in 1991, reaching 95% in 1995.

Reforms to the financial sector thus helped prevent a banking crisis, but did not result in any marked diversification in institutions or instruments; the commercial banks continued to play the predominant role. Indeed, they tended to promote concentration. Whatever indicators we use, between 1990 and 1993 concentration increased, reversing the trend since 1987 (Rojas and Vilcapoma, 1996, p. 37). The number of banks fell from 23 to 17, before increasing once again to their original level at the end of 1996. The diversification of banking activities after the introduction of the *banca múltiple* meant that banks were able to increase their income from sources other than interest rates. Non-financial income rose from 12% at the end of 1990 to just under 27% in March 1994, falling back slightly thereafter.

Bank reforms coincided with an increase in rates of dollarisation, both for loans and deposits. In December 1990, loans in dollars accounted for 69.3% of the total, peaking at 77.8% in June 1994. Meanwhile deposits in dollars rose from 65.2% at the end of 1990 to 81.1% three years later. In 1994 and 1995, levels of dollarisation fell back, but not to their initial levels. Exchange rate risk was thus minimised by the extent of dollarisation.

Banks became relatively more efficient because of the reforms. Bank employment fell fairly rapidly in the larger banks, but in the mid-1990s recovered to previous levels because of the entry of new banks into the system. The ratio of bank employees to total loans fell notably between the end of 1992 and 1996.[8] During the first part of the reform process, banks were obliged to increase their provisioning through, amongst other things, increases in their capital base. From 1993 onwards, almost all indicators of bank performance improved and fears of a banking crisis receded.

---

obligations' (indicative of short-term flows obtained abroad) stood at 2.84 billion dollars in December 1996.

[7]   The reform took place at a difficult point, during which bad debts rose from 14.6% at the end of 1990 to 16% in March 1993. With the subsequent recovery, these fell quite quickly.

[8]   *Medio de Cambio*. Documento de trabajo, November-December 1996, p. 44.

The institutional context and policy constraints

This section focuses attention on a number of rigidities which are likely to impinge on future policy-making.

Dollarisation

Dollarisation brings with it serious constraints in terms of macroeconomic management; as of 1996, 75% of all deposits were denominated in foreign currency and 74% of all loans. The central bank therefore lacked room for manoeuvre in regulating the money supply, irrespective of the exchange rate regime (Dancourt, 1997). In theory, the central bank could have controlled the monetary base and the supply of bank credit in soles by leaving the exchange rate free; the sale and purchase of foreign currency and debt paper would have allowed this. However, this option would have only allowed the authorities directly to regulate about one-quarter of the money supply, since the sale of dollars responded to stimuli other than those emanating from the central bank. Indeed, such restrictions would have been largely voluntary, given the unwillingness to regulate inflows arising from private bank borrowing abroad.

Dollarisation also made it much more difficult to use devaluation as a tool to mitigate and manage sectorially problems arising in the external sector. Indeed, having dollarised bank portfolios, companies selling in soles would have faced grave problems, given the classic impact of a devaluation on domestic demand and on the bad debts of the banking system. Furthermore, a real devaluation would have implied an increase in real interest rates payable by those with dollar debts. Banking crises would therefore have arisen for two reasons: the change in the profitability of bank clients arising from the increase in margins on tradables with respect to non-tradable goods (towards which most of their resources had been directed); and the financial burden assumed by those operating in soles, whether in tradables or not. If the devaluation was in itself a consequence of the withdrawal of deposits abroad, the effects would have been magnified.

On the other hand, the privatisation of public service utilities compounded the effects of exchange rate policy constraints. Such companies needed to remit dollars abroad and therefore had an interest in there being an overvalued exchange rate, since every sol they earned in the sale of services raised more in foreign exchange. At the same time, foreign creditors benefited from an overvalued exchange rate since every sol the government raised in tax bought correspondingly more foreign exchange, thereby easing debt payments. A devaluation would make it more difficult to finance payments, at least in the short term.

A coalition of interests thus emerged resistant to a depreciation of the exchange rate, thereby limiting policy options. The consequence of this was that the central bank was restricted in what it could do (Iguíñiz, 1997), especially in offsetting fluctuations by resort to higher unemployment rather than through lower wages. Since the struggle for employment remains a key social demand, this was an option that involved political risks for the government.[9]

The viability of the export model

Analysis of the efficacy of the export strategy is required to determine the resultant rate of growth. Neither the domestic nor the international context is the same as 50 years ago. A number of points merit emphasis at the outset. First, commodity prices are low and have not fully recovered from their fall 15 years ago. Secondly, volatility in the terms of trade persists and there is a negative correlation between this volatility and patterns of growth (Gavin, Haussman, Perotti and Talvi, 1996). Thirdly, the deals negotiated with exporting firms have tended to be favourable for these, usually at the expense of taxes, wages and the current account of the balance of payments (Promperú, 1996; Gómez, Urrunaga and Bel, 1997, pp. 64-5). Fourthly, the retention of foreign exchange to promote growth runs into a foreign debt constraint, necessitating a primary surplus to shift resources from the private sector to the state in order to meet debt commitments. Fifthly, foreign investors in the service sector remit profit without contributing to exports (Schydlowsky and Schuldt, 1996, p. 50). Finally, the process of reversing import substitution involves increased imports of consumer goods, reducing the possibility of retaining for investment purposes the foreign exchange generated by exports. Between them, these factors tend to weaken the effects of exports on growth.

In addition to the points mentioned above, it is also possible that the economy will lose international competitiveness through the effects of 'Dutch disease' (Schuldt, 1994; 1995) whose effects have been compounded by the rapid increase in consumer credit for imported goods. However, at the same time this relative decline in manufacturing has been mitigated, at least in part, by the development of industries processing raw materials for export.

The only way in which these negative factors could be offset was through an ever increasing quantity of foreign investment, so that the increase in output could offset the effect on prices and the relatively small proportion of foreign exchange made available for productive investment. Sustainability over the long term, therefore, appeared to be closely related to the ability to continue to increase export volumes.

At this point, it is important to bear in mind that Peruvian supply on world markets will probably increase fairly speedily over the next few decades. The country's productive potential has lagged behind in recent decades, and there is significant potential for both the mining and agroindustrial sectors to increase output substantially. Other sectors with considerable room for growth include timber extraction and tourism, while improvements in the efficiency of the fishmeal industry could lead to increased exports. Investments in oil and gas may have an important effect in substituting imports, while at the same time

---

[9]   It could be argued conversely that unemployment was one of the main tools in encouraging labour 'discipline'.

yielding exportable surpluses.[10] Finally, in the agricultural sector, new products like asparagus have proved dynamic, whilst output of certain traditional crops have also increased.

Projections for total exports suggest a level of some 8.5 billion dollars a year in 2000, or around 14-15% of GDP. The effect of an increase of this sort should help encourage the development of institutions and a culture to produce new export lines.

However, this sort of increase in exports cannot be taken for granted. The differential rent resulting from the quality of natural resources may be insufficient. According to one study, large-scale mining investment requires tax concessions, without which a number of projects are unlikely to go ahead, in spite of investment in exploration.[11] Signs of political and institutional instability, coupled with the approach of presidential elections, may hold back investment in sectors in which returns are only recovered over the long run.

As we indicated above, the continuity of this sort of macroeconomic policy could run into difficulties if there is a delay in the export boom taking off, whilst debt service obligations become increasingly onerous.[12] The outlook depends on a number of factors which are difficult to forecast accurately in view of the country's institutional instabilities. Sufficient foreign exchange is required but also the primary fiscal surplus for the central bank to buy it. At the same time, whilst the debt payment schedule is fairly clear, military and other areas of spending are an unknown quantity, as is the way in which presidential politics might impact on public spending. The congressional and presidential elections in 2000 appear likely to have an important bearing on fiscal spending.

As of 1998, the debt repayment calendar seems fairly well-defined. Debt service payments are programmed to total 1.52 billion dollars in 1998, 1.66 billion in 1999 and 1.7 billion in 2000. Thereafter, payments are set to peak at 1.88 billion in 2004. Meanwhile, official projections for exports suggest that they will increase at an annual rate of 10% up to 2000, bringing the total to 8.3 billion dollars. If thereafter the annual rate of increase rose to 11%, exports should hit 14 billion dollars in 2004. Debt service-to-export ratios would therefore decrease to around 20% in 2000 and 13% in 2004. [13] If the export of services is included, these ratios would fall to 17% and 11% respectively. Up to 1999, the government can also rely on privatisation revenues. However, the increase in foreign direct investment could have ambiguous effects: while on the

---

[10]   Development of the Camisea gas field in the jungle region of northern Cusco may offer a major potential for exports as well as substituting for imported fuel.
[11]   A study by Macroconsult for the Instituto de Estudios Mineros develops this point. Macroconsult (1997) (see also Chapter 3).
[12]   The fall in mineral prices in 1997 and 1998, coupled with institutional uncertainties, had the effect of postponing a number of major investment projects, such as Antamina and La Granja.
[13]   The debt service ratio was still around 29% of exports at the end of 1997, reflecting in part an increase in repayments to commercial banks following the 1996 Brady deal.

one hand it would bring in capital, on the other it also would involve imports and by stimulating the domestic economy would further add to the demand for imported goods. Often, increases in investment coincide with a worsening of the situation on the trade account.

It is therefore difficult to avoid the conclusion that in the medium-to-long term, Peruvian primary exports are likely to undergo a substantial and sustained increase, and that this should give rise to a fairly lengthy period of growth. It is also clear that such growth would have little impact on employment and could, indeed, lead to a further worsening of income inequalities and a further build-up in social and political pressures. However, it also seems that although these effects are highly probable, they are not a direct political consequence of the economic model itself or a questioning of the export strategy. At least, it is difficult to show this with any real empirical rigour. In view of this, I would prefer to leave open the question of export performance over the next two or three decades; even if there is a serious slump in the next few years, it will probably resolve itself either through the granting of further incentives to exporters or through a devaluation; any radical crisis in the export model presupposes its prior success.[14]

Capital market opening and bank reform

The volatility of short-term capital flows is a new factor inducing instability. One source of volatility is external, in the sense that these flows depend on variations in global interest rates or respond to moments of crisis in other countries. This volatility afflicts the domestic economy. These policies of institutional change which a government may consider necessary to resolve a specific problem – including that of economic vulnerability – may be considered a threat by fund managers in other countries. At the very least, policy changes have to take into account their possible effects on capital flight.

On the issue of capital market opening, a distinction has to be drawn once again between the short term and the long term. Hitherto, short-term capital inflows have boosted growth and reduced inflation. However, the longer-term effects of short-term capital are more difficult to foresee: on the one hand the liberalisation of capital markets sends favourable signals for longer-term capital investment, especially in a country with a history of state intervention with regard to property and capital controls; on the other, the increased vulnerability of the economy has the opposite effect, especially for investments which take time to mature.

Vulnerability to capital fluctuations has caused concern in different international organisations, and has been carefully monitored by them (Gavin, Haussman, Perotti and Talvi, 1996). For our purposes, we have to ask the question whether this will alter macroeconomic policy. The reason for raising this point is that for some writers a reverse causality has been established: that it

---

[14] In this respect, I would agree with the long-term perspectives adopted by Schuldt (1995).

is the economic policies of countries which really explain this volatility (Gavin, Haussman, Perotti and Talvi, 1996). However, it could be argued that the roots of such volatility are to be found in the international context.[15] Moreover, countries are subject to constant pressure from the multilateral organisations to introduce reforms to the state: this means that they face stronger pressure to reform their institutions than to introduce relative prices to deflect international volatility.

This leaves the feeling that countries have to administer volatility and to persist with international financial insertion by means of state reforms. The purpose is to guarantee the generation of primary surpluses and to provide a defence against banking crises. Given the impossibility of multilateral organisations contributing much to the mitigation of a crisis were one to happen in a number of countries at the same time, and given the high cost of financial crises worldwide, it is the developing countries which appear to bear the cost in reducing the probability of such an event taking place. Clearly, a major banking crisis would impede economic growth in Peru for a number of years, generating new forms of political instability.

The Fujimori government's banking law (DL 27702) helped forestall a number of problems and banking regulation became stricter. Nevertheless, concentration in the Peruvian banking sector is roughly double the average for the rest of Latin America, and about one-quarter of all loans in Peru still go to firms associated with the bank concerned. There are strong arguments for tighter regulation and such control mechanisms as reserve requirements or minimum capital levels are not very effective methods for controlling liquidity. The methods by which these rules are circumvented suggest the need for banking institutions to work in a more regulated framework (Rojas-Suárez and Weisbrod, 1995).

Another factor which adds to financial stability is the existence of low-volatility national savings, such as those administered by AFPs and CTSs. Although we have already indicated that in a few years these may become a significant and more stable element of national savings (thereby reducing the likelihood of bank failure), a serious banking crisis would probably wipe out both the AFPs and the new system of privatised pensions.

After 1990, it seems that the increase in external savings coincided with a decrease in national savings. Seemingly, forced personal saving in institutions is offset by the increase in consumer credit. Between 1990 and 1995, credit to the private sector tripled as a percentage of GDP (Held and Szalachman, 1996, pp. 22-5). The increase in wealth created by higher stock market valuation and higher property prices, combined with the cut-off in consumption in the late 1980s and early 1990s, all helped engender this sudden spurt in consumption.

---

[15]   My impression is that, once again, national governments find themselves with no option but to reform when confronted with problems whose origin is mainly external.

Summarising, the vulnerability of the Peruvian economy to capital movements is not very high. Its resistance to the 'tequila effect' pointed to the extent of its isolation. The strengthening of banking regulation further fortified the system. It looks relatively unlikely that Peru would be badly affected by external pressures, unless such a crisis was both pronounced and prolonged. While receipts from privatisation provided short-term immunity, long-term loans were increasing and helped provide finance for investment in mining, oil, gas and other sectors. Short-term lending and speculative inflows represented only a relatively small proportion of total capital inflows. The increase in forced saving, with movements fairly closely regulated by the government, further reduced the risk of serious problems arising. The biggest risk to the banking sector came from excessive lending to the non-tradables sector. In this context, the effects of devaluation could not be ignored.

The fiscal structure and its vulnerability

President Alberto Fujimori's ability to cope with international instabilities and defuse their impact within the domestic economy depended a great deal on fiscal management, a topic taken up and developed further by Rosemary Thorp and Francisco Durand in Chapter 11. The concentration of spending decisions within a single office, SUNAT, was designed in part to increase flexibility in response to differing economic and political conditions. Nevertheless, there was a number of more structural factors which have also affected the government's ability to respond to changing international conditions and domestic political problems.

The social base of the tax system in Peru is narrow. For instance, the number of registered taxpayers in the first four months of 1997 was 1,637,000, or around 20% of the total labour force. Of these, those who made a tax return totalled some 640,500, or only 8% of the workforce. Those who in fact paid were around 448,500.[16] The fiscal structure in Peru is similar to that of most other countries in Latin America, and this provides some useful clues as to fiscal vulnerability. One of the most important features that distinguishes fiscal deficits in Latin America from those in developed countries is their volatility. Those aspects of developed countries' fiscal systems which are most volatile are precisely those which loom largest in Latin America: non-tax forms of revenue and indirect taxes (especially on trade). By contrast, the fiscal system in developed countries relies to a much greater extent on income from social security payments and direct taxes.

The Peruvian fiscal system shows up these rigidities clearly. In 1994, sales tax and the selective consumption tax raised 65.3% of tax income, whilst other indirect taxes (excluding taxes on trade) were the equivalent of 33.5% of tax income for Latin America as a whole. By contrast, the equivalent ratio in the countries of the OECD was 27.3%. Income tax in Peru generated 20% of total revenue, as opposed to 32.5% in Latin America and 33.9% in the OECD

---

[16]   *Gestión*, 20 May 1997, p. 40.

countries.[17] In Peru, taxes on foreign trade accounted for 12.3% of tax income, a similar level to the Latin American average of 11.2% for the 1992-94 period, but much higher than the OECD figure of 0.89%. Forms of income which are least stable in developed countries are precisely those which are most important in Peru.

At the same time, the structure of spending is also very rigid, similar in most respects to other countries in Latin America. Unlike the OECD countries, the main difference is the fiscal burden of debt repayment, salaries and capital costs. Debt and public sector remunerations are particularly rigid elements in the Peruvian case.

Latin America's fiscal problem is therefore a dual one: volatility on the income side is higher than in industrialised economies, whilst changes in expenditure are more pro-cyclical. In some respects, however, Peru differs from the norm in the larger countries of Latin America. It is particularly exposed to changes in the structure of its income and expenditure, and the weight and rigidity of debt payments mean that adjustment has to take place in other areas, principally in public investment spending (as was the case in 1996). At the same time, the type of public indebtedness is less sophisticated and risky than, for instance, in Mexico or Argentina. The withdrawal of external financial support when the economy enters into a downturn and the consequent negative effect on fiscal spending is not comparatively the riskiest aspect in the Peruvian case.

Indeed, one of the 'advantages' of the strict adherence to scheduled debt payments is the reduction in the pro-cyclical volatility in external financing, which Gavin, Haussman, Perotti and Talvi (1996) identify for Latin America as a whole. For good or for bad, the government's dilemma lay not in the area of debt payment since to reduce these payments would produce a cut-off in new lending which would neutralise any advantages to be gained from non-payment. Moreover, international support was a crucial element in the government's economic and social strategy.

The rigidity with regard to debt payment was thus structural. Since low wage levels make it difficult to reduce public sector remunerations further, any adjustment would have to be made (as in the past) by reducing capital spending. In the meantime, political difficulties in finally laying to rest the old state meant that creating unemployment was not a viable route, at least not until after the elections in 2000. One option could be to resort to raising inflation levels and to use this as a way to drive down real wages. However, the most obvious way to respond to volatility is to increase the burden of direct taxation and to reduce taxes on foreign trade. Political difficulties in finally dismantling the old state structure would postpone any attempt to lay off workers in the public sector until after the presidential elections in 2000. Opting for fiscal decentralisation would not be viable whilst regional and municipal authorities are unable to levy their

---

[17]   The OECD provides a relevant contrast because of its low levels of inflation.

own taxation. Meanwhile, in the short term at least, privatisation probably provides the easiest way to reduce fiscal volatility. In this respect, it seems more likely that the political calendar, rather than any attempt to create an anti-cyclical strategy, will prevail.

Political constraints

Finally, it is impossible to ignore the political constraints that impinge on the Fujimori government and limited its scope for manoeuvre in the design and implementation of macroeconomic policy. From the early 1990s onwards, the government was influenced in its decisions by criteria of political continuity, and specifically the removal of the legal barriers to re-election. During Fujimori's second government, after 1995, such criteria persisted, underlining the need to retain popularity. Indeed, from its very early days, opinion poll findings played a key role in the sequencing of economic reforms.

By whatever standards used, Fujimori was a politician who managed to cultivate – at least up until 1997 – high levels of public approval, and this greatly assisted him in implementing what, in other circumstances, would have been unpopular economic policies. His popularity also gave him greater margin for manoeuvre in dealing with such other actors as the armed forces and the multilateral financial institutions.

The relationship between economic performance and presidential popularity was not one of cause and effect, and for this reason dissatisfaction with the results of economic policies did not necessarily lead to changes in those policies, still less in the overall strategy. For instance, Fujimori's popularity peaked in 1992, a year of continued economic difficulty, largely because of the public response to the *autogolpe* and the subsequent capture of Abimael Guzmán, the founder and leading light of Sendero Luminoso. However, between 1993 and 1995, there was a closer correlation between growth in the economy and support for the president. An important finding of the polls (which are usually conducted only in Lima) was that sympathy for Fujimori varied considerably between different age and income groups.

Furthermore, public attitudes towards specific aspects of the reform programme also indicate large variations between different sectors of the population at different times. These show up clearly, for instance, when different sectors were asked to give their reactions to such issues as state-shrinking, privatisation and judicial reform. Even among groups which would previously have been hostile to many aspects of reform – for instance among unionised workers – responses were surprisingly mixed. In large part, this reflects the greatly reduced influence of trade unions among wage-earners. It is possible that in conditions of sustained growth, unions may regain some of their lost strength, although it is hard to imagine them regaining the same degree of political influence that they wielded in the 1980s.

The reform programme appears, therefore, to have had an ambiguous appeal, even though by 1997 it seemed clear that some aspects of policy were becoming increasingly unpopular among specific sectors of the population. Privatisation policy, for instance, met with greater criticism than before. There were also indications that such issues as low wages and inadequate employment were having a more decisive impact in determining the government's popularity.

In my view, three factors seem likely to have an important bearing on social policy. The first is the influence of multilateral organisations, who are among those most interested in transferring scarce fiscal resources away from medium and high-income groups to the benefit of the poor. The second is the political pressure that could be exerted by those impoverished by years of crisis but excluded from the sort of assistance available to slum-dwellers and peasant communities. The third is budget constraints. Pressures may also emanate from the poorest sectors, in receipt of help with infrastructure, clothing and food, but which will push for such assistance to be institutionalised and made more permanent.

Conclusions

In this chapter, I have sought to avoid making definitive judgements about the longer-term viability of the Fujimori government's reform strategy. Even if Fujimori himself were no longer the lead actor, a mere change of president seems unlikely to lead to any substantial change in the overall thrust of policy. Conditioning factors, whether external and internal, historical or conjunctural, would probably stay the same for some time. My analysis has brought out what I consider to be a number of constraints limiting the government's room for manoeuvre, which may in the future force it to modify its stance in some respects. In spite of a tendency to import policy instruments and institutional models, the Fujimori government has been fairly pragmatic in its approach. There seems little reason to think that it will change in this respect and that, having no predilection for suicide, it will continue to adapt policy to perceived risks, political or other.

PART II

ECONOMIC PERFORMANCE

CHAPTER 3

Privatisation, Investment and Sustainability

Drago Kisic

This chapter aims to evaluate some of the reforms introduced by the Fujimori government in the context of macroeconomic sustainability. Specifically, it seeks to establish whether the rate of investment achieved was sufficient to sustain a growth rate of around 5% per annum, the minimum required (although not the only condition) for the country gradually to resolve its longstanding problems of poverty and unemployment. Investment levels increased substantially in the early 1990s, largely due to successful policies of macreoconomic stabilisation, market liberalisation and pacification. Initially, at least – as one would suppose – the recovery of economic activity was based on greater use of installed capacity.

The chapter begins by analysing the patterns of investment in the 1970s and 1980s, in which public sector investment predominated over private. Then, having briefly touched on some of the basic reforms of the early 1990s – trade liberalisation, financial reform and privatisation – it seeks to highlight the increase in investment achieved. It goes on to deal with the requirements for continued growth, not just in terms of investment needs but also in terms of the removal of other economic, social and political obstacles.

Investment and the public sector, prior to 1990

From 1970 onwards, the state played an increasingly important role in determining the pattern of growth, with the bulk of investment coming from the public sector. This coincided with the growth in the number of state companies, which roughly tripled in number by 1980. Under this model of 'state capitalism' (Fitzgerald, 1983), public investment quickly overtook private investment as a proportion of GDP (see Table 1).

In the second half of the 1970s, the economy entered into a period of adjustment, public investment fell, only to pick up again in the early 1980s under the Belaúnde government (1980-85). Overall investment levels increased up until 1982 when they reached a peak of 33.5% of GDP. Thereafter, following the onset of the debt crisis, climatic disturbances related to the El Niño phenomenon and the government's failure to introduce timely adjustment policies, investment fell. The heterodox policies adopted by President Alan García (1985-90) saw the public sector once again privileged in terms of policy-making.

Table 1. Saving- investment Gap, 1972-90 (as Percentage of Nominal GDP)

	Total Investment	Public Investment (1)	Private Investment (1)	Share of Public Investment (%)	Share of Private Investment (%)	Total Domestic Savings	Saving-Investment Gap
1972	14.5	5.0	7.8	35	54	14.1	-0.4
1973	16.0	5.5	7.1	34	45	13.9	-2.1
1974	18.9	8.3	6.9	44	37	11.9	-7.0
1975	19.8	8.4	9.2	42	46	8.5	-11.3
1976	18.1	8.0	8.7	44	48	10.3	-7.8
1977	14.8	6.2	8.2	42	55	8.7	-6.1
1978	14.4	5.5	8.3	38	58	12.8	-1.6
1979	21.7	5.0	15.7	23	72	27.9	-6.2
1980	28.8	6.1	18.8	21	65	28.3	-0.5
1981	34.3	7.3	21.5	21	63	27.3	-7.0
1982	33.5	8.5	21.3	25	63	27.0	-6.5
1983	24.3	8.7	15.0	36	62	20.0	-4.3
1984	20.1	8.1	12.2	40	60	19.2	-0.9
1985	18.3	6.3	12.2	35	66	18.9	0.6
1986	20.3	5.2	15.1	26	74	14.7	-5.6
1987	21.1	4.1	17.0	19	81	15.6	-5.5
1988	22.0	3.4	18.6	15	85	15.0	-7.0
1989	17.8	3.6	14.2	20	80	17.1	-0.7
1990	15.7	2.7	13.0	17	83	12.3	-3.4

(1) The difference between total investment and the sum of public and private investment between 1970 and 1985 is explained by the exclusion of stock change.

Source: BCRP

Much of the gross capital formation that took place in the 1970s was directed towards the strengthening of the public sector, and was financed largely through an increase in the foreign debt. The level of investment averaged around 18.5% of GDP, growing in 1979 and 1980 to 21.7% and 28.8% respectively. Whilst investment during this period was diversified throughout the economy, much of it was directed towards the development of the oil sector and (to a lesser extent) infrastructure. For its part, the private sector found itself excluded from a number of economic sectors by virtue of the government's policy of nationalisation.

In the early 1980s, under Belaúnde, investment reached record levels, oscillating between 33-34.5% in 1981-82. Whilst private investment recovered a larger share of the total, the continuance of policies of state capitalism meant that public investment maintained its pre-eminence, especially in such areas as infrastructure. Levels of investment tapered off towards the middle of the decade, as macroeconomic imbalances fed through into higher levels of economic uncertainty. This was particularly pronounced in the last few years of the decade when, as a result of the collapse of García's heterodox model, economic output contracted sharply and inflation ran out of control.[1]

---

[1]   The economy contracted by 8.8%, 1.7% and 3.7% in 1988, 1989 and 1990 respectively, whilst consumer prices rose by 1,722%, 2,775% and 7,650%.

During the 1970s and 1980s, the economy was affected by large distortions in relative prices (interest rates, the real exchange rate, public sector prices, tariffs etc) which encouraged inefficiencies in the pattern of investment, whilst state planning policies prioritised import-substituting industrialisation (ISI). Private sector investment diminished in relation to that of the public sector in the 1970s, whilst in the 1980s – largely because of the progressive fiscal crisis of the state – it increased once again as public sector investment fell to very low levels.

The extent of state intervention in the 1970s encouraged inefficiencies in state companies, which lacked capital for investment and which suffered from official price subsidisation policies, poor training and overmanning. Whilst in 1968 there had been 18-40 state companies (depending on the definition used)[2] generating between 1-6% of GDP, by 1980 there were 186 (Alvarez Rodrich, 1991). Of these, 136 were non-financial companies, the rest being linked to the financial system in one way or another.

State interventionism was at its height during the two consecutive military governments of Generals Juan Velasco and Francisco Morales Bermúdez (1968-80), when state economic planning sought to dynamise the economy through so-called 'strategic sectors'. The existence of state monopolies encouraged the use of price controls and led to persistent fiscal deficits.[3] At the beginning of the 1990s, there was a total of 46 legal monopolies in different areas of the economy.[4] In the area of marketing, the largest of these companies controlled food imports (ENCI), rice imports (ECASA) and the sale of minerals and metals (Minpeco). In the productive sphere, the largest were Petroperú (controlling the refining and sale of petroleum products) and Pescaperú (in the fishing and fishmeal industries). In the service sector, the main state monopolies were electricity generating and distribution, water supply and sewerage, telecommunications, ports and social security. However, around 60% of public sector assets (excluding those in the financial sector) were accounted for by only three firms: Electroperú, Petroperú and Entelperú (telecommunications).

At the beginning of the Fujimori government, in 1990, the public sector accounted for 28% of total exports and 25% of imports.

Structural reforms after 1990

The gravity of the political and economic problems that confronted President Alberto Fujimori on taking office in 1990 made reform indispensable. With the backing of multilateral lending organisations like the World Bank and the Inter-American Development Bank (IDB), he adopted a number of policies designed

---

[2]   The public sector can have either direct or indirect participation in a company.

[3]   The deficit of non-financial state companies reached 5% of GDP in 1975, and levels of over 4% in 1982 and 1988, the crisis points for the Velasco, Belaúnde and García governments respectively.

[4]   *Perú Económico*, vol. XVIII, no. 3, March 1995, pp. 1-2.

to restore balance to the country's macroeconomic variables and to mend fences with the international financial system. It became clear that stabilisation was not possible without structural reform aimed at reducing state intervention and freeing up the market system. Three key priorities in terms of structural reform became apparent: (i) a redefinition of the role of the state through the break-up and sale of state monopolies; (ii) the liberalisation of foreign trade and the encouragement of competition between domestic and foreign producers; and (iii) financial reforms aimed at improving the workings of domestic capital markets. Such reforms also sought to increase competitiveness and investment in the private sector, which henceforth would act as the driving force in the economy.

The speed at which stabilisation measures and more structural reforms were implemented led to increases in unemployment and lower wages. The recession was heightened by a new structure of relative prices, itself the consequence of stabilisation, involving real exchange rate appreciation and a sharp drop in real wages. This, in turn, provoked a fall in consumption and the closure of firms which could no longer compete. The entry of largescale capital inflows (both short-term speculative flows as well as foreign direct investment (FDI)) also encouraged an overvalued exchange rate.[5]

Trade liberalisation

The main objective of trade liberalisation was to shift the axis of economic orientation away from import substitution towards the export market. Not only did the government wish to reduce inefficiencies in the economy, but it also wanted to take full advantage of globalisation and to reduce an excessive dependence on a small local market. The main policies adopted were customs reform; an overhaul of the tariff regime; the reduction in the number of prohibitions; and a rationalisation of export incentives. These policies were complemented by various measures to liberalise both the foreign exchange and capital markets with a view to encouraging FDI.

In 1990, the government eliminated all exonerations and non-tariff barriers, reducing tariff protection to three tiers: 15% for locally-produced inputs, 25% for capital goods and food, and 50% for luxury items. Then, in early 1992, the tariff regime was simplified further: 15% for locally-produced inputs and 25% for capital goods. This reduced the average tariff to 15.6%. In early 1997, a further amendment was made to the tariff structure, when the 15% tariff on inputs was reduced to 12% and the 25% tariff on capital goods to 20%. In both cases, there were exceptions, including a temporary 5% surcharge on some items. Taxes on imported agricultural goods were in fact maintained, providing some protection for agricultural producers. The average tariff after these changes was 13.6% (see Figure 1).

---

[5]   This was estimated by the central bank at around 10% in 1995 (Banco Central de Reserva del Perú, 1995).

Figure 1. Imports f.o.b. and Average Tariff Rates

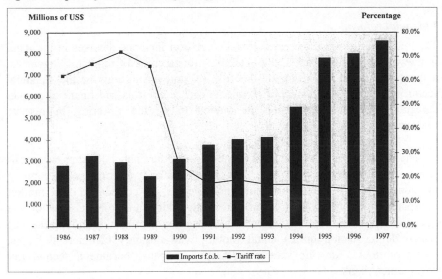

Figure 2. Imports f.o.b. and Investment as Percentage of GDP

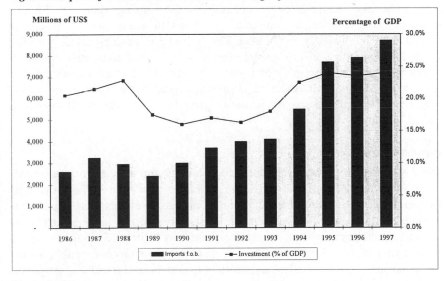

Source: BCRP

Tariff liberalisation led to an increase in imports (see Figure 1). The high correlation between the coefficient of investment and the level of imports also gives an indication of the impact of trade policy on investment (see Figure 2). The idea of reducing tariffs further in 1997 was to encourage investment by reducing the cost of capital goods and increasing the efficiency of domestic producers. However, typically, the effects of tariff reduction on investment tend only to materialise in the medium term. Meanwhile, the switch in emphasis towards export-led growth did little to ameliorate the chronic problem of unemployment (see below).

Financial reform

The main changes in the area of financial reform included changes in the legal framework governing capital markets, the strengthening of regulatory agencies, a more restrictive definition of the role of state institutions in the financial sector, the ending of balance of payments capital controls and financial market deregulation (the liberalisation of interest rates, the lowering of reserve requirements etc.).

The introduction of a new legal framework for the financial system was well-received by economic agents, since this tended to clarify the rules of the game in the longer term, whilst enhancing both levels of confidence and market transparency. In redefining areas of state participation in the financial sector, the government wound up the various state development banks and placed the Banco de la Nación on an equal footing with ordinary commercial banks. Furthermore, Cofide, the state project funding bank, became a second tier development bank.

The liberalisation of the capital account covered a number of areas, ranging from authorising dollarisation to opening up the banking system to foreign investors. This encouraged competition and led to a substantial increase in financial savings (mainly in dollars). The increase in savings helped provide credit for investment in the private sector. At the same time, diversification within the financial market – for instance the development of a more reliable stock market – made it easier to raise risk capital for investment purposes. Similarly, the privatisation of pensions provided new sources of domestic capital.[6]

Privatisation

The Fujimori government's privatisation strategy formed part of an overall market-oriented strategy to achieve greater economic efficiency and competitiveness, based on the promotion of private investment and a reduction in state participation. The inefficiency of state companies had resulted from political interference in management decisions, unrealistic pricing regimes and a bloated payroll. In order to show the effects of privatisation on the public sector fiscal accounts, Table 2 illustrates both the sale price of and the projected investment in the 100 former state companies, by sector, sold off between 1990 and February 1997. The data show up the particularly large sums raised by the privatisation of the two state telecommunications companies (Compañía Peruana de Teléfonos and Entel) and their sale to the Spanish firm Telefónica.

At the outset, the government decided not to sell the so-called 'strategic companies', preferring instead to refloat them and to improve their management.

---

[6]   Resources in AFPs (private pension plans) and CTSs (schemes for time service compensation) exceeded 1 billion dollars in 1997. See also Chaper 2.

The original plan was to sell off only 23 companies. The first two to be disposed of were the state's minority holding in Sogewiese Leasing and Compañía Minera Buenaventura, sold in June and July 1991. Subsequently, policy shifted in favour of a more radical divestment of state assets. In September 1991, a new decree was issued with a view to privatising all state companies, establishing the Comisión de Promoción de Inversión Privada (Copri) as the institution responsible for increasing productivity and efficiency overall, but with a specific remit to carry out privatisation policy, recapitalise former state companies and develop competition in the market for goods and services.

Table 2 Privatisations by Economic Sector, to February 1997 ($mn)

Sector	Amount	Projected Investment
Telecommunications	2650.19	2176.00
Electricity	1574.34	539.74
Mining	778.91	4503.97
Hidrocarbons	791.51	170.00
Manufacturing	544.00	48.50
Finance	355.93	30.00
Fishing	112.04	0.00
Transport	86.25	35.54
Tourism	47.60	23.05
Other	81.77	0.00
Total	**7022.54**	**7526.80**

Source: COPRI

In pursuit of these objectives, Copri established the basic ground rules for privatisation, and nominated the members of a special committee for the promotion of private investment (Cepri) for each privatisation. The Cepris were responsible for restructuring firms prior to their sale in order to make them more attractive to potential investors; contracting assistance from investment banks; establishing guidelines and procedures; providing technical assistance; and generally overseeing the process. In the case of companies providing basic infrastructure services – the second phase of privatisation that began in 1997 – the executive body was the Comisión de Promoción de Concesiones Privadas (Promcepri), composed of two separate bodies: an executive directorate and the special committees to deal with each case.

Given market imperfections – especially in monopoly sectors like telecommunications, oil and electricity – an effective regulatory framework was particularly important to the success of privatisation, which was geared up to promoting competitive markets and improving the quality of goods and services to consumers. Peru lacked any strong regulatory tradition outside the financial sector, where the central bank, the banking superintendency and Conasev (the securities watchdog) had long provided a reasonable service. As a result of privatisation, some notable advances were made in regulation, although much remained to be done in improving efficiency and transparency.

In order to deal with the problem of natural monopolies in sectors like energy and telecommunications, a number of regulatory agencies were established. In the telecommunications industry, for instance, a regulator known as the Organismo Supervisor de la Inversión Privada en Telecomunicaciones (Ospitel) was set up shortly after privatisation of CTP/Entel. Its purpose was to supervise the regulatory framework, to resolve disputes, to supervise tariff levels and to help improve the quality in the services offered to the public. In the oil industry, an organisation was set up early on (Perupetro) to oversee the fulfilment of contracts. In the energy sector, the Comisión de Tarifas Eléctricas was entrusted with regulatory responsibilities.

Public and private investment

Investment at the national level increased substantially during the 1990s. Table 3 shows that in 1995 investment had risen to 24.3% of GDP, up from just 16.7% in 1991. The average per annum for the first six years of the decade was 20.3%. Of this, the proportion due to private investment rose substantially. Although investment levels fell off slightly in 1996 owing to fiscal constraints and the slowdown in growth, it seemed likely that they would pick up again in what remained of the decade.

Table 3. Investment (in relation to nominal GDP)

	Investment	Public Investment	Private Investment	Public Investment (%)	Private Investment (%)	Internal Savings	External Savings	Savings /Investment
1991	16.7	2.7	14.0	16	84	13.6	3.1	-3.1
1992	16.5	3.1	13.4	19	81	11.9	4.5	-4.5
1993	18.5	3.4	15.1	18	82	13.3	5.2	-5.2
1994	22.0	3.9	18.1	18	82	16.9	5.3	-5.1
1995	24.3	4.1	20.2	17	83	16.9	7.3	-7.4
1996	23.5	3.8	19.7	16	84	17.7	5.8	-5.8
1997	24.0	na	na	na	na	18.4	5.6	-5.6

At the same time, foreign direct investment (FDI) became a much more important component of overall investment in the 1990s. This was largely due to the privatisation programme, and shows up clearly in the figures after 1993. However, there were also important new investments being made, as was the case with Gas de Camisea.[7] In part reflecting the scale of privatisation, the increase in FDI was concentrated largely in mining, manufacturing, telecommunications and the energy sectors.

Public investment fell notably in the 1990s. Between 1991 and 1996, it represented only 3.5% of GDP, whereas in previous decades it had varied between 5% and 10% of GDP, falling only below 5% in the last four years of the 1980s (See Table 1). Whilst the philosophy of the economic model was to

---

[7]   This is the potentially enormous gas field which, until they pulled out in July 1998, was being developed jointly by Shell and Mobil in the north of Cuzco department.

reduce the involvement of the state in economic development, the success of the privatisation programme involved the transfer to the private sector of those sectors which had previously absorbed large quantities of public investment. The slight increase in public investment between 1991 and 1995 was primarily the result of new infrastructure provision – basically roadbuilding and schools.

Figure 3. Foreign Direct Investment Flows (FDI)

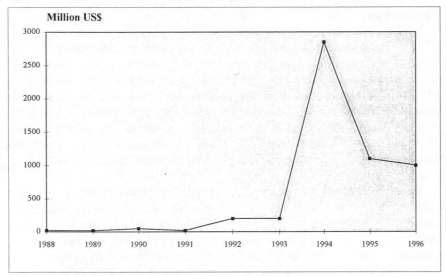

Source: CONITE

Peru's reinsertion into world financial markets

Seven years after first taking office, the Fujimori government eventually managed to complete the restructuring of its foreign debt with the implementation of a 'Brady' deal with private bank creditors. In 1996, it signed a debt restructuring agreement with bilateral official Paris Club creditors. At the same time, the government was seeking to gain better access to Asian markets through full membership of APEC.

The arrangements with its principal creditors made it easier to project with greater accuracy the exact burden of foreign debt service payments for the following 20 years. The Paris Club negotiations involved renegotiating loans falling due in 1996-98 and payments falling due between 1999 and 2007 on the basis of a rescheduling of previous debt service arrears. The Brady deal of March 1997 involved rescheduling arrears on principal falling due since 1983 (worth 4.2 billion dollars) and arrears of interest (worth 6.4 billion dollars). The initial cost of the Brady deal was around 1.4 billion dollars, financed partly by the multilateral banks and partly by the Peruvian treasury.

The refinancing of the commercial debt promised to have important effects on the economy in the medium term. By virtue of Peru's improved country risk, it would lead to a reduction in interest rates payable and an increase in the resources which could be channelled though private banks. Secondly, it would lead to new foreign banks establishing themselves in Peru, thereby improving levels of efficiency in the domestic banking industry. Finally, the resumption of repayments was expected to have an effect on the balance of payments, forcing the government to maintain a tight fiscal policy.

Sustainability

The macroeconomic situation inherited by the Fujimori government was the worst in living memory. Hyperinflation exceeded 7,000% a year in 1990, output had contracted a full 20% since 1988 and levels of investment fell to just 15.7% of GDP. Largely as a result of the policies implemented since then, annual inflation fell to 10% in 1995, rising slightly to 11.8% in 1996 but falling to 6.5% in 1997. Meanwhile, output in the economy grew by an average 5% between 1990 and 1996, accelerating in 1997 when growth was up to 7.4% with the government aiming for it to grow at 5-6% until the end of the decade.[8]

Economic growth was accomplished partly by the use of already installed capacity, but it also reflected the upturn in private investment. Indeed, the increase in the current account deficit was, in part, a reflection of this since investment brought with it an increase in the demand for imported capital goods. Economic growth depends on the dynamism of investment (gross capital formation), although it also relies on the efficiency of investment, which in turn hinges on competition and market stability. In this sense, macroeconomic stability, international competition, the relative strength of the financial system and the investment in human capital were all important contributory factors. Along with the achievement of relative price stability, an increase in investment from 16% in 1990 to 24% of GDP in 1995 was one of the major achievements of these years. Without adequate investment, no sustainable growth was possible.

However, the investment achieved in the early 1990s was not primarily the consequence of increased domestic saving, which remained low precisely because of the lack of growth in the 1980s. Unrestricted access to external financing and the removal of impediments to foreign investment were the main causes of the increase in domestic investment, especially in the first half of the 1990s. A current account deficit equivalent to 7.3% of GDP in 1995 reflected, in part, the strength of this investment. Peru's ability to sustain a large current account deficit in the last few years of the decade would depend on its ability to increase exports and to achieve a substantial increase in domestic savings.[9]

---

[8]   Growth was expected to fall to 2-4% in 1998, due largely to the adverse effects of the El Niño phenomenon and to the Asian slowdown on trade performance.

[9]   After the adjustment in 1996, the correct acount deficit fell slightly. In 1997 it reached 5.3% of GDP, but seemed set to grow once again in 1998.

International experience (Morande, 1996) suggests that in many cases domestic savings are more the result, rather than the cause, of economic growth. Table 4 shows investment and saving as a proportion of GDP, projected to 1998.

Table 4. Key Macroeconomic Indicators (%)

	GDP Growth	Annual Inflation	Current Account Deficit	Investment	Domestic Savings	External Savings
				Percentage of nominal GDP		
1991	2.9	139.2	3.1	16.7	13.6	3.1
1992	-1.8	56.7	4.5	16.5	11.9	4.5
1993	6.4	39.5	5.2	18.5	13.3	5.2
1994	13.1	15.4	5.3	22.0	16.9	5.3
1995	7.0	10.2	7.3	24.3	16.9	7.3
1996	2.8	11.8	5.8	23.5	17.7	5.8
1997	4.5	9.5	5.4	24.0	18.3	5.4
1998 [1]	5.0	8.0	5.8	24.5	18.6	5.8

(1) Forecast

Source: BCRP

It seems reasonable to suppose that if investment and growth continue at reasonably buoyant levels, domestic saving will increase and that – at some point in the future – an equilibrium point will be achieved, or even a surplus on the capital account. This is, of course, a very long-term perspective, a decade or more, during which the external balance is only sustainable on the basis of continued capital inflows from abroad. On this point, it is worth pointing out that the ratio of foreign debt to GDP fell steadily from 1990, and that following the closure of the Brady deal, it was likely to fall to around 33% of GDP. While still high by international standards, this was a considerable improvement on the ratios of up to 40% witnessed at points of fiscal and balance of payments crisis since 1970.

A study by Macroconsult (Macroconsult 1997), undertaken for the IDB, suggested that the fiscal situation would be fairly sustainable in the following few years; due to the reforms undertaken and the increase in the ratio of investment to GDP, the rhythm of growth in the economy up to 2000 promised to be in the region of 5% a year, a figure close to the government's own target. At this sort of growth rate, sufficient fiscal resources would be generated to ensure payment of the foreign debt. According to this study, the fiscal deficit would continue to fall to around zero in 2000.

With respect to foreign capital inflows into the Peruvian economy, about 80% was long-term, which meant that the situation was markedly different to that of Mexico at the end of 1994. Similarly, as of 1997, Peru had sufficient reserves (equivalent to more than twelve months of imports) and maintained a fairly flexible exchange rate policy.

There are few studies on the conditions likely to make growth in Peru sustainable. Cuba (Cuba, 1995) elaborated a model of potential GDP which related investment rates to growth rates. He calculated potential growth on the basis of past investment patterns (including the effects of depreciation) and their productivity. The model allows us to work out what the growth rate of productive capacity would be, given observed rates of investment. This is a better method than previous models, which assumed that the incremental capital-output ratio was constant and which were calculated on the basis of fairly *ad hoc* methods.

In the recent empirical literature on economic growth, apart from variables like human capital, trade liberalisation and macroeconomic stability, the most important determinant is the investment rate. Other things being equal, the economies which grow fastest are those that invest most. Cuba's model helps us to calculate the investment required to achieve a given rate of growth. The results are illustrated in Figure 4. With an investment rate of 25.3% of GDP, the model suggests that – assuming that there was no financing constraint on the current account of the balance of payments – it would be possible for the economy to grow at an average 6% a year without overheating up to 2000. It also suggests that at these investment rates it would be possible to push growth even higher thereafter. However, the reasons why such rates may not be achievable concern more the sustainability of external financing and the lack of domestic saving than the lack of productive capacity or investment *per se*.

Figure 4. Potential and Actual GDP

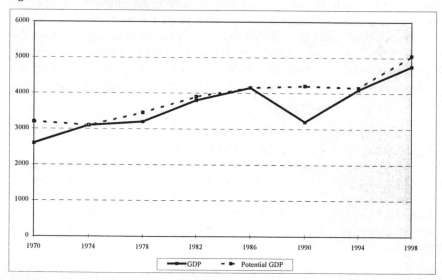

Source: BCRP

The results are fairly positive, since in recent years a new cycle of capital accumulation has been under way. In 1995, for instance, the investment rate was consistent with a growth rate of around 5%. So long as this pattern of accumulation persists, it should be sufficient to sustain annual growth rates of 6% or more. At the same time, the government took steps in 1996 to prevent the external deficit reaching dangerous proportions and domestic saving seems to have responded to growth. Therefore, if these conditions continue, it should be possible to generate sustained growth.

For there to be a 4.5% real-terms growth rate over the next ten years and for rescheduled debt agreements to be honoured, Peru would have to increase export earnings to 17.6 billion dollars a year by 2007 (Macroconsult, 1997). Of these, mining exports would have to rise to 9.8 billion dollars a year (Table 5), implying that minerals would account for 55% of total exports. This assumed (fairly conservatively) that imports would remain at 12.5% of GDP, the average for the period 1994-97. It also posited that non-traditional exports would grow at 12% a year between 1998 and 2002, and at 10% in 2003 and thereafter, whilst all other (i.e. non-mining) traditional exports would grow at 5%. The study assumed constant price levels for exports.

Table 5. GDP, Trade and Debt Servicing Forecasts ($ mn)

Year	GDP	Total Imports	Total Exports	Mining Exports	Public External Debt Service
1997	63,995	8442	6324	2845	1381
1998	68,547	8565	7008	3200	1519
1999	73,422	9174	7766	3621	1661
2000	78,644	9826	8606	4101	1697
2001	84,238	10525	9537	4642	1701
2002	900,229	11274	10568	5249	1731
2003	96,647	12076	11711	5978	1867
2004	103,521	12935	12978	6785	1879
2005	110,884	13855	14382	7689	1838
2006	118,770	14840	15937	8705	1838
2007	127,218	15896	17661	9843	1838

Note: GDP estimated on the basis of a rate of inflation of 2.5% from 1997

Source: Macroconsult (1997)

The study argued that, in order to achieve this target, a minimum level of new mining investment would need to be carried out, worth 7.5 billion dollars over the ten years between 1997 and 2007. According to information produced by the energy and mining ministry, it would be possible to achieve this target (see Table 6). In 1997, there were 206 projects (of varying sizes) either under construction or at the stages of exploration or study, representing a potential investment of 6.7 billion dollars. Of these, only 13% represented firm commitments by investors, the rest were still under evaluation. This means that the great majority of these projects still needed the go-ahead. For this to happen, again according to Macroconsult, changes would be needed to the tax regime to make investment more attractive.

In the longer term, Peru has enormous potential for mining expansion. As of 1997, only around one-third of the area considered apt for mining had been properly surveyed, the remainder (some 60 million hectares) had yet to be explored. This suggests that, beyond 2007, there would be a large mining potential still to be exploited. Given the fact that many of the world's main mining houses have established a presence in the country, there was considerable optimism that exploration would increase rapidly.

However, increased investment in mining and other relatively capital-intensive extractive industries may do little to resolve Peru's employment problems. From 1989 onwards, the level of employment fell rapidly, even when – after 1993 – new investment helped increase production levels substantially. Between 1993 and 1995, for instance, investment in mining reached just over 1 billion dollars (Table 6); nevertheless, employment levels in the mines continued to fall. In 1995, mining employment levels were 70% lower than ten years earlier.

Table 6. Estimated Expansion of Mining Investment, 1993-2005 ($mn)

	1993-1995	1996	1997	1998	1999	2000	2001-2005	Total
Expansion	545	418	444	330	177	92	92	2098
Construction	345	20	2	0	0	0	0	367
Feasibility Study	62	340	1381	1380	1294	894	160	5511
Exploration	56	164	144	187	117	109	109	886
Total	**1007**	**943**	**1970**	**1898**	**1589**	**1094**	**360**	**8862**

Source: Ministry of Energy and Mining

Continued state reform

A *quid pro quo* for sustainability is for reform of the state to be continued. State reform began in earnest in 1990-91 with the transfer of property and responsibilities from the public sector to the private. According to the 1993 Constitution, the state has responsibility for defending the country's sovereignty, guaranteeing the rights of its citizens and securing their general welfare. Although the public sector in 1997 still employed 700,000 workers (30% of the workforce) between ministries, autonomous public institutions and local government, the state had yet to prove capable of providing education, healthcare, justice and public security. Further changes were therefore required to improve the efficiency of public administration in these and other areas, and to ensure the equitable distribution of available resources to those most in need of them.

Privatisation constituted the first step towards incorporating a larger number of private investors into increasing output, and between 1990 and 1997 a total of nearly 100 companies were sold to the private sector. Among those still awaiting privatisation at the end of 1997 were many of the installations belonging to Centromin in the mining sector, the oil refinery at Talara, the northern oil pipeline, Electroperú in the electricity sector, as well as a number of smaller companies.[10]

Despite the achievements in privatising companies, a great deal still had to be done in improving the regulatory framework, with a view to encouraging best practice and competition within the private sector. In spite of the government establishing regulatory agencies in specific sectors – Osiptel in the telecommunications sector and the Organismo Supervisor de Inversiones en Energía (Osinerg) in the oil/energy sectors – it was still unclear exactly what role the state would play as regulator with regard to prices, the role to be played by other state entities like Indecopi, the institution charged with promoting competition, or Perupetro in the oil industry.

Among its objectives, the government sought to extend share-ownership as part of its privatisation strategy. Attempts in this direction began in 1994, with a view to increasing the number of beneficiaries and making reform irreversible. However, compared with Bolivia, where the 'capitalisation' scheme involved 50% of the equity of former state companies being held in trust for the public, so-called *participación ciudadana* in Peru involved an average of 5% of the equity. Up until 1997 at least, the most successful public share subscription had resulted from the sale of the government's remaining stake in Telefónica del Perú.

A second phase of privatisations was announced in 1997, related primarily to attracting private capital to construct and administer infrastructure projects. To this end, in August 1996, the government established Promcepri, whose purpose was to design, implement and regulate the awarding of private concessions. One of Promcepri's main tasks, therefore, was to facilitate concessions to the private sector, letting the state undertake less profitable public works but ones with higher social significance. Concessions were to be offered in eight areas: roads, electricity distribution, ports, communications, airports, water projects, railways and tourism.

Also pending as a medium-term goal was the creation of state regulatory authorities in the construction of infrastructure, since the private sector was not necessarily best-placed to evaluate the costs and benefits to society as a whole.

Reform of the state was also required in areas providing social services. Since a key national objective was to reduce poverty (and especially 'extreme

---

[10] The economic disruption caused in early 1998 by the return of the El Niño phenomenon caused the government to slow down its programme of privatisation.

poverty'), there was a case for enhanced private participation in such spheres as education and health, leaving it to the state to provide such services to lower-income levels. To this end, the government established in November 1996 the Superintendencia de Entidades Prestadoras de Salud to authorise, oversee and regulate both public and private entities providing health insurance cover. In early 1997, new legislation was passed by Congress (*Ley de Modernización de la Seguridad Social*) which sought to promote competition in the health insurance market and the inflow of private capital into this sector on lines similar to those adopted for private pension funds (AFPs). Effective regulation of such entities was likely to be of key importance to the success of such programmes.

In the sphere of education, a law was passed in November 1996 to provide a framework for private investment in the construction of education infrastructure of all types, although as of mid-1997 it had not been made effective through the publication of detailed regulations, leaving the rules of the game unclear for potential investors. While such investment may eventually improve educational standards, it may also make education more expensive for students.

More broadly, the state had yet to establish a new rapport with civil society in the modern world. In the words of Armand Matterland, 'today's aspiration is not so much "more market" or "more state", but more "civil society"'. Civil society is a concept that goes beyond economics and politics, with its roots in the cultural and ethical life of the people. It embraces a wide range of types of organisation – business organisations, educational associations, non-governmental organisations (NGOs), professional groupings and community groups. It represents a continuum which links the most private (the family) with the most public (the state). In Peru, the concept of civil society has emerged forcefully in recent years as the vehicle through which reforms should be channelled for the development of the country.

It is also worth pointing out that the difference between 'state' and 'government' is something which has yet to be properly defined in Peru and that this distinction is central to the longer-term success of the model. Whilst the overall direction of the reform model being implemented may be correct, it is important that it stand apart from the political interests of specific parties or individuals. It is therefore of key importance that it be protected from the vicissitudes of electoral or other short-term political considerations.

There can be little doubt that if future uncertainties are to be minimised, two key, inter-related elements must be present: a set of consistent economic policies and a relatively stable and predictable political system to back them up. Whilst advances have been made with respect to the former, there is still some way to go before a sustainable political framework is achieved which does not depend on one person or one group in order to function. In this respect, the private sector (in its widest sense of civil society) should take the lead in ensuring that the political system is not defined by individuals or specific groups but is underpinned by a broad consensus in society. There should therefore be a broadly accepted vision of the future, which prioritises economic growth and education. Growth should take into account stability, the expansion of exports and protection of the environment; education should seek to cultivate values of solidarity and ethics, raise the quality of training and the harnessing of new technologies, and allow the country to take advantage of the opportunities provided by globalisation.

The economic model implemented by the Peruvian authorities since 1990 was not invented in Peru, but sought to adapt principles adopted in other countries to modernise their economies. Whilst the Fujimori government implemented the model fairly boldly, it had little alternative but to do so. The challenge Fujimori and his successors face is to ensure that the positive results achieved come to benefit the broad mass of the population.

Conclusions

The simultaneous processes of structural adjustment, reinsertion into the global economy and political pacification may have been conducted in a disorderly way, but they were indispensable. In 1990, the country faced the real possibility of disintegration, crippled by hyperinflation, isolated from the effects of globalisation and rocked by the proliferation of terrorism, drug-trafficking, poverty and crime. Reform came about because it was a question of national survival. There were no obvious alternatives; for some the reforms were a matter of conviction, for others it was a question of necessity. What is clear, however, is that the country changed in some fundamental ways: economic stability was recovered; the government once again became an interlocutor with the outside world; the people regained some of the confidence lost in their political leaders and became more optimistic about the future.

The major question that was posed with regard to economic policy was whether Peru, once again, confronted a pendular situation which would end in a new balance of payments crisis. Would it be necessary to impose more draconian adjustment measures to avoid such an outcome, or would this be mitigated by a growth in domestic savings offsetting any shortfall of foreign savings? Would the current account of the balance of payments support the debt repayment obligations signed between Peru and its creditors?

The answers to such questions would depend on the extent and nature of economic growth. Growth, in turn, relied on sufficient investment to increase installed capacity and being oriented primarily towards increasing both exports and employment. If the economy could expand by at least 5% per annum, and could do so substantially increasing both exports and employment, the model should prove viable and sustainable over the medium term.

The government's policies to attract foreign investment, both through its privatisation programme and its incentives to foreign investors, provided a positive framework to achieve this objective. Given the extent and degree of economic dislocation in recent decades, it was reasonable to think that domestic investment would take time to recover. A period of capital accumulation, possibly building up over several years, was required for this to happen, implying further constraints on already low levels of domestic consumption.

We have argued that to achieve average annual growth rates of the order of 5%, it would be necessary to increase investment levels to 25% of GDP. During the period 1994-97, investment levels averaged 23% of GDP. The restructuring of the foreign debt, the ongoing programme of privatisation and concessions, and the opportunities that Peru offered foreign investors suggested that investment could be sustained (and indeed increased) in the short-to-medium term.

The boom in mining exploration also suggested that it would be possible to increase mining exports by around 14% a year up until 2007. If so, this would help maintain balance on the external accounts and would – other things being equal – help push up output by towards 5% per annum. For these projects to materialise, there might well have to be policy continuity and further adjustments in the tax regime. It would be necessary to transfer the boom in prospecting into a boom in investment.

However, to ensure economic sustainability, political problems still needed to be confronted. Stronger institutions were required that provided guarantees for the legitimate transfer of power from one government to another. There was also a need for the strengthening of other institutional arrangements. In an important article Shane Hunt (Hunt, 1995) argued that 'for there to be a consistent long-term model, a *strong* state is needed. However, it is important to stress that a *strong* state does not mean an *interventionist* state. A state must be strong in the sense that it has the capacity to defend itself against pressures from society, so that it can pursue a consistent line of behaviour. A small, non-interventionist state should have the strength to maintain that line.' Hunt maintains that there are three alternatives: an *autonomous* state, which he sees as authoritarian and inconsistent with liberal norms; a state supported by the ruling class, an alternative he rejects for the lack of such a class in contemporary Peru; and a state supported by a coalition of dominant interests. He sees the last of these three as the only viable alternative for Peru.

The question therefore arises of how to create such an alternative. Hunt's reply is that what is required is a 'populist' movement. By this he does not mean populism in the sense of fiscal irresponsibility and state intervention, but the establishment of a broad coalition of otherwise antagonistic interests behind a project to pursue economic progress in a context of democracy and respect for the rule of law.

CHAPTER 4

Stabilisation, Structural Reform and Industrial Performance

Luis Abugattas

As of August 1990, at the very beginning of President Alberto Fujimori's first term in office, economic policy, along with the underlying development model since the 1960s, underwent a radical change. Structural adjustment policies led to the abandoning of the strategy of import-substituting industrialisation (ISI), whilst at the same time a tough macroeconomic stabilisation programme was adopted. Price controls were thus eliminated, the exchange rate and interest rates freed, the labour market deregulated, a tax reform initiated and trade liberalised, with the elimination of all non-tariff barriers and the lowering and harmonisation of tariffs. The process of structural reform in Peru was perhaps the most intense and rapid of any Latin American country in recent times.

Industrial development had been a cornerstone of economic policy ever since the promulgation of the first industrial development law (Law 13270) in 1959, when the process of import substitution began. The reforms introduced by the Fujimori government dismantled the legal framework established to promote industrial development, leaving the role assigned to industry in national development policy far from clear. No explicit policy for manufacturing industry was announced. Indeed, it has been suggested that 'there is no better industrial policy than the absence of an industrial policy' (Tavara, 1994). By contrast, from 1990 onwards, a number of measures were taken that gave special treatment to other economic sectors. According to government statements, the country's economic future was to be based on priority given to agriculture, fishing, mining and tourism (Promperú, 1997). The economic model of the Fujimori government was thus based, primarily, on the development of primary export sectors. Meanwhile, stabilisation policies and subsequent structural reforms exposed manufacturing industry to a drastic period of adjustment designed to eliminate the last vestiges of ISI.

The purpose of this chapter is to analyse the performance of the industrial sector in the period 1990-97 and how the sector adapted itself to these new circumstances. It has become a commonplace amongst economic analysts to blame ISI for the emergence of a highly inefficient industrial sector, capable of growth only because it was sheltered by an artificial system of tariff protection, responding to policies of a 'populist' orientation. Consequently, it was widely expected that the radical shift in policy in Peru, reversing ISI, would lead to widespread de-industrialisation, since Peruvian industry could no longer compete with foreign imports and would be unable to adapt to the new circumstances. How severe was the impact of the policies introduced after 1990? Have the soothsayers been proved right? What changes have come about in the structure of production and employment? How has the manufacturing sector adapted to these changes in circumstances? These are some of the questions we seek to address in this chapter. The findings are but the first stage of a more ambitious research project currently under way, and as such they should not be taken as exhaustive or the last word on the matter.[1]

Import-substituting industrialisation in Peru (1960-90)

Before proceeding to evaluate the impact of macroeconomic stabilisation and structural adjustment policies post-1990, it is worth highlighting some of the main characteristics of the process of ISI in Peru. To some degree, these distinguish it from the classic Latin American model, and have an important bearing on the development of manufacturing and its performance in the 1990-97 period.

First, the process of ISI began relatively late in Peru compared with other countries in Latin America. Between 1948 and 1960, economic policy was oriented by the classic liberal model. ISI was adopted as a policy paradigm only in the early years of the 1960s, following the 1959 industrial promotion law and during the first Belaúnde government (1963-68). The process was consolidated and deepened by the General Law of Industries of 1974 (Law 18350) and the policies pursued by the military government, particularly during its first phase under General Juan Velasco. The industrial regime was made somewhat more flexible by the 1982 Industry Law (Law 23407) and the first attempts at economic liberalisation undertaken by the second Belaúnde administration (1980-85).

Nevertheless, manufacturing industry accounted for some 20.8% of GDP in 1954 and grew at an annual average rate of around 8% during the 1950s. Thus, industrial growth antedated specific government legislation designed to encourage import substitution. By 1974, manufacturing industry represented 26.6% of GDP when it peaked, and then fell back to around 23% of GDP for much of the subsequent period. A number of industries – amongst them food and beverages, textiles and the processing of raw materials for export – developed at the margins of ISI policies, primarily on account of their own international competitiveness. In addition, it can be convincingly argued that the role played by ISI policies in the expansion of manufactured production was limited to a number of specific sectors. At the very most, these represented less than 5% of GDP.

---

[1]   Study is handicapped by the inadequacy of the statistical material available. Industrial statistics derived from the annual survey undertaken by the Ministry of Industry, Tourism, Integration and International Negotiations (Mitinci) have only been processed up until 1992. Consequently, because of the delay in producing a new statistical base, the calculations about sectoral growth are based on their weighted structure in 1979. Calculations based on the 1994 data may produce significantly different results. Preliminary findings were presented in Luis Abugattas (1996).

Secondly, the rapid growth achieved in manufactured production under the aegis of ISI policies was basically limited to the late 1960s and early 1970s, when annual growth rates reached an average of around 7.3%. Thereafter, the relative dynamism of the industrial sector diminished. Whilst the rate of growth in industrial production averaged around 5% in the period 1970-75, it fell in the following five-year period (1975-80) to only 1.5%. Throughout the 1980s, the average industrial growth rate was negative. Thus, the dynamism instilled by the experiment in ISI was exhausted relatively quickly in the Peruvian case. A decade of rapid industrial growth ended around 1974, giving way to a period of economic instability with successive attempts at stabilisation. This relative decline was finally taken to extremes under the government of Alan García (1985-90), especially after 1988 when manufacturing industries entered a phase of extreme crisis. As we will see below, this phase arguably had a more important impact on the sector than the liberalising reforms adopted after 1990 by the Fujimori government.

Thirdly, the policies of industrial protection adopted to promote ISI were subject to multiple exceptions and special regimes conferred on specific industrial activities. Thus, although the tariff walls erected were relatively high and policies were introduced (such as the Registro Nacional de Manufacturas) which sought to create special domestic advantages for specific industrial lines, these walls and privileges were not as uniform or as solid as they might seem. At the end of the 1980s, there were 114 legal rulings in force which conferred tariff exemptions on a wide range of goods. Indeed, the effective tariff income, measured by tariffs actually paid on the value of imports, rose after the reduction in tariffs which took place alongside the elimination of all exceptions. Protection for domestic production was high during the ISI phase for consumer durables and non-durables, whereas there were multiple exceptions for inputs, intermediate goods and capital goods. These effectively limited the expansion of ISI and hastened its demise.

Finally, another characteristic of Peruvian ISI, and one which also helps explain the fairly rapid exhaustion of the model – irrespective of its intrinsic contradictions which have already been widely discussed in the literature – relates to the socio-political context in which the ISI model developed. The highpoint of ISI was during the more radical phase of the military government which ruled the country from 1968 to 1980. The distributive policies adopted by the government, the high levels of social mobilisation it stimulated, its recourse to increased state intervention, the anti-private sector official rhetoric and the various attacks on the existing property regime all influenced business behaviour in the industrial sphere, especially with regard to investment decisions and the time-horizons of other business decisions. Specific measures, such as the labour stability laws, the introduction of the industrial community, the system of worker participation in profits and management, as well as the overall climate of state intervention, were only finally revoked with the reforms of the 1990s. These factors played a key role in influencing business decisions, undermining what could have been a more harmonious period of ISI.

In spite of the problems that afflicted the industrial sector, as well as the limitations and incoherences in the programme of ISI itself, manufacturing made significant advances from the 1960s onwards and came to play an important role in the overall pattern of national production. As well as accounting for as much as 26% of GDP at its peak, the sector accounted for an added-value of close to 8 billion dollars in the early 1990s and provided employment for as much as 17% of the total workforce. In its early phase, industrial production had grown considerably faster than the economy as a whole, acting as an 'engine of growth' especially in the period 1960-74.

In sum, the manufacturing sector achieved an important measure of development during the period of ISI. However, prior to the stabilisation policies introduced in 1990 and the reforms that flowed from them, the industrial sector had already run into a crisis which reflected the exhaustion of the model. This crisis was made more acute by the macroeconomic populism of the García government and its consequences. In the 1988-90 period, industrial production underwent a severe contraction of around 30%. The main indicators of industrial health – capacity utilisation, employment, profitability, amongst others – all reflected this deterioration. The economic crisis of these years reduced the net worth of a wide range of industrial firms and led to the closure of many. This crisis had prolonged effects which impacted on the nature of the reforms introduced by the Fujimori government and the capacity of firms to adapt to them.

Thus, the behaviour patterns of manufacturing industry during the 1990s reflected not just the policies adopted by the Fujimori government but the legacy of the 1980s, and in particular the exhaustion of the ISI model. It is very difficult to isolate one factor from another. In what follows, both aspects will enter into the discussion of the various industrial sectors and how they performed during the process of economic liberalisation.

Economic liberalisation and industrial development, 1990-97

Beginning in August 1990, and as a consequence of the stabilisation package adopted and the structural reforms that ensued, the manufacturing sector was subject to a drastic adjustment. To be sure, it found itself in a difficult situation. The sector was affected by two different types of measures: (i) a radical trade liberalisation; and (ii) the effects on relative prices of the liberalisation and deregulation of domestic markets.

Firstly, as a result of the trade opening, competition from imported goods rose abruptly. Whilst all import prohibitions and non-tariff barriers were removed, tariffs were cut and made more uniform. The average tariff level fell from 66% in 1989 to 16.1% in 1992. Under the new tariff arrangements, imports paid two rates – 25% and 15% – with 87% of all items paying the lower of the two. The higher level of protection was limited to textiles, clothing, shoes, some agricultural produce and specific types of white goods. The initial trade liberalisation was the most drastic of its kind anywhere in Latin America.

Trade liberalisation underwent a second phase in early 1997, when tariffs were reduced further. The 25% tariff level was cut to 20% and the 15% level to 12%, although for a limited number of goods a degree of additional protection was offered in the form of a temporary 5% surcharge. The result of this was to reduce the average tariff to only 13%. The process of trade liberalisation was further enhanced by the various agreements entered into with neighbouring countries. Trade liberalisation led to a sharp rise in imports. In the case of consumer goods, imports increased more than fivefold from 338.3 million dollars in 1990 to 1.85 billion in 1996, an annual rate of increase of 27.4% – well above the average increase in the growth of domestic production.

Secondly, it is important to stress that trade liberalisation took place at a point when the structure of prices, costs and demand was unfavourable to domestic producers. Due to the liberalisation and market deregulation, as well as other policies applied by the government, a structure of relative prices came into being which sapped the competitive edge of domestic industries. Together, these measures raised costs of production: domestic and international interest rates rose to 40% per annum in dollars in the initial stages of the reform; prices were raised for basic public services and fuel; and the price controls on previously subsidised or controlled inputs were scrapped.

This increase in prices took place at a time when the purchasing power of consumers had been drastically reduced. Taxes were also increased, both in terms of improved methods of collection and the introduction of new taxes, such as the basic income tax (*impuesto mínimo a la renta*) and the transfer of payroll taxes (Fonavi) to employers.[2] The increase in production costs and the tax burden (which represented 24% of the gross costs of production in the industrial sector) squeezed profit margins, especially since trade liberalisation made it more difficult to pass on costs to the consumer.

Trade liberalisation in Peru also took place at a time of currency appreciation, which again distinguishes it from similar experiences in other countries. Central Bank (BCRP) data indicate that the real multilateral exchange rate appreciated against a trade-weighted basket of foreign currencies by 22% between 1990 and 1997. Other calculations of the real exchange rate, based on an index of domestic production costs, suggest the rate of appreciation may have been even higher. Currency appreciation had the effect of further reducing the real protection afforded to domestic producers and increasing the competitiveness of imported products.

Industrial output
What was the combined effect of these influences on the industrial sector? The

---

[2]   For more detail of the government's fiscal reforms, see Chapter 11 of this volume.

indicator which is often used to measure in aggregate terms the impact of a combination of influences is the ratio of industrial production to GDP. With the diminution of manufacturing in the generation of value-added in the economy, what we see in the short and medium term is a process of deindustrialisation, reflecting the lower proportion of manufactured output in relation to the output of other sectors. What we see in the longer run is the redistribution of resources towards non-tradables and the increase in production for export at the expense of import-substitutive industries.

Table 1. Evolution of the Manufacturing Sector, 1985-1997 (Selected Indicators)

Year	Share of GDP (%)	Value Added (1985=100)	Annual Rate of Growth (%)	Index of Gross Output (1979=100)	Index of Employment (1979=100)	Index of Labour Productivity (1979=100)
1985	21.76	100.00	6.20	96.80	102.50	89.83
1986	23.25	117.90	18.00	114.20	108.70	117.47
1987	24.55	134.50	14.00	130.10	117.90	123.42
1988	23.47	117.20	-12.80	113.50	115.30	110.11
1989	21.41	94.50	-19.40	91.40	102.70	99.58
1990	21.69	92.10	-2.20	89.40	100.00	100.00
1991	22.51	98.40	6.93	95.60	94.90	112.30
1992	22.25	95.50	-3.84	91.90	85.20	117.35
1993	21.91	100.10	6.25	97.80	78.30	139.30
1994	22.50	116.30	22.51	119.90	75.00	166.60
1995	21.87	121.20	7.64	129.00	75.80	174.93
1996	21.90	124.50	1.82	131.30	74.10	184.20

Source: MITINCI (elaborated by author)

Table 1 shows a selection of indicators which cast light on trends in the industrial sector between 1985 and 1996. Looking at the relationship of industrial value added to GDP, it becomes clear that there was no radical change in this ratio if we compare the post-reform period (1991-96) with the 1985-90 period. In the former, industrial production accounted for 22.15% of GDP, whilst in the latter it was only slightly higher (22.65%). Even if we compare the peaks in the economic cycle within each period, industrial production reached 23.9% of GDP in 1986-87 and 22.2% in 1994-95. These figures appear to gainsay the thesis that the economic reforms that took place after 1990 led to the deindustrialisation of the country. Taking the comparison between the two 'peaks', it would seem that the extent of de-industrialisation was in fact limited to around 1.7% of GDP. This figure compares quite strikingly with Chile and other cases, where trade liberalisation and economic reform caused industrial participation in the economy to decline from 25% (of GDP) at the end of the 1960s to 20% in the 1980s (Meller, 1992).

Rather, what we see in Peru is a progressive de-industrialisation beginning in 1974 and made more acute in the last few years of the 1980s. In other words, the phenomenon long predated the Fujimori reforms. However, confining ourselves to the period of reform in the early 1990s, it seems to be the case that Peruvian industry signally failed to initiate a period of recovery, since the ratio between industrial production and total production failed to increase during the course of the 1990s. This may suggest that the longer-term effects of the reforms have yet to make themselves felt.

While it is certainly true that the available evidence does not suggest that stabilisation policies and those associated with structural adjustment produced any notable de-industrialisation, it is also clear that there was a change in the role afforded to manufacturing in the economy as a whole. Industrial production no longer acted as a 'locomotive' of growth, as it did in the 1960s. As of 1990, the lead sectors in the process of growth were construction, fishing, non-tradables and the production of primary goods. Industrial development was shaped by the performance of these other sectors and in response to their productive needs. In contrast to the heyday of ISI, manufacturing passed to having a subsidiary role, its performance derived essentially from the demand for other sorts of goods and services. After 1990, aggregate industrial growth rates came to depend on growth rates for the economy as a whole, a structural change that reduced the elasticity of manufacturing output in relation to GDP. The loss of this leading role is also evident if we look at other indicators. The proportion of bank loans to manufacturing interests declined from above 32% in the 1980s to around 26% in 1996-97. Similarly, whilst in the 1980s it was the sector which absorbed most employment, playing a key role in establishing wage parameters for the economy as a whole, its importance in these respects after 1990 was much reduced.

The industrial sector grew between 1990 and 1997 at an annual average rate of just over 5% (see Table 2). The pattern of growth was led by industries processing primary goods, which grew on average by 6.4%. Industries like fishmeal, sugar and mineral refining were essentially adjuncts of commodity industries and their performance was closely related to the dynamism of these markets. In the short run, the main factors influencing them were those like the climate and international mineral prices, rather than the state of the domestic economy. In contrast, the rest of the manufacturing sector, reflected by the official figures produced by the industry ministry (MITINCI), saw annual average growth rates of around 4.5% during this period. Some commentators suggest that the growth achieved by manufacturing industry indicates the limited effect of the reforms on the sector. This deserves some comment.

Table 2. Annual Percentage Variation in Industrial Production, 1985-97

DESCRIPTION	1985	1986	1987	1988	1989	1990	1991	1992	1993	1994	1995	1996	June 1997	Annual Rate of Growth 90/97
Total Manufacturing Industry	**6.02**	**17.96**	**13.95**	**-12.74**	**-19.44**	**-2.22**	**6.94**	**-3.85**	**6.41**	**22.52**	**7.65**	**1.82**	**7.74**	**5.04**
Primary Processing	6.31	24.48	18.17	-13.90	-27.16	-1.44	6.49	-4.12	2.36	24.12	12.98	-0.82	8.32	4.51
Other Manufacturing	5.13	-1.72	-2.14	-7.42	13.64	-4.35	8.21	-3.21	17.72	18.68	-5.72	8.73	6.33	6.40
Consumer Goods	**5.50**	**22.50**	**15.63**	**-12.82**	**-22.12**	**-1.72**	**6.35**	**-4.00**	**2.47**	**22.34**	**9.00**	**0.07**	**10.44**	**4.35**
Non-durables	5.36	20.86	15.33	-10.89	-21.40	-2.24	5.87	-3.73	3.66	23.42	9.02	0.58	10.53	4.73
Durables	9.99	72.70	22.15	-51.81	-49.02	28.61	27.70	-13.72	-45.38	-60.57	3.34	-52.71	-61.78	-41.89
Intermediate Goods	**4.89**	**11.47**	**11.42**	**-11.64**	**-14.95**	**-4.29**	**7.76**	**-2.05**	**12.22**	**21.77**	**4.85**	**6.42**	**6.19**	**6.48**
Agriculture	-3.53	33.60	19.20	-8.42	-40.01	5.26	-15.49	13.08	-3.26	24.46	9.09	-3.58	5.27	1.57
Mining	1.14	35.49	48.63	-17.89	-46.83	-4.46	0.02	-8.70	24.78	9.61	11.42	0.68	-5.95	2.40
Industry	5.51	8.10	7.91	-12.59	-8.88	-5.02	9.24	-4.00	13.67	21.39	3.55	5.49	6.28	6.39
Construction	5.91	30.15	30.63	-2.17	-36.62	-1.67	9.74	17.36	1.16	28.01	14.89	33.85	9.13	12.66
Capital Goods	**29.16**	**32.96**	**21.04**	**-19.12**	**-35.11**	**7.83**	**2.61**	**-21.65**	**-3.92**	**36.31**	**27.24**	**-17.58**	**-1.83**	**-0.25**

Source: INEI-BCRP

Firstly, the rate of growth achieved responded mainly to the recovery of production levels in specific sectors, following the strong downturn experienced in the 1988-90 period. As can be seen in Table 2, all sectors underwent a severe contraction in output during this period, especially those industries serving the domestic market. Equally, as we can see in Table 3, industry as a whole was working at less than 50% of installed capacity, with unused capacity particularly high in sectors producing consumer durables, intermediate goods for the mining industry and capital goods. The growth achieved in this period led to a recovery of production levels achieved a decade earlier. This is clearly the case if we compare levels of capacity utilisation at the peaks of the productive cycle (e.g. 1986/87 and 1994/95). Similarly, this is also the case if we look at GDP indices and those for the volumes of production in Table 1.

Another aspect which requires emphasis is that the recovery in production levels responded first and foremost to the way in which the industrial sector grew rapidly in 1994 and 1995, especially in those industries geared to the domestic market. The figures recorded by MITINCI show growth rates of 24.12% and 12.98% for these two years respectively, in response to the measures taken by the government to increase aggregate demand in the economy. With the measures introduced in the second half of 1995 to stem growth and to avert balance of payments difficulties, the pattern of growth changed abruptly, with the sector growing by only 1.8% in 1996. Indeed, this figure was only achieved because of the relative buoyancy of the export-oriented processing industries and strong demand for inputs from the construction industry. Other industrial sectors performed very poorly. During the first half of 1997, industrial growth picked up again, achieving a 7.7% expansion in output. A clear conclusion that can be drawn is that the performance of industries producing for the domestic market was highly susceptible to macroeconomic policies and their effects on other sectors.

Table 3. Output as a Percentage of Installed Capacity, 1985-97

DESCRIPTION	1985	1986	1987	1988	1989	1990	Average 1985/90	1991	1992	1993	1994	1995	1996	June 1997	Average 1990/97
Manufacturing Sector	62.90	69.86	75.22	64.02	51.20	49.97	62.20	52.73	50.47	52.46	61.88	63.14	62.44	65.43	57.31
Primary Processing	59.32	69.06	76.22	64.38	46.89	46.22	60.35	49.22	47.19	48.26	57.90	63.50	61.79	64.24	54.79
Other Manufacturing	76.89	73.08	70.94	62.54	68.52	64.87	69.47	65.83	62.38	66.27	74.74	62.10	63.66	68.11	66.00
Consumer Goods	63.77	71.17	76.82	65.42	50.95	50.07	63.03	53.25	51.12	52.32	62.66	67.27	65.67	69.01	58.92
Non durables	64.48	71.31	76.74	66.72	52.44	51.27	63.83	54.28	52.25	54.09	65.28	70.05	68.66	72.19	61.01
Durables	47.73	68.34	78.47	37.81	19.28	24.79	46.07	31.66	27.31	14.92	5.88	6.08	2.87	0.62	14.27
Intermediate Goods	64.97	70.25	74.58	64.31	53.79	51.24	63.19	53.57	51.94	55.36	63.28	60.15	61.44	64.21	57.65
Agriculture	51.07	68.23	73.78	66.74	40.04	42.14	57.00	35.61	40.27	38.96	48.49	52.89	51.00	50.41	44.97
Mining	54.70	69.38	81.23	65.96	35.07	33.50	56.64	33.51	30.59	38.17	41.84	46.62	46.94	46.99	39.77
Industry	67.53	70.69	74.01	62.99	56.24	53.11	64.10	55.93	53.04	56.70	64.65	59.72	60.46	63.41	58.38
Construction	53.20	67.48	78.13	75.15	47.63	46.84	61.41	51.40	60.33	60.62	66.87	74.86	92.09	96.51	68.69
Capital Goods	40.27	53.55	62.32	48.87	31.71	34.20	45.15	35.09	27.49	26.42	36.01	45.81	37.76	39.81	35.32

Source: INEI-BCRP

Employment

An issue which has given rise to considerable controversy is the effect which economic stabilisation and liberalisation, particularly trade liberalisation, had on industrial employment. Evaluation of this point is impeded by the absence of reliable statistics on employment in the industrial sector. However, the evidence at our disposal suggests that from 1990 onwards there was a considerable fall in employment in manufacturing in the formal sector of the economy, with workers displaced into subsistence activities in the informal sector, and that this led to an overall decrease in both wages and productivity.

The only official set of figures is the monthly survey of firms with more than 100 employees, conducted by the labour ministry. According to these, the industrial sector saw a sustained contraction in its workforce. In the period 1990 and 1995, employment in these larger firms fell by 26% (see Table 1), with numbers falling through 66 consecutive months from 1990 onwards. In these firms, 248 in total, around 25,000 jobs were lost overall. Taking into account all industrial firms, we would estimate that the total numbers of jobs lost was in the region of 220-250,000. The problem of employment was aggravated further in the second half of 1995 and thereafter, when the rate of growth in the economy slowed down. For example, a study on the textile industry, an industry which provides a substantial proportion of jobs throughout the sector, suggested that in 1995 and 1996 there was a 20% fall in blue-collar employment and a 13% fall in white-collar jobs (Sociedad de Industrias, 1996). This contraction in employment responded to a number of factors. A large number of jobs were lost as a result of the paralysis in production in numerous firms, whilst other firms reduced the numbers of shifts they operated or eliminated certain lines of production. Another important cause was the practice of rationalisation introduced by many firms which led to a shift in the ratio of labour to capital.

However, one study undertaken using the 1981 and 1993 census returns and the national income level surveys (ENNVIs) in 1985, 1991 and 1994, came to the conclusion that total employment in the manufacturing sector expanded between 1990 and 1994, by a total of over 100,000 jobs from 676,000 to 771,000. It went on to argue that a radical shift had taken place in the structure of employment in manufacturing, with employment in large firms decreasing whilst payrolls in small and medium-sized firms increased (Consorcio de Investigación Económica, 1996). These conclusions need to be looked at carefully, since they are not entirely consistent with other indicators at our disposal. Furthermore, in view of the structural changes experienced in industry, estimates based on the employment elasticity of the manufacturing sector, which indicates growth in sectoral employment as of 1993, are not very reliable (Jiménez, 1996).

In any case, it remains clear that there was a decrease in industrial employment in firms in the formal sector of the economy, not just in those with 100 workers or more but in other strata too. The displacement in employment appears to be mainly towards firms with six workers or less, the so-called *micro-*

empresa, in which conditions and work practices were not comparable with manufacturing industry as such.

Sectoral breakdown

Even if it is the case that industry managed to maintain almost unaltered its share of GDP and to regain levels of production reached a decade earlier, the liberalising reforms had the effect of changing the structure of industrial production. These changes have taken place within different industrial sectors and between them. Within each sector, the ease with which different firms adjusted varied considerably, creating significant changes in the relative market share of individual firms, not least because of a paralysis in output in a considerable number.

The changes in industrial structure can be analysed by grouping together different sub-sectors in terms of the average growth rates achieved by each in the period between 1990-97 and in terms of variations in their use of installed capacity over the same period. Installed capacity is measured in relation to the highest level of production in each sub-sector over a time series. Persistent under-use of installed capacity would indicate a change in the structure of production in that sub-sector by virtue of the dismantling of the industrial apparatus. The annual average rate of growth indicates the capacity of different sectors to react to changing economic circumstances. In accordance with the variations in these two different indicators, it is possible to identify four different situations within the industrial sector which help show the differential impact of the economic reforms.

Table 4. Classification of Industrial Subsectors by Growth Rate and Average Annual Installed Capacity Utilisation 1990/97 (%)

ISIC	Description	Inst. Capac. Aver. 90/97	Growth Aver. 90/97
GROUP A			
3000	Fishmeal	48.47	5.05
3111	Prepared meat conserves	46.85	6.68
3113	Fruit and vegetable conserves	46.31	12.36
3620	Glass	49.41	8.89
3699	Non-metallic products (various)	47.11	5.05
3811	Iron tools and artefacts	35.16	1.31
3819	Metallic products (various)	29.90	10.50
3831	Electrical machinery (various)	33.94	8.72
GROUP B			
3112	Milk products	66.76	5.26
3115	Oils and fats	71.04	1.30
3116	Grain milling	67.11	5.19
3118	Sugar	62.87	1.10

3121	Food products (various)	70.97	7.42
3122	Animal feed	71.82	4.98
3133	Malt and beer	68.16	1.25
3134	Soft drinks	57.18	8.06
3140	Tobacco	53.08	0.51
3211	Textiles and clothing	69.70	1.70
3213	Knitwear	67.79	11.77
3215	Ropemaking	76.28	19.95
3412	Paper and cardboard containers	52.69	9.43
3420	Printing	51.72	2.84
3511	Basic chemicals	73.26	5.89
3513	Synthetic resins	52.57	0.77
3521	Paint and varnish	62.94	9.27
3523	Cleaning products	65.57	12.02
3529	Other chemicals	73.35	7.29
3530	Oil refining	78.63	1.64
3551	Tyres	70.92	1.88
3560	Plastic products	62.84	10.87
3610	China and porcelain	79.06	22.40
3692	Cement	78.61	6.66
3710	Iron and steel	66.22	7.07
3720	Non-ferrous metals	85.65	9.57
3839	Electrical goods (various)	52.31	2.83
3909	Industrial goods (various)	58.36	6.29
GROUP C			
3114	Fish conserves	41.88	-0.30
3131	Distilling	11.9	-13.27
3231	Tanning	36.55	-2.6
3240	Leather products and shoes	34.93	-11.79
3411	Paper and cardboard	27.33	-7.70
3512	Fertiliser and pesticides	12.1	-22.85
3522	Pharmaceuticals	41.13	-5.99
3559	Rubber goods	21.95	-7.2
3829	Machinery and equipment (various)	35.69	-1.93
3832	Television and radios	14.90	-47.04
3833	Electrical household appliances	11.34	-30.45
3843	Automobile	23.19	-9.08
GROUP D			
3117	Breadmaking	71.91	-7.53
3119	Chocolates and confectionery	56.42	-8.32
3220	Dressmaking	53.73	-7.68

Source: INEI-BCRP

Table 4 sets out a classification of different sub-sectors in line with these variables. In terms of installed capacity, we have adopted 50% as a dividing line. Although arbitrary, it bears some relation to industrial performance prior to the reforms. Appendices 1 and 2 show trends in the growth rate and in the use of installed capacity between different industrial activities in the period between 1990 and 1997.

The activities included in Group C are those most seriously prejudiced by the process of economic reform. These are the sectors which produced negative annual average growth rates for the period and which were operating at very low levels of installed capacity. Of these, the worst affected appear to be firms producing domestic electrical appliances (3833), radios and televisions (3832), fertilisers and crop sprays (3512) and distilleries and manufacturers of spirits (3131). These sectors experienced negative annual average growth rates of 15% or more. The most extreme example was domestic appliances (TVs and radios), for which output suffered an annual average contraction of 47%. These industries worked at an average of between 11% and 23% of capacity over this period, and in each case unused capacity increased. In 1996, their use of installed capacity varied between 0.3% and 8%.

Within Group C, we also find other industrial subsectors, such as vehicle manufacture (3843), in which average use of capacity was 23.2% and in which production contracted on average by 6.5%; rubber products (3559) working at 22% of capacity and suffering an average contraction of 7%; paper and cardboard (3411) at 27.3% of capacity and output contraction of 8%; leather products (3240) and shoes (3240) at 35% of capacity each; and machinery and equipment (3829) at 35.7% with negative growth rates. In most cases, the collapse in production was a consequence of the 1988-90 economic crisis and the failure of industries to recover thereafter because of the economic adjustment. In this context, we need to remember that the auto assembly industry was practically dismantled prior to 1990, reduced to a single factory assembling trucks and one or two plants producing bodywork. Similarly, in the pharmaceutical industry, 14 foreign companies closed their laboratories in Peru, but well before 1990. In this sector, average use of installed capacity for the period 1990-97 was 41%, whilst output contracted at an average annual rate of 5.6%.

Predictably, the main casualties of the economic reforms were those industries which had developed behind high tariff walls during the ISI period. These sectors were least able to recover from the crisis of the late 1980s and to meet the competition from imports. The case of the pharmaceutical industry was somewhat different, since the closure of laboratories was a response taken by foreign firms relocating production in other countries. The Peruvian-owned pharmaceutical firms managed to adapt to the new situation and continued in production.

A second group of industries is represented in Group A, which – despite capacity utilisation levels of below 50% – managed to achieve growth in their annual average output over the 1990-97 period. These industries appeared to be undergoing recovery, increasing their levels of capacity utilisation. Four sub-sectors of metal-working industries fall under this category: tools and hardware (3811), diverse metal products (3819), diverse electrical tools (3831) and diverse non-metallic products (3699). Similarly, in the food industry, two sectors came under this heading: meat conserves (3111) and tinned fruit and vegetables (3113), whilst this was also the case for the glass industry (3620). Although all hard-hit by the crisis of the late 1980s, these industries managed to weather the reforms of the early 1990s. Each industry, of course, exhibits individual traits. In the case of the food industry and the production of non-metallic minerals, capacity utilisation had moved ahead of 50% by 1997. However, industries in the metal-working sector were still working at around 40%, showing less capacity to adapt and a greater exposure to competition from imports. Whether or not these sectors will recover their historic levels of output remains to be seen.

Industries falling into Group D are those in which average capacity utilisation was above 50% but where average growth was negative. They included breadmaking (3117), chocolates and confectionery (3119), clothing (3220). In the case of the first two, the lack of adequate data obscures the true picture. These are industries dominated by small-scale enterprises and which therefore generally fall outside the coverage of industrial performance statistics. Nevertheless, the buoyant export performance of the clothing industry from 1994 onwards is a good example of a positive response to the change in policy orientation. Performance in the chocolate and confectionery sector appears to be rather similar to the industries in Group C. Following a relative recovery in the period 1990-92, these sectors deteriorated thereafter in spite of the rapid growth rates in the economy as a whole. Faced with tough foreign competition, a number of firms were forced to close their doors. During the first half of 1997, this industry was working at only 31% of installed capacity.

Finally, Group B includes those sectors which were not prejudiced by the market opening and other reforms. These managed to achieve positive annual average growth rates in the years after 1990 (although to varying degrees of success), and working at over 50% of installed capacity. It was the relative dynamism of these that enabled industry as a whole to recover the production levels achieved prior to 1988. They share a number of common characteristics and they were sectors less afflicted by the crisis of the late 1980s, a point that becomes clear if we note the relatively high levels of capacity use in 1990. In general, these were industries which showed sustained recovery power after 1990, in many cases exceeding the average capacity-use rates for the 1985-90 period, and in some cases reaching new production peaks (see Appendix 2).

Group B incorporates a heterogeneous collection of subsectors, but ones which had tended to perform robustly in the pre-ISI period. For instance, output of intermediate goods for the construction industry was buoyant, such as cement

(3692), ceramic goods and porcelain (3610), iron and steel (3710), paint, varnish and polish (3521) and plastics (3560). All these had high average growth rates and high use of installed capacity. In the first half of 1997, for instance, these industries were all working at 90% or more of capacity. Such products benefited from expansion in the construction industry, and most did not suffer competition from cheaper imports. The food industry (including beverages and tobacco products) also managed to recover well from the downturn of the late 1980s, although it was less buoyant than those sectors producing construction materials. It was more vulnerable to foreign competition and more subject to volatility in domestic demand. The textile industry (3211) and knitwear (3213) also managed to stage a recovery from the years of crisis. In the case of the former, growth in the first half of the 1980s was modest, but capacity utilisation rose from 67% in 1990 to 81% in 1997. The knitwear industry proved much more dynamic, with an average annual growth rate of 11%. The most successful sub-sectors of the textile industry were those geared to the export market. In the case of the chemical industry, most sectors reveal fairly rapid annual growth rates after 1990, varying between 6% (basic chemicals) and 12% (cleaning fluids) on average, with utilisation rates of 78-92% in 1997. Another sector which managed to defend itself from foreign competition with some success was tyre manufacture. The two manufacturers involved did so by specialising in specific types of tyre, but these both were linked to transnational producers which accounted for most imports.

Finally, Group B also encompasses those industries dedicated to the processing of primary raw materials for export. Growth rates for these industries were, in general, superior to those industries producing mostly for the domestic market. Whilst average annual growth rates exceeded 6.4% for these products, the growth rate for other industries was around 4.5%. These industries worked on average at higher rates of capacity than the others, although the rates were not greatly influenced by the reforms. Their performance was much less influenced by considerations of macroeconomic policy and was dependent more on the buoyancy of world markets. However, in the case of sugar refining, output rates reflected the longstanding problems of the sugar cooperatives, whilst the poor growth record in oil refining reflected management problems in the state-owned oil company, Petroperú. The most dynamic primary processing industries were non-ferrous minerals (closely linked to the mining industry) with a 9.6% annual average growth rate, and fishmeal (5%). Nevertheless, the fishmeal industry ran at relatively low levels of capacity utilisation with production levels notoriously dependent on climatic factors and fish stocks.

The foregoing breakdown provides a synthetic picture of industrial performance in the 1990-97 period. However, it should also be borne in mind that a great deal of variety is to be found within sectors at the level of individual plant and firms. Even among those sectors which were worst affected by economic conditions, there were firms which managed to restructure themselves or reorient their marketing strategies. Equally, amongst those sectors which were better placed to prosper, there were cases of firms which failed to adapt and which fared poorly. The key to understanding this variety is the mixed abilities of businessmen to tap financial resources and manage their firms. One of the key variables here was the extent of their indebtedness at the point at which the new policies were introduced. The sharp increase in the cost of credit during the first few years of the adjustment phase was an insoluble problem for many industrialists, especially those unable to tap new sources of fresh money.

Closures

The industrial restructuring which took place in Peru in the early 1990s led to the paralysis of a fairly large number of firms. The exact number of firms which went into liquidation or which suspended output temporarily or for longer periods is difficult to assess. In many cases, firms which shut down did so without complying with legal formalities, especially smaller enterprises. Also, many firms switched from one activity to another, availing themselves of their knowledge of local market conditions and so turning from manufacturing to importing activities. In such cases, a firm might well have continued to operate under the same name and on the same legal footing, whilst undertaking a wholly different set of activities. Irrespective of the shortcomings of the available statistics, it is still possible to get an idea of the impact of the reform programme on factory closures by using the monthly survey of industrial establishments conducted by the industry ministry.

Table 5 classifies the firms included in the survey by industrial sector and shows the number of firms in which production was at a standstill in June 1997. Of the 268 firms included, just over one-quarter (69) were effectively paralysed on this date. The table shows the breakdown by industrial sector. Thus, in the machine tools industry, one-half of the firms involved were not producing; in the rubber industry the proportion was 40% and in other sectors it varied between 13-37.5%, with many in the 30% range. But in other sectors – tobacco, china, porcelain, non-metallic minerals, iron and steel, non-ferrous minerals – there were no firms at a standstill. Thus the data corroborate the findings enumerated above in our sectoral breakdown. However, to establish more precisely how many firms were forced to close, temporarily or permanently, would require a more detailed study than is possible here.

A phenomenon that is closely related to that of closure is the migration of production abroad. In view of the unfavourable conditions prevalent on the domestic market, some firms opted to alter their business strategies and to relocate production in other countries – principally in other member states of the Andean Pact – and export to Peru instead of producing there. This was particularly commonplace in the chocolate and confectionery industry, the production of industrial and domestic cleansers, the tyre industry and the paper industry (which practically disappeared). The practice tended to be simplest for transnational firms with pre-existing productive bases in other countries.

The economic programme that was applied in Peru in 1990 and thereafter thus triggered a series of changes in the industrial sectors, which we discuss below. Firstly, it is important to stress once again the speed at which these changes took place and the impact which they had in all areas of industry.

Table 5. The Number and Percentage of Firms where Production was Paralysed, June 1997

ISIC	Description	No. firms.	No. paralysed	%	Mergers/ Takeovers	%
311-12	Food products	15	5	33.3	1	6.7
313	Beverages	13	1	7.7	3	23.1
314	Tobacco	2	0	0.0	0	0.0
321	Textiles	49	17	34.7	3	6.1
323	Leather	12	4	33.3	0	0.0
341	Paper	10	3	30.0	0	0.0
351	Industrial chemicals.	20	4	20.0	3	15.0
352	Chemicals (various)	31	5	16.1	9	29.0
355	Rubber goods	5	2	40.0	0	0.0
356	Plastics	23	3	13.0	2	8.7
361	China and porcelain	2	0	0.0	1	50.0
362	Glass	8	3	37.5	0	0.0
369	Non metallic minerals	6	0	0.0	0	0.0
371	Iron and steel	4	0	0.0	0	0.0
372	Non-ferrous metals	6	0	0.0	1	16.7
381	Basic metals	22	7	31.8	3	13.6
382	Non-electrical machinery	12	6	50.0	0	0.0
383	Electrical machinery	14	7	50.0	2	14.3
384	Transport goods	6	2	33.3	0	0.0
390	Other manufactured goods.	8	0	0.0	0	0.0
	TOTAL	268	69	25.75	28	10.4

Source: MITINCI

Investment and productivity

The process of industrial restructuring involved a significant amount of investment, geared towards modernising the productive structure and the introduction of new forms of management and organisation. There are no figures which allow us to measure quantitatively the investment involved in this process of industrial restructuring. However, since the investment that took place involved a high imported component, the data for the import of capital goods for industry provides us with some idea of the amounts.

Table 6. Peru: Imports of Capital Goods (Millions of US dollars)

	1990	1991	1992	1993	1994	1995	1996	1997*	TOTAL
Capital goods	879.85	958.69	1,993.00	1,234.46	1,804.74	2,350.11	2,368.79	704.51	12,294.15
For industry	550.21	576.22	598.16	747.73	1,054.57	1,458.70	1,688.67	505.72	7,179.98
1. Office machinery	71.02	107.08	116.18	134.25	191.17	299.33	312.44	75.29	1,306.76
2. Tools	21.15	17.22	15.65	20.29	32.87	45.09	38.23	10.28	200.78
3. Parts and accessories.	125.86	110.94	92.09	145.43	190.03	136.46	135.80	40.22	976.83
4. Industrial machinery	269.89	223.88	257.16	338.36	454.48	606.71	791.53	268.74	3,210.75
5. Other fixed equipment	62.30	117.10	117.09	109.39	186.02	371.10	410.67	111.19	1,484.86
3+4+5	458.05	451.92	466.34	593.18	830.53	1,114.27	1,338.00	420.15	5,672.44

*Jan-March

Source: Customs Service

Table 6 shows that after 1993 there was a large increase in capital goods imports for industry, rising from an annual average of 574 million dollars for the 1990-92 period to 747 million in 1993 and continuing on a sharply rising curve in subsequent years. A similar increase can be detected for the import of industrial machinery, another useful proxy but an item which also includes other goods than those used strictly for industrial investment. Imports of industrial machinery between 1990 and 1997 were worth a total of 3.2 billion dollars. It seems that around 70% of this was actually machines used in industry. Taking this figure, and adding to it the costs of installation and the locally-produced components of investment, it would seem that total investment in new assets alone would have been in the order of 3 billion dollars. The behaviour of industrial investment in the context of liberalising reform is a topic which has yet to be properly studied for Peru.

Much of the new investment was geared towards bringing in and applying new productive technologies which, linked to the rationalisation of the workforce and the new methods of administration and management, helped generate a significant increase in productivity. In column 6 of Table 1, we included data on labour productivity for the period 1985-96. As can be seen, labour productivity underwent a sustained increase after 1990, rising to levels well above those prevalent in the second half of the 1980s. The index of productivity reflects shifts in the physical volume of aggregate production and those in industrial employment. Since the index is based on the survey of the 268 largest firms (those with more than 100 employees), it does not necessarily reflect accurately trends within industry as a whole. It may well exaggerate the rise in productivity. Nevertheless, estimates for different firms confirm the broad trend towards higher productivity.

Another consequence of the reform process has been the trend towards industrial concentration through mergers and acquisitions. The very fact that many factories have closed is, itself, indicative of greater concentration. Mergers became more frequent after 1993, following legislation that year to facilitate them. The move towards fewer suppliers was particularly evident in the beer industry, among producers of ceramic goods, in the flour and pasta industry, the soft drinks sector and among producers of electrical conductors. The industry ministry figures set out in Table 5 provide information on the number of firms involved in mergers. Of the firms mentioned in the survey, over 10% were involved in mergers. Between 1993 and 1997, there were some 100 mergers and acquisitions, although in some cases these involved simply the fusion of the productive and commercial operations of the same firm. But in many other cases, mergers took place between what previously were direct competitors. The experience of other countries would suggest that this was a process which was just beginning in Peru.

Table 7. Manufactured Exports 1989-1997 (millions of US dollars)

SECTOR	1989	1990	1991	1992	1993	1994	1995	1996	1997*
Textiles	344.90	364.30	392.10	343.00	324.30	395.80	440.70	454.50	217.00
Metalworking	47.60	42.90	40.30	43.70	42.20	39.70	39.80	48.70	18.50
Chemicals	93.10	89.50	86.80	74.20	74.30	101.90	132.80	167.10	74.60
Steel	161.20	151.30	125.20	125.30	123.00	119.80	145.20	141.20	77.60
Non-metallic minerals	16.00	15.60	18.20	22.80	25.10	29.40	30.00	37.30	18.30
Others	96.50	98.60	84.80	97.10	103.40	101.50	157.40	205.60	141.60
Total	759.30	762.20	747.40	706.10	692.30	788.10	945.90	1,054.40	547.60

*January-May

Source: BCRP

The reform process also stimulated, to a certain degree, foreign direct investment (FDI) in the industrial sector. The stock of foreign investment remained practically unchanged throughout the 1980s. In 1987, this amounted to 408 million dollars. However, by 1997, it had increased to 1.09 billion dollars. Between 1990 and 1993, there was no significant increase in FDI. However, from 1993 onwards, there was a sharp upturn. This went hand-in-hand with a proliferation of joint ventures between Peruvian and foreign firms. One of the characteristics of FDI during this period is that it was oriented primarily towards already existing firms and investment in new projects was fairly insignificant. Another feature is that FDI went to relatively few industrial sectors. Some 21.5% of the total arose from the privatisation of oil refineries, which absorbed 147 million dollars. Just over 16% went to the industry producing oils and fats, a product of the acquisition of two leading producers and the establishment of a new processing plant. Around 10% of the total was in chocolates and confectionery, with the acquisition of the main producer by a transnational enterprise. Investments in these three sectors alone account for nearly one-half of the total new FDI. Other sectors to receive foreign investment were the textile industry, parts of the food industry and basic chemicals. Likewise, these investments were geared almost entirely to the acquisition of existing plant.

Manufactured exports

Finally, another effect worth mentioning is the growth in the export of manufactured goods. Table 7 shows how up until 1993 industrial exports remained relatively stagnant, even declining slightly in relation to the 1980s. The increase in export activity became more noticeable thereafter, rising by 13.8% in 1994, 19.9% in 1995 and 11.5% in 1996. Preliminary figures for 1997 suggested that this trend continued. Amongst the most successful sectors in this respect was the textile and garment industries, which represented 43.4% of total manufactured exports in 1996. Also, exports of jewellery played a significant part. The value of jewellery, of course, reflected in large part the value of the metal included in the product. It is possible that the high international market prices for some goods, like jewellery, exaggerate their importance in the overall structure of industrial exports. From 1994 onwards, the manufacturing sector exported approximately 10% of its production. However, except in the case of textiles and garments, foreign demand still played a fairly secondary role in the overall development of the manufacturing sector.

The effects of the economic reforms on industry have yet to work themselves through. Although the effects are still preliminary, this chapter has sought to provide an initial evaluation of the process.

Appendix 1. Annual Percentage Variation in Industrial Production, 1990-97

ISIC	Description	1990	1991	1992	1993	1994	1995	1996	June 1997
TOTAL	**Total Manufacturing Sector**	**-2.22**	**6.94**	**-3.85**	**6.41**	**22.52**	**7.65**	**1.82**	**7.74**
	Processed Primary goods	-1.44	6.49	-4.12	2.36	24.12	12.98	-0.82	8.32
	Other Manufacturing	-4.35	8.21	-3.21	17.72	18.68	-5.72	8.73	6.33
	Consumer Goods	**-1.72**	**6.35**	**-4.00**	**2.47**	**22.34**	**9.00**	**0.07**	**10.44**
	Non-durables	-2.24	5.87	-3.73	3.66	23.42	9.02	0.58	10.53
	Durables	28.61	27.70	-13.72	-45.38	-60.57	3.34	-52.71	-61.78
	Intermediate goods	**-4.29**	**7.76**	**-2.05**	**12.22**	**21.77**	**4.85**	**6.42**	**6.19**
	Agriculture	5.26	-15.49	13.08	-3.26	24.46	9.09	-3.58	5.27
	Mining	-4.46	0.02	-8.70	24.78	9.61	11.42	0.68	-5.95
	Industry	-5.02	9.24	-4.00	13.67	21.39	3.55	5.49	6.28
	Construction	-1.67	9.74	17.36	1.16	28.01	14.89	33.85	9.13
	Capital Goods	**7.83**	**2.61**	**-21.65**	**-3.92**	**36.31**	**27.24**	**-17.58**	**-1.83**
30	**Fish-meal and fish-oil industry**	**3.06**	**8.88**	**-11.76**	**52.83**	**36.66**	**-25.98**	**4.05**	**9.60**
31	**Food products, beverages and tobacco**	**1.07**	**7.57**	**-2.88**	**2.81**	**16.84**	**5.00**	**-1.87**	**10.54**
311-12	Food products	0.58	-3.05	0.00	3.97	20.17	5.53	-2.94	12.02
3111	Prepared meat products	-27.75	31.73	-4.65	12.74	11.81	5.79	26.81	1.96
3112	Dairy products	6.33	14.18	-4.94	1.52	19.53	7.01	6.88	11.03
3113	Fruit and vegetables preservations	-0.08	6.31	-2.05	-28.07	53.14	57.61	-3.03	46.53
3114	Fish preservation	8.65	-45.67	-5.01	55.60	31.31	-11.48	-16.57	30.07
3115	Vegetable and/ or animal oils and fats	5.42	-12.93	-2.75	10.24	13.30	1.94	1.83	9.35
3116	Grain milling	-19.58	31.67	10.47	10.47	8.42	-2.93	1.48	-4.96
3117	Breadmaking	-5.32	16.21	-0.32	-0.33	24.41	-2.34	n.d.	n.d.
3118	Sugar	2.74	-5.77	-21.39	-8.74	35.17	18.67	-5.32	26.31
3119	Chocolate and confectionary	-2.71	7.52	22.14	-7.62	-13.18	-10.08	-23.65	-17.54
3121	Food products (various)	6.28	3.08	6.97	6.25	22.41	10.72	12.57	6.50
3122	Animal feed	9.11	-9.96	26.65	-2.86	20.58	16.83	-4.14	3.86
313	Beverages	0.63	29.22	-6.32	1.30	12.34	3.68	-3.84	10.90

3131	Distilling	-20.40	-21.22	-47.99	-30.26	51.64	-15.06	-7.17	70.63
3133	Malt and beer	0.46	15.81	-3.32	8.49	-5.68	14.81	-4.05	4.27
3134	Soft drinks	6.99	62.01	-5.49	-5.53	35.53	-6.11	-3.46	16.20
314	Tobacco	9.67	3.68	-8.64	0.40	10.39	7.86	11.94	-6.63
32	**Textiles, clothing and leather goods**	**-9.05**	**-0.47**	**-7.24**	**-3.67**	**37.12**	**7.96**	**10.86**	**7.10**
321	Textiles	-10.35	-2.75	-7.37	-4.96	40.66	9.70	6.74	7.40
3211	Spinning, weaving and finished goods	-8.95	-1.55	-7.86	-6.18	26.92	5.56	-0.48	11.51
3213	Knitwear	-15.73	-9.88	-8.75	-2.56	102.91	19.45	23.23	-2.90
3215	Cordmaking	-10.96	17.08	18.76	13.09	36.84	22.59	16.07	28.77
322	Dressmaking	-2.18	11.72	-7.04	1.20	40.02	n.d.	n.d.	n.d.
323	Leather and skins	-7.35	-15.41	6.49	-4.00	-3.68	1.40	1.71	-3.76
324	Leather shoes	1.67	32.04	-15.29	7.00	-5.86	n.d.	n.d.	n.d.
33	**Timber and furniture-making**	**-5.57**	**24.85**	**n.d.**	**21.50**	**20.32**	**n.d.**	**n.d.**	**n.d.**
34	**Paper**	**11.91**	**-9.36**	**-5.94**	**-0.97**	**79.76**	**41.50**	**-52.75**	**1.46**
341	Paper industry and products	14.71	-24.37	-38.51	4.98	96.69	37.23	-1.43	1.46
3411	Paper and cardboard	12.81	-25.05	-44.38	9.04	62.47	39.03	-22.03	-14.73
3412	Paper and cardboard containers	18.46	-23.10	-27.79	-0.73	149.60	35.42	19.85	13.46
342	Printing and Publishing	10.14	0.50	10.17	-2.62	74.72	42.93	n.d.	n.d.
35	**Petroleum-derived chemicals**	**-1.75**	**4.22**	**-1.59**	**10.80**	**13.03**	**12.54**	**-0.91**	**10.15**
351	Industrial chemicals	-1.90	1.10	-13.08	12.80	7.86	5.95	12.26	7.99
3511	Basic chemicals	-10.28	9.61	-10.18	13.66	11.25	10.07	18.11	5.08
3512	Fertilisers and pesticides	-0.44	-43.49	-29.18	-19.74	2.52	-28.06	22.91	-22.19
3513	Synthetic resins	13.63	-0.70	-15.64	15.10	2.39	0.93	-0.45	16.82
352	Chemical products (various)	3.37	8.58	4.22	7.93	17.32	28.76	-8.85	13.82
3521	Paint, varnish and laquer	-20.25	-19.77	69.36	28.08	9.62	8.97	-1.54	14.33
3522	Pharma-ceuticals	-0.49	-0.44	-13.44	-11.27	14.80	58.62	-49.24	13.71
3523	Cleaning Products	20.74	26.47	-6.87	3.98	22.90	37.78	2.42	19.01
3529	Other Chemicals	1.02	4.72	12.49	13.89	16.28	13.28	-5.32	3.81

353	Oil refining	-3.23	2.10	0.67	4.42	3.52	-1.80	-0.67	-0.31
355	Rubber	-2.46	-14.18	-7.46	8.93	2.37	6.94	-3.29	15.73
3551	Tyres	-2.12	-9.50	-10.22	25.61	5.94	6.21	-8.16	18.94
3559	Rubber goods (various)	-3.45	-27.77	2.60	-44.21	-23.24	14.12	41.60	0.11
356	Plastic products	-13.99	17.55	9.47	28.83	30.08	1.47	2.58	14.40
36	**Non-metal industries**	**-1.15**	**3.74**	**-1.08**	**16.95**	**28.71**	**22.15**	**8.79**	**10.65**
361	China and porcelaine	-4.94	25.15	15.07	16.93	44.75	29.33	20.22	21.13
362	Glass	-2.50	-8.91	-9.26	-14.76	22.41	48.06	32.71	19.05
369	Non-metallic minerals	0.12	2.63	-3.34	24.39	24.94	15.59	-0.46	3.88
3692	Cement	2.67	-2.46	1.46	12.50	31.77	17.98	0.91	9.71
3699	Non-metallic minerals (various)	-4.95	13.52	-12.19	49.68	14.03	11.17	-3.13	-6.88
37	**Basic metal industries**	**-10.25**	**17.29**	**0.75**	**4.74**	**15.46**	**7.98**	**14.47**	**4.81**
371	Iron and steel	-12.57	11.85	4.63	7.21	35.85	5.06	10.46	8.31
372	Non-ferrous metals	-9.66	18.61	-0.14	4.15	10.44	8.87	15.64	3.84
38	**Metal and machinery**	**7.20**	**7.24**	**-18.20**	**-1.00**	**20.91**	**30.39**	**-11.64**	**0.51**
381	Metal goods except machinery	-4.84	7.75	-11.79	40.17	18.21	39.40	2.28	5.49
3811	Tools and ironmongery	-3.57	-0.44	-12.36	5.78	59.95	-13.78	-7.74	23.72
3819	Metal goods (various)	-5.11	9.46	-11.68	46.65	12.54	49.69	3.40	3.82
382	Machinery and equipment	19.12	14.43	-18.24	-14.78	38.10	30.48	-37.45	-3.48
383	Electrical machinery and equipment	7.10	3.29	-17.87	-11.22	-0.66	46.27	-5.65	-0.63
3831	Electrical machinery (various)	-14.86	10.40	2.47	16.03	59.60	40.24	-29.78	19.17
3832	Television and radios	29.03	19.50	-8.77	-35.82	-61.68	0.25	-55.44	-79.41
3833	Electrical household appliances	26.23	74.31	-33.01	-96.11	36.25	79.44	-15.05	15.39
3839	Electrical Goods (various)	3.40	-10.21	-25.44	8.32	3.99	56.11	10.37	-3.69
384	Transport materials	16.69	11.95	-25.98	-18.29	74.38	-8.85	-36.84	-9.04
39	**Manufacturing industry (various)**	**6.68**	**9.72**	**12.43**	**0.53**	**47.26**	**1.33**	**-8.45**	**-3.13**

Source: INEI-BCRP

Appendix 2. Annual Installed Capacity Utilisation (%), 1990-97

	Description	1990	1991	1992	1993	1994	1995	1996	June 1997	Ave-rage
TOTAL	Total Manufacturing Sector	49.97	52.73	50.47	52.46	61.88	63.14	62.44	65.43	57.31
	Processed Primary goods	46.22	49.22	47.19	48.26	57.90	63.50	61.79	64.24	54.79
	Other Manufacturing	64.87	65.83	62.38	66.27	74.74	62.10	63.66	68.11	66.00
	Consumer Goods	50.07	53.25	51.12	52.32	62.66	67.27	65.67	69.01	58.92
	Non-durables	51.27	54.28	52.25	54.09	65.28	70.05	68.66	72.19	61.01
	Durables	24.79	31.66	27.31	14.92	5.88	6.08	2.87	0.62	14.27
	Intermediate goods	51.24	53.57	51.94	55.36	63.28	60.15	61.44	64.21	57.65
	Agriculture	42.14	35.61	40.27	38.96	48.49	52.89	51.00	50.41	44.97
	Mining	33.50	33.51	30.59	38.17	41.84	46.62	46.94	46.99	39.77
	Industry	53.11	55.93	53.04	56.70	64.65	59.72	60.46	63.41	58.38
	Construction	46.84	51.40	60.33	60.62	66.87	74.86	92.09	96.51	68.69
	Capital Goods	34.20	35.09	27.49	26.42	36.01	45.81	37.76	39.81	35.32
30	Fish-meal and fish-oil industry	59.28	52.11	43.13	49.91	60.41	37.13	38.63	47.17	48.47
31	Food products, beverages and tobacco	51.22	55.10	53.51	55.01	63.44	66.28	63.96	67.69	59.52
311-12	Food products	57.24	55.50	55.49	57.70	67.73	70.86	66.80	69.07	62.55
3111	Prepared meat products	29.98	39.49	37.65	42.45	47.47	50.22	63.68	63.89	46.85
3112	Dairy products	56.00	63.94	60.79	61.71	73.76	73.79	69.40	74.72	66.76
3113	Fruit and vegetables preservations	40.24	42.78	41.91	30.14	46.16	65.53	50.50	53.23	46.31
3114	Fish preservation	49.78	27.05	25.69	39.97	52.49	46.46	38.76	54.88	41.88
3115	Vegetable and/ or animal oils and fats	71.15	61.95	60.24	66.41	75.24	76.70	78.11	78.56	71.04
3116	Grain milling	44.42	58.49	64.62	71.38	77.39	75.12	76.23	69.21	67.11
3117	Breadmaking	63.37	73.64	73.40	73.16	74.84	73.09	n.d.	n.d.	71.91
3118	Sugar	67.67	63.76	50.12	45.74	61.83	73.37	69.47	70.99	62.87
3119	Chocolate and confectionary	57.27	61.58	75.21	69.48	60.32	54.24	41.41	31.87	56.42
3121	Food products (various)	53.90	55.56	59.43	63.15	77.30	84.37	84.68	89.38	70.97
3122	Animal feed	57.34	51.63	65.39	63.52	76.60	89.49	85.79	84.76	71.82
313	Beverages	42.54	54.96	51.49	52.16	58.60	60.75	58.42	66.17	55.64

3131	Distilling	23.18	18.26	9.50	6.62	10.04	8.53	7.92	11.13	11.90
3133	Malt and beer	57.27	66.33	64.13	69.57	65.62	75.34	72.29	74.73	68.16
3134	Soft drinks	34.21	55.42	52.38	49.48	67.06	62.96	60.78	75.18	57.18
314	Tobacco	50.25	52.10	47.59	47.78	52.75	56.89	63.69	53.62	53.08
32	**Textiles, clothing and leather goods**	**58.93**	**58.65**	**54.41**	**52.23**	**68.72**	**72.89**	**77.32**	**79.81**	**65.37**
321	Textiles	65.14	63.35	58.68	55.51	73.90	79.18	79.77	82.04	69.70
3211	Spinning, weaving and finished goods	67.15	66.11	60.91	57.15	72.53	76.56	76.19	81.00	69.70
3213	Knitwear	58.26	52.50	47.91	46.68	77.65	88.00	88.31	83.00	67.79
3215	Cordmaking	60.55	70.89	84.19	78.47	76.26	71.43	78.09	90.34	76.28
322	Dressmaking	44.83	50.08	46.55	47.10	65.95	67.85	n.d.	n.d.	53.73
323	Leather and skins	41.65	35.23	37.51	36.02	34.69	35.59	36.20	35.54	36.55
324	Leather shoes	30.95	40.86	34.61	37.28	35.09	30.79	n.d.	n.d.	34.93
33	**Timber and furniture-making**	**34.09**	**42.56**	**n.d.**	**42.44**	**51.07**	**46.61**	**n.d.**	**n.d.**	**43.35**
34	**Paper**	**43.92**	**39.81**	**37.44**	**37.08**	**49.13**	**51.96**	**24.20**	**24.72**	**38.53**
341	Paper industry and products	38.51	29.13	17.91	18.80	36.98	50.75	47.29	48.31	35.96
3411	Paper and cardboard	36.96	27.70	15.41	16.80	27.30	37.95	29.59	26.90	27.33
3412	Paper and cardboard containers	41.81	32.15	23.22	23.05	57.52	77.90	79.09	86.79	52.69
342	Printing and Publishing	48.38	48.63	53.57	52.17	55.20	52.36	n.d.	n.d.	51.72
35	**Petroleum-derived chemicals**	**50.85**	**52.99**	**52.15**	**57.78**	**65.15**	**72.13**	**70.99**	**73.77**	**61.98**
351	Industrial chemicals	52.22	52.80	45.89	51.76	55.83	59.15	64.80	67.37	56.23
3511	Basic chemicals	59.14	64.82	58.22	66.17	73.62	81.04	91.06	91.97	73.26
3512	Fertilisers and pesticides	29.14	16.47	11.66	9.36	9.60	6.90	8.49	5.19	12.10
3513	Synthetic resins	53.23	52.86	44.59	51.32	52.55	53.04	52.80	60.17	52.57
352	Chemical products (various)	45.24	49.12	51.19	55.25	64.39	79.50	72.46	73.74	61.36
3521	Paint, varnish and laquer	38.02	30.50	51.66	66.16	72.53	79.03	77.81	87.80	62.94
3522	Pharma-ceuticals	44.41	44.21	38.27	33.96	38.98	61.83	31.38	36.04	41.13
3523	Cleaning Products	43.99	55.63	51.81	53.87	66.20	86.00	88.07	78.98	65.57
3529	Other Chemicals	54.52	57.10	64.23	73.15	82.37	85.60	81.04	88.84	73.35

353	Oil refining	73.74	75.29	75.79	79.14	81.93	80.45	79.91	82.82	78.63
355	Rubber	56.78	48.73	45.09	49.12	50.28	53.77	52.01	59.85	51.95
3551	Tyres	68.94	62.39	56.01	70.35	74.53	79.16	72.70	83.26	70.92
3559	Rubber goods (various)	37.54	27.12	27.82	15.52	11.92	13.60	19.26	22.81	21.95
356	Plastic products	35.64	41.89	45.86	59.08	76.84	77.97	79.98	85.44	62.84
36	**Non-metal industries**	**49.06**	**50.89**	**50.34**	**58.47**	**64.64**	**76.90**	**76.77**	**81.40**	**63.56**
361	China and porcelaine	53.08	66.44	76.45	85.01	84.55	94.87	81.49	90.59	79.06
362	Glass	43.03	39.19	35.56	30.31	37.11	54.94	72.91	82.24	49.41
369	Non-metallic minerals	50.20	51.52	49.80	61.95	67.02	77.47	75.79	77.18	63.87
3692	Cement	68.71	67.02	68.00	76.50	76.89	90.72	88.80	92.26	78.61
3699	Non-metallic minerals (various)	31.84	36.14	31.74	47.50	54.17	60.22	58.34	56.95	47.11
37	**Basic metal industries**	**62.40**	**73.19**	**73.74**	**77.24**	**89.12**	**88.38**	**90.22**	**88.73**	**80.38**
371	Iron and steel	44.30	49.55	51.85	55.59	75.51	79.33	87.30	86.28	66.22
372	Non-ferrous metals	69.27	82.16	82.05	85.45	94.28	91.44	91.07	89.47	85.65
38	**Metal and machinery**	**27.92**	**29.95**	**24.50**	**24.25**	**29.32**	**38.24**	**33.79**	**35.07**	**30.38**
381	Metal goods except machinery	19.16	20.65	18.21	25.53	30.18	42.07	43.03	44.83	30.46
3811	Tools and ironmongery	31.08	30.95	27.12	28.69	45.89	39.56	36.50	41.48	35.16
3819	Metal goods (various)	17.74	19.42	17.15	25.15	28.30	42.37	43.81	45.22	29.90
382	Machinery and equipment	32.42	37.10	30.33	25.85	35.70	46.58	29.14	30.03	33.40
383	Electrical machinery and equipment	34.72	35.86	29.45	26.14	25.97	37.99	35.84	37.78	32.97
3831	Electrical machinery (various)	19.71	21.76	22.30	25.88	41.30	57.92	40.67	41.93	33.94
3832	Television and radios	25.60	30.59	27.91	17.91	6.87	6.88	3.07	0.33	14.90
3833	Electrical household appliances	21.01	36.62	24.53	0.95	1.30	2.33	1.98	1.98	11.34
3839	Electrical Goods (various)	52.64	47.26	35.24	38.17	39.70	61.97	68.40	75.12	52.31
384	Transport materials	25.69	28.77	21.29	17.40	30.34	27.66	17.47	16.92	23.19
39	**Manufacturing industry (various)**	**41.04**	**45.02**	**50.62**	**50.89**	**74.94**	**71.49**	**65.45**	**67.44**	**58.36**

Source: INEI-BCRP

CHAPTER 5

The Impact of Structural Adjustment on Agricultural Performance[*]

Raúl Hopkins

This chapter seeks to investigate the impact of the structural reforms carried out by the Fujimori government on the agricultural sector. The severity of the economic adjustment in the economy as a whole was mirrored in the agricultural sector. A number of structural reforms were implemented: goods and factor markets were liberalised; there were severe staff reductions in the various state agencies (the agriculture ministry and the Banco Agrario) and closure of other public monopolies; and a law was promulgated to promote private investment in agriculture.

We seek to examine the effects of these reforms, and in particular, the extent to which agriculture performed better, or worse, than in previous periods. At first sight, the policies appear to have been fairly successful. In the period 1993-97, agricultural output experienced an annual average rate of growth well above 8%. Our aim is to investigate the extent of this success. Are we witnessing a substantial improvement in agricultural growth performance, or was this rapid expansion merely a short-run recovery from very low output levels?

The link between agricultural performance and government policy is complex. Firstly, agricultural performance is affected by a large number of variables (such as the demand for primary commodities in the industrialised world and changes in other sectors of the economy) and is not just a response to government policies. Secondly, the expansion came after a severe drop in agricultural output (-16.5% in the 1988-92 period), partly due to the initial effects of the stabilisation process. In such a context, it is therefore relevant to ask the degree to which this growth is just a short-run recovery and whether it can be sustained in years to come. Thirdly, climatic conditions were, up to 1997 at least, remarkably favourable.

Finally, we examine whether, in the light of the structural adjustment programme, private agents have become efficient providers of those goods and services previously supplied by public enterprises. Special attention is given to the case of credit and agricultural extension.

From 1975 to 1990, Peru suffered its deepest economic and social crisis of the century and one of the most serious of its history. As we have seen in

[*] I am grateful to Jorge Agüero (GRADE) and Pedro Llontop (IEP) for their valuable research assistance, and to the Instituto de Estudios Peruanos for its support during my visit to Peru.

previous chapters, the most tangible manifestations of this crisis were hyperinflation, terrorism and the paralysis of the productive apparatus. At its heart lay deep social differences, long unattended, and a populist and ineffective handling of economic policy. High levels of inflation and falling GDP per capita affected rural producers as well as urban ones, whilst the effects of political violence were felt particularly acutely by the agricultural sector, both in terms of the death toll, the effects on agricultural investment in the areas concerned and the acceleration in urban migration.

Between 1975 and 1990, the rate of growth of agricultural output was 1.9%, well below the rate of population growth. Agricultural output for local markets, produced basically in the highlands (*sierra*), the poorest area of the country, fell at an average annual rate of 0.58% (Hopkins, 1995, Table A3). The backwardness and relative stagnation of agriculture led to a substantial decrease in its contribution to the overall economy. In 1950, agriculture accounted for 23% of GDP. By 1989, it stood at around 12% (Webb and Fernández Baca, 1996, Table 18.8). This decline is even more marked in relation to the trade balance. While in 1950 exports of cotton, sugar and coffee represented more than one-half of total exports, their proportion fell to 10% at the end of the 1980s. The agricultural trade balance, which was traditionally positive, has been in deficit in most years since 1980.

Despite this decline, agriculture is one of the leading sectors in terms of employment. Around 30% of the labour force works in agricultural activities. It is also a critical sector in terms of poverty. A comparison of standard of living indicators shows that the situation in the rural areas is worse than the corresponding national averages, and is particularly acute in the highlands (Hopkins, 1995, Table I.3; IFAD, 1991, Table 11). As Adolfo Figueroa shows in Chapter 7, in terms of rural-urban differences, the incidence of poverty is much higher in rural areas (see in particular his Table 3).

It is against this background that the policies of President Alberto Fujimori must be judged. He promised to give priority to the agricultural sector. Being himself an agronomist, his election generated expectations of a better future for this sector.

Policy agenda

As is discussed elsewhere in this volume, the structural adjustment programme adopted by the Fujimori government was notable both for its drastic nature and its effects on almost all sectors of the economy. The main policy areas and reforms are listed in Table 1, which in each case highlights the main policy innovations as these affected the agricultural sector. The reforms altered the institutional framework in some fundamental ways, the main objective being to free up market mechanisms in the allocation of resources.

Table 1: Main Policies Implemented by the Government

Type of policy	Macroeconomic instruments	Policies for the agricultural sector
1. Price	• Price deregulation in goods and factor markets	• Withdrawal of price controls for foodstuffs and agricultural inputs
2. Fiscal	• Reform of tax system • Fall in government deficit	• Staff reduction in Ministry of Agriculture
3. Monetary and financial	• Floating exchange rates; elimination of the MUC *a* • Interest rates market determined • Restrictive monetary policy	• Agricultural Bank closed • Interest rates market determined
4. Trade	• Withdrawal of quantitative restrictions on trade • Reduction in dispersion of tariff rates from average of 56% to only two rates (15% and 25%)	• Additional protection rates for agricultural goods, through system of surcharges • Elimination of quantitative restrictions on trade
5. Institutional reform	• Deregulation of goods and factor markets • Creation of institution to supervise intellectual property and free competition	• Elimination of public monopolies in foodstuffs and agricultural inputs • Creation of institutions in charge of research in natural resources and sanitary control (Inrena)
6. Investment and property rights		• Investment Promotion Law, promoting private investment and the development of the land market

Source: Based on various sources, following the framework suggested by Norton (1987).

a – MUC stands for Mercado Unico de Cambios, a multiple system of exchange rates created by the government of Alan García. Under the MUC, foodstuffs were imported at the lowest exchange rate, with the effect of reducing their price in the domestic market.

Goods and factors markets were thus deregulated, in agriculture as well as other sectors. Although price liberalisation of many of the main foodstuffs had been initiated in 1988, in 1990 price controls were virtually eliminated. In the factor markets, the changes took place more than a year after the introduction of the stabilisation programme. The Employment Promotion Law (DL 728) appeared in November 1991 with the aim of deregulating the link between employees and employers, and promoting formal sector employment. A key reform in this respect was the curtailment of labour stability.[1]

In addition, structural reform involved the reduction in the size of the state, starting with a reduction in the number of employees and the privatisation of public enterprises. State monopolies were done away with, and in the case of agriculture, ENCI and ECASA, the entities responsible for the purchase of production and the distribution of food subsidies, were wound up.[2] In 1990, the

---

[1]   A discussion of the changes in the regulation of the labour markets, from a legal perspective, is found in Varillas (1994) and Pasco (1994). See also Thomas, Chapter 9, in this volume, for an assessment of the changes introduced by the government in the functioning of the labour market.

[2]   ENCI was the *Empresa Nacional de Comercialización de Insumos* (National Enterprise for the Import of Agricultural Inputs). ECASA was the *Empresa de Comercialización de Arroz* (Rice Marketing Enterprise). Both had their origin in the policies of the first phase of the military

subsidy on foodstuffs made by ENCI and ECASA was reduced by 20% on the previous year. The subsidy was dropped on products such as maize.

According to Escobal (Escobal, 1994), the stabilisation programme impacted on agricultural policy in three main ways: (i) price policy led to the elimination of controls on the prices of foodstuffs and inputs, whilst deregulation also affected interest rates by eliminating preferential rates for farmers; (ii) trade liberalisation eliminated many of the restrictions which had acted as an anti-farming bias as a result of import substitution policies; (iii) institutional reforms made the sector more attractive to investors.

The fiscal and monetary policies applied by the Fujimori government had a negative short-run effect on agricultural production. The reduction of subsidies on agricultural inputs negatively affected output, whilst raising costs. Similarly, the elimination of preferential interest rates increased production costs. However, their impact was lessened by the relatively small number of producers with access to credit. In addition, the contraction of demand because of a fall in purchasing power also damaged the sector.

The passage from a state-controlled economy (where capital does not necessarily flow to the area of greatest efficiency but rather seeks short-term benefits) to a full market economy is a complicated transition. The effect of this transition, like the effects of stabilisation policy, can also lower output. The fact that factors of production are assigned to more profitable activities implies that less efficient farmers are replaced by others who operate more effectively. In the short or medium term, however, the process of developing a more competitive agricultural sector can involve significant costs in terms of output and employment.

The effect of economic policy on labour markets is difficult to assess. Firstly, much of the labour force in this sector works on a temporary basis.[3] Secondly, statistics in rural areas are scarce and often unreliable. Some partial studies suggest, however, that the impact of structural adjustment on labour markets varied according to the type of activity and location. In a study of agriculture in Cusco, Baca (Baca, 1996, p. 32) emphasises the intensification of temporary migration in the early 1990s. Urrutia (Urrutia, 1996) in a study on Cajamarca, points out the structural characteristics of labour markets there: temporary, unspecialised, irregular, with uneven wages, unstable and beyond the effective scope of the law. Alvarez, in this volume (Chapter 6), discusses some of the local effects of coca production. Webb and Fernández Baca (Webb and Fernández Baca, 1996, Table 16.13) show an important increase in real wages in 1995 and 1996 for agriculture-related activities in Lima, probably related to the

---

government (1968-1975), although some important modifications were introduced during the following governments. An analysis of the marketing policy of the military government is found in Alvarez (1983).

[3]   In the third agricultural census, carried out in 1994, 97% of the workers were classified as temporary.

rapid growth of this sector during this period.

Short-run recovery or sustainable growth?

The aim of this section is to examine the impact of government policies on agricultural performance. Our analysis is set out in three stages: firstly, we look at the relevant data on output and prices; we then discuss the extent to which output performance may be sustainable in the medium and long term; and finally, we briefly assess the link between output trends and rural poverty.

Output and prices

Table 2 summarises agricultural output performance. Two periods can be distinguished. The first extends from 1990 to 1992 and is characterised by a sharp output fall (an annual average fall of 4.0%) and a drop in agricultural prices, discussed below.[4] This fall in production started in 1989 during the government of Alan García. However, after 1993 we observe an impressive recovery in agricultural output (with an annual average rate of growth of 9.2% for the years 1993-96). This positive trend continued in 1997 with an output growth of 4.9%. Taking the 1990-96 period as a whole, output expansion was less spectacular but above previous historic trends: a rate of growth of 3.3%, compared with 2.1% in the period 1950-1989. There was a severe drop in agricultural production in 1998 due to the El Niño phenomenon in 1998.

Another important feature of Peruvian agriculture in these years was the fall in relative prices for agricultural goods. This is shown in the first three columns of Table 3. In the first period, agricultural prices fell in relative terms by 16.2% (annual average). In the second period, agricultural prices grew at a positive, but moderate, rate of 1.3% (annual average). Overall, the value of production fell in the period 1990-96.[5] These tables suggest that the rise in farmers' income was insufficient to offset the fall in relative prices. In real terms, the value of agricultural output at the end of 1996 was below its 1990 value. Nevertheless, it was growing at a positive rate.

In order to give an idea of farmers' purchasing power, agricultural prices have been deflated by the Consumer Price Index (CPI). Although this is a standard procedure,[6] it may yield biased estimators because of high inflation rates in the early 1990s. The CPI is estimated taking as given the quantities

---

[4]   The inclusion of 1990 as part of the Fujimori government is problematic. Fujimori became president on 28 July 1990. His administration therefore bore no responsibility for the agricultural harvest in the first half of the year. However, the shock measures adopted in the second half caused an abrupt fall in agricultural prices, reducing farmers' incomes.

[5]   The fall in relative prices for agricultural goods was due to the appreciation of the domestic currency and, also, to the recession of the economy. The link between exchange rates and agricultural prices is examined in Hopkins (1993).

[6]   This is, for example, the method used by Cuanto (Webb and Fernández Baca, 1996, Table 16.4) in its estimation of real wages.

consumed for each commodity in the base year (using Laspeyres' formula). This method is reasonable when prices are fairly constant. However, it may produce inaccurate results when inflation is high and there are abrupt changes in relative prices. Under these circumstances, assuming a fixed consumption basket becomes unrealistic, as households adapt their consumption patterns to these changes, reducing consumption of those commodities which rise in price most quickly. This problem has been addressed by Escobal and Castillo at GRADE (Escobal and Castillo, 1994) who have produced alternative estimates for the CPI.

Table 2. Agricultural Output Performance, 1990-96 (% annual average rates of growth)

	Previous trend	Fujimori government		
	1950-89	1990-92	1993-96	1990-96
Agricultural GDP	**2.1**	**- 4.0**	**9.2**	**3.3**
Agriculture		*-17.0*	*16.6*	*0.5*
Rice	4.3	-8.8	6.5	-0.3
Maize 'amilaceo'	0.3	-17.1	19.4	2.1
Beans	2.0	-9.4	11.6	2.1
Potatoes	-0.6	-16.0	24.1	5.0
Wheat	-0.9	-22.9	24.3	1.3
Cotton	-0.7	-30.5	22.2	-4.0
Maize 'duro'	3.3	-20.7	9.1	-4.9
Coffee	6.3	-6.5	7.9	1.5
Livestock		*4.8*	*4.4*	*4.5*
Poultry	8.1	16.0	7.9	11.3
Lamb	-0.8	-1.0	1.2	0.2
Pork	1.9	-0.3	3.3	1.8
Beef	1.9	-0.3	0.6	0.2
Eggs	n.a.	3.7	5.4	4.7
Milk	1.3	-1.4	3.6	1.4

Source: See Appendix 1

As an additional exercise, therefore, we have estimated the trends in agricultural prices using the GRADE Consumer Price Index. The results (see Appendix 2) broadly confirm the sign of the previous results, outlined above. At the same time, however, they indicate that the magnitude of the fall in relative prices may have been exaggerated by the official figures. The annual average rate of contraction in relative prices for 1990-96 was -4.8%, substantially less than the -6.7% shown in Table 2. The overall rate of change in the gross value of production remains negative (-2.3%) for 1990-96, but not as much as the -4.3% shown in Table 2.

Table 3. Agricultural Prices and Value of Production (% annual averages rates of growth)

	Agricultural Prices			Value of Production
	1990-92	1993-96	1990-96	1990-96
Total	**-16.2**	**1.3**	**-6.7**	**-4.3**
Agriculture	*-13.8*	*3.2*	*-4.5*	*-4.0*
Rice	-13.8	6.0	-3.0	-3.3
Maize 'amilaceo'	-7.4	0.9	-2.8	-0.7
Beans	-22.0	-1.4	-10.8	-8.9
Potatoes	-12.2	-0.4	-5.7	-1.0
Wheat	-23.5	0.5	-10.6	-9.4
Cotton	-16.9	1.8	-6.7	-10.5
Maize 'duro'	-11.5	-2.8	-6.6	-11.2
Coffee	-14.9	24.0	5.6	7.1
Livestock	*-18.8*	*-0.9*	*-9.0*	*-4.5*
Poultry	-23.2	0.4	-10.5	-0.4
Lamb	-10.0	-0.5	-4.7	-4.5
Pork	-19.3	-4.7	-11.2	-9.7
Beef	-16.1	0.2	-7.2	-7.0
Eggs	-21.9	0.9	-9.6	-5.4
Milk	-15.9	-2.5	-8.5	-7.2

Source: See Appendix 1

Sustainable growth?

A frequent question asked by observers is whether the rapid growth rates of these years could be sustained. One way of approaching the subject is by examining the possible link between the output figures shown in the previous section and the measures adopted by the government presented at the beginning. The key question is the extent to which government policies modify the quantity and quality of the basic resources with which agriculture operates.

It is clear, in the first place, that there was an improvement in the social and economic context within which agricultural activities took place. The decline in the incidence of terrorism and inflation brought greater stability to the economic system and diminished the uncertainties for investment. It may be no exaggeration to suggest that improved economic and social stability was one of the most important factors determining output performance. Other economic changes which also had significant effects include: (i) an increase in road-building, thereby diminishing the transport costs of foodstuffs to the cities; (ii) the process of awarding land titles undertaken by the government;[7] (iii) deregulation of the land market and promotion of investment in rural areas; and (iv) the withdrawal of price controls on foodstuffs.

---

[7]   The number of land titles awarded between 1992 and 1996 was 158,648, covering a surface area approximating eleven million hectares (Webb and Fernández Baca, 1996, Table 19.1).

The deregulation of the land market is particularly important. This was provided for by Decree Law 653, the *Ley de Promoción de las Inversiones en el Sector Agrario*, promulgated in July 1991. This increased the maximum area of agricultural land that can be privately owned. It also reduced restrictions on access to this type of ownership, most of which originated as a consequence of the 1969 Agrarian Reform Law. One of the differences between the 1993 Constitution and the 1979 Constitution is that the former allowed peasant communities to sell or cede their land. Although it did not specify the terms under which this could be done (which is the object of the *Ley de Tierras* and its detailed regulations), it opened the way up for a more dynamic and less protected land market.[8]

In addition to fostering the more favourable economic climate mentioned above, these measures encouraged a gradual increase in agricultural investment. Figures 1 and 2 summarise the information on this point. Although there are always difficulties in interpreting investment data and consequently the figures must be interpreted with caution, they provide a useful approximation.

Figure 1 refers to central government investment during the period 1980-95. It shows a sustained fall in public investment up until 1988, followed thereafter by a recovery. Central government investment in agriculture remained relatively constant throughout the entire period, with far less marked fluctuations. This would suggest that expenditure on irrigation projects (the most important single component of public investment) was not substantially affected by the country's general economic malaise.

Figure 2 provides data on two key areas of agricultural investment: (i) spending on land improvement (*gastos en mejora de tierras*), and (ii) investment in machinery and equipment. This figure covers both the public and private sectors. The figures on land improvement remain stable throughout the period, with an appreciable increase after 1992. As public sector investment remained constant in this period (Figure 1), they suggest an upturn in private investment. On the other hand, investment in machinery and equipment grew substantially in the early years of Alan García's government, falling drastically in 1988 and 1989. Since that time it has remained relatively constant.

---

[8]   A summary of the recent laws related to the land market is presented by Mújica (1994). The possibility of a new process of land concentration (and the resulting *bimodal* growth pattern) has been pointed out by influential institutions working in this field, such as the Centro Peruano de Estudios Sociales, CEPES (which publishes *Debate Agrario*, one of Peru's most prestigious and serious-minded agricultural journals).

Figure 1. Investment by Central Government, 1980-95 (Millions of nuevos soles at constant 1979 prices)

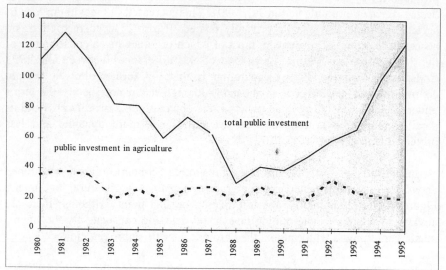

Source: INEI (1992 and 1996)

Figure 2. Investment in Land Improvement and Agricultural Machinery, 1980-95 (nuevos soles at constant 1986 prices)

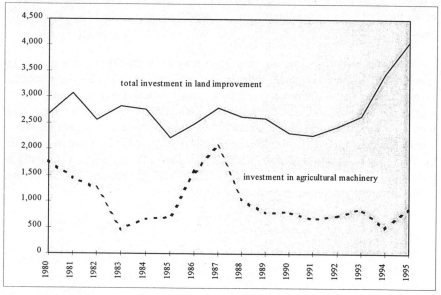

Source: Webb and Fernández Baca (1993 and 1996)

In all, then, the figures suggest an improvement in some important components of private investment, in part as a result of policies implemented by the government. It is interesting to add, on the other hand, that structural adjustment began in 1988 and 1989, before Fujimori came into government.

This is confirmed by the drastic fall of total investment in 1988-89. In this respect, Fujimori's adjustment continued a trend that had already begun.[9]

An alternative approach to discussing the sustainability of agricultural growth is to examine the data for agricultural production for the period 1990-96 and to compare it with the preceding decades. Had the trends registered in the preceding period remained constant, one would expect the values since 1990 to fluctuate around the projected values. An exercise of this nature was carried out both at a national level (shown in Figure 3) and at departmental level. The data has been fitted econometrically to a semi-logarithmic function.

In the majority of cases, production figures show a fall below the historical trend in the initial years, followed by an unmistakable rise above that tendency. Although the available evidence is still too limited to perform a rigorous statistical exercise, the figures suggest a possible structural rupture from 1993.

During visits to rural areas I attempted to collect additional information relating to these issues, conversing widely with farmers and agrarian specialists, in both the private and public sectors. An initial observation resulting from these visits was that the situation differed widely between natural regions.[10]

In the coastal area, agricultural exports emerged recurrently as a topic of conversation but, at the same time, so did complaints about lack of credit and of technological assistance. The closure of the Banco Agrario created a shortage in the provision of credit which the private banks were unable to cover. Two credit mechanisms promoted by the government – the *Cajas Rurales* (a kind of cooperative bank) and *Fondos Rotatorios* (rotating funds) – clearly proved insufficient.[11] Agricultural extension services were dismantled in the final years of the García government and there has been no serious attempt since to meet farmers' demands. In both cases – credit and technical assistance – recent Peruvian experience highlights the difficulties for the market to meet these requirements.

The farmers' dominant perception in the *sierra* was of the inability of the state to reach a significant proportion of communities. Some peasants mentioned the activities of government agencies (such as Foncodes and Pronamach)[12] but their predominant view was of sparse government assistance, or none at all. When I asked open questions about the state of agriculture, a frequent reply referred to climatic conditions. It was obvious that in the early 1990s these had

[9]   A similar situation is also observable with respect to fertilisers (see INEI, 1993 and 1996).

[10]   The fieldwork was carried out in April 1997. It included La Libertad on the coast (*Costa*), areas around Huancayo in the *Sierra* and La Merced in the jungle fringe.

[11]   See below.

[12]   Foncodes (Fondo de Desarrollo y Compensación Social) is the government's social development fund. Pronamach (Programa Nacional de Manejo de Cuencas Hidrográficas y Conservación de Suelos) is the leading government programme working on the preservation of natural resources.

been particularly favourable. However, it was also acknowledged that the decline in terrorism and inflation played a crucial role.

My visit to La Merced in the jungle fringe (*ceja de selva*) to the east of the Central Andes also revealed some contradictory assessments. Despite recovery in the area from an economic decline in the early 1990s, there still existed a certain fear of large-scale investment (as a result of the problems brought about by drug-trafficking and terrorism) and the spread of a fruit-fly pest, a matter on which the state had taken little decisive action.

Figure 3. Agricultural Output, 1950-97 (1969=100)

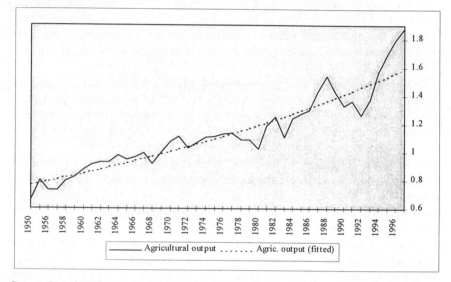

Source: *Period 1950-1989*: Hopkins (1995, Table A3). This is a quantity index estimated following the Fisher formula. *Period 1990-1996*: Webb and Fernández Baca (1996, Table 18.8). *Year 1997*. Website of Instituto Nacional de Estadística.

Note: The trend was estimated by fitting the quantity index to a semi-logarithmic function (period 1950-89). The trend for 1990-1997 is the set of forecast values (i.e. the values of the quantity index if agriculture had continued growing at the same exponential rate as before).

Output trends and rural poverty

This section examines the link between rural poverty and the performance of agricultural output. Recently there has been an important debate in Peru about the impact of government policies on poverty, a topic which is addressed by other writers in this volume.[13] This section seeks to place this issue in the context of our previous discussion.

The results of the National Survey on Standards of Living suggest that between 1985 and 1996 there was a fall in total household expenditure in rural areas and, at the same time, a decline in inequality measured in terms of food

---

[13]   See in particular Adolfo Figueroa in Chapter 7 in this volume.

consumption. Between 1985 and 1991, there was a fall of 48% in total per capita expenditure. This trend was partially reversed between 1991 and 1994 (an increase of 41%), which was nevertheless insufficient to achieve the levels prevalent in 1985. The inequality measures are shown in Table 4. Between 1985-86 and 1991 there was a decline in the level of inequality (as measured by the Gini coefficient), but it remained roughly constant between 1991 and 1994.

Table 4. Distribution of Expenditure and Nutrients among Rural Households, 1985-94

	Gini Coefficient, %		
	1985-86	**1991**	**1994**
Total expenditure (soles per year)	44.8	38.1	38.5
Expenditure on food (soles per year)	46.1	35.6	34.8
Calorie consumption (kg. per day)	33.2	29.7	27.9
Protein consumption (gr. per day)	45.3	32.9	32.9

Source: Estimated on the basis of Escobal and Aguero (1996)

There is an important connection between these results and the production patterns shown above. Several of the products showing a substantial output increase are produced in the highlands, where income levels tend to be lowest. Hence the good performance of these crops may have had a positive influence on income distribution. By the same token, however, the performance of these crops in years to come will also affect the pattern of income distribution.

An additional factor that must be taken into account is the impact of foreign aid, which has been considerable in the 1990s. Between 1990 and 1994, the value of multilateral and bilateral aid was 1.82 billion dollars, an annual average of 364 million dollars (Hopkins and Grenier, 1996, p. 4). This represents around 10% of the value of imports. Part of these funds were devoted to support infrastructural projects in rural areas.[14] Food aid also grew rapidly. Expressed in volume terms, it increased from 198,000 tons in 1989 to 397,000 tons in 1994. This had the effect of reducing the incidence of poverty, although most of the programmes were located in the urban areas.

The new role of government after structural adjustment

A retreat of the state?

Institutional reform has been one of the important changes promoted by the

---

[14]   These funds came from bilateral aid (69.5%), multilateral agencies (21.8%) and non-governmental organisations (8.6%). It should be mentioned that the above figures are still an underestimate, since a significant proportion of aid to non-governmental bodies is not included in official figures.

government. The new role of the agriculture ministry is to lay down rules and to promote agricultural development, not to involve itself directly in the provision of goods and services. As a result, the organisation of the ministry was simplified. A number of public agencies were closed down (ECASA, Banco Agrario and Senama[15]), and there were drastic cuts in staff: 80% between July 1990 and January 1993 (Vásquez Villanueva, 1993, p. 75).

In the branches of the ministry I visited during my fieldwork, the dismantling of its activities was evident. In Huancayo, for example, we were informed that in the department of Junin the total staff had been reduced from 1,300 to 140. The main impression I gained of the role played by the state during these years was one of disorderly retreat. In some areas, the numbers of personnel are quite inadequate for the workload, which is some respects has been increased (such as credit provision and the supervision and management of machinery).

However, the reduction in the ministry's payroll does not necessarily betoken an overall retreat of the state. There has been a large increase in expenditure by other ministries whose work impacts on the agricultural sector. Such is the case of the ministry of the presidency, whose budget represented 22.6% of total government spending in 1996. It is also important to note that new agencies were created within the agriculture ministry, such as Senasa and Inrena)[16] and others (like Pronamach) received increased support from the government. As a result, the ministry's overall share of government spending remained relatively constant at around 1.7% of GDP between 1993 and 1996 (Webb and Fernández Baca, 1996, Table 30.19).[17] Similarly, the overall share of public expenditure, as a proportion of GDP, remained constant between 1990 and 1995, falling slightly from 29.2% to 29.1% (Webb and Fernández Baca, 1996, Table 3.14).

The supply of credit

The supply of credit to agriculture declined substantially after 1988 (Figure 4). This was due to the adjustment process initiated in the last years of the García government and the subsequent closure of the Banco Agrario. The year with the lowest supply of credit was 1992, when the bank was closed. After 1992, the main source of agricultural credit was the private financial sector. However, private banks demand a number of requirements that small farmers usually found impossible to satisfy.[18]

---

[15]   Senama is the *Servicio Nacional de Maquinaria* (the government agency in charge of machinery).

[16]   Senasa is the *Servicio Nacional de Sanidad Agropecuaria* (the government agency in charge of sanitary and health conditions in the agricultural sector). Inrena is the *Instituto Nacional de Recursos Naturales* (the National Institute of Natural Resources).

[17]   Changes in the organisation of the public sector make comparisons difficult. Between 1992 and 1993, for example, there was a substantial fall in the expenditures of the prime minister's office, from 21.4% to 14.6%, probably explained by the increase in that of the Ministry of the Presidency.

[18]   In my fieldwork, I had the opportunity to visit a number of private banks. Before considering lending money, these required property titles (which many small farmers do not possess), an established profitable business and usually a minimum of 10 hectares of cultivable land. It is

Figure 4. The Supply of Agricultural Credit (million soles at constant 1990 prices)

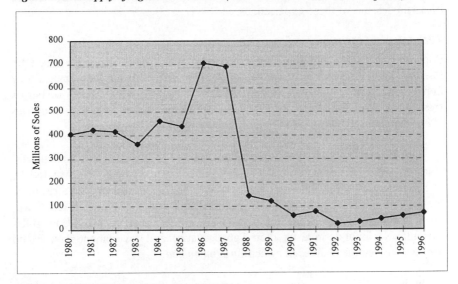

Source: Instituto Nacional de Estadística e Informática.

The response to the shortage of credit was the creation of new institutions to provide rural credit. The most important were the *Cajas Rurales*.[19] Their importance grew rapidly, and by 1997 they provided around 6% of the total supply of credit. The requirements to farmers are lower than those set by private banks but the cost of credit is expensive and akin to the market rates.

The agriculture ministry also started its own credit schemes through the *Fondos Rotatorios,* and similar services are provided by the Ministry of the Presidency through Foncodes. Thcsc funds are intended to be self-financed through the interest paid by farmers. In practice, this has not been the case. The interest rate is usually low and these schemes can operate only because their running costs are financed by the government. It is somewhat paradoxical that after the severe criticisms made of the Banco Agrario, the government itself embarked on the provision of services for which it lacks expertise.

In a recent article on the supply of agricultural credit in Peru, Alvarado (Alvarado, 1995) points out that in order to reach small farmers it is indispensable to develop new credit methodologies based on the experiences carried out by informal lenders and, more recently, by non-governmental organisations.[20] One of the shortcomings of the *Cajas Rurales* and the *Fondos*

---

interesting to note, in relation to the latter, that only 15.7% of farms in Peru have more than 10 hectares of land, according to the 1994 agricultural census.

[19]   The coffee producers' cooperatives had an important role in the creation of the *Cajas Rurales* as a way of providing funds to farmers, given the lack of public sources of finance and the demanding requirements of private banks.

[20]   Among other lessons, Alvarado indicates the importance of peer monitoring, the need to reduce transaction costs – and initial external financial assistance to cover the costs – of starting a

Rotatorios promoted by the government is that they do not sufficiently take on board the lessons of these experiences.

Technological assistance

Poor output quality and low yields are two of the main obstacles faced by farmers. Pests also currently constitute a major difficulty for the expansion of Peru's fresh food industry. Sanitary barriers restrict the sale of much of Peru's fresh produce in the United States, Japan and other Latin American countries (*Peru Reporting*, 1997, p. 31).

In previous decades, the government carried out significant agricultural research and extension activities. The key public agency in this field was INIPA (*Instituto Nacional de Investigación y Promoción Agropecuaria*). As a result of the economic crisis and structural adjustment, this institution was closed down. Its research activities were transferred to a new smaller institution INIA (Instituto Nacional de Investigación Agropecuaria), and government agencies no longer involved themselves in agricultural extension.

In November 1992, the government created Senasa, located within the agriculture ministry. Its purpose was to raise health standards and ensure access to fresh food markets. Although the establishment of Senasa was a positive step, its main limitation was its small budget which was insufficient for it to achieve its objectives.

Fruit flies are an example of such problems. They inflict an estimated 100 million dollars worth of damage to Peruvian produce every year (*Peru Reporting*, 1997, p. 33). In order to tackle this problem, Senasa has four separate programmes to destroy the fly by various methods. Although the programme has funding from an Inter-American Development Bank (IDB) loan, there was concern about raising the funding necessary to keep the programme running.

Technological assistance for small farmers in the highlands is even more complicated, due to: (i) the geographical remotness of producers, scattered over a vast territory; (ii) the diversity of their production; and (iii) the small scale of their operations. The government has some programmes working in rural areas (such as Pronamach and Foncodes) but their outreach is limited and they provide little by way of technical assistance.

Conclusions

Has Peru under Fujimori started a new phase of rapid agricultural development? What is the new role of government in the wake of structural adjustment? These have been the questions that we have attempted to address here. The answers are mixed. The immediate effect of economic stabilisation was a dramatic fall in

new credit programme.

agricultural output and prices. After 1993, however, the figures indicated a positive expansion, well above previous trends. On the whole, for the period 1990-97, output expansion was positive, but not dramatically so. The effect on farmers' income was smaller due to the fall in relative prices.[21]

The data reviewed suggest that government policies had a positive impact on agriculture until 1997, but (i) it was far from spectacular, and (ii) it was highly dependent on the performance of the economy as a whole and on climatic conditions. This final section discusses the change in the role of the government after structural adjustment.

The overall figures on government spending indicate that, as a share of GDP, it remained virtually constant throughout the period 1990-96, although there was an increase in public investment (Figure 2).[22] Hence, despite the rhetoric, the 'size' of government was similar, if not greater, than in the previous period. What was important, however, was the change in the composition of expenditure within the public sector. Whilst the bureacracy in the agriculture ministry experience savage cuts, other public sector institutions were created or expanded.

There was a clear belief in government circles that the leading role in agricultural development should be played by the private sector. As Absalón Vásquez Villanueva, then Minister of Agriculture, emphasised in 1993:

> government agricultural policy aims to promote farmers' efficiency, profitability and competitiveness, together with the rational exploitation of natural resources and the conservation of ecosystems. The role of the state is to establish norms, to guide and to promote, replacing the paternalistic, interventionist and bureaucratic role it used to play in the previous two decades (Vásquez Villanueva, 1993, p. 11).

What the Peruvian experience shows, however, is that it takes time to increase the participation of the private sector, and that it cannot be expected immediately to fill the vacuum left by the retreat of the public sector. In this chapter we have examined two cases where the presence of the government was dominant: the supply of credit and the provision of technical assistance.

In the case of credit, the government was quick to close the Banco Agrario without offering an alternative way to provide agricultural credit to farmers. Subsequently, the supply of credit gradually increased, but it was far inferior to the levels required by small farmers. Something similar happened with the

---

[21]   As these conclusions were being revised (in March 1998) the El Niño phenomenon was causing severe damage to the Peruvian economy, particularly in the agricultural sector. This points out, once again, the vulnerability of crop production in Peru to climatic conditions, despite the programme of preventive and emergency measures taken by the government.

[22]   As a share of GDP, public investment increased from 2.5% in 1990 to 4.1% in 1995 (Webb and Fernández Baca, 1996, Table 30.14).

provision of technical assistance. The system of extension was terminated in the last years of the previous government and further cuts were introduced in INIA by the Fujimori administration. The hope that private agents would take the leading role in technological transfer did not materialise, with the exception of provision for a very few, profitable crops.

The experience of agricultural policy in Peru also shows that the delimitation of functions between the public and the private sector is still inadequate. At the same time, there was a high degree of fragmentation between various government agencies and a need for a greater sense of direction and purpose. As was mentioned above, the state found itself in a process of disorderly retreat. Peru needs a small government sector, but one that is highly professional and effective.

Finally, if there is a single lesson to be drawn from the previous 15 years of economic crisis, it is that it is politically difficult to sustain a pattern of development that systematically excludes important groups of the population. Of equal importance to achieving fiscal and monetary equilibrium is the establishment of an equitable set of rules and initiatives which offer more widespread growth opportunity. This is particularly important in the highlands, where private market institutions are not a sufficient condition for achieving high and sustainable rates of growth.

Appendix 1:
Sources and Methods of Estimation of Table 2

The source for estimating the rate of growth of agricultural GDP for the period 1950-1989 is Webb and Fernández Baca (1991, Table 11.8). It was estimated fitting a semi-logarithmic regression, $LQa = a + rt$, where LQa is the log of agricultural GDP, t is time and r is the GDP rate of growth. For the period 1990-95, the source for agricultural GDP is Webb and Fernández Baca (1996: Table 18.8). The data for 1996 is a preliminary estimate.

The output figures (agriculture and livestock) for the period 1950-89 are based on Hopkins (1995, Table II.2). The output rate of growth was estimated fitting a semi-logarithmic regression (as in the case of GDP growth). The period covered was 1950-90. The periods 1990-92, 1993-96 and 1990-96 are average rates of growth. The source for the crops and livestock figures are Ministry of Agriculture, I and II, *Compendio Estadístico Agrario*, and Webb and Fernández Baca (1996, chapter 19).

The sources for agricultural prices are as follows: 1989, Webb and Fernández Baca (1991, chapter 12); 1990-93: Ministry of Agriculture, *Segundo Compendio Estadístico Agrario 1990-1993*, Vol. III, Table 7.1; and Webb and Fernández Baca (1996, Table, 17.31). The 1996 figures are preliminary, based on a comparison between the 1996 and 1995 January-June series. Nominal figures were deflated by the consumer price index, taken from Webb and Fernández Baca (1996, Table 17.3).

Appendix 2
Comparative Estimates of Agricultural Prices (% annual averages rates of growth)

	1990-92	1993-96	1990-96
Using the Official Inflation Index			
Total	-16.2	1.3	-6.7
Agriculture	-13.8	3.2	-4.5
Livestock	-18.8	-0.9	-9.0
Using the GRADE Inflation Index			
Total	-13.5	2.3	-4.8
Agriculture	-11.0	4.3	-2.6
Livestock	-16.2	0.2	-7.2

Source: Using the Official Inflation Index: from Table 3 of this chapter. *Using the GRADE Inflation Index*: the sources and methodology are as before but the deflator is the Geometric Price Index estimated by GRADE. The assistance of GRADE is gratefully acknowledged.

CHAPTER 6

Economic Effects of the Illicit Drug Sector in Peru[*]

Elena Alvarez

When President Alberto Fujimori was inaugurated in mid-1990, he inherited a country not only in economic and political disarray but also with an important illicit drugs sector. Seven years later, things have changed. The economy has been stabilised and the guerrilla organisations appear to have been brought more under control. Yet the illicit coca sector continues, although at declining rates. What has been the economic impact of the illicit drug sector during the Fujimori administration? What has Fujimori done to stop the illicit drug sector? Will the illicit drug sector persist?

At the outset, Fujimori declared the guerrilla problem his priority issue. Despite the preferences of US officials, the drug issue was subordinated to the 'pacification' of the country. The so-called 'Fujimori doctrine' sought to distinguish between coca growers and drug traffickers. It focused on support for a policy of 'alternative development', involving the implementation of a number of projects within a free market to encourage the substitution of illicit crops. The illicit coca sector may have upset overall macroeconomic adjustment by promoting currency overvaluation, but at the same time it created employment and incomes that otherwise would not have been available. I argue that while in the late 1980s and early 1990s there may have been incentives to clamp down on the coca sector – after all, it aided guerrillas to fund their war against the government – by the late 1990s such incentives no longer existed to the same degree. In the early years, the positive economic effects of coca were offset by the political instability and violence engendered by the alliance between guerrillas and traffickers (Alvarez, 1992). Later, the coca sector appeared to have more positive economic effects, on balance.[1] Coca preceded Fujimori, and it seems likely it will also outlive his administration.

The purpose of this chapter is to describe and discuss the illicit drug sector in Peru, its economic impact at the local and national levels and some of the institutional and political conditions which promoted it. Its local impact will be discussed in more detail because the data bank developed for some coca growing areas is more reliable than the national estimates.[2] It is important to

[*]   This chapter is based partially on research directed by the author and sponsored by the United Nations Development Programme, New York, and the North-South Center of the University of Miami, Coral Gables, Florida. The project was undertaken in cooperation with Cuanto S.A. in Lima (Alvarez, 1993a and 1993b).

[1]   In Bolivia, the coca sector created incomes and employment, but none of the problems that the alliance of guerrillas and traffickers have caused in Colombia and Peru.

[2]   Assessments of the impact of coca byproduct output at the local level are based on surveys

stress that I refer specifically to coca and its byproducts, even though there is growing evidence of increasing production of marijuana and opium poppy seeds.[3] Furthermore, readers should be on their guard for the quality of the data, which needs refinement and whose validity rests upon many assumptions.

The coca sector in Peru

I have dealt elsewhere with the reasons behind the expansion of the illicit coca sector in Peru (Alvarez, 1991; Alvarez and Cervantes, 1996). In addition to the lure of external demand and Peru's comparative advantages as a producer, a combination of rural poverty, ineffective land reform, urban biases in policy, government ineptitude and high wages and profits associated with coca production seem to explain this growth. The political and institutional context favouring coca has been carefully documented by Cotler (Cotler, 1996).

The process of production starts with crude cocaine or coca paste, a mixture of alkaloids that is about two-thirds cocaine. It is produced by dissolving dried leaves in sulfuric acid and precipitating the alkaloids with sodium carbonate. The result is coca paste (PBC), which is later converted into a salt by solution in hydrochloric acid and further treatment to remove the other alkaloids. Cocaine base (PBL), a transparent crystalline substance, requires further purification.[4] It takes between 100-200 kgs. of dried leaves to produce 1 kg. of cocaine paste, and approximately 2.5 kgs. of paste are required to produce 1 kg. of pure cocaine hydrochloride (HCl) (Weiss and Mirin, 1987, p. 9). Tables 2 and 3 contain some 'recipes' used in Peru for producing PBC and PBL (Alvarez, 1993a).

A type of cocaine hydrochloride is usually what is sold to the international traffickers. Colombia is still the leading cocaine exporter, though Bolivia and Peru appear to have increased their share of the cocaine exported through other countries, notably Mexico and Brazil (Thoumi, 1997). Bolivia and Peru produce coca leaves and process coca mainly to the cocaine base stage. However, in the second half of the 1990s, Colombia appears to have increased considerably its importance as a coca grower (Uribe and Mestre, 1997).

Key features of the illicit drug sector in Peru.

The illicit drug sector had its origins in the late 1970s. It is gradually accounting for a smaller share of GDP and appears to be a declining revenue activity (see Table 1). This is the result of the trend in prices. Coca production has declined

---

conducted by Cuanto S.A. in 1993 and 1995 (Alvarez, 1996).
[3]   According to DINANDRO (Dirección Nacional de Drogas) marijuana seizures increased significantly between 1994 and 1996. Different Peruvian journalistic sources have pointed to the increases in poppy seed production. Opium seizures also increased.
[4]   Cocaine base purification can be accomplished by two different methods. One uses petroleum ether, methanol, and hydrochloric acid; the other utilises a mixture of acetone and benzene (Grinspoon and Bakalar, 1976, esp. pp. 73-5).

from an estimated 8% of GDP in 1988-89 (Alvarez, 1993a) to levels below 1% of GDP in 1995. Although there are estimates of up to 300,000 hectares being devoted to coca production, using a more refined and careful methodology we would estimate that it ranged between 145,000 and 175,000 hectares (Alvarez, 1993a).[5] The coca sector performs an important employment creating function; about 7% of the rural economically active population (150,000 to 175,000 people in 1993) is presumed to be employed directly in the sector. This figure would be higher if indirect employment were added.

Table 1. Peru: coca sector value-added by stages, 1992-95 (in millions of current US dollars)

	1992		1993		1994		1995	
	high	low	high	low	high	low	high	low
Coca Leaf	290	246	220	182	185	154	20	20
Coca Paste	399	334	291	206	387	288	288	233
Cocaine Base	332	279	335	219	426	291	162	131
HCl (cocaine)	103	86	71	30	62	26	70	56
TOTAL	1,124	945	917	637	1,060	758	540	440
% GDP	2.7	2.3	2.3	1.5	2.1	1.5	1.0	0.8

Source: Alvarez (1996). Two estimates have been developed, a high and a low. Data for Peru's GDP come from Cuanto S.A.'s various yearbooks.

The raw coca leaf makes up only a small share of the wholesale price, and an even smaller share of the retail price of the final product. This extreme price mark-up is a function of the escalation of risk involved as coca passes along the production chain from farmgate raw material to wholesaler and eventually to its point of sale. The extra profit is the premium paid for the risk imposed by law enforcement, mainly at its final point of distribution. Ironically, strong control activities create the conditions for the extra profits associated with illicit activity.

The declining price trend in the coca sector has had various implications:

• Although there was some recovery from the very low levels reached in 1995, the per capita coca income is still higher than the incomes that can be generated by legal crops. Our estimate for 1997 ranges between 1,400 and 2,300 dollars. Recent rural household surveys suggest that incomes from legal crops are very low and range between 420 and 720 dollars, less than a third of what could be earned in the coca sector. That is, coca incomes are not extremely high, but licit incomes are very low.

---

[5]   A new methodology was developed, based on labour allocation in rural areas of Peru, satellite data for different areas, various 'recipes' of coca byproducts in different areas, productivity parameters and data for prices of coca byproducts (Alvarez, 1996).

- Declining incomes in the coca sector may have persuaded former cultivators to become involved in the higher levels of vertical integration within the cocaine industry, as growers shifted into more clearly illicit aspects of drug production.

- The coca sector has increased all input prices, especially labour and the price of goods consumed in the growing areas, which has then lowered the profitability of other local activities, both agricultural and non-agricultural. The coca boom is thus responsible for 'Dutch disease' (DD) symptoms in such areas.

- Although the coca sector may be a declining revenue activity, the inflow of foreign exchange still has an impact on the real exchange rate, thus affecting the overall macroeconomic situation.

Another important characteristic relates to the linkages between coca/cocaine and the rest of the economy. Coca's backward linkages (the purchases which the sector makes from others) show that they may be higher than previous estimates suggest. For instance, 15-17% of the sector's intermediate demand is for chemical products and 16-17% for transportation and storage (Alvarez, 1996, appendix B) The implications of this are significant: the coca sector 'employs' indirectly many more people than was previously estimated. This is the case not just for rural areas, but also for urban areas where many of the inputs for the industry are produced.

Finally, as in other (licit) agricultural activities, wholesalers appropriate most of the profit. Previous calculations indicated that the 'wholesalers' (or traffickers) received annual incomes in the million-dollar range, while the 'agroindustrial' producers received well-below 15,000 dollars per annum.

Estimates of net farm incomes[6]

Three estimates of net farm income generated by coca cultivation and byproducts are discussed in this section. One for mid-1992, one for late 1995 (see Tables 2 and 3) and the other for January 1997. The calculations for the latter year follow the same methodology as the other two tables, and suggest that the situation for producers of coca byproducts was profitable, especially when compared with 1995. Data from the US Drug Enforcement Administration (DEA) suggest that in January 1997 a coca grower producing cocaine base on a typical 1.5 hectare farm unit could obtain between 7,099 and 11,396 dollars. This means that the coca sector per capita income for a family of five at January 1997 prices would range between 1,420 dollars and 2,279 dollars, which is above the per capita average national income. By contrast, in 1995, given the setbacks associated with the excess supply and interdiction, coca byproduct output was a relatively low-income activity, yielding roughly similar income

---

[6]   Unless stated otherwise, estimates are presented in current US dollars.

levels as licit alternatives. Data processed by Cuanto S.A. for the Rural Households Living Standards Survey indicated that rural income per capita for 1994 ranged between 420 dollars (in the Andean region) and 720 dollars (for coastal agriculture). Income per capita in rural areas of the jungle was between these figures. Our coca income estimates for 1995 were comparable to the jungle rural average per capita income, about 300 dollars. However, these calculations are based on assumptions regarding many of the major parameters involved. If such assumptions change, the conclusions will differ.

On a per hectare basis, and using the DEA average yields for Peru, 1.8 tons of coca leaf produced a gross value of 3,060 dollars at June-July 1992 prices and at 1.70 dollars/kg of coca leaf (see Table 2). Assuming that all labour involved is family labour, that 5% of the gross value (153 dollars) was paid for protection to Sendero Luminoso, the police or the military, and subtracting the cost of inputs (e.g. fertilisers and herbicides), the net income per hectare generated by cultivating coca leaf worked out at about 607 dollars. Using Morales's (Morales, 1989) recipe for the production of PBC, which includes kerosene, sulfuric acid, lime, sodium carbonate and water, the value of these inputs in the producing areas was estimated at 80 dollars per kg.[7] Using the June-July 1992 prices of 380 dollars/kg, farmers earned gross revenues of 6,218 dollars per hectare, assuming a yield of 1.8 MT/hectare and a technical coefficient of 1:110. Deducting costs associated with processing materials (chemicals), some transportation and a 5% Sendero Luminoso tax,[8] the estimated net farm income amounted to 4,543 dollars per hectare – the net farm income in a typical 1.5 hectare farm unit generated about 6,815 dollars which was 1.7 times higher than the coca leaf estimated net income for the same family farm unit.

If the same coca growers decided to go a step further into the processing of coca paste and produce PBL, their net family income at those prices would have been only a little higher. Assuming a technical coefficient of 1:2.2 and 780 dollars/kg per PBL, one hectare would generate 7.45 kg of PBL or 5,811 dollars in gross revenues. Once the cost of chemicals for cocaine base processing and the assumed 5% guerrilla tax are deducted, the net revenue would have amounted to 5,055 dollars or 7,582 for a typical 1.5 hectare farm unit. On a per capita basis, this would have meant 1,517 dollars for a family of five, slightly higher than the national average, placing these producers in the upper quartile of

---

[7] *Materials Required to Prepare Three Kilos of Coca Paste*

Material	
Coca leaves	340 Quantity.8 kg (or 30 *arrobas*)
Sulfuric acid	15 kg
Kerosene	90 litres
Lime	24 kg
Sodium Carbonate	3 kg
Water	3,900 litres

Source: Morales (1989), p. 74. The prices for these inputs were provided by the World Bank (internal data).

[8] Based on information gathered from coca growers in the Huallaga valley.

Peru's income distribution.

Table 2: Coca Budget per Hectare (June-July 1992)

Leaf Production	
Yields	1,800 kg
Price	$1.70/kg
Gross Revenues	$3,060
Costs:	
Fertilisers, other inputs and transportation	$300
Sendero Luminoso tax *(a)*	$153
Total Costs	$453
Net Income per hectare	$2,607
Net Income for a typical farm unit (1.5 ha)	$3,911
Coca Paste Production (PBC)	
Technical Coefficient	1:110
Yields	16.4 kg
Price	$380/kg
Gross Revenues	$6,218
Costs:	
Processing materials (chemicals)	$1,312
Transportation	$52
Sendero Luminoso tax *(a)*	$31
Total Costs	$1,675
Net Income per hectare	$4,543
Net Income for a typical farm unit (1.5 ha)	$6,815
Cocaine Base (PBL)	
Technical Coefficient	1:2.2
Yields	7.45 kg
Price	$780/kg
Gross Revenues	$5,811
Costs:	
Processing materials (chemicals)	$465
Sendero Luminoso tax *(a)*	$291
Total Costs	$756
Net Income per hectare:	$5,055
Net Income for a typical farm unit (1.5 ha)	$7,583

Sources: Alvarez, 1993a. Data for prices: UNDCP/UNDP, 1994; yields: USAID, 1995, data for cost of production: Morales, 1989; and Núñez and Reátegui, 1990.

(a) The 'tax' levied by Sendero Luminoso varied depending on the area (Núñez and Reátegui, 1990 and Gonzales, 1989).

If we proceed on a similar basis with data for late 1995 (see Table 3), two obvious conclusions seem to arise: i) that in 1995 coca leaf production was not profitable; and ii) that coca growers had to produce illicit coca byproducts to do better. In fact, in the calculations that follow – based on 1995 prices gleaned on a UNDP field trip – net farm income nearly doubled by going into production of PBC (Table 3). Using October-November 1995 prices of 121 dollars/kg, farmers earned gross revenues of 1,984.40 dollars per hectare, assuming a yield of 1.8 MT/hectare and a technical coefficient of 1:110. Deducting costs associated with processing materials (chemicals) at 87 dollars/kg, the estimated net farm income amounted to 558 dollars. Therefore, the net farm income of a typical 1.5 hectare farm unit would have been around 836 dollars, twice that of the producer of coca leaf.

Table 3: Coca budget per hectare (October-November 1995)

Leaf Production	
Yields	1,800 kg
Price	$0.32/kg
Gross Revenues	$576
Total Costs ($0.63/kg x 1,800 kg)	$324
Net Income per hectare	$252
Net Income for a typical farm unit (1.5 ha)	$378
Coca Paste Production (PBC)	
Technical Coefficient	1:110
Yields	16.4 kg
Price	$121/kg
Gross Revenues	$1,984.40
Total Costs ($87/kg x 16.4)	$1,426.80
Net Income per hectare	$557.60
Net Income for a typical farm unit (1.5 ha)	$836.40
Cocaine Base (PBL) Commercial and Direct	
Technical Coefficient	1:2.2
Yields	7.45 kg
Price:	$ 256/kg for commercial $320/kg for direct
Gross Revenues:	$1,907.20 to $2,384
Total Costs	($174/kg x 7.45 and $180.25/kg x 7.45)
Net Income per hectare	$614.03 to $1,041.00
Net Income for a typical farm unit (1.5 ha)	$921.05 to $1,561.5

Source: Author's estimates, based on data in Núñez and Reátegui, 1995.

If the same coca growers went into cocaine base production, their net family income at these prices would have been slightly higher. Two PBL varieties were identified as being produced by growers: commercial and direct. The latter is of somewhat better quality than the former. Assuming again a technical coefficient of 1:2.2 and prices of 256-320 dollars/kg per PBL, commercial and direct respectively, one hectare would yield 7.45 kg of PBL, or 1,907-2,384 dollars in gross revenues. Once the cost of chemicals for cocaine base processing are deducted, the net revenue would amount to 614-1,041 dollars, which for a typical farm unit (1.5 hectares) meant a net revenue of between 921.05-1,561.5 dollars. This, in turn, would mean a per capita income of 184-312 dollars for a family of five, close to the rural jungle per capita income, and well below the national average.

The economic impact

Macroeconomic consequences

Analysis of the economic impact of coca must take into account the following points:

- The paradoxical possibility that the coca boom can ultimately increase poverty in the areas concerned. The reasoning behind this is that the additional foreign exchange generated by (illicit) coca exports creates at least two types of perverse effects – on the food growing sector which competes with imported foods (De Janvry, 1987, pp. 485-96) and on producers of tradable goods – even though the overall impact on the economy may be positive.[9] The first negative effect is a shift of resources into coca production and non-tradables (services and construction), to the detriment of food production.[10] In Peru, coca competes with rice and yellow maize (used for poultry feed), both major foodstuffs in urban areas, and cassava and tropical fruits. The demand for construction and services increases as a result of the income effects from the coca export sector.[11]

- The adverse impact on domestic prices for food products and the domestic prices of imported goods in general (De Janvry, 1987). This results from the inflationary push created by the revenue derived from the coca economy and the resulting tendency of the real exchange rate to appreciate. The availability of foreign exchange averts the need for devaluations, and enables low domestic prices for food and industrial goods to be maintained.

- The production of coca byproducts has harmful environmental effects, since producers dump many of the chemicals used in processing coca derivatives into the rivers, killing wildlife and ultimately impacting negatively on the

---

[9]   Tradable goods consist of exportables and importables. Exportables, in turn, consist of actual exports as well as close substitutes for exports that are sold domestically. Importables consist of imports as well as goods produced domestically and sold domestically that are close substitutes for imports, i.e., import-competing goods. Tradables have their domestic prices determined by the world market. Non-tradables consist of all those goods and services the prices of which are determined by supply and demand domestically, and generally consist of services (Corden, 1981, p. 8).

[10]   Coca competes with many other foodstuffs and agricultural products from other ecological areas because workers migrate to the coca-producing areas. In other words, the competition is for labour and not for land, since land is widely available in the jungle.

[11]The construction sector was very dynamic in certain years. Growth rates rose above 10% growth in the following years: 1980-81, 1986-87, 1992-94. These years coincided with the first two years of the Belaúnde, García and Fujimori governments respectively.

health of the population in producing areas.

• Despite negative effects at the local level, the net economic effect of coca expansion may be positive at the national level, since the decrease in non-coca agricultural activity (food and non-food) may be offset by the overall increase in the economic activity (agricultural and non-agricultural) derived from, and associated with, the coca expansion.

• The first two perverse economic effects hypothesised here for the agricultural sector apply regardless of the legal nature of the commodity exported. It may be true, however, that the illegal nature of coca exports worsens the situation (e.g. environment, public health) because the government cannot avail itself of additional tax revenues to compensate those sectors which suffer as a result of the coca export boom.

The Dutch Disease (DD) framework seems to be applicable to the analysis of both the local and national effects. Schuldt (Schuldt, 1994) deals with the DD framework to assess the sustainability of the Peruvian development model.[12] The DD framework has also been used to assess the macro impact of the illicit export incomes generated by coca byproducts. The DD framework is usually used to analyse export booms and devise appropriate policies to manage these booms effectively.[13]

How does this 'disease' work? In essence, a massive increase in unexpected foreign exchange income exercises two effects: one on expenditure and the other on resource allocation. The first refers to a modification in relative prices, as the available increase of national income leads to a price increase in the industries of non-tradable goods in relation to tradable goods. The latter reflects the real revaluation of the exchange rate in national currency. This is because a rise in effective demand for non-tradable goods will increase their price, given the rigidity of supply in the short-term. In the case of tradable goods, prices are adjusted by quantity either being imported or through exporting surplus supply. The resource allocation effect works in two ways: one is through the wage increases of labourers hired in the boom industry concerned, or the transfer of labour towards that industry on account of higher wages in that sector. The other is the multiplier effect of the extraordinary gains which push up demand for goods in industries such as construction, government and most services.

For some authors, DD takes place because of the distorting effects generated by an export boom, leading eventually to the 'de-industrialisation' of the economy concerned, especially in those industries which do not benefit directly or indirectly from the export boom. For others, DD starts when the export boom

---

[12]   The term Dutch Disease was first used to refer to the adverse effects on Dutch manufacturing of the natural gas discoveries of the 1960s, essentially through the subsequent appreciation of the Dutch real exchange rate (Schuldt, 1994). Because of the clarity of Schuldt's exposition, I will use his summary of DD in this section.

[13]   The real exchange rate is often defined as the ratio of the price of non-tradables over the price of tradables.

ends, foreign exchange flows fall off, and a painful and prolonged process of adjustment is required for wage earners and in government spending.

The literature on coca incomes and DD in Peru is sparse. A common denominator, however, has been the argument that coca incomes have had slight impact on exchange rate appreciation (Vega and Cebrecos, 1991 and Cruz-Saco et al, 1994). Cervantes (1996) has analysed the literature in detail. In his assessment, these conclusions are based on very short time series, and often – as in the case of Cruz Saco et al. – involve inconsistencies in the way technical analysis was conducted. Alvarez and Cervantes (1996) analysed the impact of the illicit coca byproduct export inflows on Peru's exchange rate and the overall macroeconomy in mid-1993. Using coca byproducts data developed with well-defined methodologies for the period 1979-92 and well-established econometric techniques (Alvarez, 1993a), they concluded that coca exports exercised a significant, direct influence on the extraordinary inflow of foreign exchange, especially between 1979 and 1986. Subsequently, the influence of coca exports seems to have been more indirect.

Cervantes (1996) later refined this analysis. He studied the macroeconomic repercussions of the illicit drug industry, using quarterly data from 1981 to 1995. His analysis suggests that despite the decreasing importance of the illicit drug sector, it has had and continues to have important macroeconomic effects.[14] The analysis also suggested that the monetisation of income generated by the sector was greater during the period 1981-88 than in more recent years. He also pointed out that illicit drugs had an impact on the stock market, especially the price of the stocks which seem to have been used as a means of money laundering.

At the regional level, in the Huallaga area, the importance of coca agriculture is made clear from the following indicators. The main findings are similar to those for Colombia (Thoumi, 1997), with coca producing areas exhibiting DD symptoms: labour costs are higher, there is licit crop displacement in favour of coca growing, and service and transportation sales increase. In these areas the price of the non-tradable goods tended to increase considerably in relation to the rest of the country. It is also true that the coca growers' incomes were higher than those of other legal agricultural producers in other parts of the country. It will be obvious also from the discussion that follows that the illicit coca industry has been the main dynamic of growth in the Peruvian jungle in the last two decades.

The largest areas of coca growing are in the departments of San Martín and Huanuco, which together encompass 57% of the total planted area. However, in the early 1990s, coca cultivation expanded to the departments of Amazonas, Ucayali, Junin, Ayacucho and Puno.[15] Edmundo Morales (Morales, 1989, pp.

---

[14] Cervantes's work shows the existence of 'cointegration' amongst rates of inflation, the real exchange rate, international reserves and exports of coca byproducts.

[15] It is estimated that 11 of the 24 departments of Peru are currently producing coca or have the

94-7) calls the prosperity arising from coca 'cosmetic development' because, in his assessment, the expansion has not brought real economic progress in these areas. His assesment is shared by many coca growers interviewed in the Huallaga Valley in mid-1995. In the words of one anonymous coca grower:

> The coca boom has brought just a lot of frivolity and waste of money ... dancing every Sunday and corruption for the youth. Some have taken advantage of coca profits and purchased lands where they're building their houses; these are the minority, however; most waste their money ... those who have surely benefited from the coca boom are the owners of taverns, bars, canteens and orchestras.

And according to Morales, in Tingo María, the administrative and commercial capital of the Upper Huallaga region:

> Local residents complain about the condition of their streets and services such as electricity and water supply. They argue that given the tremendous amounts of money handled 'the city should be paved with marble'. It is true that Tingaleses (people from Tingo María) come in contact with large amounts of cash, yet, unfortunately, money that comes to Tingo María is neither invested to create a solid and independent local economy nor used to generate tax revenues for the welfare of the community.

Morales asserts that when he first visited Tingo María in 1966 it was a 'small town' whose main street was the dirt road connecting Lima with Pucallpa. In 1978, the main street was a commercial nexus: major national banks had opened branch offices there; the city boasted a university campus; there were scores of restaurants and hotels which had opened there. In 1996, Tingo María was considered one of the most important cities in the Peruvian jungle, with several daily flights from Lima.

While Morales may believe that this expansion was 'cosmetic' growth, the illicit coca sector has been the main growth activity in the jungle economy in recent decades. Indeed, the coca export boom has spawned large movements of population, especially from the highlands towards the jungle; it has led to the development of significant urban settlements in what were previously remote and inaccessible areas; it has also forced governments to fund 'special projects' to substitute coca growing, and to devote resouces to roadbuilding and other infraestructure.[16]

---

potential to become major production areas. These include from north to south, Loreto, Amazonas, San Martín, Ucayali, Huanuco, Pasco, Junin, Apurimac, Ayacucho, Cuzco and Puno (USAID, 1995, p. 1).

[16] As of 1994, Peru had spent over 500 million dollars on 'special projects': constructing roads, providing electricity and clean water (all of which are important conditioning factors for economic development) and this included zones in coca-producing areas (Alvarez, 1995).

According to Hidalgo (1985 p.15), the area covered by the Programa Especial del Alto Huallaga (PEAH) saw its population grow between 1961 and 1972 by 55.4%. Between 1971 and 1981, the population grew more than three-fold from 39,274 to 129,865 inhabitants. Population growth rates averaged 7.6% annually, while nationally the population grew by 2.9%. Population expansion continued between 1981 and 1993, according to Gallo, Tello and Rivera (1994, pp. 56-7), albeit at a slower rate of 3.4% a year. The national average for this period was 2.2%. During the 1972-92 period, the growth in areas under agriculture also grew faster than the national average. The growth for annual crops was about 11% per year, suggesting that the amount of land devoted to crops tripled. The agricultural frontier expanded by about 16% each year, much higher than the national and regional averages (Gallo, Tello and Rivera, 1994).

Through the US Agency for International Development (USAID), the United States became formally involved in alternative development strategies in 1981, with the implementation of the Upper Huallaga Area Development Project (UHAD), the precursor of PEAH. The original purpose of UHAD (1981-93) was to support government efforts to develop a narcotics control strategy in the Upper Huallaga valley by strengthening public sector agricultural support services and expanding rural and community-level development activities. Total UHAD project funding for the twelve-year implementation period were 53.6 dollars million, of which 31.2 million came from the US government (16.2 million was granted and 15 million came as a loan). The remaining 20.3 million dollars was provided by the Peruvian authorities (USAID, 1995b) A new stage of 'alternative development' started in 1996, which was due to receive 30 million dollars in special source funds over a five year period from the US government. The Peruvian government was to contribute 14 million dollars.[17] The United Nations International Drug Control Programme (UNDCP) between 1984-93 funded a number of small rural development projects whose major purpose was 'supply reduction' – encouraging crop substitution. These were worth about 39 million dollars over five years; an additional 1.5 million dollars was spent by UNDCP on demand reduction (656,000 dollars) and control activities (864,000 dollars) (UNDCP-PNUFID, 1994).

Needless to say, these projects would not have been allocated funds in these areas had it not been for illicit coca expansion.[18] Over at least the last two decades, the allocation of resources for jungle agricultural development has been led by the expansion of the illicit processing of coca and its derivatives.

Findings at the local level

Specific conditions in the Upper Huallaga were revealed in a series of surveys

---

[17]   The government's contribution included 10 million dollars in host country-owned local currency generated from PL 480 Title III resources and 4 million from Treasury funds (USAID, 1995b, p. 9).
[18]   It is interesting to observe that Bolivia in the same period between early 1980s to early 1990s received over 220 million dollars for alternative development projects (Alvarez, 1995).

conducted by Cuanto S.A.[19] These refer to urban/rural living standards in four districts in the departments of San Martín and Ucayali: Nueva Cajamarca, Shamboyacu and Tocache in San Martín (surveyed in April and May 1993); and Padre de Abad in Ucayali (surveyed in November 1995). Each community represents a different type. Nueva Cajamarca was a district mainly of rice production, where coca growing was incipient but none of those surveyed admitted to producing it; Shamboyacu produced mainly coca and two out of three farmers declared they produced it. Tocache is an old coca-growing area, but plantings had diminished and only one out of three farmers admitted to producing it. Pedro de Abad is a district which previously grew coca, but which at the time of the survey was producing other crops like bananas, yellow maize and cassava.

Summarising some of the indicators of living standards, we reach a number of conclusions. Public services in coca growing areas are often less available than in the non-coca growing areas. Households in coca growing areas (old or new) have additional goods which denote higher income. With regard to access to electrical appliances, the data for both urban and rural areas show that households in the more established former coca growing area of Tocache had better-equipped households. In Shamboyacu, a newer coca growing area, households had greater access to certain items such as station wagons in urban areas. Per capita consumption data suggested that Shamboyacu and Tocache, the two biggest coca growing areas, had greater access to certain food items, such as poultry, bread, beer, evaporated milk, sodas and kerosene. Table 4 summarises income and living standards in the four communities.

The survey shows that the households in coca growing areas had higher incomes and higher consumption levels than those in non-coca growing areas. The 1993 data for the San Martín districts showed that the monthly income of a coca-growing family ranged between 200 dollars (wage earner in the coca activity) and 700 dollars (if coca growers were titled proprietors of their lands and processed cocaine paste). Coca growers' incomes were 8% higher than those of non-coca growers, comparing rural incomes in Shamboyacu vis-à-vis those of Nueva Cajamarca.

The inhabitants of Shamboyacu declared receiving the highest income, on average 1,049 soles per month (or 549 dollars); Padre Abad residents declared 778 soles (or 345 dollars in 1995); Nueva Cajamarca 561 soles (or 294 dollars); and Tocache 537 soles (or 281 dollars). In terms of consumption, Shamboyacu was still first with 767 soles (402 dollars), followed by Tocache 624 soles (327 dollars); and Nueva Cajamarca 503 soles (263 dollars). This seems to indicate concern in Tocache in declaring their real income. According to these data, a predominantly coca area (Shamboyacu) would have double the income level of a non-coca area (Nueva Cajamarca). In terms of income distribution, in Tocache, the top two deciles had 43% of total income, in Nueva Cajamarca 45%

---

[19] Surveys were developed for the UNDP research project mentioned above.

and in Shamboyacu 48%. The income of coca growers was transformed into savings and higher consumption (e.g. beer and meat), boosting the income of retailers. In Shamboyacu, residents saved 28% of their incomes in contrast with 10% in Nueva Cajamarca.

Table 4. Surveyed areas in departments of San Martín and Ucayali: some indicators

Districts	Nueva Cajamarca	Shamboyacu	Tocache	Pedro de Abad
Population (inhabitants)	21,157	2,257	28,966	22,757
Housing ownership (%)	89	92	79	82
Average arable land (in hectares)	3.8	3.7	2.4	3.7
Main crops	rice, coffee	coca	banana, cassava, rice and coca	banana/yellow maize, cassava, coca
Income (in dollars/month)	294	549	281	345
Expenditures per month in dollars	263	402	327	n.a..

Sources: Based on surveys conducted in 1993 and 1995 in these areas by Cuanto S.A.

Coca processing may have contributed to a deterioration in health. Because of the chemicals being dumped into the rivers, it is not surprising that a higher proportion of the population showed signs of recent illness: in Shamboyacu 37% and Tocache 35%. The proportions for Nueva Cajamarca and Padre Abad were 24% and 20% respectively.

Economic costs

Tullis (Hollist and Tullis, 1987) was one of the first scholars to point out the likely negative effects of the drugs trade on food production in Bolivia and Peru. He found strong evidence for adverse effects on production and prices of basic foods. His argument was based on coca production displacing land which would otherwise have been used for licit agricultural production. In his assessment, this displacement increased food prices because it decreased licit supply. Although I do not agree with the 'mechanics' of his evaluation, he was right in pointing out that coca production led to price increases because available labour left the licit agricultural sphere to process coca. However, Tullis was incorrect in his views on land displacement. The reason is simple: land is abundant in the jungle and coca bushes do not require 'good' land to grow. Price increases were triggered by the increased demand from coca growers and labourers. This had a 'positive' effect for merchants selling foodstuffs and other goods and services, but may have had a negative impact for those not involved in the drug trade.

There is much anecdotal evidence about the rise in wages caused by coca growing. For instance, Laity (1989) points out the higher wage rates paid by coca growers as opposed to those paid for licit agriculture, though he fails to present a time series here. The increase of wages probably had a negative impact for employers not involved in the drug trade. The surveys for the three areas studied in 1993 indicate that almost all items in Shamboyacu had higher prices for most foodstuffs (between 5 and 35%). In the case of kerosene, an item used in the households but also as an input for coca paste processing, the price paid in Shamboyacu was four times higher per litre than elsewhere.

Thus one of the first negative effects in producing areas may have been a shift in resources towards coca production, especially labour as opposed to land, and non-tradable goods (eg. services such as restaurants and bars) to the detriment of food production. The second is an adverse impact on domestic prices for food products and, more generally, those of imported goods because of exchange rate appreciation. On this, Gallo, Tello and Rivera (1994, p. 53) in their local assessment of the Upper Huallaga, state the following:

> The coca economy has directly engaged over 50 % of the rural population of the upper jungle areas, whose production of only 10 or 15% gets into the warehouse of ENACO[20] for its legal marketing. At the same time the coca economy has favoured the situation of the illegal informal market which, coupled with a free foreign exchange market, contributes additionally to the money laundering of narcodollars. The latter in turn becomes a 'de facto' regulator of the foreign exchange market.

Environmental costs

Coca also damages the environment.[21] Several studies have documented the rationale behind deforestation in the late 1980s (see Bedoya, 1990)[22] in the Amazon region and attempted preliminary assessments of the jungle cover lost to deforestation (Dourojeanni, 1989). Environmental pollution was assessed by Marcelo (1987). Bedoya concluded that the illegality of coca encouraged extensive agriculture both among farmers, whether producing legal crops or not. Extensive agriculture – slash-and-burn – encourages deforestation. Legal cultivators lack the wage labour to help provide permanent agriculture because coca crops pay higher wages, whilst eradication programmes force producers to migrate ever further from the eradicators. Sendero Luminoso also played a role in deforestation by forcing cultivators to plant coca along with self-subsistence crops. The guerrillas would charge a 'tax' (*cupo*) for protection, financed by

---

[20]   ENACO is the Empresa Nacional de la Coca, whose function is to market legal production of coca. Most legal production comes from La Convención in Cusco.

[21]   Although this literature is somewhat dated, there do not seem to be any new studies, either by independent or governmental organisations, which document recent environmental damage arising from coca processing. Our discussion on the impact on health seems to be consistent with the damage that dumping of chemicals may have had on people and the environment.

[22]   Agriculturalists who used the land not very intensively had to deforest on an average 18.93 hectares in order to avail themselves of 3.52 hectares. That is, farmers who used their land extensively deforested on an average 5 hectares in order to have 1 hectare (see Bedoya, 1990, and Dourojeanni, 1989).

coca production (Bedoya, 1990).

According to Dourojeanni (1989, p. 5) coca was mainly planted on land appropriate for forestry, further damaging the environment. Coca caused deforestation of hundreds of thousands of hectares in areas not appropriate for agriculture. Deforested land included coca plantations, plantations of subsistence crops (cassava, banana and corn) belonging to coca growers, areas used by peasants fleeing those regions dominated by drug traffickers and guerrillas, land used by coca growers fleeing police repression, and areas deforested for landing strips, camps and laboratories. Dourojeanni calculated that about 700,000 hectares had been deforested directly and indirectly because of coca, equivalent to about 10% of total deforestation in the Peruvian Amazon this century.

The major consequences of this are, as Dourojeanni (1989, pp. 5-6) puts it:

> the loss of soil through sudden or cumulative erosion; the extinction of genetic resources; the alteration of the hydrological system; flooding; the reduction of the hydroelectric potential; increased difficulty in river navigation; the lack of wood and firewood; the lack of game animal for hunting, etc. Moreover, under these circumstances burning off the woods and ground cover produced by clearing the land is almost obligatory, bringing other consequences like air pollution, the loss of soil nutrients and damage to topsoil.

Furthermore, as Dourojeanni explains, whereas history from pre-hispanic times shows that coca can be planted in ways to preserve natural resources, the methods used today promote erosion. The plant has even been given the epithet 'the Attila of tropical agriculture' (Dourojeanni, 1989, p. 10).

Marcelo studied the impact of chemical waste dumped by coca paste producers into the rivers. In his words:

> In 1986, the volume of these substances [refers to toxic waste dumped in the rivers] was estimated at 57 million litres of kerosene, 32 million litres of sulphuric acid, 16 thousand metric tons of lime, 3,200 metric tons of carbide, 16,000 metric tons of toilet paper, 6.4 million litres of acetone, and 6.4 million litres of toluene (Marcelo, 1987, p. 2).

Cuanto S.A. has estimated similar chemical dumping on the basis of 1992 data, pointing to the threat to the region's aquatic resources. Many species of fish, amphibians, aquatic reptiles and crustaceans have already disappeared from the rivers and streams in areas where maceration pits are located, and the contamination of these rivers in the Upper Huallaga valley already exceeds pollution standards established by the World Health Organisation (WHO) for fresh and inland water (Marcelo, 1987, p. 4).

Measuring the costs

It is important to distinguish between short-term and long-term effects and between social and private costs and benefits. From a long-term and social cost perspective, the results that follow indicate that coca production may offset the short-term benefits for some specific members of society. However, ignoring social costs, the private short-term benefits outweigh the private costs for coca producers.

It is difficult to put a price on losses in nature. Some of the deforested land may be recovered, but disappearance of animal species native to these areas may not. What price can be put on the loss of the 700,000 hectares of deforested land? A report prepared by a consulting firm to assess the substitution programme, sponsored by USAID, quoted 600 dollars per hectare in lands producing legal crops in the Upper Huallaga (Econsult, 1986) as the annual average value from cultivating legal crops, such as coffee and cocoa. The value in relation to coca was 4,500 dollars/hectare/year in 1985. Cuanto's data on income per capita for rural households in 1993 ranged between 420 dollars (rural *sierra*) to 720 (rural coast). A UNDP study (Salazar, 1990) quoted prices per hectare of possible coca substitutes, such as cocoa at 1,615 dollars/hectare/year, coffee at 1,114 dollars/hectare/year, palm oil at 833 dollars/hectare/year, rice at 885 dollars/hectare/year, using the best technologies as of February 1990. Lacking better data, we will take 500 dollars and the 1990 data for coca substitutes (mentioned above) as the lower and upper limits respectively, to value the hectareage losses or income that cannot be produced. This yields 350 million dollars (i.e. 500 dollars x 700,000 hectares = 350 million dollars lost income) and 778 million dollars (or 1,615 dollars x 175,000 hectares) + (1,114 dollars x 175,000 hectares) + (885 dollars x 175, 000 hectares) + (833 dollars x 175,000). In other words, while coca produced between 945 dollars and 1,124 million dollars in 1992, it may have created losses in the order of 350 and 778 million dollars. A figure in between these two is probably realistic, since our second example assumes that Peru will encounter no obstacles in selling the extra export production. How about the animal losses? There is probably no price that can compensate for this. What about water contamination? Can the rivers be cleaned? Does this affect just South Americans, or others further afield? Valuation of such costs is obviously subjective and problematic, but whatever the assigned value the damage in many cases is irreversible and irreparable.

Weak state, corruption and drugs

Julio Cotler (1993) has documented the institutional and social context surrounding the fight against drugs in Peru. Further, Gorriti[23] has argued persuasively that many of the factors which gave rise to the guerrilla violence of the 1980s were also important in explaining the expansion of coca. In this

---

[23]   See Gorriti (1988), pp. 193-212 and Gorriti (1990).

section, I shall discuss some of these conditions and the persistence of the illicit drug trade in Peru.

According to Cotler, the growth of drug trafficking can be attributed largely to the traditional weakness of the Peruvian state, its limited ability to centralise authority and to enforce laws throughout the country. In such conditions, the armed forces have been able to acquire significant collective power, which has given them a fairly high level of autonomy from successive government administrations and from a fragile social organisation.

Fujimori decided early on in his first administration to fight the guerrillas first, and confront all else later. This was meant to allow the military to lead the fight against guerrillas, irrespective of concurrent allegations of human rights abuse. Evidence from US government agencies, such as the Drug Enforcement Administration, respected investigative journalists and the inhabitants of coca growing areas suggests that various groups within the armed forces have received payments from drug traffickers in exchange for allowing them freely to operate in the drug producing areas. Although the US State Department's former Bureau of International Narcotics Matters stresses that 'corruption' amongst narcotics enforcement personnel is individual, not institutional, Bureau officials have also asserted that 'corruption is endemic in virtually all Government of Peru institutions' (BINM, 1993, p. 124). If this is so, it suggests that members of the military stand to benefit so long as the coca trade persists.

Fujimori framed his approach to illicit drugs within the so-called 'Fujimori doctrine', drafted by Hernando de Soto, at a time when de Soto was an important adviser to his government. It basically calls for alternative development and free-market policies to encourage economic growth which, in de Soto's framework, also meant the removal of governmental constraints to the development of free markets. The 'alternative development' programme started with a small USAID-backed project in various coca growing areas, and as discussed earlier, many projects were launched during Fujimori's presidency in different regions which formed the basis for alternative developments to coca. However, hopes that there would be a rapid process of substitution proved misplaced. On the one hand, most alternative agricultural products are low-income elasticity products which means that their markets are not dynamic. On the other hand, cocaine prices at wholesale levels continue to be only a small fraction of retail prices in consuming countries. Thus, traffickers may increase prices at local (wholesale) levels, making it difficult for the legal alternatives to become competitive. Coca byproduct prices, which were very low in 1995, recovered subsequently and continued to provide good incomes to those involved. In 1997, a number of media exposés indicated the extent of corruption in the armed forces.

Conclusions

Although the coca sector is an activity which may be yielding declining incomes, it seems to provide considerably higher incomes than the legal agricultural alternatives. Unlike the situation in the 1980s and early 1990s, it is my view that the illicit coca sector – excluding long-term social costs – provides higher short-term private benefits than the costs associated with environment degradation and public health.

As our discussion at the local level shows, the impact of coca is clear: growers enjoy a higher standard of living and consumption levels than agricultural workers involved in legal types of production. Although coca growers and growing areas are affected by higher contamination and pollution levels, this study has shown that the potential losses in agricultural income arising from deforestation were (at those prices) less than the gains provided by the illicit sector. Cities like Tingo María, located in the coca-growing area, attribute their growth over the last 20 years to the coca boom. Growth in the Amazon region in recent decades cannot be divorced from coca and its derivatives. Without it, incomes and employment levels would be greatly reduced. In view of this, the coca economy seems likely to persist. Meanwhile, although it is difficult to know the extent to which coca is a corrupting influence amongst agencies of the state, there can be little doubt that there are many who have a vested interest in its continuance. This may be particularly the case amongst those whose responsibility it is to repress it.

PART III

DISTRIBUTION

CHAPTER 7

Income Distribution and Poverty in Peru

Adolfo Figueroa

A World Bank study has shown that income inequality in the Third World is persistently high (Deininger and Squire, 1996). It is said that Humboldt was amazed to observe the high degree of social inequality in many Latin American countries. Nearly two centuries after his visit, it is still a characteristic of the region. Theoretically, this is surprising. Relative prices, including real wages, undergo drastic changes everywhere, and yet the distribution of income does not change much. This empirical observation would contradict the predictions of most economic theories. Are there other factors that keep income distribution unaltered? If so, what are they?

In this chapter, I submit that there is a structural aspect in the social process that keeps reproducing the same social structure. A new theoretical framework, which I call exclusion theory, is developed to investigate this problem. It is a theory about markets and non-market relations; about social integration and social exclusion.

Exclusion theory

My model is a society that is organised as a capitalist democracy, which means that it has both a market system and a democratic system. Regarding the market system, I assume that the society is over-populated, in the sense that the Walrasian equilibrium real wage is zero, or close to zero. Moreover, I assume a society composed of multi-cultural and multi-ethnic social groups.

The concept of social assets

In a capitalist democracy, individuals participate in economic exchange endowed with a given set of assets. There are three types of assets: economic assets, which refer to productive resources such as land, physical capital, financial capital, and human capital; political assets, which refer to the access of people to rights established by society; and cultural assets, which relate to social values with regard to personal characteristics, such as language, race, sex, kinship, education, occupation, religion and geographical origin. The hierarchy of these social values is established by the cultural values of the society, which I assume as given. Taken together, these three types of assets are referred to as 'social assets'.

While economic assets indicate what a person *has*, political and cultural assets indicate who a person *is*. In these terms, citizenship is a political asset; and the individual's personal characteristics (identity) are his or her cultural assets, providing the individual with either social prestige or social stigma leading to discrimination and segregation. Clearly, an individual with a given set of personal characteristics would have a different mix of cultural assets if the system of cultural values changed. Unlike most economic assets, political and cultural assets are intangible; they are not tradable, so they do not have market values. However, as I will argue below, political and cultural assets play a significant role in the process of production and distribution.

At any given point in time, individuals are endowed with different quantities of these assets. Whilst economic inequality is inequality in economic assets, social inequality is a combination of inequality in economic, political and cultural assets. A society where social inequality is based on differences in economic assets alone could be called a 'liberal society', in which political and cultural assets are distributed evenly.

Market exclusion

Exclusion from the economic process will mean here exclusion from exchange in some basic markets. For this analysis, a distinction must be drawn between Walrasian and non-Walrasian markets. A market is Walrasian when individuals can buy or sell as much as they can and wish of a commodity at the prevailing market price. A Walrasian market always clears. Thus, under a competitive market structure, neither excess demand nor excess supply can prevail. Consequently, market rationing operates through prices. By contrast, a non-Walrasian market operates according to quantitative rationing; people cannot buy or sell the quantities they may wish to. A non-Walrasian market may operate with either excess demand or excess supply. For example, the potato market operates like a Walrasian market, whereas the labour, credit, and insurance markets are non-Walrasian.

Credit markets function as non-Walrasian markets because banks are concerned about interest rates they receive from loans and the riskiness of these loans. However, the interest rate a bank charges may itself affect the degree of risk attached to a pool of loans by either (a) sorting potential borrowers (the 'adverse selection' effect), or (b) affecting the actions of borrowers (the 'perverse incentive' effect).[1] Both effects arise from the residual imperfect information which is present in credit markets after banks have evaluated loan applications. 'When the price (interest rate) affects the nature of the transaction, it may not clear the market' (Stiglitz and Weiss, 1981, p. 393).

In conditions of uncertainty, where there is imperfect information, market

---

[1] 'Adverse selection' is the process by which 'undesirable' members of a population of buyers or sellers are more likely to participate in voluntary exchange, thus excluding those that are most 'desirable'. 'Perverse incentive' refers to the 'undesirable' actions that people would take induced by an economic incentive.

exchange is subject to risks. The bank's expected return depends on the riskiness of repayment; therefore, the bank would like to identify good borrowers, and to do so it is required to use a variety of screening devices. The interest rate an individual is willing to pay may be one such device: those willing to pay high interest rates may, on average, represent worse risks. As the interest rate rises, the average riskiness of borrowers increases, possibly lowering the bank's expected profits. This is the adverse selection effect. The perverse incentive effect applies when higher interest rates induce producers to undertake projects with higher returns but higher risk.

Consequently, there is an optimum interest rate that maximises the expected return to the bank. Clearly, it is conceivable that at this optimal interest rate the demand for funds exceeds the supply. However, the bank would not give a loan to an individual who offered to pay more, for such a loan is likely to be a worse risk.

Logically, market equilibrium with excess supply of funds in credit markets is a possible outcome because the interest rate directly affects the quality of the loan in a manner that matters to the bank. Non-Walrasian markets generally share the property that the expected quality of a commodity (or a service), demanded or supplied, is a function of its price.

Modern labour market theory is based on the axiom that the quality of the labour supplied depends on the real wage that employers pay (Bowles, 1985; Shapiro and Stiglitz, 1984; Solow, 1990). Although labour may be abundant, employers would still face problems in securing a supply of reliable and trustworthy workers. Higher wages (so-called 'efficiency wages') induce workers to satisfy these requirements. In this case, there is no adverse selection problem and the incentive effect is not perverse. The excess supply of labour is, however, the result of this logic. Hence, excess supply operates as a worker discipline device.[2]

In sum, in Walrasian markets people are excluded from exchange in a particular market because their real income, or their productive capacity, is too low; the quantities they demand or supply, at prevailing market prices, are very limited. In non-Walrasian markets people are excluded from exchange not because of demand or supply limitations, but because the logic of the market exchange implies that some who are capable and willing to participate will not be able to exchange what they want.

---

[2]   In the case of insurance markets, the theoretical proposition also considers that these markets function as if they were non-Walrasian markets. Due to the moral hazard problem, they would operate with some form of rationing. Insurance firms will be willing to provide more insurance, but if they do, those consumers will rationally choose to take less care, and profits will thus decline. Not all consumers can obtain as much insurance as they want to buy at the current prices. Also, insurance markets will not exist for risks that are not measurable, that is, where the probability distribution of events is not known. In this context, insurance firms will not be able to make actuarial calculations. For instance, risks associated with climatic variations will not be insurable.

Under market exchange, therefore, individuals' real income depends on their initial endowments of assets, relative market prices, and the quantities of goods or services that they can exchange in non-Walrasian markets. In a pure Walrasian market system, the real income of individuals would depend on asset endowments and relative prices only, for market rationing is done through prices. I assume here that the economy of this particular society operates with Walrasian and non-Walrasian markets. The latter includes labour, credit, and insurance markets, markets which play a key role in the accumulation of workers' economic assets, because they determine their incomes and the way in which they reduce risks. I will call them 'basic' markets.

Two mechanisms may then be distinguished which lead to income inequality: (a) the determination of the set of relative market prices; and (b) the extent of exclusion from basic markets.

What factors determine relative prices? The set of exogenous factors in most economic theories includes initial endowments of economic assets, institutions, technology, preference systems and state policies. In relation to initial endowments, our theoretical framework suggests that social assets should be considered as the relevant variable, as people participate in market exchange endowed not only with economic assets, but also social assets. In order to simplify the analysis, I assume that the two most important exogenous variables in the determination of relative prices are the initial distribution of social assets and the set of state policies.

Who would be excluded from market exchange in basic markets? Exchange within non-Walrasian markets is carried out under conditions of imperfect information and uncertainty, and it is based on promises (to work hard, to repay a loan, or to reduce risks). In this context, asset endowments will provide signals in the rationing process. I will therefore assume here that exclusion from non-Walrasian markets is not a random process; it depends on people's social asset endowments: those poorly endowed with social assets are more likely to be excluded.

State policies can also influence the access to non-Walrasian markets, especially where the quantity of goods and services to be rationed in such a market depends upon such policies. For example, state policies affect the level of economic activity, which in turn affects the level of employment, and hence the number of jobs to be rationed among workers. They also define the credit supply, and hence the amount of credit to be rationed.

For a given set of state policies, individuals' real income will depend on the asset endowments they possess, and the quantity of goods and services they can acquire in the non-Walrasian markets. If individuals are excluded from the labour, credit, and insurance markets (or sent to less profitable segmented markets) their income will be lower and more at risk. Their capacity to accumulate economic assets will thus be lower.

For a given market structure, the ultimate cause of income inequality lies in the distribution of the initial endowments of social assets, and in state economic policies.[3] In such conditions, the following endogenous variables are determined in the labour market: the quantity of wage-employment, the level of real wages and profits. Given the labour supply, the total quantity of surplus labour is then determined. In an over-populated economy, surplus labour will take the form of unemployment and self-employment, and wages will be higher than the incomes of the self-employed. This income difference among workers is necessary for the functioning of the system since it creates an incentive for workers to seek wage employment. Those excluded from the labour market become the poorest.

Who are those excluded from the labour market? For a given type of labour, workers with the lowest political and cultural assets are most likely to be excluded. Those who belong to different subcultures tend to be viewed by employers as the least reliable workers. They may also think that linguistic and cultural barriers raise the cost of extracting economic surplus from this type of labour. Thus, through the workings of the labour market, people bearing a social stigma for the capitalist class tend to be placed at the end of the line in the rationing process. The rate of surplus labour would vary according to ethnic and cultural characteristics of the workforce.[4] Moreover, some of the surplus labour would become 'superfluous labour', playing no role in the labour market, not even one of reinforcing discipline amongst the rest of the workforce.

Most surplus labour is also excluded from credit and insurance markets. Banks and insurance companies do not expect to profit by doing business with the self-employed or informal enterprises. They discriminate against small firms when, due to imperfect information and the consequent high transaction cost, they rely on property as collateral. Why, then, are informal lenders able to do business with small units? Whilst theoretically, informal lenders share the same economic logic as banks, in practice they have better information and better control over the actions of borrowers. The 'adverse selection' and 'perverse incentive' effects are both smaller. Credit market segmentation is a corollary of this theory: large units participate in the formal credit market, whereas small units do so in the informal credit market where the price of credit is higher.[5] For surplus workers, this is the secondary mechanism of market exclusion which

---

[3]   The set of relations of this theoretical model can be summarised as follows: Let $Ij = f(Sj, Qj, P)$, where Ij is the real income of individual j; Sj, his or her endowments of social assets; Qj, the quantity of goods or services obtained in non-Walrasian markets; and P, the set of market relative prices. If we call X the set of state policies, we postulate that $P = g(Sj, X)$, and $Qj = h(Sj, X)$. Then, the f function becomes $Ij = F(Sj, X)$.

[4]   This theoretical proposition is consistent with US data on unemployment; unemployment rates for US blacks are usually twice those for whites (Barro, 1990, Table II.2, p. 261).

[5]   Market segmentation occurs when the same good or service operates under two separate markets with two market prices. The economic logic of this situation originates in the belief of buyers or sellers that these goods or services are different in some respects (for example, in the degree of risk or trust). This arises from incomplete information. Another reason for the difference is the existence of legal norms (formal property rights against informal property rights). Segmented markets may be Walrasian or non-Walrasian

means that they cannot escape from being the poorest. The essential market mechanism that generates income inequality in this economy thus operates through the labour market. The outcome for prices and quantities in the labour market implies a specific distribution between profits, wages, and income from self-employment; it also implies the exclusion of a segment of the labour force from wage employment and from the credit and insurance markets.

In this world of uncertainty, economic inequality will persist and even increase, due to the unequalising nature of market exchange. There are several reasons for this: (a) people with high incomes will save and accumulate more assets; (b) the wealthy are better placed to embark on projects with high returns and high risks because their capacity to bear those risks and to profit from those returns is higher; and (c) the poor are excluded from basic markets. Where borrowing is difficult, the wealthy need to borrow less and have a higher capacity to invest.

Distribution of economic rights

Why do rights exist in a capitalist society? Okun (1975) argued that a capitalist democracy operates with a double standard: the market system implies inequality, but the political system preaches equality. How is this contradiction resolved? Okun sought to do so by suggesting a theory in which rights set limits to inequality, thus making society viable.

What are the factors that determine the set of rights in a particular capitalist society? Conceptually, we can distinguish between factors of demand and supply. On the demand side, there are factors such as social pressure, tolerance to inequality, the existence of a culture of inequality, the degree of democracy, and the income level of the poor. On the supply side, there is a society's productive capacity (the production frontier), the preferences of the ruling classes in allocating scarce resources to ensure rights of access to public goods, and international agreements. The extent of rights will therefore depend on pressures of demand or supply.

How are economic rights distributed? Most rights are provided for through the fiscal budget. This is clearly the case for economic rights in the form of goods and services supplied by the state (schools, health service, food, shelter), and they are free of charge. Some non-economic rights are also financed through the fiscal budget in the form of public goods, such as the right to vote, access to justice and social protection. These goods and services are withdrawn from the market and delivered to the population in the form of rights, the objective being that money should not buy everything in society. However, this objective is not always achieved since money impacts on the delivery of rights.

I will assume that effective exclusion from rights depends on the rationality of the ruling class. Although elites seek political legitimation through the establishment of rights, they also have an incentive to exclude people from rights. In the absence of rights, government expenditure will be used to generate political support in a clientelistic fashion.

Two particular rights merit discussion: (i) property rights and (ii) social protection rights.

(i) Property rights are essential to the efficient functioning of the market system, as Coase (1960) has insisted. Besides, they are also essential for the understanding of social inequality. If legal rights to private property are not guaranteed, exchange contracts cannot be legal. As a result, 'informal contracts' and 'informal markets' arise. Market segmentation is probably based in many cases on the absence of property rights. Credit markets are an example, as property cannot be used as collateral if there is no legal title. I assume that the poor are those who generally lack these rights because the relative cost of obtaining legal title to property is greater for them. Non-market exchange will predominate in the economic transactions of the poor.

(ii) With respect to social protection, the state has ways to insure risks associated with health and income in the form of health insurance, unemployment insurance and retirement pensions. Who are those excluded from these rights? Another postulate is introduced here: elites have an incentive to include in these insurance programmes wage earners only, so that employers can contribute to the financing of these rights. This has an economic logic, as employers create an incentive system for workers to search for wage employment. Those excluded from wage-employment are thus excluded from these rights.

To summarise, Walrasian markets clear, non-Walrasian markets do not; labour markets operate with excess supply, and credit and insurance markets operate with excess demand; economic rights are not universal but benefit wage-earners. One outcome of the economic process is a high degree of inequality: a first order inequality exists between capitalists and wage-earners; a second order exists among workers, that is between wage earners and those excluded from the labour market.

Finally, I introduce the proposition that the system cannot function with a very high degree of inequality, as there is a limited social tolerance of inequality. Thus, one condition for social equilibrium is that the distribution of income should lie within the set of income distribution values that are socially tolerable. A multi-cultural society may have a higher degree of tolerance of inequality than a more homogeneous society, but all the same it must operate within certain bounds. If inequality goes beyond the threshold of social tolerance, a situation of 'distributive crisis', social disorder and political instability in the democratic system will emerge.[6]

---

[6]   A formulation of this theory can be found in Figueroa (1993).

Some basic hypotheses

Taking this theoretical framework and applying it to a capitalist democracy with overpopulation and composed of multi-cultural and multi-ethnic social groups, we should observe the following:

- Social inequality is very pronounced. Economic, political, and cultural assets are highly concentrated. Those at the bottom of the economic pyramid are also at the bottom of the political and cultural pyramids.

- The labour market operates as the basic mechanism of social exclusion. Thus, worse than being exploited is *not* to be exploited; that is, the non-exploited (non-wage earners) are the poorest and most excluded group in society.

- The ownership of economic assets becomes more unequal over time. The accumulation of economic assets (stocks) depends upon the distribution of national income (flows) in each period. In a dynamic system, this process occurs as follows: given the initial endowments of social assets, the market system determines a distribution of income; this defines in turn a new set of individuals' economic assets (through savings and capital accumulation), which in the next period will determine a new distribution of income, and so on. In this dynamic process, the rich accumulate proportionately more wealth than the poor. Inequality in the distribution of economic assets becomes more unequal over time as those initial conditions lead to an increasingly skewed distribution of national income in each subsequent period.

- An equalising tendency in political and cultural assets. As economic development takes place, the demand for and supply of rights increase. Modernisation also tends to equalise cultural assets through education expansion and rural-urban migration. These represent the dynamic relations between economic and social inequalities.

- The democratic system will be fragile and prone to distributive crises. Pronounced inequality makes the social order unstable, as it generates social disorder, which leads to authoritarian government. As democratic rules of social order are inconsistent with excessive inequality, democratic and authoritarian regimes will tend to intermingle.[7]

- The set of state policies and the *initial* endowments of social assets are exogenous variables. Hence, history (through the initial conditions) does matter in this theory. Changes in these exogenous variables will modify the trajectory of the endogenous variables of the social system. The parameters of the system are set by the functioning of the market mechanism, the

---

[7]   Maslow's well known theory of hierarchy of human necessities would suggest that income inequality generates social inequality in the sense that people with higher real income would satisfy necessities of a higher order, such as self-realisation, participation in politics, art, and altruism, with a *qualitatively* different basket of goods and services. As more people become richer, the demand for democratic institutions will increase.

political system, and by the culturally determined ideology and social values of the society. Causality relations can then be established.

- Social exclusion is one of the basic mechanisms through which the exogenous variables generate social inequality. A capitalist democracy is a system of social relations, of social integration. But at the same time it is a system that operates on the basis of social exclusion. Indeed, social exclusion is inherent in the functioning of the capitalist system.

Within this framework, social exclusion becomes a theory, rather than a description of an *outcome* of the social process (such as poverty); it is a construction that helps explain that outcome. Exclusion from basic markets (labour, credit, insurance) is a *cause* of poverty; exclusion from other markets, such as those for some consumption goods (for example, a car, a telephone, durables and tourism), would be an *effect*.

Empirical evidence: the Peruvian case

Peru is a multi-cultural and multi-ethnic country. At least six ethnic groups can be identified: Andean Indians, Amazonian Indians, blacks, whites, Asians and those of mixed race. As for languages, in addition to Spanish, several native languages are spoken, such as Quechua and Aymara in the Andes, and Ashaninka and others in the Amazonian region. According to the 1993 national census, 13% of the adult population was illiterate in Spanish.

Poverty and inequality

In Peru, data on poverty are more abundant than on inequality. Overall poverty can be measured by per capita GDP. As shown in Table 1, the evolution of GDP per capita since 1950 can be divided into three periods. The first period, 1950-75, shows rapid growth at an average rate of 2.5% per year; the second period, 1976-93, saw considerable variations, with a declining trend and the steepest fall in 1989-93; the third period (1994-96) shows a partial recovery, with an average rate of increase of 3.3% per year.

The most recent recovery is only partial, as the 1996 per capita GDP is roughly similar to that of 1965, 30 years earlier. Moreover, it is 15% below the level of 1987, the previous peak; and only 10% above the level of 1989, the year when inflation peaked at its highest rate in Peruvian history. There can be no doubt that Peruvians have undergone a significant degree of pauperisation over the last two decades.

Table 1: Indicators of Living Standards (1970-96)

	Real GDP per capita (1985=100)	Real wages (1985=100)		Poverty (head counting) (%)
	(1)	Private (2)	Minimum (3)	(4)
1950	61.4			
1955	73.3			
1960	82.6			
1965	96.2			
1970	103.7	178.2	219.4	
1971	104.9	193.0	218.7	
1972	104.9	207.7	231.0	
1973	107.6	218.0	225.8	
1974	114.6	212.4	230.0	
1975	115.2	201.6	213.6	
1976	114.1	185.6	196.1	
1977	111.9	160.2	173.2	
1978	109.2	139.4	132.0	
1979	112.4	133.7	147.7	
1980	114.6	141.8	182.8	
1981	116.8	141.4	155.9	
1982	114.1	148.7	143.3	
1983	97.8	125.2	145.8	
1984	99.4	111.5	116.2	
1985	100.0	100.0	100.0	41.6
1986	107.1	130.5	103.0	
1987	113.6	139.6	113.9	
1988	102.0	91.0	84.0	
1989	88.3	61.2	44.6	
1990	81.7	43.8	39.5	
1991	82.2	52.5	27.5	53.6
1992	78.1	50.7	28.8	
1993	82.0	54.1	20.2	
1994	91.2	64.2	26.5	49.6
1995	96.3	59.2	27.0	
1996	97.3	na	na	51.3

Source: Cuanto

The decline in real wages has been even more significant than that of per capita GDP. Real wages in the private sector in 1995 were equivalent to 60% of those in 1985, whereas for per capita GDP the figure is 96%. Minimum real wages underwent an even steeper fall compared to mean real wages in the private sector. In spite of a significant recovery in 1994-95, employment in the modern sector remained at a very low level (Table 2).

Table 2: Performance of the Labour Market (1980-95)

		Proportion of Lima's Labour Force (%)		
Years	Employment in Modern Sector	Underemployed	Unemployed	
			Total	Female
	(1)	(2)	Total	Female
1980	109.1	26.0	7.1	11.2
1981	110.5	26.8	6.8	11
1982	110.9	28.0	6.6	10.6
1983	106.7	33.3	9.0	11
1984	98.9	36.8	8.9	12.6
1985	98.6	42.2	10.1	s.i
1986	102.9	42.6	5.3	8
1987	108.8	34.9	4.8	6.2
1988	108.0	37.0	7.1	s.i
1989	100.5	73.5	7.9	10.7
1990	98.2	73.1	8.3	11.4
1991	92.4	78.5	5.9	7.3
1992	82.4	75.7	9.7	12.5
1993	76.3	77.6	9.9	12.2
1994	76.7	na	8.8	11.8
1995	76.1	na	7.1	8.7

Source: INEI and BCRP, *Memorias.*

(1) Employment in firms of 100 workers or more (January 1990=100).

(2) Occupied workers with earnings below minimum real wages of 1967.

For Lima, a measure of poverty can be derived from the statistics for underemployment.[8] As can be seen in Table 2, the proportion of the occupied labour force earning less than the real minimum wage of 1967 has increased substantially since 1989, after which time it has remained almost constant at around 77%.

Head count data on poverty is available for four years only. National household surveys, conducted in accordance with the Living Standard

---

[8] Underemployment is defined as including workers who earn less than the minimum wage.

Measurement Studies of the World Bank, show that nearly 42% of the population was below the poverty line in 1985. This figure jumped to over 50% in the 1990s (Table 1). In terms of the rural-urban differential for poverty, it is clear that the incidence is much higher in rural areas (See Table 3).[9]

Table 3. Poverty Levels (Percentages per population group)

Areas	1985	1991	1994
National	41.6	53.6	49.6
Lima	27.4	48.9	37.6
Rest of urban areas	41.0	na	44.5
Rural	53.5	na	68.2

Source: Cuanto, No. 68, Vol. 6 (December 1994), pp. 8-12.

The detailed study on Peru's income distribution carried out by Webb (1977) showed that, in the mid-1970s, Peru was among the countries with the highest inequality in the world. The study also described the process of income concentration in the period 1950-73. Another study, which made some recalculations for the period 1950-80, found similar trends of income concentration (Figueroa, 1984). For more recent periods, no such studies exist. From household survey data some estimates of income inequality have been made, but they refer to the distribution of labour income, not national income.

An approximation to the share of labour in national income can be reached by using the data on per capita GDP and real wages presented in Table 1. If we take the ratio of wage labour participation as constant − it changes but not greatly, as will be shown below − the rate of change in labour's share can be suggested by measuring the difference between the rates of change of real wages and per capita GDP.[10] Real wages increased by 13% and per capita GDP by 11% between 1970 and 1975, implying an increase in labour's share. The two rates were -23% and -9% respectively in the period 1983-88 (vis-à-vis 1976-82); and -55% and -20% in the period 1989-93 (over the previous period), indicating a sharp fall in labour's share. In the 1994-95 period, labour's share increased slightly, with rates up 18% and 14% respectively. Another way to show this is to use an index of real wages over per capita GDP: 1.00 in 1980, 0.54 in 1990, 0.70 in 1994 and 0.61 in 1995.

---

[9]   A revised estimation based on the same household survey data suggests that this is the case for a poverty line of 30 dollars a month per household member. Below 15 dollars a month, the trend goes in the opposite direction. Since the poverty (Lorenz) curves for 1985 and 1994 cross at the 20 percentile, it seems more meaningful to use the 30 dollar line. My calculations will appear in Lance Taylor and Enrique Ganuza, eds. (forthcoming).

[10]   Labour share can be written as the ratio $wL/yN = (w/y)(L/N)$, where w represents the mean real wage, L the quantity of wage-labour, y per capita income, and N total population. If L/N is constant, and if the growth rates of per capita GDP and per capita income (national income) are equal, changes in labour share can be measured as the difference between growth rates of the mean real wage and per capita GDP.

Around the mid-1970s, Peru's social structure could be divided into five social groups: the capitalist class, the middle class, the wage-employed (including the public sector), the urban self-employed and the rural self-employed. The economic and social differences separating these groups were very marked, particularly between the capitalist class and the rest. At that time, the top 1% received a third of the national income, and the bottom third received only 5% (Webb, 1977). In the absence of studies on changes in the income pyramid for the most recent decades, I can only offer some partial information and some guesses.

At the top, the property-owning class still remains a very small group. Peru's distribution of *economic assets* is still highly concentrated. Several studies have shown how Peru was still an oligarchy in the 1950s and 1960s. However, in the 1980s concentration of property was still very marked: large firms belonged mostly to 330 families, of which 80 formed part of a few major economic groups centred on a bank (Malpica, 1989). In 1989, for instance, the top 13 economic groups, owned by twelve families, produced an equivalent of 17% of Peru's GDP (Campodónico et al, 1993, p. 122). These twelve families were still the most powerful economic groups in Peru in 1996 (Durand, 1996).

The middle class can be defined as those with a university education, in which human capital is concentrated. According to the 1993 census, only 6% of the adult population had completed university education, as compared to 3.3% in 1981. Whilst the middle class has grown numerically during the period, it is the sector which suffered the largest loss in real income due to the fall in real wages and the crisis of the state.

In the mid-1970s, the base of the income pyramid was constituted by the peasantry, with the poorest groups in the income pyramid to be found in the peasant communities of the Andes and small jungle communities. These groups remain in this position partly because the land reform excluded them. The more educated, younger and wealthier sectors of the peasantry were those who tended to migrate to the cities. In the centre of the pyramid, social mobility was both high and volatile, a kind of 'social magma'.

Market exclusion

Census data for 1972, 1981 and 1993 reveal the high degree of exclusion of workers from wage employment. Measured as a percentage of the total labour force, these rates were 54%, 55%, and 57% respectively for Peru as a whole, and 35%, 35%, and 44% for Lima. Of course, not all workers outside the area of wage employment can be considered as excluded from the labour market. Some are not willing to work as wage earners, being better off as they are. Nevertheless, it is clear that the degree of exclusion is high in Peru.

The unemployment rate for Lima (shown in Table 2) underestimates the real level of exclusion from the labour market. Whilst there is no systematic information on the socio-cultural differences between wage earners and those excluded from the labour market, it is widely believed that there is discrimination by race, origin of birth, family name and gender. For instance, the rate of unemployment among female workers is considerably higher than the average.

Table 4: Concentration of Commercial Bank Credit (in percentages)

	1968	1990	1993
Sectors	100	100	100
Commerce	43	27	30
Manufacturing	31	45	39
Other	26	29	31
Regions	100	100	100
Lima	77	82	83
Arequipa	3	6	5
Elsewhere	20	12	12

Source: Superintendency of Banks and Insurance.

In formal credit markets in Peru (e.g. the banking system), credit allocation is highly concentrated. Commerce and manufacturing account for the bulk of credit: 75% in 1968, 72% in 1990 and 70% in 1993. In regional terms, the allocation of credit is concentrated in Lima: 77% in 1968, 82% in 1990, and 83% in 1993 (Table 4). Classified by type of recipient, large firms obtained most of the credit. Unpublished data for one of the largest banks in Peru show that the top decile of debtors holds 74% of the bank's total loans and the top 30% holds 92%. The Gini coefficient, calculated by deciles, is 0.78.

Table 5. Peru: Total Bank Credit and Share of Development Banks, Selected Years

Year	Total Real Credit (Index)	Share of Development Banks
1978	100.0	49.8
1982	163.4	42.2
1986	126.5	46.5
1987	118.4	50.0
1988	39.1	41.5
1989	26.6	33.1
1990	19.3	31.8
1991	31.0	24.5
1992	39.1	15.9

Source: INEI, *Compendio Estadístico, 1992-1993*, Tables 20, 27, p. 154

Those excluded from commercial credit may have access to the credit supplied by development banks. Indeed, development banks appear to lend to smaller firms, but the majority of firms receive little or no formal credit. In addition, the amount of credit from development banks has declined more than from commercial banks. Credit from development banks was 50% of formal credit in 1978 and declined to 25% in 1991, constituting a smaller share of a smaller amount, as total formal credit declined in real terms during the recession. In 1990, this credit was only 15% of its 1982 level (Table 5). As part of the adjustment process, development banks were closed down in the 1991-92 period (see Chapter 5).

Thus, most firms – particularly small and micro firms – are excluded from formal credit. They must seek credit in the informal market, creating a segmentation in the credit market.[11] This is consistent with the hypothesis that, in addition to labour markets, economic exclusion also operates through credit markets. The self-employed, excluded from the labour market, are also prevented from accumulating economic assets by virtue of the exclusion they face in the credit market. This double exclusion helps perpetuate their relative poverty.[12]

Exclusion from economic rights

The distribution of economic assets can be measured in accordance with the following headings (Figueroa, Altamirano and Sulmont, 1996):

Social protection. Such rights are very limited in Peru. The numbers of those included in the public social security system are but a small fraction of the total population. In 1986, 42% of the labour force (which represents only 51% of total wage-earners) belonged to the social security system (the Instituto Peruano de Seguridad Social). Urban-rural differences were very pronounced in this respect. Whereas 72% of the labour force in rural areas is outside the social security system, the percentage is nearer 60% in urban areas. That only half of all wage-earners are included in the social security system is a clear indication of the precariousness of wage employment. The coverage of the social security system with regard to retirement pensions is also very low. In 1990, two-thirds of the population aged 65 years lacked this right. Moreover, pensions payable per person are very low, and there is no system of unemployment insurance.

Social services. During the 1980s and 1990s, public expenditure on basic social services (education, health, housing and employment programmes) fell in relative terms. As a proportion of GDP, expenditure on such social services also declined: from 4.6% of GDP at the beginning of the 1970s to 3.4% at the beginning of the 1990s. As a proportion of government expenditure, the relative fall was less noticeable. Around 25% of the government budget was allocated to social expenditure at the beginning of the 1970s, falling to 19% in the first half of the 1980s and recovering somewhat to 23% at the beginning of the 1990s. However, the fall was more dramatic in absolute terms: in 1992, the level

---

[11]   Informal financial firms seem to operate under very risky and precarious conditions. The bankruptcy of many such firms has been a feature of the recession (1988-92).

[12]   The insurance market is so small in Peru that there is little need to study it in order to show that there is exclusion.

represented only 49% of its 1980 value. In per capita terms, the fall is more striking still: in 1992 it was barely 30% of what it had been in 1980 (Table 6). The fall in resources produced a dramatic decline in the quality of public services.

Table 6: Government Expenditure on Education, Health, Housing and Employment (1970-92) percentages

Year	Real Expenditure (Index: 1970=100)		As a percentage of	
	Total	Per capita	GDP	Government Expenditure
1970	100	100	4.5	26.4
1971	105	102	4.6	24.7
1972	114	108	4.8	25.3
1973	127	116	4.8	24.2
1974	127	113	4.5	23.9
1975	133	115	4.6	23.2
1976	135	114	4.7	23.5
1977	120	99	4.3	19.0
1978	113	90	4.0	17.5
1979	121	95	3.9	19.0
1980	154	118	4.6	20.0
1981	153	114	4.6	21.1
1982	136	99	4.0	19.2
1983	119	85	4.2	16.9
1984	125	87	4.1	16.8
1985	124	84	4.0	16.7
1986	158	105	4.7	21.7
1987	121	79	3.4	18.0
1988	121	77	4.3	26.0
1989	81	51	4.1	25.0
1990	53	33	3.4	19.0
1991	51	31	3.2	24.0
1992	61	36	3.7	27.0

Source: INEI and BCRP.

Labour rights. The right to participate in labour organisations is very restricted in Peru. According to the law, the right of unionisation is limited to workers in firms with 20 or more employees. In 1992, only 15% of the labour force were affiliated to workers' unions in urban areas and only 5% in rural areas. The law meant that in Lima in 1981 only 63% of wage earners enjoyed the right of unionisation. In 1993, the percentage had fallen to 52%, revealing a shift in employment away from large firms to smaller ones. In fact, unionisation (wage-earners in firms with 20 or more workers who are affiliated to unions) was 65% in Lima in 1981, dropping to 50% in 1993. This seems to reveal changes in the importance attributed to union membership by workers, a facet of the economic crisis.

The income pyramid: continuities and changes

The social group at the bottom of the income pyramid remains the same: the Indian population, mostly composed of peasant families. The Indian peasantry of the Andes and the Amazonian area are not only the poorest, but also share different sets of cultural and social values. A significant proportion do not speak Spanish, are illiterate and live in remote areas with poor communication systems; they are therefore effectively excluded from the modern cultural process.

The size of this social group can be approximated by means of the rates for illiteracy and non-Spanish-speaking. According to census data, the rate of illiteracy in Peru was 27% in 1972, 18% in 1981, and 13% in 1993; non-Spanish-speaking rates were lower: 12%, 9%, and 5% respectively. However, if we use less restrictive definitions, such as primary education (up to three years) as a proxy for 'illiteracy' and the language used in communication within the family for 'non-Spanish-speaking', the rates become significantly higher. We would guess that the relative size of this group – those with the highest degree of cultural exclusion – may be around 20% of the population.

Socially, the Indian population has never been fully integrated into the 'national society' of Peru. But is it becoming more integrated now? In terms of economic integration, the answer is positive; the peasantry is more integrated into the rest of the economy through market exchange. A study showed that by the end of the 1970s, in the southern Andes – Peru's most traditional region – peasants exchanged nearly 50% of their production, while also selling labour in casual labour markets. With the expansion of the road network, a commercial revolution has taken place in rural areas (Figueroa, 1984a).

In terms of political integration, the situation has also improved. For a long time the Indian population was excluded from citizenship. The Andean peasant communities received legal recognition in 1923, and the Amazonian communities in 1969. Prior to these developments, they were not considered to be Peruvian citizens (the Republic of Peru was established in 1821) and lacked property rights. The extension of the franchise to illiterates was promulgated only in 1979, but even then native languages were not officially recognised. However, since the 1960s, rural education has been greatly extended. Cultural integration has also increased. With the growth of education in rural areas, the proportion of Spanish speakers has increased. Access to mass media is also much more significant now, due not only to the widespread ownership of transistor radios, but to the greatly expanded outreach of television.

The most important mechanism of social integration of the indigenous population has been migration. Peru has gone from being a predominantly rural to a predominantly urban country in the last fifty years. In 1940, 35% of the population lived in urban areas; in 1993, 70% did so. Although the level of population growth is high, it has grown at a decreasing rate: 2.9% in the 1950s and 1.7% in the 1990s. The 1993 census shows that only 22% of the population lived in the Andean rural areas. The indigenous population has moved to the cities in large numbers. By moving to towns, the Indians have become more integrated, economically, politically and culturally.

Cultural integration has taken place not only because Indians have adopted 'western' values, but because they have reproduced their own original cultural practices and values in the city. This could be called the 'size effect' of migration: if one individual migrates from a particular region, he or she has no choice but to adopt the culture of the city; if thousands migrate from the same area, they adopt urban culture but they also disseminate their own culture. Peru's large towns have undergone cultural adaption; there has been a process of cultural and racial mixing. In Lima, nobody is a foreigner now; as in New York, no group is in the majority.

There has also been a 'feed back effect', as migrants maintain ties with their place of origin. These are kept going by continuous visits, transfers of money, participation in the local *fiestas*, and so on. Migrants form associations which provide a social network in the city and, through them, contribute to the economic development of their place of origin, which, because of all these interactions, undergoes cultural changes as well. Thus, both effects contribute to a reduction in urban-rural differences and, hence, to a more homogenous society.

Migration has not only been internal. Migration abroad has also occurred. An interesting example is the temporary migration of Peruvian peasants to the United States, to work as shepherds on the ranches in Utah, Montana and California. In 1990, some 3,000 were involved (Altamirano, 1992).

The extent of this massive migration over the last few decades has caused a social revolution in Peru; a revolution that has brought with it a higher degree of social integration, but which has produced social effects that were unexpected. Governments have long tried to encourage social integration through specific policies (like the *Programa de Integración de la Población Aborigen* launched in 1963), but such policies have been unable to achieve the effects that migration has. Even the land reform programme, implemented between 1969 and 1975, did not change social conditions much, since, by design, the large majority of Indian peasants were excluded from its scope (Webb and Figueroa, 1975).

In spite of this progress, social integration is far from complete. Indians still tend to be excluded from basic markets. They have had their access to economic rights curtailed, due to policies implemented during the recession. Culturally, they still face social discrimination and stigma. Indians who remained in the rural communities lack the social assets of those who migrated. In sum, the indigenous population is still at the base of Peru's social pyramid. However, it is a social group that is becoming smaller and smaller; it is also more integrated, closer to the centre of the social pyramid, to what we called the 'social magma'.

The indigenous population has suffered most from the political violence that has afflicted Peru since 1980 through the activities of two guerrilla groups, Sendero Luminoso and the Movimiento Revolucionario Túpac Amaru (MRTA). Violent conflict has led to the death of some 23,000 people, most victims coming from areas where the indigenous populations predominate. Many have found themselves forced to leave their communities and migrate to the cities, mainly Lima. They have become the 'new excluded' in the city. It is important to note that the political discourse of the subversive groups had greater acceptance amongst those with the highest degree of exclusion. The same discourse tended to be rejected within labour unions in urban areas, suggesting the existence of a relationship between exclusion and political violence.

Between the indigenous population on the one hand and the elite on the other, there is a space that includes about 75% of the population. Here, at the centre of the social pyramid, mostly urban, there is an area of significant social mobility. This is where the races and cultures mix, where informal (illegal) markets operate (including local coca dealers) and where migrants from rural areas will find a place to live and work. Indeed, this is where 'the action' is, as some sociologists and anthropologists put it; this is where the 'new face of Peru' is to be found (Matos Mar, 1984; Portocarrero, 1993).

While the economic and social demands of this group have increased, the capacity of the market system and the state to meet those needs has not developed to the same degree. Indeed, because of the economic crisis of the late 1980s and early 1990s this capacity has declined. A social eruption is therefore unsurprising. There has been a redistribution of income because of political violence and the growth of the coca industry. At the same time there has been a process of informal privatisation of public and private goods by these emerging groups. Streets and plazas have been occupied by vendors; idle urban land has been squatted; private property has been challenged. The informal economy, where property rights and contracts are illegal, has increased (De Soto, 1986; Thomas, Chapter 8 of this volume). New forms of collective action in the productive sphere (networks of small firms, whose entrepreneurs are of Andean origin) have emerged, as have *comedores populares* in areas of consumption. Most people who belong to this 'social magma' operate under precarious conditions of employment, but use their membership of different social networks to facilitate social mobility and risk reduction.

Although the social composition of the capitalist class is also changing – with the entrance of new family names and non-white faces – the capitalist class still predominates over the social process through the mechanisms of exclusion.[13] The same can be said of the state. Although the political class has new entrants as well – symbolised to some extent by second generation immigrants like Alberto Fujimori himself – the acquisition of rights has not been widened but narrowed. Clearly, the traditional oligarchic system of 1950s Peru has disappeared, since political and cultural exclusion has become weaker. In this sense, Peru no longer fits the image of a traditional dual society. All the same, the social system still operates with social exclusions, which contribute to social inequality, particularly in exacerbating economic inequality. Over time, the Peruvian data suggest that political and cultural assets are becoming more evenly distributed, whilst economic assets are becoming more unequally distributed.

Fujimori's Policies Towards Inequality and Poverty

The stabilisation and structural reform policies followed by the Fujimori government have involved consideration of distributional problems. However, the option chosen has been one in which equity had low priority. The Social Emergency Programme that accompanied the 'Fujishock' of 8 August 1990 had a largely political logic: to make shock therapy politically viable. This choice is perhaps surprising if one remembers the figures shown in Table 1 on poverty and inequality: per capita income and real wages had reached such low levels that the problem of pauperisation could not be ignored.

Table 7: Government Budget Allocation to Poverty Reduction Programmes (percentages)

	1993	1994	1995	1996
Total (US$ million)	287	503	984	1055
As percentage of GDP	0.8	1.0	1.7	1.8
Programmes				
Foncodes (social support, employment generation and institutional support	53.2	40.8	22.2	17.4
Glass of milk programme	18.3	15.4	10.2	8.9
Pronaa (popular kitchens)	9.2	8.8	9.4	7.5
Support for agriculture in emergency zones	10.4	7.8	8.9	8.3
School meals	4.9	3.3	3.4	4.8
Sub-total	96.0	76.1	54.1	46.9
Others	4.0	23.9	45.9	53.1
Total	100.0	100.0	100.0	100.0

Source: INEI

---

[13]   The 'new rich' includes the 'coca lords', a group culturally distinct from the traditional upper and middle classes.

In 1991, the emergency approach changed, with the establishment of the National Fund for Compensation and Social Development (Foncodes), whose basic idea was to help the poor through small-scale investment projects. In 1992, the government created the National Food Assistance Programme (Pronaa) to help poor areas, urban and rural, with food supply. In 1992, the ministry of the presidency was created to coordinate assistance to the poor.

Expenditure on poverty alleviation was 89 million dollars in 1990, 161 million in 1991 and 225 million in 1992 (Ministerio de Economía y Finanzas, 1993; p. II-30). After 1993, the government developed a new programme of poverty reduction, whose central target was to reduce the poverty level of near 50% to 20% by the year 2010. The budgets for poverty relief are shown in Table 7. The magnitudes of funds made available were increased significantly, due, in part, to the resources generated through the privatisation of state firms; part of the funds raised in this way must by law be spent on poverty relief. However, none of these programmes and organisations are geared towards creating *rights*. On the contrary, many rights have been eliminated. Within the government, some have fought to create a '*gasto social básico*' to finance rights to basic education, health-care and judicial services. However, this is a minority position struggling against the mainstream view in favour of discretionary expenditure.

Why does the government oppose the creation of rights? Governability in Peru is fragile and the popularity of the government is volatile. Clientelistic types of spending are ways to make governance viable, a theme developed further in Chapter 13, below. At the core, the problem lies in the increased degree of inequality and poverty that the Fujimori government has itself helped to generate; as was shown in Table 1, the shock therapy brought a sharp fall in per capita GDP in 1990-92. In a society already trapped in a distributive crisis, the effect of this additional impoverishment was critical, threatening increased political instability and a growing problem of governability within a democratic framework. The *autogolpe* of April 1992 was endogenous. Since Fujimori's social policies will not solve the problem of social exclusion, it seems highly probable that extreme inequality will persist.

Conclusions

By introducing the concepts of social assets and non-Walrasian markets, we have been able to construct a theoretical framework for understanding social inequality in a particular society: a capitalist democracy, over-populated, multi-ethnic and multi-cultural. In such a context, the workings of a capitalist democracy generate mechanisms of social integration and social exclusion at the same time. Social exclusion is, thus, a mechanism built into the workings of the system: the excluders are the ruling classes.

Exclusion theory, simply put, states that economic inequality is generated not only through exploitation, surplus extraction, unequal distribution of initial resource endowments and a regressive tax system, but also through exclusion from basic markets and economic rights. Over time, the system tends to be equalising in terms of political and cultural assets, but the opposite in terms of economic assets. In spite of modernisation, a society that is born very unequal will tend to remain so.

Thus, the effect of exogenous variables upon economic inequality operates through market mechanisms, the political system and cultural values. The exogenous variables include both the initial distribution of social assets among individuals and a set of state policies. The theory predicts that changes in these variables will shift the trajectories. Another prediction is that the nature of democracy will be imperfect and fragile.

The empirical evidence for Peru, a country with a marked multi-ethnic and multi-cultural mix, seems consistent with such predictions. Peru has a persistently high degree of inequality because it is an overpopulated economy that functions with market exclusions and a segmented distribution of economic rights. The Indian population remains at the bottom of the income pyramid since market exclusion and exclusion from economic rights affects them most.

As far as trends towards exclusion are concerned, the hypothesis appears to be confirmed. An outcome of the social processes is that the distribution of economic assets tends to be increasingly concentrated over time. Cultural change fosters greater national integration through rural-urban migration and the growth of education. However, such changes are slow and ambivalent. Even though ethnic discrimination continues, the lower proportion of the indigenous and rural population in the national population as a whole implies that this source of inequality in cultural assets will diminish. Today, discrimination on account of cultural assets means less in terms of participation in the labour market than it did 50 years ago; rationing in the labour market is more dependent on chance and less centred on cultural assets than in the past. Also, political participation is less restricted by ethno-cultural differences.

However, progress towards a more equal distribution of rights has not occurred, as predicted by our dynamic theory, in the absence of changes in exogenous variables. The debt crisis and the hyperinflation of the 1980s constituted changes in exogenous variables which modified the original trajectory. The economic crisis of the 1980s gave rise to lower income per capita and fewer public goods to help sustain economic rights. In spite of this setback, I still consider that Peruvian society is moving slowly towards being a liberal society in which the weight of economic assets is the fundamental factor behind social inequality.

The hypothesis that, given the extent of impoverishment in the 1980s, Peru has crossed the threshold of social tolerance with regard to poverty and inequality, entering into a situation of distributive crisis, seems to receive empirical confirmation. Clearly, this is an extreme result arising from the effects of hyperinflation and social exclusion, a situation in which social protection policies have lost any priority.

This distributive crisis implies a quantitative change in the ways in which society works. Political violence, redistributive violence (i.e. transgression of property rights), chaos and corruption are its characteristics. Since the democratic system does not have the capacity to prevent this distributive crisis, the political class tends to lose its legitimacy and political instability thus becomes endogenous. As this is what has taken place during the Fujimori administration, the hypothesis of a fragile democracy has empirical support.

The distributive crisis, of course, involves political costs for society, since it implies some backward movement in the construction of democracy. The economic costs of the distributive crisis are also large. Over the short term, Peruvians have been obliged to devote scarce resources to defending property rights. Indicative, for example, is the fact that the number of those involved in the protection industry (bodyguards etc.) is similar to those working in the modern industrial sector. Substantial resources need to be devoted to the administration of justice, police and prisons, costs related in one way or another to the costs of inequality. Over the long term, Peru has lost substantial amounts of private investment because of social and political instability: per capita private investment has fallen noticeably since 1983 (Figueroa, 1993).

If society continues to be affected by a distributive crisis, the thresholds of tolerance may fall further and the inequality and poverty which were previously considered intolerable may then become more acceptable. The ability of the majority to resist impoverishment may lessen. The factors which engendered the distributive crisis may lead the economy onto a trajectory of continuous deterioration, leading possibly to a new social equilibrium, but at a lower level. At this new equilibrium, the new level of poverty might reproduce itself socially, producing a new culture of inequality. This process seems to have occurred in Peru. The economic policies followed by the Fujimori government may have already led society to a lower level of equilibrium, at which wages are lower, poverty higher, inequality more pronounced and public social expenditure per person is reduced. Social equilibrium under these conditions is unstable. Under such initial conditions, it is very likely that economic growth and social development will follow a slow and unstable path.

CHAPTER 8

The Labour Market and Employment

Jim Thomas

Having been elected with what Peruvian voters thought was an economic package that would avoid austerity measures, President Alberto Fujimori produced the 'Fuji shock' and launched Peru into a structural adjustment programme that has been notable for its severity. Many aspects were conventional, with policies focused on gaining fiscal control of the economy to fight hyperinflation, removing subsidies and freeing markets, and restructuring tariffs to improve international competitiveness. In some respects the emphasis in the Peruvian programme differed from adjustment programmes in other countries; this was true in the case of the labour market.

In commenting on early structural adjustment programmes in Latin America, Sebastian Edwards noted that policies concerning the labour market had often been low on the list of priorities:

> Surprisingly, labor market reforms have been absent from most adjustment programs. Labor markets are the forgotten sector, and discussions of speed, sequence, intensity and conditionality have many times proceeded as if labor markets are irrelevant.

> But some of the most severe distortions in Latin America are in labor markets – government workers tend to have instant tenure, bargaining is poorly regulated, labor taxes are extremely high, dismissal costs are enormous, and backward-looking indexation introduces significant inertia to the inflationary process. In sequencing reforms, countries (except Chile and Peru) have chosen to leave labor market deregulation until last. This is a poor choice, because under most circumstances an early reform of the labor market is highly beneficial, helping reduce the transitional costs of adjustment. If labor markets are not deregulated, there is a danger that the effects of other reforms will be minimal – even negative (World Bank, 1993, pp. 3-4).[1]

---

[1] Labour market 'reforms' include changing labour contracts to make it easier for employers to lay off workers, reducing the powers of trade unions and reducing the real value of minimum wages by not adjusting for inflation. For a full discussion of the role of labour markets in structural adjustment, see Horton, Kanbur and Mazumdar (1994). The latter contains case studies of Argentina, Bolivia, Brazil, Chile and Costa Rica. Lagos (1994) provides an analysis of the links between deregulation of and increasing flexibility in the labour market and Lagos (1995) is a case study of labour market deregulation in Chile. See also Thomas (1996) and Diwan and Walton (1997).

As the quotation suggests, the World Bank sees labour market reforms as being crucial to the adjustment process, but the political costs of challenging strongly entrenched labour movements has deterred politicians from undertaking such changes in many countries. President Fujimori has neither ignored nor neglected the labour market, which has undergone some major changes in recent years. This chapter sets out to examine these changes and to answer three questions in relation to the labour market:

(i)   Is what happened to the labour market under the Fujimori government really different from what went before?

(ii)   Is what happened to the labour market under the Fujimori government different from/the same as what is happening/has happened in other Latin American countries?[2]

(iii) How sustainable are the changes? This raises further questions, namely are the changes likely to be maintained and could they be reversed by a new president of a different political persuasion?

This discussion of the labour market concentrates on the *urban* labour market, because (i) this represented about 67% of the Economically Active Population (EAP) in 1994 (Webb and Fernández Baca, 1996, p. 491, Table 15.22), and (ii) Raúl Hopkins in this volume (Chapter 5) covers rural questions, including those involving the labour market.[3]

A number of analysts have examined the link between structural adjustment and poverty and, in particular, the possibility that adjustment programmes may have worsened the very unequal distribution of income that characterises most countries in Latin America (see Baer and Maloney, 1997; Berry, 1997; Bird and Helwege, 1996; Morley, 1995; Psacharopoulos et al, 1997; van der Hoeven and Stewart, 1993; and Zuvekas Jr., 1997). While it is difficult to quantify any direct links that may exist between programmes of structural adjustment and changes in income distribution (see Bulmer-Thomas, 1996), Berry (1997, p. 34) argues that a 'tentative guess would be that the elements of reform packages related to trade and the labor market may underlie most of the negative trends in figures reported on distribution.'

As we shall see, a number of developments in the labour market, such as the weakening of the power of trade unions, have contributed to the process of social exclusion discussed by Figueroa in this volume (Chapter 7). This point will be discussed in the concluding section of the present chapter.

---

[2]   As background to the economic situation in Peru before 1990 and to provide a comparison with what has happened in other Latin American countries, see Altimir (1994), Dornbusch and Edwards (1991), Gonzales de Olarte (1996), ILO (1994), Instituto Cuanto (1991), Lago (1991), LondoZo (1995), Lustig (1995), Paredes and Sachs (1991), Tulchin and Bland (1994) and World Bank (1995a and b).

[3]   In some respects the coverage of my chapter will be more limited than this, as much of the statistical data available relates to Metropolitan Lima.

Employment trends[4]

Growth in the labour force

The economically active population (EAP) of Peru grew from 5.587 million in 1980 to 8.046 million in 1992, or by 44.0%.[5] The non-agricultural EAP grew from 3.364 million persons in 1980 to 5.388 million in 1992, an increase of 60.2%, with the result that the non-agricultural EAP increased from 60.2% to 67.0% of the total EAP. For Lima and Callao, the increase in the EAP was from 1.832 million in 1980 to 2.870 million in 1992; 56.7%, during the period. These are relatively high rates of growth and raise questions concerning the ability of the economy to generate employment for the growing urban labour force.[6]

Figure 1. Annual Growth in GDP and Manufacturing Output in Real Terms, 1981-95

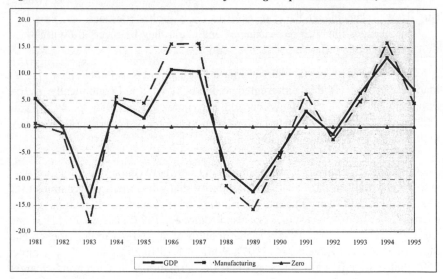

Source: Webb and Fernández Baca (1996).

As Figure 1 shows, between 1980 and 1995 gross domestic product (GDP) measured in real terms suffered a number of severe negative fluctuations, as well

---

[4]   Various issues of Webb and Fernández Baca's *Perú en números* have been used to provide consistent time series on labour market variables, but in some cases the series do not cover recent years. In such cases, I have tried to fill the gaps with data taken from a variety of other sources. Valverde (1997) notes changes in the methodology for measuring underemployment that may make it difficult to compare figures in the future.

[5]   According to ILO (1996a), between 1990 and 1995, the EAP in Peru grew at an average annual rate of 3.4% per annum, compared to a weighted average of 3.2% for Latin America and the Caribbean.

[6]   While INEI (Peru's National Institute of Statistics and Information) predicts that the annual number of births will decrease from 626,000 in 1990 to 594,000 in the year 2009, this still represents a rapid rate of population increase. The population of Peru is predicted to rise from 21.6 million in 1990 to 29.5 million in 2009 and 35.5 million in 2025. Fertility rates are higher for rural than for urban households, but high rates of rural-urban migration lead to high rates of growth of the urban population (see Webb and Fernández Baca, 1996, Tables 4.1, 4.13 and 5.2).

as several years of high growth. The net effect was that the positive and negative swings more-or-less cancelled out and add up to a small positive overall growth during the period. Manufacturing output (in real terms) also showed large fluctuations and very little real growth over the period.[7] This combination of a growing non-agricultural labour force and little real growth in the output of the Peruvian economy might lead one to expect to find high levels of unemployment over the period

Levels of employment

While in developed countries one might expect the EAP to be composed of those workers who are employed plus those who are unemployed, in developing countries, the situation is more complex. In most developing countries, *underemployment* best describes the situation of many workers. Underemployment may be defined from two points of view, by *hours* and by *income*. Underemployment by hours, or visible underemployment, corresponds to the intuitive concept of those workers who would like to work for more hours than they do, but are unable to find the extra work. Underemployment by income, or invisible underemployment, corresponds to the concept that, at the other extreme, many workers may be working long hours but failing to earn an adequate income. Technically, in Peruvian statistics the underemployed by income are defined to be those who work 35 or more hours per week, but fail to earn more than the minimum wage (in real terms). This second definition covers an important component of underemployment in much of Latin America and it is included in the data on Peru.[8]

Those who are neither unemployed nor underemployed are said to be adequately employed. Figure 2 shows the distribution of these three categories from 1980 to 1994 and a number of points may be noted.

First, despite the severity of the economic crisis and the hyperinflation experienced in Peru, the level of unemployment showed very little variation between 1980 and 1994. This reflects the fact that in a country without unemployment benefits and social security payments, not many workers could afford to be unemployed.

Second, the striking feature of the graph is the great increase in the number of workers who were underemployed, rising from 37.0% in 1988 to 73.5% in 1989 and remaining at around this level from 1989 to the end of the period shown in the graph.

---

[7] Peruvian manufacturing output remains largely concentrated in Lima and Callao: in 1970 the percentage produced there was 60.6%, in 1980 it was 61.1% and in 1995 it was 58.4% (see Webb and Fernández Baca, 1996, p. 566, Table 18.36).

[8] See ILO (1990) for a further critical discussion of the definitions of these concepts.

Figure 2. Percentage of Economically Active Population with Adequate Employment, Underemployment or Unemployed

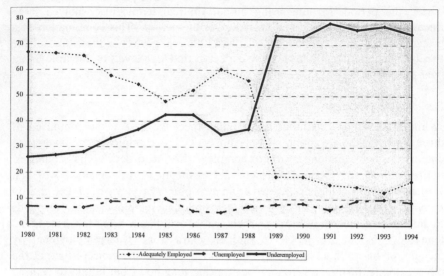

Source: Webb and Fernández Baca (1992 and 1996)

The sharp increase in the number of underemployed had a variety of causes. First, it reflected the serious downturn in economic activity that reduced the number of those in adequate employment by forcing many workers out of formal employment into the Urban Informal Sector – to be discussed in the next section. Secondly, it reflected the effects of the hyperinflation, which represents an 'inflation tax' on those who could not avoid paying it by switching into dollars. This group is primarily, though not exclusively, the poor and they had to respond to the tax by working longer hours, but often for lower incomes.[9]

Infante (1995) presents further information on the unemployed in Metropolitan Lima for the period from 1984 to 1993 (see Table 1). With respect to age, there was a fall in the proportion of the unemployed aged between 14 and 24 and an increase in those over the age of 45. When disaggregated by sex, the effect was more marked for men than for women. With respect to level of education, there was a decrease over the period in the proportion of the unemployed with only primary education and an increase in those with higher education. When disaggregated by sex, the decrease in primary education effect was more marked for women, while both men and women showed an increase in unemployment for those with higher education. Thus, broadly speaking, by the end of the period a higher proportion of the unemployed were older and better educated.[10]

---

[9]   In many cases the extra hours were obtained partly by working overtime, but also by working at other activities. These may well have been in the Urban Informal Sector. An example would be a public sector worker who drove his or her car as a taxi in the evenings and/or at weekends. One suspects that some proportion of those claiming to be unemployed may actually be moonlighting.

[10]   Given a high positive correlation between education and income, the better educated could

Table 1. Composition of Open Unemployment by Age and Level of Education in Metropolitan Lima, 1984-93

Characteristic \ Year	1984	1986	1987	1989	1990	1991	1992	1993
AGE: TOTAL	100.0	100.0	100.0	100.0	100.0	100.0	100.0	100.0
14 – 24 years	52.6	50.9	54.1	51.4	48.7	49.5	40.5	43.4
25 – 34 years	26.7	28.9	23.0	28.8	28.2	29.1	28.3	24.7
35 – 44 years	10.0	11.0	13.8	9.9	14.5	7.0	13.8	13.3
45 years or more	10.7	9.2	9.1	10.0	8.2	14.3	17.4	18.6
MEN	100.0	100.0	100.0	100.0	100.0	100.0	100.0	100.0
14 – 24 years	49.4	58.7	50.5	54.6	47.4	47.8	40.1	41.2
25 – 34 years	26.2	19.5	24.8	23.5	28.9	25.1	26.3	18.8
35 – 44 years	7.1	8.3	9.9	5.5	13.8	6.1	12.7	11.8
45 years or more	17.3	13.5	14.8	16.5	9.9	21.0	21.0	28.2
WOMEN	100.0	100.0	100.0	100.0	100.0	100.0	100.0	100.0
14 – 24 years	55.8	46.4	57.3	48.7	49.8	51.3	40.9	45.8
25 – 34 years	27.2	34.3	21.4	33.1	27.6	33.1	30.1	31.0
35 -44 years	12.9	12.6	17.3	13.6	15.8	8.0	14.9	14.9
45 years or more	4.1	6.7	4.1	4.5	6.7	7.5	14.0	8.3
EDUCATION: TOTAL	100.0	100.0	100.0	100.0	100.0	100.0	100.0	100.0
No education	1.0	2.5	0.6	1.4	0.7	0.0	1.2	0.6
Primary	17.7	11.6	10.9	13.9	17.9	12.9	16.0	11.6
Secondary	65.7	65.9	70.6	61.6	56.0	60.3	57.4	62.7
Higher	15.6	20.0	17.9	23.1	25.4	26.8	25.4	25.1
MEN	100.0	100.0	100.0	100.0	100.0	100.0	100.0	100.0
No education	0.0	1.4	0.0	0.8	0.7	0.0	0.0	0.0
Primary	16.6	11.2	6.2	15.7	15.7	17.0	13.8	15.9
Secondary	66.9	72.0	81.5	59.1	59.1	64.0	61.8	60.5
Higher	16.5	15.4	12.3	24.4	24.6	19.1	24.4	23.6
WOMEN	100.0	100.0	100.0	100.0	100.0	100.0	100.0	100.0
No education	2.1	3.1	1.1	1.9	0.7	0.0	2.4	1.2
Primary	18.8	11.9	15.1	12.3	19.7	8.8	18.0	6.9
Secondary	64.5	62.4	60.9	63.6	53.5	56.5	53.3	65.1
Higher	14.6	22.6	22.9	22.1	26.2	34.6	26.3	26.8

Source: Constructed from Infante (1995), p. 44, Table 17.

Unemployment in Lima was not spread equally among different sectors of economic activity. Disaggregating by sector and taking 1984 = 100 as the base year for an index of employment in large firms (i.e. those employing more than 100 workers), Infante (1995, Table 8c) shows that between 1984 and 1990 the index had fallen to 96.2 in manufacturing, 94.8 in commerce and risen to 105.6 in services. Between 1990 and 1993, however, the index fell in all three sectors: to 75.4 in manufacturing, 60.8 in commerce and 85.3 in services.[11]

The structure of the labour market

As in many developing countries, the urban labour market in Peru may be

---

afford to be unemployed. For further discussion of women in the labour force see UN (1995).

[11] Abugattas (1996, p. 23) shows that an index of employment in industry with 1979 = 100 as the base year fell from about 85% in January 1990 to 61% in January 1996.

classified in terms of the urban formal sector (UFS) and the urban informal sector (UIS). The concept of the UIS was developed by the ILO (International Labour Organisation) in a country study of Kenya (ILO, 1972) and subsequently there have been many theoretical arguments concerning the usefulness of the concept.[12] In the data that have been compiled for Latin America by PREALC[13] the UIS is defined in terms of self-employed workers (other than professionals) and those working for enterprises employing less than ten workers. The UFS consists of self-employed professionals (such as doctors, lawyers, etc.), those working for enterprises employing ten or more workers and those working in the public sector. In addition to these two sectors, there is a further category of domestic servants.

Figure 3. Structure of Urban Labour Market, Metropolitan Lima, 1981-95 (percentages)

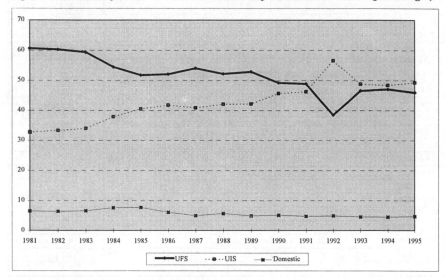

Source: Webb and Fernández Baca (1992 and 1996)

Figure 3 illustrates what has been happening to the structure of employment in Metropolitan Lima between 1981 and 1995. There has been a steady downward trend in the level of employment in the UFS (from 60.7% of the EAP in 1981 to 46.0% in 1995), while employment in the informal sector has grown from 32.8% of the EAP in 1981 to 49.3% in 1995.[14]

---

[12] In the context of Peru, the informal sector is probably best known through the writings of Hernando de Soto (de Soto, 1986). However, his somewhat simplistic equation of 'informality' with 'illegality' has been widely criticised in academic circles; see Thomas (1995), Tokman (1992) and Tokman and Klein (1995).

[13] *Programa Regional del Empleo para América Latina y el Caribe*, the Spanish title of the ILO's regional office in Santiago as part of its World Employment Programme. It was dissolved in December 1993 after 25 years of distinguished operation in providing excellent analysis of the labour market in Latin America and the Caribbean.

[14] There are relatively sharp declines in the UFS in 1983, possibly reflecting the disruption caused by *el Niño*, in 1989 probably reflecting the effects of hyperinflation and in 1992, reflecting

Table 2. Growth in the Number of Paid Workers by Size of Enterprise in Metropolitan Lima, 1984-93 (1984=100)

Size of enterprise	1984	1987	1990	1993
9 or less workers	100	123.9	147.9	214.3
10 to 19 workers	100	136.2	161.6	173.9
20 to 99 workers	100	115.9	151.1	172.6
100 or more workers	100	112.7	91.0	109.0

Source: Infante (1995), p. 36, Table 8a.

Not only has there been a shift in employment from the formal sector to the informal sector, but within the formal sector there has been a shift in the balance between large and small firms. Table 2 shows indices of the growth in the number of paid workers by size of enterprise for selected years between 1984 and 1993 and it can be seen that paid employment in enterprises employing nine or fewer workers has more than doubled during the period, reflecting the growth in the informal sector. Within the formal sector, the expansion in paid employment in enterprises employing fewer than 100 workers has been much greater than in enterprises employing 100 or more workers.

Table 3. Distribution of Paid Workers by Size of Enterprise in Metropolitan Lima, 1984-93 (percentages)

Size of enterprise	1984	1986	1987	1989	1990	1991	1992	1993
9 or less workers	30.2	33.9	31.3	28.3	34.6	34.2	36.7	40.0
10 to 19 workers	10.3	12.8	11.8	10.5	12.9	12.1	12.5	11.1
20 to 99 workers	22.4	23.8	21.8	27.3	26.2	22.5	25.3	23.9
100 or more workers	37.1	29.5	35.1	33.9	26.2	31.2	25.5	25.0
Total	100.0	100.0	100.0	100.0	100.0	100.0	100.0	100.0

Source: Infante (1995), p. 36, Table 8b.

Table 3 shows that whereas in 1984, 30.2% of paid workers were employed in enterprises with 9 or fewer workers and 37.1% were employed in enterprises with 100 or more workers, by 1993 40.0% of paid workers were employed in enterprises with 9 or fewer workers, as compared with 25.0% in enterprises employing 100 or more workers.[15]

---

increasing informalisation of the economy in response to changes in the labour market.

[15] The changes in the percentages for the other two size categories are relatively small, but it cannot be assumed that there is a direct transfer from the largest to the smallest enterprises, as there may be considerable movement between enterprises within the UFS that would not be revealed by these figures. What is clear is that there was a net movement of paid workers from the UFS to the UIS.

Wage Trends

Like most Latin American countries, Peru has had a strongly regulated labour market in which a minimum wage played an important role in setting a lower bound to what could be paid in the UFS and helping to determine the level of severance pay and pensions.[16]

If prices are stable, once the level of the minimum wage has been set, its real value remains approximately constant. However, where there is inflation, the real value of the minimum wage declines unless its nominal value is adjusted upwards periodically. The formula for such an adjustment may be formalised, such as was the case in Brazil, where wages were indexed and rose automatically (though with a lag) when prices rose. In the absence of indexation, the adjustment of the nominal value of the minimum wage may be more sporadic.

Structural adjustors tend to disapprove of a legal minimum wage, on the grounds that it distorts the operation of the labour market:

> A dynamic and flexible labor market is an important part of the market-oriented policies. It helps reallocate resources and allows the economy to respond rapidly to new challenges from increased foreign competition. Moreover, freeing the labor market of distortions improves the distribution of income because it encourages employment expansion and wage increases in the poorest segments of society. In most Latin American countries, labor market distortions have been segmented, with protected and unprotected sectors coexisting side by side. Removing the most serious distortions usually increases the unprotected sector wage rate, reduces the protected sector wage rate, and increases overall employment (World Bank, 1993, p. 92).

The result has been that in some countries in Latin America that have experienced high rates of inflation, as was the case in Peru, the real level of the minimum wage has not been maintained through nominal adjustments.[17]

---

[16] One of the characteristics of small enterprises in the UIS is that many of them do not pay the legal minimum wage. See Tokman (1992) and Tokman and Klein (1996).

[17] On an index of the minimum urban real wage (MURW) with 1984 = 100, in 1992 the value of the MURW was 44.5 in Argentina, 55.4 in Brazil, 42.0 in Mexico, 11.5 in Paraguay, 16.3 in Peru and 61.5 in Uruguay. Sebastian Edwards concludes that 'Textbooks usually mention minimum wages as the predominant labor market distortion to be removed in market-oriented reforms. But this is not the most pressing issue in Latin America today. With few exceptions, minimum wages have declined throughout the region in the past few years and have largely become a nonbinding restriction (Table 6.7). This of course does not mean that (potential) hikes in minimum wages will not hurt employment in the future' (World Bank, 1993, p. 93, Table 6.7.)

Figure 4. Indices of Real Remunerations for Metropolitan Lima, 1984-93 (Base Year = 100)

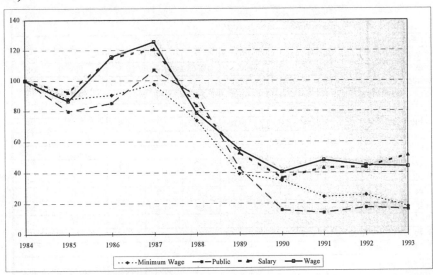

Source: Infante (1995).

Figure 4 presents indices of average salaries (SALARY) and average wages (WAGE), based on surveys of firms in Metropolitan Lima employing 10 or more workers, and average public sector remuneration (PUBLIC), for central and local government, as well as the average legal minimum monthly wage (MINWAGE). The period covered is 1984 to 1993 and all variables are measured in real terms with 1984 = 100. After rising between 1985 and 1987, all four series fall sharply until 1990. Thereafter, they behave somewhat differently, with SALARY and WAGE rising slightly, while PUBLIC stabilises at a very low level and MINWAGE continues to fall.

The picture that emerges in Figure 4 is further illustrated by the information presented in Table 4, which contains aggregate data on real average hourly earnings (RAHE) in Metropolitan Lima (in constant June 1994 soles) for selected years between 1984 and 1993. The clear picture that emerges from Part 1 of the table is that the RAHE fell for all the categories of employment given in the table, the sharp fall coming between 1987 and 1989. The losses were not uniform and, in some cases, those working in the UIS were relatively better off than those working in the UFS by the end of the period. It is notable that while there is a considerable earnings differential between white and blue collar workers in the UFS, there is no systematic differential between the two corresponding groups in the UIS.

Table 4. Average Hourly Earnings in the Formal and Informal Sectors in Metropolitan Lima, 1984-93

Year	1984	1986	1987	1989	1990	1991	1992	1993
1. Average hourly earnings (in constant June 1994 soles)[18]								
1.1 Formal sector								
Private sector								
Employer	20.8	23.5	27.1	10.7	11.4	10.4	5.4	6.1
White collar	11.1	10.9	12.1	4.1	5.3	3.1	4.0	3.5
Blue collar	6.4	5.1	5.8	2.4	2.4	1.8	2.0	1.9
Public sector								
White collar	11.2	8.0	9.6	3.5	4.2	1.6	2.2	2.1
1.2 Informal sector								
Micro-enterprises								
Employer	8.5	11.6	17.6	4.2	4.8	3.5	3.2	4.1
White collar	4.7	5.5	5.6	2.2	3.9	1.2	1.6	1.3
Blue collar	4.5	4.0	4.4	2.0	1.9	1.4	1.6	1.3
Self employed	6.9	6.4	7.6	3.3	3.2	2.2	2.3	3.2
Street seller	4.7	5.0	5.6	1.8	2.9	1.6	1.7	1.4
2. Index of average hourly earnings (1984 = 100)								
2.1 Formal sector								
Private sector								
Employer	100.0	113.3	130.5	51.7	55.0	49.9	26.0	29.2
White collar	100.0	97.8	109.2	37.0	48.0	28.1	35.8	31.1
Blue collar	100.0	80.3	91.6	38.2	37.5	28.1	31.4	29.1
Public sector								
White collar	100.0	71.4	86.4	31.6	37.9	14.0	19.9	18.4
2.2 Informal sector								
Microenterprise								
Employer	100.0	136.7	208.1	50.0	56.4	40.9	38.3	48.2
White collar	100.0	117.7	119.4	46.4	82.9	24.8	33.1	28.6
Blue collar	100.0	88.1	96.6	44.8	42.9	32.1	34.4	29.0
Self employed	100.0	93.1	110.1	48.3	45.7	31.7	32.6	45.8
Street seller	100.0	106.5	119.7	38.8	60.7	33.9	36.0	30.1
3. Dispersion of average hourly earnings in relation to private sector[19]								
3.1 Formal sector								
Private sector								
Employer	187.1	216.8	223.7	261.2	214.7	331.8	135.6	175.4
White collar	100.0	100.0	100.0	100.0	100.0	100.0	100.0	100.0
Blue collar	57.3	47.1	48.1	59.2	44.7	57.3	50.2	53.6
Public sector								
White collar	100.6	73.4	79.5	85.9	79.3	50.0	55.8	59.4
3.2 Informal sector								
Microenterprise								
Employer	76.2	106.5	145.3	103.0	89.7	110.9	81.5	118.1
White collar	42.3	50.9	46.2	53.0	37.0	37.3	39.1	38.9
Blue collar	40.7	36.7	36.0	49.3	36.4	46.4	39.1	37.9
Self employed	62.1	59.1	62.6	81.2	59.2	70.0	56.7	91.5
Street seller	42.3	46.1	46.4	44.3	53.5	50.9	42.5	41.0

Source: Constructed from Infante (1995), pp. 46-7, Tables 19 and 20.

---

[18] In June 1994, 1 US dollar was worth about 2.2 Soles.

[19] The comparison is made with white collar workers in the private sector as the reference category.

Part 2 of the table illustrates how each group fared in relation to its starting point in 1984. On this comparison, all groups lost, but it seems that UIS employers lost least and ended up with RAHE at 48.2% of their starting level, while white collar workers in the public sector did least well, ending up with only 18.4% of their 1984 level.

Part 3 of the table provides a comparison over time of each group with the reference category of the average white collar worker in the UFS. This comparison emphasises the relative gains made by employers and the self-employed in the UIS and the relative loss sustained by white collar workers in the public sector. The differential between the earnings of white and blue collar workers in the UFS hardly changes over the period.[20]

Overall, the evidence presented here suggests that on average there were no winners in the labour market and that earnings fell for all groups, though not all lost equally badly. However, the largest fall was between 1987 and 1989 and predates the period of the Fujimori government.[21]

Labour relations

Legislation concerning labour relations in Latin American countries was generally favourable towards labour employed in the UFS, with legislation covering the minimum wage, employers' contributions towards pensions and other benefits, and strict rules governing the conditions under which an employer could dismiss workers.[22]

Restrictions on the ability of an employer to sack workers has been seen by structural adjustors as a major labour market imperfection. For example, in Peru an individual worker can only officially be laid off on the grounds of (i) a grave fault on the part of the worker, (ii) a penal prosecution of the worker or (iii) if the worker is unfit.[23] Legislation has been introduced in a number of Latin American countries to reduce workers' protection. In Peru, legislation was introduced during the presidency of Alan García that reduced workers'

---

[20] MacIsaac and Patrinos (1995) present some evidence suggesting that there may be some labour market discrimination against indigenous workers in Peru and that a large portion of the indigenous/non-indigenous wage gap is unexplained by human capital and other observable differences, but this issue will not be explored further here. See, however, Chapter 7.

[21] Two recent articles in the North American Congress on Latin America (NACLA) *Report on the Americas* suggest that entrepreneurs may have been gainers since 1990 – see NACLA (1996 and 1997).

[22] Calder\n (1993) and IILS (1993) provide overviews of changes in the situation facing trade unions in Latin America during the 1980s and a number of country case studies. On Peru see Marshall (1991), Verdera (1993) and Yépez del Castillo (1993). Labour legislation is generally confined to the formal sector and workers in the informal sector have few if any rights (see US Department of Labor, 1992).

[23] See ILO (1996a, pp. 22-7) for a discussion of the costs of dismissal of workers in Latin America.

protection by making available to employers a number of different short-term contracts for workers, during which time they were not entitled to protection and benefits. The number of such contracts issued was 35,000 in 1990, 91,000 in 1991, 130,000 in 1992 and 176,000 in 1993.[24] Thus, while the Fujimori government did not introduce the first legislation to put more workers on temporary or other short-term contracts, it has passed laws to extend this flexibility. According to ILO (1995, p. 22), 'In Peru, the share of workers with temporary work contracts has bloated, especially since the new labour standards were implemented at the start of 1992. Hence, this participation surpassed 38 per cent in 1985 to 41 per cent in 1990 and to more than 50 per cent at present'.[25] It should be noted, however, that employers' contributions continue to be high for workers with permanent contracts, but the proportion of such workers has been reduced, thus lowering overall labour costs.

Figure 5. Number of Strikes, Number of Workers Involved (in thousands) and Number of Hours (in thousands)

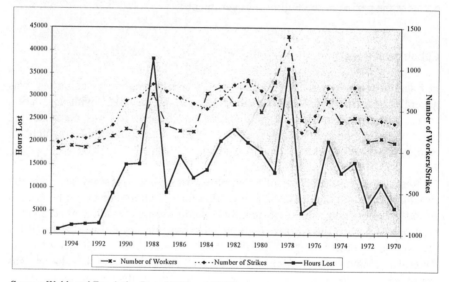

Source: Webb and Fernández Baca (1992 and 1996)

Figure 5 analyses changes in labour relations in the Peruvian labour market by presenting annual data from 1970 to 1995 on the number of strikes, the number of workers involved and the number of manhours lost through industrial

---

[24] Data from information supplied by the Labour Ministry to an IMF mission to Peru in September 1994.

[25] One measure was the elimination of the *comunidad laboral*, which was established during the Velasco government of 1968–75 as a form of worker participation in decision making, profit sharing and, progressively, ownership of an industrial enterprise (see Pinzás, 1996). Pasco (1993) and Varillas (1993) contain further details of legislative changes during the early part of President Fujimori's period in office. Verdera (1996) claims that the number of workers employed in state enterprises fell from 87,100 in 1990 to 24,300 in 1995 and, of those, the proportion on temporary contracts rose from 6.9% in 1990 to 23.6% in 1995.

action. The graph shows a strong overall correlation between the variables, as one would expect, but also reflects the fact that there may be periods during which a large number of strikes occur involving small number of workers and manhours lost, while a general strike may involve a large number of workers and manhours lost. The peak in the number of workers involved and hours lost through industrial action in 1978 corresponds to the active role of trade unions in organising popular protest against the military government of General Francisco Morales Bermúdez through national strikes.

The peak in all three variables in 1988 represented the efforts of trade unions to obtain concessions over wages from the government and employers to offset the effects of the hyperinflation on earnings in the absence of the indexation of nominal wages (see Crabtree, 1992). The failure of the unions in 1988 to influence government policy weakened their power and the data indicate a considerable decrease in all three variables since 1990, a result that is consistent with a labour market in which many workers are on temporary contracts, trade unions are weak and underemployment is at a very high level.[26] In addition to their economic problems, Mauceri (1995) points out that the unions were also faced with political problems. Sendero Luminoso tried to infiltrate trade unions and murdered a number of union leaders in the process, while the security forces (suspicious of Sendero's influence) took a repressive attitude to the labour movement. This combination of factors greatly weakened the trade union movement and made it easier for Fujimori to issue new decrees reducing labour rights. Verdera (1996) shows that the percentage of private sector workers in trade unions fell from 34% in 1987 to 13% in 1995.[27]

Employment in the public sector is more directly under the control of the government and, during the period from 1990 to 1995, the percentage of non-agricultural employment in the public sector in Latin America has fallen from 15.3% to 13.2%. For Peru the figures were 11.6% in 1990 and 8.9% in 1995, making it one of the lowest percentages in 1995, along with Brazil (9.6%), Chile (7.7%) and Colombia (8.4), in contrast to Costa Rica (17.9%), Mexico (22.5%), Panama (23.4%), Uruguay (17.7%) and Venezuela (19.5%) – see ILO (1996, Table 1 B).[28]

---

[26] At least one key member of the Fujimori government did not regard trade unions with much enthusiasm. Thus, according to Carlos Boloña: 'Trade unions, often monopolistic, often fail to reflect the interests of their members but rather benefit at their members' expense. For instance, when a union successfully negotiates a salary increase which surpasses the market rate, this improvement is made at the expense of nonaffiliated workers. Unions also often limit the availability of workers and use violent, coercive methods against both employees and employers. Certain unions, moreover, obtain protection from the government through pressure or negotiation. This protection is effected by means of legislation regulating minimum salaries, maximum working hours, wage scales, and work by minors' (Boloña, 1996, p. 211).

[27] Mauceri (1995, p. 23) notes that in late 1991 Fujimori used his power to issue decrees to reduce worker participation, union organisation and job security.

[28] Boloña (1996, pp. 243-4) noted that not much had been done in relation to downsizing the state: 'Regarding personnel reduction, 70,000 employees out of a total of 645,000 active central government workers have been relocated at a cost of over $80 million. The central government should be reduced by decreasing the number of ministries from fourteen to eight.' However, Kay

Deregulation of the economy

Privatisation[29]

The main motivation for privatisation within structural adjustment programmes tends to be related to the IMF's strategy of imposing fiscal discipline on the government involved, since selling off loss-making public sector enterprises has two effects: (i) it reduces the government expenditure involved in subsidising public enterprises and (ii) the sale produces government revenue. These two effects work in the same direction to improve the government's fiscal position. In addition, to the extent that the public enterprises are sold abroad, the sales may generate large quantities of foreign exchange and help the government solve (at least in the short run) a balance of payments deficit. For example, in Peru, between 1991 and December 1995 the privatisation programme generated a total income of about 4.4 billion US dollars, much of which involved foreign investment, such as the 1.4 billion US dollars that were paid by a Spanish consortium for ENTEL, the Peruvian telecommunications company.[30]

However, privatisation has implications for the labour market, as the process of selling off public sector enterprises often involves shedding labour, either by the government before the event, as part of the preparation for privatisation in order to make the public enterprise more profitable and therefore more attractive to potential buyers, or by the new owners after privatisation has taken place as a way of achieving higher productivity and greater profits.

While the financial transactions involved in the privatisation of Peruvian public enterprises have been completed in a number of cases, the period is too short for there to have been much adjustment of the labour force involved. However, if the labour market adjustments are similar to those observed in other Latin American countries that have privatised state enterprises, the effects may be dramatic. For example, Tandon (1994, p. 63) reports in relation to Mexico that after privatisation the labour force in Aeroméxico fell from 11,500 to 6,500.

While one may anticipate labour shedding as part of the privatisation process, the overall welfare gains and losses are complex and depend on many factors and assumptions. For example, if labour shedding does lead to higher productivity, lower prices and a better product, demand may expand and the labour force with it. Hachette, Lüders and Tagle (1993) in a study of five

(1996, p. 60) argues that there has been a much larger reduction in public sector employment, but that as a result of the increased control of the economy from the president's office, the state is now stronger than it was in the past.

[29] See Devlin (1994) for a general discussion of privatisation programmes in Latin America and Van der Hoeven and Sziraczki (1997) on privatisation and labour issues. On Peru, see the chapters by Abugattas and Kisic in this volume.

[30] According to UN (1996, Table III-1), the value of Peruvian privatisations (in million US dollars and as a percentage of all privatisations in Latin America) was 3 (0.01%) in 1991, 208 (1.39%) in 1992, 317 (3.11%) in 1993, 2,578 (30.23%) in 1994 and 946 (25.07%) in 1995. As the volume of total privatisations in Latin America declined from a peak of 16.7 billion US dollars in 1991 to 3.8 billion US dollars in 1995, Peru's programme became the largest individual component.

privatised Chilean enterprises between 1973 and 1989 show that while employment in one enterprise fell from 11,900 in 1973 to 4,402 in 1984, it had recovered somewhat to 5,453 in 1989 and that overall, for the other four enterprises, total employment fell from 17,617 in 1973 to 7,421 in 1984 and had increased to 14,224 in 1989.

Clearly post-privatisation employment will depend on the nature of the activity in which the enterprise is involved. If it is a high technology, capital intensive business, such as telecommunications, it is likely that privatisation will lead to more capital investment in computer technology and a demand for a relatively smaller but more highly trained labour force.[31]

Social security and pension reform

Writing in 1992 in a comparison of the situation in Costa Rico, Mexico and Peru, Carmelo Mesa-Lago was not optimistic about the feasibility of extending the social security system in Peru to cover the UIS, as it was not capable even of providing for the needs of those in the UFS:

> The financial situation of the Peruvian Social Security Institute (IPSS, Instituto Peruano de Seguridad Social) is the most unsuitable for extension. The sickness-maternity program has a permanent deficit covered by transfers from the pension program, which has thus suffered gradual capital depletion. The latter has generally had a surplus, but this is decreasing in comparison to income and, in 1988, the two programs faced a serious crisis. The 1988 emergency plan tried to restore the balance by increasing contributions to both programs, tightening control of evasion and arrears, improving investment profitability, complying with the state's obligations, and reducing staff costs. However, the serious economic crisis in 1988, a rate of inflation of around 2,000 percent and the high rate of contribution (higher than Mexico's) jeopardized the success of this plan (Mesa-Lago, 1992, p. 201).

The impact of the earlier social security and pensions system on the labour market came in the form of the contributions paid by both the employer and the employee as a component in labour costs.[32] Mesa-Lago (1994, p. 40, Table 2.7) notes that in 1989-90, while employees were supposed to contribute 6% of wages or income, for employers the figure was 16%, which was the fourth highest level in Latin America behind Argentina (31%), Uruguay (25.5-33.5%) and Brazil (17.8-18.8%) and about the same level as Colombia (14.5-17.8%). In 1986 in Peru, 68.9% of contributions came from employers, which was a marginally larger percentage than Mexico (68.8%) and considerably larger than

---

[31] Having surveyed a number of studies of the labour market effects of privatisations in developing and transitional economies, Van der Hoeven and Sziraczki (1997) conclude that while the short-run effects on employment are either negative or preserve the status quo, it is less clear what will happen in the longer run.

[32] Marshall (1991) noted that over 70% of private sector workers on temporary contracts were not protected by the social security system as they were not affiliated to the IPSS.

other Latin American countries, such as El Salvador (52.9%), Colombia (52.7%), Brazil (52.5%) and Costa Rica (49.2%). At the other extreme was Chile with employers contributing only 2.0% to the system (Mesa-Lago, 1994, p. 42, Table 2.8).

The model used by a number of Latin American countries when planning reforms of their social security and pension systems is that developed in Chile, which moved from a state system to one that depends largely on private social insurance (see Mesa-Lago, 1994, 1997 and Arenas de Mesa and Bertranou, 1997).

In Peru, the reform of the state system has not followed the Chilean route entirely, but has set out to establish a private insurance scheme alongside the existing state system. In November 1991, a decree-law was enacted by the executive to introduce a private pension scheme that was almost identical with the Chilean one and included a number of features, such as lower employer contributions, that were incentives for employers to pressure employees into joining the private scheme. This scheme was scheduled to come into operation on 28 July 1992, but after the 1992 *autogolpe* a new decree-law (published on 16 July 1992) replaced the 1991 law with one that moved closer to the Chilean system by making it mandatory to join the private scheme for those who had not previously been insured in the state scheme and for all new entrants to the labour force and those who ceased to be covered by the state scheme. Mandatory employer contributions were replaced with voluntary ones. By 1995, about 29% of those who were insured were in the private scheme and that percentage will grow over time.

The changes in the social security and pension systems will affect the labour market through the potential reduction in labour costs to employers as contributions are shifted away from employers and onto employees. Workers who transferred from the state to the private scheme were given a salary increase to compensate them for paying a larger contribution to replace the employers' component, so employers will not make all the gains in the short run. However, in the long run, as new entrants come to dominate the work force, the gains to employers should be substantial.

All of these reforms and changes are relevant to the UFS, but leave those in the UIS largely where they were – outside the private system and dependent on the state system, if they have access to it. To the extent that Peru moves towards the Chilean system and transfers state funds to the private sector in social security, the poor and needy who are dependent upon the state for what little they can get may be worse off. To the extent that the private schemes are not required to accept high risk cases, such as the old and the sick, those who are excluded from the new system may lose their access to health care and financial support, even though this may have been limited in scope under state schemes. This constitutes a further dimension of social exclusion.

Conclusions

Having described some important features of the urban labour market in Peru, it is time to summarise the evidence relating to the questions raised at the beginning of this chapter. A summary of the conclusions is presented in Table 5. Obviously, such a presentation is impressionistic and, in the case of the third question, sustainability is speculative.

Table 5. Summary of Conclusions on the Effects of President Alberto Fujimori on the Peruvian Urban Labour Market

Variable	Different to before 1990 in Peru?	Different to policies in other LA countries?	Sustainable/ reversible?
Employment: high levels of unemployment and underemployment	No	No	In theory reversible
Structure: large UIS and growing informality	No	No	In theory reversible
Wages: erosion of real minimum wage	No	No	In principle reversible, if a government decides to legislate an increase
Labour relations: growing use of temporary contracts and weak trade unions	Yes	Varies	Probably reversible
Privatisation: reduction of number of state enterprises	Yes and No	No	Probably sustainable
Social security: private pension and insurance schemes	Yes	No	Probably sustainable

(i) Is what is happening to the labour market under the Fujimori government really different from what went before?

With respect to employment, the structure of the labour market and wages, the answer is *no* as the major discontinuity with the past occurred during 1988-89 before Fujimori came to power. While the move towards increased flexibility in the labour market has been encouraged by Fujimori, it was started under the presidency of Alan García. Considering labour relations, the answer is *yes*, as the number of strikes, the number of workers involved and hours lost in industrial action have all been lower since 1990 than they have been since the early 1970s. Concerning privatisation, the reaction of Belaúnde and his advisors to the extension of the state that occurred under the military government between 1968 and 1980 was to favour privatisation. However, very little was achieved (see Crabtree, 1992) and what is new about the Fujimori government's privatisation programme is its speed and full-blooded commitment. Finally, the introduction of a private social insurance scheme in parallel with the state system does represent a new development. The point to stress is that the economic chaos and the hyperinflation that characterised the final years of the García administration had a profound political effect that allowed Fujimori to undertake economic measures that would have been blocked by opposition forces in earlier years.

(ii) Is what is happening to the labour market under the Fujimori government different from/the same as what is happening/has happened in other Latin American countries?

Here the answer is *no* with respect to all but one of the variables considered. High levels of unemployment and underemployment have existed in many Latin American countries, which have also experienced an expansion in the relative size of the UIS and falling real minimum wages. Privatisation is part of the structural adjustment programme in many Latin American countries and a number of them have introduced some degree of private insurance cover into their social security and pension systems. With respect to labour relations, the picture has been mixed. Some countries, such as Venezuela, have witnessed widespread national protests against the introduction of structural adjustment programmes, while others have seen less industrial resistance to change.

(iii) How sustainable/reversible are the changes?

Turning from what has happened to what might happen is to move into the realm of speculation and the interaction of predictions concerning future economic events and possible political reactions to them.

With respect to employment, the structure of the labour market and wages, standard economic trade theory would predict that as Peru has a surplus of labour to capital it should move towards an exporting structure involving more labour-intensive production and this should lead to more employment. The majority of workers in the UIS are in commerce and services, which are mainly non-traded, and as the terms-of-trade move against non-traded goods there should be a movement of workers out of the UIS.

However, in the short run, there is not much evidence of this happening in other countries that have been involved in export oriented readjustment, such as Chile. It is possible that success in export markets may involve competition in moderately capital-intensive activities, since in many manufacturing activities, such as clothing and the production of sports goods, labour is even cheaper in parts of Asia and Africa and countries in Latin America may not have a comparative advantage in labour. On balance, it seems reasonable to predict that Peru will continue with high levels of underemployment, a large UIS and low wages for some years.

Wages represent another area in which different outcomes are possible. On the one hand, in a free market economy, an excess supply of labour is likely to keep wages at a low level in the short run. On the other, it would be possible for a president with a different political agenda to reactivate the Real Minimum Wage at a level at which it would become a binding constraint on the labour market.

Labour relations have been less troubled under Fujimori than during the 1980s and this may reflect a combination of the failure of the trade unions to protect their members from the effects of the hyperinflation and the increasing number of workers now on temporary and other short-term contracts. This is likely to continue in the short-run unless the unions are able to find an issue around which to rebuild support or a new president is elected with a mandate to reactivate the trade unions.

The privatisation programme is likely to be sustainable. It is a major component in structural adjustment programmes and it seems unlikely that a president would be elected with a programme to re-nationalise enterprises that have been privatised or extend a process of nationalisation to new enterprises, though a new administration might slow down the speed and extent of privatisation and hence change the nature of the programme.

The social security programme is also likely to be sustainable. As the proportion of the labour force in the private insurance scheme grows, it will become more difficult to reverse the process back to a state pension and social security system.

Three of the variables analysed in this chapter (employment, the structure of the labour market and wages) are largely outside the control of the president and his government and hence the changes in these variables were not intentional, as they commenced before 1990. The changes in labour contracts, privatisation and the social security system were intentional.

Could the changes have been avoided? Yes, in the case of privatisation and the reform of the social security system, since the initiative came from the government and wages could have been indexed. However, these policies would have been inconsistent with the overall economic policy of the government. It is less clear in the case of the other variables. The major changes occurred before 1990, so the question is not could Fujimori have avoided the changes, but could he have reversed them or lessened their impact on the labour market?

It is difficult to see how he could have reversed the trends within the labour market, given the constraints of a structural adjustment programme, and still maintained the confidence of the international bankers. The severe negative effects of García's heterodox economic programme on the Peruvian economy suggest that there is no easy fix.

However, once the economy had been brought under control, it might have been possible to devote more resources to reducing the high level of poverty directly, through special work schemes or other programmes that targeted the poor. This was a feature of the adjustment process in Chile under the military dictatorship and seems to have reduced the basic level of poverty there (see Graham, 1993). In August 1991, Foncodes (Fondo de Compensación y Desarrollo Social) was established with funds from a 425 million dollar trade sector loan from the Inter-American Development Bank to 'finance ... social investment projects in matters of employment, health, nutrition, basic education and other areas benefitting the population in poverty' (Kay, 1996, p. 78). This was controlled from the presidential office and while Kay suggests there was a high correlation between the location and scale of public works programmes and Fujimori's vote in the 1995 election, he concludes that 'a deepening alliance between the executive and a more politised military, combined with the creation of agencies linked to the executive branch, the recentralisation of authority, and the disintegration of the party system afforded Fujimori the opportunity to use the state's economic resources to enact a sweeping programme of social investment and infrastructure reform' (*Ibid.*, p. 89).

In Peru, polls of Fujimori's popularity tend to be carried out in Lima and may not fully represent the views of voters outside the capital, but opinion does seem to have shifted and some of those who supported the 1995 re-election of the man who had stopped the hyperinflation in 1990 may have become frustrated with the situation of 'jobless growth', in which Peru's GDP rises by impressive increments, but high levels of underemployment continue.

Adolfo Figueroa has pointed out the problem of 'social exclusion' that greatly complicates the process of economic advancement for many in Peru (see Figueroa, 1995, and Figueroa, Altimirano and Sulmont, 1996). The failure of the Fujimori government to provide support for the poor may undermine the will of the voters to continue with the neo-liberal experiment. This is a danger that may affect other countries which have few winners and many losers in the short-run and where income inequality exacerbates the problem:

> With slower growth, perhaps brought on by the pressing need to correct balance of payment deficits, the problems of income distribution may yet lead to the gradual unravelling of neo-liberalism. The test that lies ahead is whether the neo-liberal paradigm proves sufficiently adaptable to define a constructive role for the state in strengthening the balance of payments, redistributing income and establishing foundations for sustainable growth without reverting to the excesses of the past. ... Declining growth rates in the region suggest that Latin American governments have been living on borrowed time as well as borrowed money (Bird and Helwege, 1996, pp. 32-3).

The politics of Latin American countries provides many examples of presidential candidates who promise much, in terms of economic reform and progress, but fail so dramatically and cause so much economic damage that one may ask how they could possibly have been elected. One would hope that Peru will not be blessed by such a president in the future. However, given past history, one can only hope.

PART IV

INSTITUTIONS

CHAPTER 9

Justice, Legality and Judicial Reform

Javier de Belaúnde

Justice and governability: the conditions for judicial reform

The judiciary in Peru suffers from low public esteem. Even though this is by no means a new problem, in recent years it has been one of the institutions which has inspired least public confidence. In part, at least, this distrust is a historical problem. The judiciary has never enjoyed the political autonomy required for it to protect individual rights against abuse by the state or from the excesses of the country's rulers. One of the reasons for this – but not the only one – has been the interference in the appointment of judges. In the 1979 Constitution, the president was given the right to nominate judges, members of superior courts (*vocales superiores*) and the Supreme Court (*vocales supremos*) from a list of names suggested by the Consejo Nacional de la Magistratura. In the case of the Supreme Court, presidential nominees needed to be approved by the Senate. Prior to 1979, the system was essentially the same. The use of these powers by the executive has reinforced the political dependence of the judiciary.

Another historical characteristic of the judiciary has been a lack of adequate funding and poor working conditions. Although legally the judiciary has a right to a certain proportion of all budget outlays, in practice this has never been applied. Inadequate funding has meant low wages for those working in the judiciary, often dilapidated or inappropriate buildings, poor working conditions and the lack of documentary back-up. Frequently, the judicial authorities lack even the resources to acquire the official gazette in which all legal dispositions are published. The judiciary has suffered years of neglect under successive governments. More than just a coincidence, this would seem to reflect politicians' distaste for a strong, assertive judiciary. The internal organisation of the judicial system is also archaic and irrational, with some Lima judges burdened with case-loads of up to 5,000 cases.

A consequence of these conditions is that corruption is widespread throughout the judiciary, exacerbated in recent years by the extent of drug-related crime. At the same time, the capabilities of many judges appear to have declined. This is hardly surprising in view of their very poor remuneration. Most lawyers with a reasonable training are attracted by the lure of the private sector, where working conditions and pay are infinitely better than in the public sector.

Legal procedures are also often obsolete and inappropriate to the needs of the population. Proceedings can drag on for long periods, normally to the detriment of those demanding justice and to the benefit of those who have violated the law.

As a consequence there is a very large prison population awaiting trial. The view is entrenched that the justice system is slow and unreliable. Verdicts are by no means predictable from judges who are often ill-equipped to deal with the cases that come before them. The problem is partly one of ignorance of pertinent aspects of the law, but more often one of ideology. Typically, judges are hidebound by an overly formal application of legal norms and are reluctant to give opinions on problems in which law and reality appear to be at odds. Furthermore, litigants frequently simply ignore the rulings of judges.

Consequently, most people have little faith in the workings of the judicial system, even when they are able to gain access to it. The man in the street sees the law as something arcane, remote and divorced from his everyday interests. Many people therefore seek to avoid the justice system, preferring to resolving their problems in informal ways which, often, are simply illegal. In so doing, they further undermine the rule of law, which ultimately is the guarantor of a democratic system.

Long neglected, the problems afflicting the judiciary have been a source of considerable discussion in recent years. A number of factors help explain this interest. Perhaps one of the most obvious is the increase in the incidence of violence. Spurred by terrorism, drug trafficking and the increase in common crime, this has posed a threat to the very existence of a democratic state. It has become evident that human rights and freedoms mean little without an operative, democratically inspired justice system. It has also become clear that a market-based economic system cannot work unless specific rights are respected and enforced. Such concerns have led to something of a consensus that without an independent and efficient justice system, there can be no democracy.

Some of these concerns were aired in a report known as 'Agenda Perú', whose authors stated that 'the institutional framework of Peruvian society has shown itself incapable of responding to rapid social change over the last four decades. Over this time, the forms by which power is exercised and authority wielded with regard to economic and social matters has collapsed. Peru has had to confront a series of crises of democratic governability and good governance' (Sagasti, 1994 p. 30). Thus the whole question of governability emerges, understood as the possibility for power to be exercised efficiently, efficaciously and legitimately in the pursuit of economic and social objectives. This is tightly bound up with the question of legitimacy, or 'the sense that the citizens recognise the right of those who rule over them to exercise power and authority, and that they identify with the institutions of the state, so long as these are subject themselves to certain pre-agreed limits and respect for the rules of the game' (Sagasti, 1994, p. 20). The report goes on to state that 'probably the most serious obstacle to the population identifying itself with the institutions of the state has been the inoperance, the arbitrariness and the corruption of the judiciary'.

It is for this reason that in civil society the notion is growing that governability requires the creation of institutions that enjoy strong legitimacy, especially in the justice system. The demand for judicial reform has thus gained momentum, not just in professional and academic circles, but within society as a whole. These demands have met with a government response. Our aim here is to examine the strengths and limitations of that response.

Whilst there may be a growing consensus in Peru about the need for judicial reform, there is less agreement on what this means, still less in designing specific policies to carry it out. Basically, the judiciary should fulfil two main functions: to ensure the supremacy of the constitution and respect for basic rights, and to provide a mechanism for the resolution of conflicts between individuals. In view of the problems of violence, human rights abuse, impunity and the need to respond to rapid changes in society, judicial reform, is not just a problem of improved procedures and greater technification, but the establishment of a system by which citizens can depend on the rule of law (Binder, 1993, pp. 245 et seq.). For this reason, any reform has to be based on such fundamental principles as the unity of jurisdiction, the impartiality of judges, the exclusivity of their jurisdiction and the use of specific jurisdictions for those specific purposes only. Judicial autonomy is a key principle, with judges acting within established hierarchical norms. For this, three basic guarantees need to be met: (i) judges are bound by the judicial norms set out in the constitution and to adjudicate strictly in accordance with constitutional principles; (ii) judges should not be subject to dismissal, unless they fail to carry out their allotted tasks; and (iii) levels of remuneration should be guaranteed to remove the threat of other powers undermining judicial autonomy by manipulating the pay received by judges.

Judicial reform should be structural and multi-dimensional. These dimensions include (i) a normative dimension: the law itself must set out the principles of jurisdiction and the way it is organised, providing a legal system that responds to the demands placed upon it; (ii) an administrative dimension: the introduction of administrative systems that relieve judges of responsibility for endless non-judicial tasks, leaving them time to dedicate themselves to judicial activities; (iii) an informational dimension: although the use of computerised information systems is not the solution to the judiciary's problems, they would help make the system more efficient; (iv) a statistical dimension: linked to the previous point, the adequate use of statistical information is an important adjunct in the formulation of policies and other aspects of planning; (v) an infrastructural dimension: courts and other places where hearings are conducted should provide good facilities, especially for those accused; and (vi) a financial dimension: the justice system needs to have the funds required for it to operate adequately.

The Fujimori government and the judiciary (1990-95)

From his inaugural speech to Congress on 28 July 1990 onwards, President

Alberto Fujimori adopted a critical stance towards the judiciary, echoing public concerns about the performance of judges. For this reason, it is important to analyse how the Fujimori government responded to the challenge of judicial reform, especially in light of the opening up of the economy to the international market.

Between 1990 and 1992, the government promoted a number of reforms that affected the judiciary. These included a General Law of the Judiciary (*Ley Orgánica del Poder Judicial*), a new penal code, a Civil Procedural Code (*Código Procesal Civil*) and a Criminal Procedural Code (*Código Procesal Penal*).[1]

The General Law of the Judiciary, dealing with judicial organisation, was promulgated in 1991, the result of a lengthy period of discussion. It was a serious attempt to strengthen the judiciary institutionally. In particular, the new law made a number of administrative changes within the judiciary, designed to overcome its inability to plan ahead and spearhead reforms from within. Previously, the administrative functions within the judiciary had not been clearly set apart from those of jurisdiction. To this end, the new law established an Executive Committee (Consejo Ejecutivo de Poder Judicial) with responsibility for forward planning and other administrative functions. Although some of the individual innovations included in the law were not ideal, in general it represented a serious attempt to grapple with a number of major problems.

The Civil procedural core, along with the new penal code, established a solid system of penal guarantees. The Criminal procedural core also introduced important reforms to systems of penal procedure, putting the public prosecutor's office (Ministerio Público) in charge of penal investigations for adjudication by a penal judge.

However, the palace coup (*autogolpe*) of April 1992 interrupted the implementation of the new General Law, whilst lack of finance impeded implementation of the Civil procedural core. A number of legislative changes (not just in relation to terrorism but also other special penal regimes) ended in disfiguring the penal code. According to one authority, this represented 'the consolidation of authoritarian penal law' (Rivera Paz, 1997, p. 21). Furthermore, largely because of pressures from the police, which did not wish to be beholden to the public prosecutor's office, as well as because of a lack of resources, the Criminal procedural core, promulgated in 1991, had yet to take effect in 1997.

Fujimori's speech on 5 April 1992, justifying his actions against the legislative and judicial branches, laid considerable stress on judicial corruption, arguing that judges were incompetent, partisan and even accomplices in terrorism. A few days later, most of the judges of the Supreme Court were

---

[1]   The Congress of Peru's new website (http://www.congreso.gob.pe/congreso/leyes/leyes.htm) contains an archive of all Peru's laws.

dismissed, along with the attorney-general (*Fiscal de la Nación*), the judges of the Tribunal of Constitutional Guarantees (set up under the 1979 Constitution), the members of the Consejo Nacional de la Magistratura and a large number of other judges at lower levels in the judicial hierarchy. Thereafter, the government proceeded to nominate new provisional members of the Supreme Court, who were given authority to dismiss judges of lesser rank. Many judges were therefore removed from their posts without right of appeal, and replaced by provisional designees.

Yet again, it seemed that judicial reform had been interpreted largely as a change of personnel. Not only was the coup, in itself, unconstitutional, but it replaced judges with a number of provisional appointees in a way that was the very antithesis of respect for judicial autonomy.

The *autogolpe* also paved the way for the promulgation of wide-ranging new anti-terrorist laws and the creation of a special system of justice to deal with this problem. Public criticism of the workings of the justice system had extended to its role in dealing with terrorism. An important study on this pointed out that: 'one of the state institutions which had suffered most severe criticism from public opinion with regard to its incapacity to deal with terrorism in recent years has been the judiciary. Delays in passing sentence, leniency, poor judicial decisions with regard to those accused of terrorism, as well as corruption and the tendency of some judges to accede to blackmail in not condemning those accused of drug-trafficking and terrorism, as well as some political authorities are facts ... The government's decision to put the trial of terrorists and those accused of treason in the hands of military tribunals was the direct consequence of the low public estimation of the judicial process' (Cobián Vidal, 1993, pp. 30-8).

The first laws designed to repress terrorism date from 1981 and 1987. Investigations were put in the hands of public prosecutors (*fiscales*) and trials were conducted in ordinary courts, with due concern for the rights of those accused. However, it became clear that 'by skilful use of legal and democratic procedures, known members of terrorist organisations were on occasions absolved by judges on the grounds of inadequate evidence' (Cobián Vidal, 1993, p. 36).

The new penal codes introduced in 1991 sought to deal with the problem of terrorism. Nevertheless, according to Cobián Vidal, the new code introduced 'norms that gave guarantees to those accused, including those of terrorism. The provisions were suspended by the anti-terrorist legislation promulgated after April 5 ... According to the government authorities, the norms of the penal code were insufficient within a context of internal war'. After the *autogolpe*, the penal codes relating to terrorism were radically changed. A new law was drafted which defined and punished terrorism. The minimum penalty was 20 years in prison with a maximum of life imprisonment. Military tribunals were put in charge of judging those accused of terrorism, whilst the charge of treason *(traición a la patria)* for terrorist leaders was included. As Cobián Vidal puts it 'you have to remember that the repression of terrorism in Peru takes place within a general framework of legislation of states of emergency, in which the armed forces are given responsibility for re-establishing domestic order upset by subversion' (Cobián Vidal, 1993, p. 37).

As part of its attempts to construct new institutions in the wake of the *autogolpe*, the government called elections at the end of 1992 for what it called a Democratic Constituent Congress (CCD), which had responsibility for writing a new constitution (put subsequently to a referendum) as well as acting as a normal legislative assembly. The elections resulted in a large majority for the supporters of Fujimori.[2]

With respect to the widespread dismissals of members of the judiciary, a somewhat *sui generis* mechanism was introduced to deal with this problem. In March 1993, pending ratification of the new constitution, the Congress approved a constitutional law by which it established the Jurado de Honor de la Magistratura on a transitional basis, whose tasks included: (i) receiving appeals from members of the Supreme Court who had been dismissed; (ii) evaluating those who had been appointed on a provisional basis and reporting back to Congress; (iii) producing a list of nominees for other members of the Supreme Court whom the Congress would finally ratify; and (iv) receiving appeals from judges from other levels and organising a public forum to designate vacancies.

The appointment to the Jurado[3] of five jurists, all with a reputation for independence and moral rectitude, did much to allay fears and raise hopes that there would be an improvement in the functioning of the judicial system. Nevertheless, the Congress would have to respect the non-partisan views of the Jurado. Initially, the Jurado could only fulfil the first of these four tasks. In receiving appeals from those dismissed from the Supreme Court, it resolved (and its decision was upheld by Congress) that none of those who had been dismissed should be reappointed. Thereafter, in evaluating the role of the provisional members of the Supreme Court, the Jurado came to the conclusion that five of its eleven members should be reappointed without the necessity of other candidates being publicly sought. Congress received this suggestion, but months passed before it pronounced on the matter. Eventually, it chose to reserve judgement until such time that the Jurado produced a list of new names. Subsequently, Congress decided to prorogue the Jurado and let it nominate new members. Thus, following months of delay, the Jurado designated nine new members of the Supreme Court, as well as a large number of judges and public prosecutors in the Lima judicial district. Although the latter were responsible for over one-half of the total number of cases presented, this left provisional judges in post elsewhere. The appointments made by the Jurado were, by and large, good ones and relatively free of political bias.

---

[2]   This is dealt with more fully by John Crabtree in Chapter 1 in this volume.

[3]   Trazegnies Granda (1996), pp. 81-94, gives greater detail of the activities of the Jurado del Honor de la Magistratura.

In October 1993, the referendum on the new constitution was held, approving it by a narrow margin. Although by and large the 1993 Constitution upheld the overall design of the judicial system, it included modifications to it. An important change was to give to the Consejo Nacional de la Magistratura the faculty of selecting and appointing judges. Thus, to the surprise of many, politicians relinquished control over one of the mechanisms which had helped them subordinate the judiciary. This represented an important advance. Another useful innovation was the establishment of the Academia de la Magistratura to provide training to those seeking to enter the judiciary and further training to those already within it. The establishment of the post of 'Defensor del Pueblo', a sort of ombudsman, was widely greeted as a positive step, as was the creation of a new Constitutional Tribunal to undertake similar functions to the old Tribunal of Constitutional Guarantees. Also worthy of note was the decision to recognise legally the authorities of peasant and jungle indian communities, along with their codes of customary law.

At the same time, the new constitution created new norms which affected the unity and exclusivity of the judicial branch. For instance, Article 139 repealed the earlier rule that military tribunals were barred from trying civilians, except in cases of those seeking to evade military service or guilty of treason in times of foreign war. The 1993 Constitution (Article 173) allowed military tribunals to judge civilians in cases of treason or terrorism. In the case of treason, this was no longer to be limited to cases of conflict with other countries, its application being extended to internal conflict.[4]

Reforms in practice (1995-97)

We have seen how Fujimori took up the issue of judicial reform as a matter of national concern from the earliest days of his presidency. For the first time since the military government of 1968, the government treated this as a priority issue. Initially, reform was instituted using conventional legislative means. After 1992, more high-handed methods were used to substitute personnel and to hand over particularly sensitive areas of the law to special jurisdictions (in this case, military courts). The military government had used such tactics in the 1970s, substituting judges, announcing the reorganisation of the judiciary and setting up specific jurisdictions (like agrarian and labour courts) in specific areas of the law.

In 1995, following Fujimori's re-election victory, there were signs that the government was seeking to introduce a more systematic reform. In this, it received enthusiastic backing from the World Bank, the Inter-American Development Bank (IDB) and the United Nations Development Programme (UNDP), all of which released funding for judicial reforms. For such agencies,

---

[4]   In May 1998, a law was passed that extended this regime in a bid to crack down on common crime.

this was congruent with other policy recommendations, especially in the economic sphere. Foreign observers tended to be somewhat bemused by the way in which a market economy was being espoused, along with respect for the rule of law, without there being an efficient and active judiciary that commanded wide respect. How could a market economy function, if there was no authority which guaranteed the fulfilment of contracts, punished those who infringed them and provided some sort of compensation for those affected by non-compliance? How could a market function unless economic agents and citizens generally were confident of legal remedies if attacked in the street or involved in a traffic accident? What sort of rule of law could there be where the judiciary is tied to decisions made by government diktat and incapable of countermanding the decisions of those in power? How could the virtues of democracy be proclaimed without means for people to resist government excesses or uphold individual liberties? (Bustamante, 1993).

In November 1995, by means of law 26546, the Comisión Ejecutiva del Poder Judicial was established (whose functions were subsequently widened) to initiate reforms in the administrative sphere. For the period of a year, the commission took over control of the administration of the judiciary, thus substituting for the Consejo Ejecutivo set up as a consequence of the General Law. It was formed by three members of the Supreme Court, the presidents of each of its three divisions, who were to continue as commission members even when no longer presidents of those divisions. The commission also elected an executive secretary who would be responsible for the judiciary's budget and whose precise functions were to be specified at a later date in a more detailed law. In Peru, the person with the responsibility for budgets is always the top executive official, since he is the person whose job it is to develop the activities and functions of the entity in question, set targets each year, distribute budget resources and who, ultimately, is responsible for the uses to which those resources are put. Previously, in the judiciary, this had been the responsibility of the president of the Supreme Court. The person appointed executive secretary was a retired admiral, José Dellepiane, who had previously run various other public sector departments.

In June 1996, Congress approved Law 26623, establishing the Consejo de Coordinación Judicial, whose initial remit included the power to increase the functions and responsibilities of the Comisión Ejecutiva del Poder Judicial,[5] and that of its executive secretary. These new functions included the ability to regulate matters concerning the courts (*despacho judicial*), career structures and

[5]   The law has 5 articles and 12 transitional dispositions. The articles define the composition and functions of the definitive CCJ, which is made up from organisations and institutions related to the judiciary. They were made responsible for (amongst other things) coordinating the overall development of institutions working in the fields of justice. In the transitional norms, however, a transitional CCJ was established, made up from the judiciary, the public prosecutor's office (Ministerio Público), the Consejo de la Magistratura and an executive secretary. This organisation was given responsibility for the reorganisation of the administration of justice. It was to exist until December 1998, although the law anticipates that this limit could be prorogued.

the status of judges. It could also dismiss judges who do not carry out their duties in a correct fashion.[6] At the same time, the recently-established Academia de la Magistratura was included in the reorganisation, and the functions of its ruling council were to be assumed by the executive secretary of the Comisión Ejecutiva.

Even though formally we might be able to conclude that the decision to reorganise the judiciary and substitute many of its authorities was compatible with constitutional norms, a number of fundamental problems arose:

1.   The way in which the reforms were enacted. Both were approved by the single-chamber Congress without debate either on the floor of the chamber or in the media. It was therefore impossible to achieve a consensus amongst those involved.

2.   The way in which members of the Comisión Ejecutiva were chosen, on the basis not of the job they had to perform but who they were. Its members continued to be members of the commission even when they were no longer holding the office which had allowed them to become members in the first place.

3.   Depriving the president of the Supreme Court of responsibility for budgets. This key function was given to a more lowly official, who had already amassed wide-ranging powers.[7]

4.   The ignoring of views of important institutions in the legal sphere, including universities and the College of Lawyers.

5.   The establishment of a transitional institution with powers that affected the autonomy of the judiciary.

6.   The granting of new functions to the Academia de la Magistratura. The law creating the Consejo de Coordinación Judicial gave the Academia the additional role of evaluating the suitability of judges to occupy their posts. The attributes of the Academia had been clearly set out in the constitution. In our view, this clashed directly with the guarantees in the constitution regarding the status of the judiciary[8] and with the constitutional role of the Consejo Nacional de la Magistratura to ratify appointments. This requirement created instability amongst judges since it rendered their jobs

---

[6]   This attribute was declared unconstitutional by the Constitutional Tribunal on 6 November 1996. This declared that the ability to dismiss judges was an exclusive function of the Consejo Nacional de la Magistratura. However, dismissal for non-fulfilment of duties in accordance with Article 214 of the Basic Law could be included amongst the attributes of the Comisión Ejecutiva. The constitutional attributes of the Consejo Nacional de la Magistratura in respect to the power to dismiss judges has since been modified, by Law No. 26933.

[7]   As of 1997, the detailed regulations as to exactly what were the functions and attributions of the executive secretary had still not been published in the official gazette.

[8]   The 1993 Constitution, in Article 146, guaranteed the autonomy of the judiciary subject to the constitution, the permanence of appointments (subject to consent from the judiciary itself and subject to satisfactory fulfilment of duties) and remuneration which assures the incumbent a 'standard of living worthy of his mission and status'.

subject to the will of the Comisión Ejecutiva. At the same time, we believe that the new role given to the Academia extended its faculties into areas well beyond those of teaching and training.

Although the reforms were originally couched in administrative terms, in fact they went well beyond this. According to a document published by the executive secretary of the Consejo de Coordinación Judicial, entitled 'Integral Plan for the Reform of the Judiciary', the objective was to achieve a judiciary geared towards 'the demand for judicial services which protects the rights of the citizen, and which the citizen will find accessible, speedy, fair and efficient' (Consejo de Coordinación Judicial, 1997, pp. 3-4). Nevertheless, this was linked with administrative aspects. The document went on to say that: 'the strategy of the reforms in the process of modernising the structures of the judiciary are centred on administrative aspects, with emphasis on organisational and technological needs, breaking traditional paradigms and oriented to giving priority to serving the citizen' (ibid, p. 4).

Thus, the Comisión Ejecutiva had defined three areas of action for itself. The first of these was administrative reform, the objective of which was to establish an efficient organisation that responded to the needs of the justice system. In this context, attempts were made to introduce business practices derived from the private sector by means of the establishment of a general management team. The objective was that rationalisation in the use of personnel would lead to higher productivity. A scheme for voluntary redundancies was introduced amongst administrative and auxiliary staffs, coupled with internal programmes for the retraining of employees. The objectives also included the creation of systems of oversight and control, financial administration and incentives for productivity. Furthermore, the reforms sought to define a new, more decentralised organisational structure, develop more efficient systems for documentation, introduce greater use of mechanised systems of information and computation, and upgrade premises etc. In this respect, too, the idea was to implement anti-corruption programmes.

The second reform related to the system of judicial back-up aimed to help judges improve the services they offered the public. These reforms related to a number of specific areas, including (i) reduction of the backlog of cases by creating temporary courts *(salas transitorias)* in the Supreme Court and superior courts, in the ad hoc teams of judges *(juzgados transitorios de carácter colectivo)* and a specialist court to deal with drug trafficking offences; (ii) to cut administrative paperwork through mechanisation and thus to reduce the length of trials; (iii) to provide greater back-up to judges through special teams of lawyers and assistants, as well as other qualified personnel; (iv) to revise the demarcation of judicial districts to enable them better to reflect demographic pressures and facilitate ease of access to legal services; and (v) to create alternative systems of justice, such as the establishment of centres for conciliation and mediation.

The third area related to improving the quality of judges. In this context, the idea was to encourage highly qualified and committed people to become judges by enhancing job stability in the legal profession. To this end, three main proposals were made: (i) the passage of a judicial career law, designed to provide more attractive working conditions; (ii) improvement in the training facilities available to judges, encouraging them to continue upgrading their capacities throughout their professional careers; and (iii) the creation of conditions to improve the 'ethical culture' of judges and thereby enhance their prestige in society.

As can easily be seen, the reforms sought to move from administrative areas into other spheres of judicial activity. At this point, it is worth stressing that never before had the political climate been so conducive to pushing ahead with a programme of reform. Never before had such assistance from abroad been available. And never before had the conviction of the need for change been so strong amongst the judges themselves.

Attempts were also mounted at this time to reform the state prosecution service, the Ministerio Público. Law 26623, which set up the Consejo de Coordinación Judicial, declared that the Ministerio Público was to be reorganised. Following the model of the judiciary, it too set up a Comisión Ejecutiva. And, in similar fashion, the government had someone in mind to head it. In 1992, days after the *autogolpe*, Fujimori dismissed the then attorney-general and replaced him with a personal appointment, Nélida Colán Maguino, who was successively reappointed through special laws extending her mandate successively until 1996. As a consequence of Law 26623, Colán was appointed president of the Comisión Ejecutiva of the Ministerio Público. During 1996, a number of legal changes were decreed which, in practice, removed many of the functions previously conducted by the attorney-general and gave them to the Comisión Ejecutiva. These included responsibility for managing reforms in the Ministerio Público, managing it on a day-to-day basis and taking control over budgetary matters. Then, subsequently, Law 26738 suspended most of the other remaining functions left in the hands of the attorney-general, reducing this post to a pale shadow of its former status.

There can be no doubt that these reforms, both in the judiciary and in the Ministerio Público, had some positive results. First and foremost, they broke the climate of inertia which had pervaded the judicial system. Also, they had favourable consequences in improving administrative methods through the adoption of more business-like attitudes and the implementation of a greater degree of administrative control in ways that would have been hard to imagine previously. Progress had been made in upgrading the physical infrastructure of the judiciary and providing it with more modern systems of technology. Steps had also been taken to reduce the numbers of those held in prison without trial, including the creation of new courts and the trial of prisoners within prison itself. A number of studies had been carried out to improve understanding of the judiciary's financial needs and to come up with suggestions of how best to meet them. In the area of training, the Comité Ejecutivo had backed a variety of courses for judges, in coordination with the Academia de la Magistratura, even though failing to provide an overall plan to meet future training needs.

Controversial changes in relations between judges and lawyers and in the redesign of court procedures had been presented by the Comisión Ejecutiva as promising greater transparency and helping to resolve problems of congestion. These claims still needed to be analysed with greater hindsight, but it appears that the 'cloistering' of judges and their isolation from lawyers led to a large numbers of problems which otherwise would have been avoided if there had been more contact. Meanwhile, there was a climate of chaos in the justice system. Whilst those involved said that these were teething problems and would be temporary, others argued that they arose from the poorly-conducted adoption of foreign models of jurisprudence, a problem made worse by the large numbers of new, inexperienced personnel.

Beyond such considerations, there were a number of aspects of the reform process which gave rise to concern. Firstly, there was a very marked centralisation in decision-making, amplified by the lack of proper public consultation. There were few means by which members of the judiciary could contribute to or make criticisms of the reforms. Secondly, the way in which the Comisiones Ejecutivas were established ran contrary to notions of transparency and renewal. To use laws to appoint specific people and to give them free rein throughout the process of reform was not, it seemed, the best way to uphold judicial autonomy.

At the same time, many of the basic premises behind the reforms (outlined above) were ignored in practice. In many instances, the fairness of trials was sacrificed to the demands of administrative efficiency; bit by bit, the process of reform had gone beyond what had seemed sensible objectives, especially with regard to the appointment and dismissal of judges and interference in their areas of competence and status. The provisional character of judges had been accentuated by requirements for them to serve elsewhere and by the policy of their 'rotation'. The fact that several judges may be involved in a single case undermines some of the principles of good justice upheld in the penal codes.

A number of innovations undermined the sense of job stability and security that judges required. An example was the adoption of a system of bonuses, designed to compensate for the lack of an adequate budget and to reward certain judges for 'productivity'. Not only did the use of bonuses show up the failure of the executive branch to provide the judiciary with adequate funding, but it opened the way to unfair influence and political manipulation. The process of weeding out poor judges also lent itself to executive interference, whilst the process of evaluation was open to abuse.

Conflicts of jurisdiction

A number of other problems arose as a consequence of the judicial response to the violation of human rights, the increased competence of military tribunals and attempts by the executive to influence the course of judicial decisions.

Human rights and impunity

The initiation of subversive attacks in May 1980 – selective killings, sabotage of state property, massacres of individuals, attacks on police and military installations, ambushes etc. – unleashed a spiral of violence that shook the whole country. Human rights organisations consistently denounced such practices as forced 'disappearance' and the indiscriminate use of torture in those parts of the country under military control. Such concerns were echoed by international agencies like the Inter-American Commission on Human Rights.

We have already mentioned the response of the judiciary to the problem of terrorism. Here we need to look at its role in relation to protecting individual rights and liberties against the activities of the security forces, as well as the response of political authorities when the judiciary was called upon to pronounce in such cases.

As the influence and radius of activity of Sendero Luminoso spread in the early 1980s, large parts of the country were declared 'emergency zones' in which individual guarantees were suspended in accordance with Article 231 of the 1979 Constitution. In December 1982, Law 23506 was promulgated with relation to rights of habeas corpus and defence (*amparo*). Article 38 of the law suspended these rights in cases of military intervention, creating considerable confusion over the extent to which this suspension affected the judicial rights of individuals affected (Eguiguren Praeli, 1989, p. 279).

A literal interpretation of the constitution and the law would lead to the conclusion that, during states of emergency, the threat to public order and society as a whole justified extraordinary measures. However, it was less clear whether judicial authorities could, having examined the circumstances, decide whether the use of those extraordinary faculties (powers that arose from the constitution and were designed to uphold the rule of law) was in proportion to the reasons for which states of emergency were established in the first place. On the literal interpretation, there would be absolutely no pretext for any involvement of the judicial authorities to protect individuals from abuse, irrespective of their constitutional duties.

Several studies have demonstrated the way in which Peruvian jurisprudence on the question of habeas corpus wavered towards the more restrictive interpretation, leaving the population in the emergency zones at the mercy of the extraordinary powers assumed by the executive branch.[9] It may seem

---

[9]   It is important to point out that this view did not go unchallenged, and that jurisprudence

paradoxical that judges, despite the job entrusted to them in the constitution, opted to accept such restrictions on their duties. However, judges are not people removed from the society in which they live, and their decisions are influenced by – amongst other things – their perception (conscious or not) of the problems affecting society. Often, it was not so much a question of violence itself which was at issue, but against whom it was directed and the degree of violence used (Tamayo and Vásquez, 1989, pp. 25-6).

In June 1995, Law 26479, better known as the Amnesty Law, was promulgated, in which Art. 1 extended an amnesty to all members of the armed forces, the police and to members of the public who had been denounced, were under investigation, tried or imprisoned for military or civilian crimes arising out of the fight against terrorism, whether acting alone or in a group, between May 1980 and the date of promulgation. At the time, a trial was pending for those responsible for the killing of 16 persons in the Barrios Altos district of Lima. These included members of the National Intelligence Service (SIN) convicted of the killing of a university professor and nine students at La Cantuta University in 1992. According to repeated accusations in the media and among human rights specialists, these two killings involved top military officers, as well as leading government officials.

The judge, Antonia Saquicuray considered the Amnesty Law inapplicable in this case, since she believed that it represented a clear violation of international treaties signed by Peru in defence of the rights and life of individuals, citing the superiority of the constitution over individual laws in cases in which these clashed. The reaction of the government was to promulgate Law 26492 a few days later. This represented a gross violation of the autonomy of the judiciary; it interpreted the Amnesty Law in such a way as to state that it did not violate judicial norms or international commitments on human rights and that, since it related to a pardon, it was not subject to any revision by the judicial authorities. Moreover, it widened the scope of the amnesty, including in it those who had not been denounced by the cut-off point. Faced with this, the superior court in Lima dealing with the case acquiesced; those held were immediately freed.

These two laws can be looked at from two points of view. The first is from that of their effects on jurisdiction. On the one hand, faced with a decision of a judge that the law was unconstitutional, the government responded by enacting another law seeking to correct a judicial decision by imposing a new decision which would take preference. On the other, the second article of Law 26492 stipulated that the amnesty was not subject to judicial decision (*un acto no justiciable*). Suffice it to say in this regard, that any attempt to prevent an act of government being subject to judicial interpretation was itself unconstitutional since the constitution recognises the right to judicial protection[10] (*tutela*

gradually took on board the concepts of reasonableness and proportionality in the emergency zones (Espinoza-Saldana Barrera, 1995)

[10]   Art 139 of the 1993 Constitution states that 'the observance of due process and judicial protection' are key principles and rights of the judicial branch.

jurisdiccional efectiva).

The second point of view is that of the defence of human rights in a state of law.[11] In this context, the granting of an amnesty could only be justified with respect to crimes against the state, not those committed by those working as agents of the state. In this case, the amnesty is directed specifically to the benefit of military officers involved in serious allegations about human rights violations committed since 1980. In other words, it was a case of the Peruvian state absolving itself by virtue of an amnesty which, prior to it being announced in Congress, had neither been suggested nor discussed. Secondly, the Amnesty Law overrode the duty of the state to protect human life and to end the use of torture. Such duties were derived from various international treaties and other agreements, against which the Amnesty Law conflicted.

Military justice

Another problem area was that of military jurisdiction. According to an international commission of jurists, 'military justice constitutes a special jurisdiction which should only be applied to military crimes committed by members of the armed forces or the police, and not to civilians without military duties or to deprive civil justice of its jurisdiction' (International Commission of Jurists, 1994, p. 69). During Fujimori's first term, military justice saw its faculties widened and created political controversy in view of the fact that some of its rulings were considered contrary to the constitution and the laws.

In 1992, a number of decree laws were published increasing the area of responsibility of military courts by giving them sole responsibility for crimes of treason and terrorism. The crime of treason means, in reality, extreme forms of terrorism (*terrorismo agravado)*. This included attacks perpetrated by leading members of subversive organisations and membership of organisations involved in the physical elimination of persons or in causing large explosions.[12] Normally, military courts tried such crimes summarily, with judges hiding their identity and over 90% of those accused being convicted. The lack of guarantees meant that many of those convicted were victims of miscarriages of justice. Public protests drew attention to these problems, demanding that justice be done.[13]

In August 1996, at the initiative of the Defensor del Pueblo, Law 26655 was promulgated, creating a special commission to look into such cases and to propose to the president a list of those deemed worthy of pardon.

---

[11]   See the important article by César Landa Arroyo (1996), pp. 151-208.

[12]   For a detailed analysis on the typifying norms of such crimes and their compatibilty with international standards, see International Commission of Jurists, 1994, pp. 45-51.

[13]   Instituto de Defensa Legal (IDL, 1994) gives a case-by-case listing of miscarriages of justice.

Judicial autonomy: official discourse and beyond

The 1993 Constitution proclaimed the need for judicial autonomy. The Fujimori government also repeatedly claimed the need for independence in the administration of justice. The Comisión Ejecutivo did likewise. However, beyond the official discourse, it is possible to find signs of the opposite being the case in practice.

Here we highlight three cases of judicial autonomy being infringed both by government and military authorities. The first of these is related to the independence of jurisdiction and the prohibition against interference with it. In July 1992, when violent subversion was at its height, the kidnapping and forced disappearance of a professor and nine students took place at the National University of Education (better known as 'La Cantuta'). They had been sleeping in a dormitory in the university, which was under military guard. Investigations by journalists and human rights experts revealed compelling evidence that troops had taken part in their kidnapping. Subsequently, proceedings took place in both civilian and military courts, in which the main accused were military officers on active duty. As was to be expected, rival claims were presented as to whether the case should be heard in civil or military courts. This dispute was due to be settled in February 1994 by the Supreme Court, in line with the code for penal procedure and the code of military justice.

When it came to a vote, three members of the Court voted for the case to be adjudicated in military courts, two in civil courts. This was not the majority required, since the Supreme Court had to vote by at least four-to-one. In such circumstances, the General Law of the Judiciary contemplated the possibility of summoning new members of the Court until such time as the required majority was achieved. However, in this case, Congress immediately approved Law 26291, which stated that in circumstances such as these a simple majority was sufficient and that the new law was directly applicable to the case in hand without the need for more votes on the matter.

Thus it was that Congress resolved this key dispute over legal jurisdictions, overriding established procedures. This was a serious breach of judicial autonomy, involving lawmaking that was retroactive in its effects. It was also an egregious example of ad hoc legislation, a law made applicable to a single case and one which violated constitutional norms.

Another case which demonstrated the way in which military jurisdiction had assumed extraordinary and disproportionate powers was the illegal detention of retired General Rodolfo Robles. Robles had retired after denouncing the participation of military personnel in the Barrios Altos killings and the Cantuta kidnapping and disappearances. In 1996, he was violently detained without a judicial warrant being shown and was then accused of military misdemeanours (*delitos de función*) on the basis of declarations he had made to the press. When arrested, his family interceded with a writ of habeas corpus. This was upheld by a judge and an order was made for his immediate release. Thereupon, a military judge refused to accept the jurisdiction of the civilian judge. Robles's trial for supposed indiscipline and insults to superior officers continued, even though President Fujimori recognised publicly that his detention had been an abuse. A few days later, Congress approved Law 26699, which amnestied Robles, followed by Law 26700, which amnestied the military judges who had been denounced for contempt (*desacato*).[14]

The fact that an amnesty had to be given to a single person to restore his rights, coupled with the refusal to act on dispositions of civil courts, revealed the weakness of the civil jurisdiction in cases where military justice was determined not to accept judgements in defence of basic liberties. It also revealed the weakness of the institutions of civil society and a corresponding strengthening of the military apparatus which, overriding its constitutional functions, appeared to act with a will of its own.

A third instance which revealed the problem of judicial autonomy related to the Constitutional Tribunal.[15] The role played by the Tribunal's predecessor, the Tribunal of Constitutional Guarantees, is held to have been disappointing (Eguiguren Praeli, 1991, pp. 15-59). In the debate in 1993 over the new constitution, the idea of including the Constitutional Tribunal had initially been rejected but it appeared in the final draft and was included in the document subsequently ratified by referendum. The legislation governing the workings of the Constitutional Tribunal were approved only in 1995, and appointments were only made the following year, amid considerable difficulty in agreeing on nominations. When it finally took up office, the Tribunal faced an immediate problem arising from the law itself: since it had seven members, six votes were required to declare a law unconstitutional, which in practice greatly limited its ability to fulfil its allotted function.

In January 1997, the Constitutional Tribunal was called upon to resolve a claim of unconstitutionality against an interpretive law which would have enabled Fujimori to stand for re-election for a second time. On this occasion, the Constitutional Tribunal declared the law inapplicable in Fujimori's case, with three of its members voting against it and the rest abstaining. The ruling appeared to sink Fujimori's attempts to stand for the presidency in 2000, since although it did not declare the law unconstitutional, it made it inapplicable in this instance. A few weeks later, amid accusations that confidential documents had gone astray, Congress initiated an investigation which resulted in a

---

[14] The judge who had issued the habeas corpus writ, Greta Minaya, was immediately removed from her post by orders from the president of the Lima Superior Court and given a job as a sentencing judge, a category which had been created to sentence prisoners in trials that were already well advanced. These judges are not allowed to hear habeas corpus cases. A few days later, following a wave of public protest, this disposition was changed and Minaya returned to her original job. Minaya was a provisional judge.

[15] The Constitutional Tribunal does not form part of the judiciary, but as an independent entity charged with the job of protecting the constitutionality of the laws and defending basic rights, it forms a critical part of the justice system.

constitutional accusation against four of the Constitutional Tribunal's members. Setting aside the technicalities of the case, this ended in the dismissal from the Tribunal of the three magistrates who had voted against the law.[16]

The issue of judicial independence remains a live one. Beyond being a desire, it constitutes an everyday challenge for judges. The above cases are those which probably excited most controversy and public attention, but they show a consistent and worrying tendency of interference on the part of the Fujimori government in the independence of the judiciary.

Conclusions

The 1990s saw growing public interest in and appreciation of the importance of an effective, honest and independent judiciary. This was parallelled by a growing awareness of the links between economic reform and the need for a professional and dependable justice system. The Fujimori government responded to this need, giving judicial reform greater priority than before. The 1993 Constitution included some welcome developments that promised to strengthen aspects of the system. Improvements were also introduced at the administrative level (Dellepiani, 1997) and in reducing delays in adjudicating cases. Perhaps most important, a current of opinion made itself felt within the judiciary which highlighted the need for greater honesty and independence.

At the same time, other more worrying developments took place. The Constitutional Tribunal was, in part, neutralised by a law which effectively made it almost impossible to declare a law unconstitutional. Although the 1993 Constitution upheld the principle of judicial appointments being autonomous, a law was passed which suspended the mechanism by which this was supposed to take place; as a result a large number of provisional judges maintained their positions. In the sphere of the Ministerio Público, norms were issued which undermined the powers of the attorney-general to the benefit of an appointed official of lower rank who, as a previous attorney-general, had proved to be a faithful supporter of the president. The role of the Supreme Court, and particularly its president, was also diluted in favour of an executive commission. However, the creation of the post of Defensor del Pueblo represented an advance, especially in relation to correcting previous miscarriages of justice.

One of the most worrying aspects of all concerned the lack of respect by the Fujimori government for the constitutional responsibilities and attributes of the judiciary in ways that have compromised its jurisdiction. An area of acute political sensitivity was the relationship of civilian to military jurisdiction and

---

[16]   After she was removed from the Constitutional Tribunal, one of its members – Delia Revoredo – was elected (in November 1997) as the head of the Lima College of Lawyers. Subsequently she was denounced, along with her husband, as being allegedly involved in contraband. She and her husband were given political asylum in Costa Rica on the grounds of political persecution.

the tendency of civilian judges to accept the intrusion of the latter. The government's decision in May 1998 to extend the use of military courts to judge cases of common criminality in response to a growing crime wave threatened to undermine civil jurisdiction still further. Use of military jurisdiction not only to judge cases of alleged terrorism but other types of criminal activity threatened further to undermine the due process of law and augment the violation of individual freedoms.

CHAPTER 10

Fujimori and the Military

Enrique Obando

Ever since the time of Plato's 'Republic', political thinkers have wrestled with the problem of how to bring military establishments within the control of the governments and societies which they serve. In modern times, a number of methods have been used, of which I identify five main types: the Prussian model; the 'party control' model; the Anglo-Saxon model; the Swedish model; and finally the cooptation model.

The Prussian model seeks to maintain a distance between the military and politics by emphasising the former's professionalism and its absolute obedience to political authority (Huntington, 1964, pp. 30-58). This was the model that evolved in Prussia prior to the First World War, although it had emerged previously in France at the time of the Napoleonic Wars (Howard, 1976, chapter 6). It becomes problematic when military and political authority become one and the same, as was the case during the Third Reich (Leach, 1973, p. 7). In Latin America, where the model has had strong influence, it has also caused problems when the military, at times of political crisis or power vacuum, has imposed its own ideology, generally stressing authoritarianism and nationalism. Such ideologies have tended to jar with the ideologies of civil society. This was also a problem in Japan in the 1920s and 1930s (Smethurst, 1974, p. 164 and *passim*), in Spain before the civil war (Thomas, 1961), and (in more modern times) in Turkey (Tamkog, 1976) and Greece (Clogg and Yannopoulos, 1972; Woodhouse and Montague, 1985).

The 'party control' model, in which a well-organised, hierarchical and authoritarian party infiltrates the armed forces and forms a line of command subservient to the party, is exemplified by Communist systems of government (Colton and Gustafson, 1990; Bartov, 1992), although it was also characteristic of the Nazi infiltration of the German *Wehrmacht* (Dupuy, 1997). In Latin America, Cuba followed the Soviet model. Elsewhere, however, political parties have seldom (with the possible exception of the Mexican PRI) developed the necessary level of organisation to achieve this dominance. For many years, this was the model which inspired Peru's APRA, based in part on the party's experiences prior to the 1932 Trujillo rising. Under President Alan García (1985-90), there were moves by the party to infiltrate the army and to increase the authority of the police.

The Anglo-Saxon model is typical of the United Kingdom and many of its former colonies, as well as of the United States. In such countries, democracy defines a national identity and the military exists to defend that identity

(Huntington, 1964, parts II and III; Avant, 1994; and Kohn, 1994, pp. 23-31). This ideology was at its most explicit during the Second World War, and subsequently during the Cold War, in the fight for 'democratic' as opposed to 'totalitarian' values. In Latin America, the weakness of democratic institutions has handicapped the evolution of this sort of model. Moreover, democracy has tended to be valued in 'instrumental' terms, i.e. as a means rather than an end, with the end being such goals as economic development and public well-being. When democracy was seen as not necessarily leading to such ends, its value was questioned.

The Swedish model is a variation on the Anglo-Saxon theme, the main difference being that there is no difference between civilians and the military in terms of prerogatives or separate systems of justice. Such a system does not exist in Latin America. It tends to require a homogenous society, both politically and economically.

The 'cooptation' model has been the preferred model in Latin America, and it is its implementation in Peru which is the subject of this chapter. It was the model used by Carlos Andrés Pérez in Venezuela and that which León Febres Cordero sought to implement in Ecuador. Cooptation is nothing new in Peru. It was attempted by Augusto Leguía in the 1920s (Villanueva, 1977). It involves granting to the senior echelons of the armed forces special privileges (promotions, political appointments and economic favours) in return for their support for the regime. It is a system which, at least in the short run, encourages a degree of stability in civilian-military relations. However, it also generates discontent in middle and junior levels of the armed forces. García introduced cooptation as his model for dealing with the military during his government; since 1990, Alberto Fujimori has taken it to new lengths.

Power in the military prior to 1985: the system of 'rings'

In order to understand the changes that the cooptation system has brought about within the military in Peru, it is necessary to understand the system in place prior to 1985. Traditionally, the Peruvian military has combined an open, official system of power distribution – vouchsafed by the *Ley de Situación Militar* – with a concealed system.

The official system was institutionalised in the 1950s, and it stipulates that the commander-in-chief (*comandante general*) of each branch of the armed forces, the highest ranking officer, should be its most senior officer, until his eventual retirement. The age of retirement varied between the different services, but in the army it came after 35 years of active service or at 58 years of age. Seniority was determined by the first to become a divisional general *(general de división)* before other generals of the same rank. Up until the rank of colonel, promotions were made on the basis of examinations; in the case of generals, promotion was on the basis of a decision by the High Command as well as the curriculum of the officer concerned. This system proved highly predictable, making it relatively simple to guess in advance who would become commander-in-chief in any given year.

However, behind the formal system of promotions lay a less overt system, based on the principle of 'rings' (*argollas*) united in support of one particular candidate for commander-in-chief. Those who aspired to reach the top in each of the services began forming these rings at least ten years before they would be eligible to become commander-in-chief. Since the system was stable and predictable, it was relatively easy to identify those who would be eligible in any one year. Officers seeking preferment would therefore join the ring to court favour from the ringleader, whose power was derived from the fact that he could offer 'goods' to his followers. Such 'goods' included not just promotions but promises of appointments (some appointments were more sought after than others), grades, and the offer of remunerative activities – both licit and illicit.[1]

The system of rings had the effect of cementing rivalries within the armed forces, since preferment involved being part of a ring, and to reach the top involved being a ringleader. Confrontation between rings was therefore the norm. A classic instance of one ring vying against another was the struggle for supremacy in the airforce at the end of the 1980s between Lieut.-General Germán Vucetich and Lieut.-General César Gonzalo, when it transpired that airforce intelligence was tapping the telephone of Vucetich and sending the taped conversations to a television programme in order to bring him into disrepute.

Rings included officers upwards from the rank of major to that of general. The predominant ring of an incumbent commander-in-chief would often seek to encourage a preferred subordinate ring on the grounds that its leader might provide a dependable replacement on his retirement. If, however, a commander-in-chief fell into disgrace for any particular reasons, the members of his ring would suffer the consequences.

Originally, rings seldom reflected different ideological positions or special institutional leanings; rather they were formed to distribute power within a hierarchical institution. However, in the mid-1960s, ring-making took on a more overtly political dimension. In view of the preponderance of a conservative, masonic ring within the army in the 1950s and 1960s, a leftward-leaning Catholic ring came into being, organised around the *Cursillos de Cristiandad*. The *Cursillista* ring articulated a belief in the need for radical social change, and proved to be an important antecedent to the 1968 coup and the subsequent

---

[1]   The information on how the system worked before 1985 is the result of participant observation in the anthropological sense of the term. It comes from a large number of interviews with military officers (colonels and navy captains) in 1983 when I was a student at the Centre for Higher Military Studies (CAEM), in 1984 (for three months) at the National Intelligence School, and in 1984-89 when I acted as advisor to the National Secretariat of Defence.

Velasco government.[2] During the 1965-80 period, the system of rings underscored some of the ideological divergences that occurred during this time within the armed forces. The struggle within the military was not simply for goods, but for the power to influence the direction of policy. At the end of the military government, the rings within the armed forces became once again a method for distributing power and influence within the military.

With the return to civilian government under Fernando Belaúnde (1980-85), in order not to alienate the military, Belaúnde opted to leave them alone, and the system of rings unchanged. Parallel to this policy, Belaúnde gave the military the weapons it requested during the first two years of his administration. However, it proved more difficult to ensure good civil-military relations in other spheres. For example, there was little collaboration over the implementation of the National Defence System, which required civilian participation. Such mutual distrust was particularly damaging coming at a moment when Sendero Luminoso was in the ascendant. Then, in 1982, the onset of the debt crisis resulted in a marked reduction in military budgets which affected officer incomes.

As inflation increased, the income of generals during the second Belaúnde government fell to the equivalent of 550 dollars a month.[3] In military circles, this was seen as deliberate revenge for the fact that it was the armed forces under Velasco which had toppled Belaúnde's first government. One consequence of the fall in military wages during this period was the tendency for the rings to use contacts and influence to distribute illegal goods, especially with the growth of drug trafficking in this period. Whilst the navy and the airforce finally managed to control the problem of drug-related corruption, this was to prove more difficult within the army.

Cooptation of the Military: lessons from the García government

As we have already said, cooptation was nothing new in the Peruvian armed forces. Early in the century, the Leguía government (1919-30) successfully coopted the high command of the armed forces. By doing so, it broke the chain of military command, since middle and low-ranking officers came to realise that the upper ranks of the hierarchy no longer represented their interests or those of the military as an institution. It was a lieutenant-colonel, Luis M. Sánchez Cerro

---

[2]   Inteview with 'Colonel A' who requested anonimity (2 July 1992). The Velasco government was influenced by many forces, among them former members of APRA (Carlos Delgado, for instance, belonged to this group), different left-wing parties (Héctor Bejar of the FLN was director-general of youth organisations within SINAMOS) and the left of the Catholic Church. Amongst the latter was the Christian Democrat Party as well as the *Cursillos de Cristiandad*. The *Cursillos* were courses given generally by leftward-leaning priests. They focused on social injustice. Many officers met within them and their ideological leanings led them to establish a ring in opposition to the more conservative ones.

[3]   In constant December 1992 dollars. This is derived from my own calculations (Obando, 1994, pp. 122-3).

who led the coup which overturned the so-called *oncenio* of Leguía (Villanueva, 1977; Thorndike, 1969).

.There was a long history of enmity between the armed forces and APRA, and Alan García, the party's first-ever president, looked for ways to control the armed forces when he came to office in 1985.[4] Another reason why García needed to control the military was that his policy towards human rights in the counter-insurgency war against Sendero Luminoso and the MRTA was different from that of Belaúnde. Belaúnde had given the military considerable latitude to fight Sendero Luminoso, irrespective of concerns over human rights. García sought to challenge the military over human rights, even ordering the removal of the head of the joint chiefs of staff, the commander of the second military region and the military commander in Ayacucho.[5] Thus, whilst Belaúnde had respected the autonomy of the armed forces, ultimately acceding to spending requests for new equipment, García took a more interventionist approach. Cooptation took the form of cementing an alliance with the dominant ring in each of the services, providing them with appointments in government or abroad as ambassadors.[6] Where the leading ring resisted this approach, García coopted its rival and helped it win the struggle for power within that branch of the services.

In this struggle, the National Intelligence Service (SIN) played an important role. By law, this institution was under the control of the presidency, and García used it to keep tabs on military leaders.[7] This was a particularly potent weapon, given the increased scale of corruption within the army, since it provided the president with a way of maintaining discipline and preventing acts of disloyalty. At the same time, the García government sought to create a parallel force to the

---

[4]   APRA and the military had been at odds since the 1932 Trujillo rising and the massacre that followed it. In 1933, a military president, Luis M. Sánchez Cerro was assassinated by an Aprista militant. The armed forces effectively operated a veto against APRA in the elections of 1936, 1939, 1945 and 1956. They staged a coup in 1948 to bring to an end Aprista influence over the Bustamente government. They prevented an APRA victory in 1962. Each year a pilgimage was held to the tombs of those members of the military who had been assassinated in the 1932 rising. By 1985, however, this enmity had diminished. The military government (1968-80) saw a rapprochement, and by 1980 APRA seemed the natural inheritors of the sort of interventionist policies it espoused. The sons of important military leaders became Aprista militants. The armed forces ended their annual pilgrimage. There was no need to fear a military coup in 1985. However, García's cooptation policy fostered the enmity it was supposed to control.

[5]   García's policy on human rights ended in the military avoiding its responsibilities with respect to counter-insurgency unless commanders in the field received clear written instructions to avoid any possibility of them subsequently shouldering the blame for human rights violations. This helped Sendero Luminoso to expand its operations, until it seemed that the 1990 elections would not be able to be held. Some members of the military believed that this was a deliberate ploy by García to prolong his presidency.

[6]   An example helps to explain how this cooptation was carried out. The identity of our source here has to be kept in reserve. The commander of one of the military regions was the most respected general in the army. He was but one of two with sufficient standing to mount a coup against the government. He was offered the job as Peruvian ambassador to Madrid when he retired. He loyally waited three years for this position, but when he eventually retired he was given nothing.

[7]   I obtained evidence of phone tapping in 1989, whilst I was at the National Secretariat of Defence. Employees normally assumed their phones were tapped by the SIN.

military establishment by control of the police through the interior ministry. Specialist police groups began to receive armaments,[8] whilst paramilitary groups within the police – most notably the Comando Rodrigo Franco – were used to intimidate the regime's opponents.

The prevalence of the cooptation system, linked to low pay in the military and the high level of incompetence exhibited in dealing with Sendero Luminoso and the smaller Castroite MRTA,[9] led to a growing dissatisfaction among middle-ranking officers. These came to consider that their commanding officers no longer represented their interests or those of the military as an institution. They therefore began to organise themselves in opposition groups and to plan the possible removal of both the government and the high command. Two such groups became identified: Comaca, an acronym meaning 'colonels, majors and captains', and León Dormido ('Sleeping Lion'). These were not rings, since they were not organised around military leaders with the rank of general; they had no generals in them, the most senior officers being of the rank of colonel. Indeed they mobilised within the officer corps, seeking to denounce the highest ranks for having 'sold out' to politicians.

The rings within the armed forces which had not been coopted got wind of the plans being laid by Comaca, and ended up making coup preparations with a view to assuming control of the military themselves. They thought that they would be able to justify this if García sought to prolong himself in office after 1990, citing the prevalent economic and political chaos as a reason to postpone presidential elections. They set to work on a plan for uninterrupted government that would last 20 years. This became known as the 'Green Book'.[10] It consisted of a plan of government, elaborated by a group of military officers and pro-military civilian sympathisers. The document is particularly important in that it reflected a shift in military thinking. In the 1960s and 1970s, the military had devised a plan of government, the so-called Plan Inca, involving a series of radical reforms including agrarian reform, the nationalisation of key extractive enterprises, a redistribution in the pattern of wealth, protection of union activity (both in the urban and rural spheres), protection of national industries and a major dose of state control over the regulation of key prices in the economy.

By contrast, the Green Book represented the adaptation of military thinking to the liberalised market economy. It highlighted the need for radical restructuring with the sale of key nationalised industries and a drastic reduction in the extent of state intervention. At the same time, it stressed the importance of mounting a determined campaign to root out subversion, and to this end it advocated a model of tight political control. In other words, it was liberal in the economic sense and authoritarian in the political. The underlying foundation was

---

[8]   The army prevented the hand-over of half-track vehicles bought in Israel for the police. Under pressure from the military, these vehicles were eventually handed over to the army.
[9]   For a review of the counter-insurgency strategy, see Obando (1991), (1993).
[10]   Excerpts from the Green Book were published in *Oiga*, No. 647, 12 July 1993 and 19 July 1993.

a civil-military alliance, working in favour of the interests of the business class, but seeking support in civil society. This therefore represented a clear departure from *Velasquismo*, even though some of the officers involved had been Velasco-supporters in the 1970s. The failure of *Velasquismo*, along with the challenge from groups like Sendero and the MRTA had pushed the military clearly to the right.

Although in a programmatic sense this was something far removed from the ideas embodied in the Plan Inca, the basic objective was something similar: the military wanted to play a protagonistic role in the attempt to restructure society on more stable foundations, and by avoiding the sort of recurrent, periodic crises which had plagued Peru in recent decades, they wanted the country to play a more hegemonic role in the region.

The state of civil-military relations became as chaotic as the overall political and economic context. With the armed forces divided and with both middle-level officers and the high command both planning anti-regime coups, political stability was safeguarded by the 1990 presidential elections. These difficulties within the armed forces acted as a warning of the sort of difficulties arising from a strategy of cooptation. However, this was a lesson that Fujimori failed to absorb: under his government, the cooptation strategy reached new heights.

Civil-military relations under Fujimori (1990-95)

As the 1990 elections approached, the main opposition to APRA had come principally from the right-wing Frente Democrático (Fredemo) whose candidate was the novelist, Mario Vargas Llosa. Vargas Llosa had spearheaded the opposition ever since Alan García's frustrated attempt in 1987 to nationalise the domestic commercial banking industry. When, as a result of the first round, Alberto Fujimori emerged as the main obstacle to Vargas Llosa's ambitions, García afforded the former the decided support of the National Intelligence Service (SIN).

Through these initial contacts with the SIN, Fujimori learnt of the ways in which García had sought to control the military through his policies of cooptation. In this regard, a former army captain, Vladimiro Montesinos, who had been working in the SIN, came to play a leading role. Montesinos proved his usefulness early on. With Fredemo seeking to pin on Fujimori charges of tax evasion in relation to a real estate business through which he and his wife had derived income, Montesinos, a lawyer with good contacts in the judiciary, managed to help Fujimori in changing the judge in charge of the case for another who obligingly saw no case to be answered.[11]

Montesinos also proved himself an asset in dealing with Sendero Luminoso.

---

[11]   Interview with a SIN official, who requested anonymity.

During the last years of the García government, a group of SIN analysts, which included Montesinos, had developed a counter-insurgency strategy, which García had never implemented. The essence of this plan was fourfold: (i) the unification of all the various systems of state intelligence, (ii) full support for the so-called '*rondas campesinas*' as bulwarks against subversion in rural areas, (iii) giving the military full political control of areas declared to be in a state of emergency, and (iv) drastically increasing the penalties for those accused of terrorism and introducing incentives for those captured to denounce insurgents still at large.[12] This plan gave Montesinos access to Fujimori as a specialist in anti-subversive strategy, an area in which the two preceding governments had so conspicuously failed. By this time, Sendero Luminoso's armed insurrection, now in its tenth year, appeared to be growing out of control. The civil war had resulted in an estimated 23,000 deaths and loss of property calculated at 20 billion dollars.

Montesinos also proved his usefulness in other ways. As a former army captain, he had knowledge of who was who within the higher ranks of the armed forces, many of whom were officers of his own generation. All this helped Fujimori in developing his relations with the military. Fujimori was concerned that, bereft of a political party or other organised back-up in civil society, he might be a possible victim of a coup. Although his image as an independent had been a valuable asset in electoral terms, his isolation made him vulnerable. Montesinos proved himself a valued advisor in telling Fujimori whom to promote, whom to retire and whom to put in charge of key garrisons. This was a source of concern amongst *institucionalista* officers who, as with García, opposed this sort of intervention from outside. The offence was doubly galling since Montesinos had been dishonourably discharged from the army during the military government.[13]

Fujimori's system of cooptation proved rather different to that of García. Whilst García had coopted the high command, those who had reached this level had done so through the institutional system of promotions based on seniority and the system of allegiances based on rings. On Montesinos's advice, Fujimori eliminated the use of both systems, deciding himself whom to promote to the high command. A new military law was approved in November 1991,[14] specifying that the president would personally nominate the commanders-in-

---

[12]   Interview with 'Colonel C', who requested anonymity.

[13]   Montesinos was accused of selling Peruvian military secrets to the United States, specifically relating to Russian materiel acquired in the 1970s. He was seen walking out of the Pentagon in the company of General Miguel Angel de la Flor, then foreign minister. Although not found guilty of treason, he was discharged for deceipt and insubordination. He was seen in Washington when supposedly on sick leave in Lima. This information came from an interview on 17 February 1994 with a retired army general who requested anonymity.

[14]   Decree Law 752, Ley de Situación Militar. *El Peruano,* 12 November 1991, No. 4130, pp. 101700-708. The decree was approved when Congress gave Fujimori special faculties to legislate. Afterwards, typifying the disregard of civilians for military and security matters, there was no discussion in Congress about the decree. It is also symptomatic of the lack of democratic institutionality that the army lacked allies in Congress to oppose the law.

chief of the various services and that these did not necessarily have to retire after 35 years of active service. In effect, this meant that Fujimori no longer had to coopt a new commander-in-chief every year; he could name a person of trust to head the armed forces and leave him in that position for as long as he saw fit. In practice, this is what happened with General Nicolás Hermoza, who became commander-in-chief in 1991. Fujimori sent into retirement those generals who, according to seniority, were in line to become commander-in-chief.[15] According to sources within the army, Hermoza was chosen because he was someone who could be trusted not to take unilateral decisions without prior consultation with his superiors.[16]

The introduction of this new system of power distribution had important implications. It removed the need for the ring system, since it removed the basis for institutional competition for preferment; in future there would be but a single ring – those who enjoyed the confidence of Hermoza. However, even this ring no longer worked as before since the top job within the armed forces was already occupied. The possibilities for goods to be distributed were therefore more limited than before. At the same time, the new system provided few outlets for discontent, which could only be vented outside the hierarchy. There was also considerable resentment among the retired generals who had seen their own ambitions frustrated. Furthermore, the new system had the defect that promotions were awarded more on the basis of political loyalty than military proficiency. The old system had also been based on loyalty to the leader of the ring, but preferment within the ring was conducted on the basis of professional reputation. Within the new system, there was a latent conflict between those preferred on the basis of political loyalties and those more skilled soldiers who had been obliged to retire. Although it was not always the case that the least proficient candidates were promoted, this tended to be the case. As one (anonymous) commentator put it, 'the peacocks were removed by the vultures'.

In fact, Fujimori's fears about a possible coup were misplaced. In the past, coups were conducted either for ideological reasons or because civilian governments proved themselves incompetent. The coups staged against APRA to prevent it winning elections from the 1930s onwards had been of the first variety; the coup that removed Belaúnde in 1968 had been of the second. There were few reasons for the military to stage a coup against Fujimori on ideological grounds, since he had put pragmatism at the very centre of his political agenda. Furthermore, Fujimori quickly confounded the sceptics and proved himself to be an efficient president, unafraid to take some of the bold actions that some of his predecessors had failed to take. However, the fear of a coup was kept alive when, in November 1992, a coup attempt was uncovered. Ironically, the very system adopted to prevent a coup generated such discontent that it encouraged some military officers to mount one with a view to ending the system of

---

[15]   These were General Luis Palomino and General José Pastor, who were due to become commanders-in- chief of the army in 1993 and 1994 respectively.
[16]   Interview with 'Colonel D', who requested anonymity.

cooptation which Montesinos had advocated. However, the coup plot, although easily dealt with by the government, strengthened Montesinos's hand since it provided precisely the evidence he wanted to justify the approach he had advocated.

Although the November 1992 coup attempt was ostensibly a protest at the decision by Fujimori to close down Congress after his *autogolpe* of the preceding April – a coup in defence of democracy – in fact it also responded to such other concerns as the restoration of the status quo in terms of promotions and appointments. It was thus a coup perpetrated by the *institucionalistas* within the armed forces against the system of control introduced by Fujimori. The leader of the coup was General Jaime Salinas, who had been retired a year before by Hermoza. Salinas should have been chief of the army's general staff in 1993. Similarly, General José Pastor, also retired in 1991 and who should have been the army commander-in-chief in 1994, was implicated. Along with these two generals, some 40 other officers were involved, from captains up to the rank of general, both retired and on active service. However, Fujimori's closure of Congress proved to be an extremely popular move, both within the military hierarchy and among the population as a whole. Given the unpopularity of Congress with its image as an obstacle to change, it was an inappropriate moment to launch a coup in favour of the status quo.

One of the main reasons for the closure of Congress was its veto at the end of 1991 of a series of laws designed to strengthen the military's capabilities in dealing with Sendero (Cobián Vidal, 1993), at a point at which its war had entered an even more aggressive phase. The most important law vetoed (and in fact replaced by a different law) was the creation of the National Defence System. This law was Montesinos's creation, but enjoyed military support. It gave greater power to military commanders all round the country, giving them control not just of the military and the police but of the civilian administration as well. Congress believed that this represented a further militarisation of a war which was essentially political. Congress advocated a tripartite approach to counter-insurgency, with decision-making in the hands of the regional prefect (as representatve of the president), the democratically-elected regional president and the local military chief. Since in war the indivisibility of command is a key principle, it was obvious that the proposal would not work. The idea behind it had been to give a wider responsibility to civilian authorities, especially in those parts of the country where the struggle against Sendero Luminoso appeared to be more of a political than a military battle. However, with command split into three, and with all the complications to which this was likely to give rise, it did not appear to be an appropriate way to pursue counter-insurgency. This was an issue on which all in the military – whether institutionalists or loyalists – found common ground. The great majority backed the closure of Congress.

1992 was a good year for Fujimori. His government had been successful in taming inflation, whilst the capture of Sendero's founder, ideologue and guiding star, Abimael Guzmán, had proved a major blow to the guerrilla movement. And finally, the military leaders who had been planning a coup had been arrested. Reflecting these successes, Fujimori's popularity rose to levels well in excess of 70% in the opinion polls; he had made conspicuous progress in areas where his two predecessors had failed. This allowed Fujimori, who was under pressure from the Organisation of American States (OAS) to call elections for a new Congress, to do so and win a large majority, whilst simultaneously recouping some of his legitimacy abroad.

Arguably it was a moment for magnanimity, for the announcement of an amnesty for Fujimori's military opponents. His response was far from conciliatory. Suspicious of those who were not obvious loyalists, he retired more officers and removed others from key positions. This had two main effects.

The first was that in trying to root out all sources of criticism, he alienated a group of *institucionalistas,* well disposed towards Fujimori not because they had been coopted but because they considered him to be following the right policies. This group had acted as a buffer between Fujimori's opponents in the military and the loyalists, but at this point some passed over to the opposition thereby removing the buffer and heightening the chances of direct confrontation. Amongst them was General Rodolfo Robles, commander of the key third military region, who was put in charge of the military's academic institutions. Another was General José Valdivia, chief of staff of the joint chiefs of staff, who had played a leading role in the elaboration of the military's anti-subversive strategy. He was placed under house arrest during the coup attempt, and was then removed from his post, transferred first to the Inter-American Defense Board in Washington and subsequently to the Ukraine as military attaché.

The second effect was that the opposition began to attack Hermoza himself, first on account of human rights violations committed in the war against subversion, then over alleged involvement in drug trafficking. Under attack from within the military, Hermoza responded by creating a batallion to protect himself and by mounting his own system of intelligence within the armed forces.[17]

Human rights violations had been an endemic feature of the counter-insurgency effort, both under Belaúnde and García. However, under Fujimori and Hermoza, infighting within the armed forces led to members of the military opposition passing to the media proof of its involvement in extra-judicial killings. Of these violations, the most blatant examples were the Barrios Altos killings, when army commandos assassinated several people attending a party in this district of Lima, and the kidnapping and disappearance of a teacher and nine students from the 'La Cantuta' university. Robles, formerly a pro-Fujimori *institucionalista*, denounced the killings, thereafter seeking asylum in Argentina. The government sought to deny military responsibility, but the evidence was so compelling that it became impossible to continue avoiding a full investigation.

---

[17]   Interview with 'Colonel D'. The officers who were requested to attend any meeting in which the commander-in-chief was present were asked to hand over their weapons. Some felt slighted by this, since they were required to be armed under military regulations.

In order to forestall a congressional investigation, General Hermoza resorted to bringing out the tanks onto the streets of Lima in a show of force.

This sort of authoritarian and intimidating response created more problems than it solved for Fujimori and the government, which had been seeking to repair its human rights image abroad. Hermoza's actions in accusing the press of being accomplices in subversion, his attempts to cover up facts that were clearly true, his attempts to persecute military opponents who accused him of violating human rights and his use of threats to browbeat Congress did little to promote a clean image. Nevertheless, Fujimori defended Hermoza, basically because he appears to have believed that in a counter-insurgency war such excesses were bound to happen.

Meanwhile, by 1993, civilian and military courts found themselves locked in battle over their respective jurisdiction in dealing with those accused of involvement in the La Cantuta killings (see Chapter 9). Just as it seemed that the civil courts had the upper hand, the pro-Fujimori majority in the Congress changed the rules of the game. The Supreme Court had voted by three to two in favour of the case being dealt with in the military courts, less than the four-fifths majority required. Thereupon, Congress voted a new law which stipulated that a simple majority was all that was required, and that the original vote therefore stood. Although the case was finally judged by a military tribunal, such was the outcry on the matter that the court gave the officers responsible a prison sentence.

Hermoza was also accused of being involved in drug trafficking. Under the old system of competing rings, as we have seen, the leading ring provided its members with access to goods of various sorts. The new system involved only one ring and its period of predominance was no longer pre-set. Given the number of enemies created by this innovation, the leading ring had to create its own system of rewards in order to survive. In a context in which the incomes of the officer corps did not improve markedly (having fallen rapidly in real terms under Belaúnde and García),[18] there was a constant temptation to use illegal sources of wealth as an adjunct to compensate for low wages. Whilst García had resisted the temptation to deploy the army in anti-drug trafficking operations, Fujimori, under pressure from Washington, succumbed. This opened up new possibilities for lucrative gain; casting a blind eye towards the cultivation, elaboration and trans-shipment of cocaine could be hugely profitable (see Chapter 6).

It was in this context, that Hermoza's enemies within the army began to accuse him and Montesinos of being involved in drug trafficking. An investigation was mounted into drug-related corruption and over 100 officers

---

[18]   Reductions in the real incomes of officer and NCOs was dramatic. Assuming that each had earnings equivalent to 100 in January 1988, in September 1990 a divisional general's salary was worth 21.3, a lieutenant-colonel 21.7, a second lieutenant 26.3, a senior technician 20.7, a third-class technician 22.3 and a third class NCO 24.7.

were punished as a result. However, the main members of the predominant ring escaped punishment. Some, for intance, were discreetly removed from their posts and sent to embassies abroad as military attachés. Although some opposition officers denounced this, they were forced to flee abroad, their lives threatened. Such corrupt activities had a debilitating effect on military unity and discipline. It even produced intra-service clashes, as in 1994, when the airforce (which had successfully dealt with corruption in its ranks) came into conflict with the local army chief in the Huallaga region. The airforce shot down an aircraft transporting cocaine, rather than capturing it; the airforce chief believed that if the cargo had fallen into the hands of the army, it would have been misused.

Aware of the political costs of maintaining Hermoza as commander-in-chief, Fujimori suggested to him at the end of 1993 the possibility of replacing him and making him defence minister instead. Hermoza declined the offer, itself a sign of his own power and autonomy. It became clear that the president no longer had the ability to remove the head of the army. This may have been an inevitable outcome of the cooptation strategy. As long as Hermoza was able to control his all-powerful ring within the armed forces, he would have the ability to resist the president. There was no parallel force to delimit the power of the army, as had been the case, for instance, with the SS in Nazi Germany. There was only the SIN, which was aware of developments in the army, but which believed that Hermoza's strength was functional to the strength of the regime as a whole.

The February 1995 border war with Ecuador over an ill-defined stretch of frontier in the Cordillera del Cóndor exposed a critical weakness of the system. Despite the inferior size of its armed forces, Ecuador was able to inflict humiliating military losses on Peru, whose lack of preparation for this conflict indicated serious failings in military intelligence. Hermoza's conduct of the brief war was criticised, both surreptitiously within the army but with greater fanfare on the part of retired generals. Once again, Hermoza tried to silence his critics, ordering the arrest of some retired generals and sending into retirement those on active service. The cooptation system, it seemed, had had negative effects on the degree of professionalism at the top of the military hierarchy.

Fujimori's electoral triumph in April 1995, when he achieved re-election with 64% of the vote, provided him with an opportunity to change the whole military high command and to turn the page on the past. However, whilst Fujimori changed the commanders-in-chief of the navy and airforce, he retained Hermoza in post. One possible explanation for this was that Hermoza argued that the delicacy of the border situation with Ecuador was such that it made it inadvisable to change the leadership of the army. Another explanation was that criticism of Hermoza's role in the Ecuadorean conflict had affected Fujimori as well. To insist on Hermoza's departure would have been interpreted as acquiescence to political pressure from the opposition.

Rather, at Fujimori's instigation, Congress passed a law in June 1995 granting an amnesty to all members of the armed forces who had been accused of human rights violations since 1980. However, since this was a highly contentious matter, he was also obliged to announce a parallel amnesty for those former members of the military who had been involved in the 1992 coup preparations and those imprisoned since then for their criticisms of Hermoza.

Fujimori's second government: a symbiotic relationship

A symbiotic relationship existed between Hermoza and Fujimori during the first two years of his second government (1995-97), during which the former tenaciously held on to his post as commander-in-chief of the army. Whilst it is important to stress the fact that there were no fundamental disagreements between the two, Hermoza remained a political liability in the sense that his continuance in office was a source of grievance within the armed forces, amongst political groups opposed to the regime and in the international arena. Latent tensions came to the surface in October 1996, when Hermoza ordered the arrest of Robles who, since 1992, from his position in retirement, had made little secret of his hostility to Hermoza. Robles's detention caused an uproar, forcing Fujimori first to order his release and, when that failed, to push through Congress a hastily-prepared bill to give him a specific amnesty. Hermoza was eventually forced to back down.

Hermoza's defiance forced Fujimori to count more on Montesinos. Unlike Hermoza, Montesinos lacked power of his own and depended more on the president. Through his control over the intelligence community, Montesinos had had some success in building up rings loyal to Fujimori. The navy and airforce commanders appointed in 1995, Admiral Antonio Ibarcena and Lieut.-General Elcsvan Bello, had emerged from the intelligence sections of their respective services. As such, they were close to Montesinos in his capacity as effective head of the SIN. However, neither enjoyed the status to make them commanders-in-chief. Nevertheless, established rules were again bent in order to ensure their promotion. Within the army, this was seen as a clear victory for Montesinos in isolating Hermoza. However, the hostage crisis of December 1996 – when an MRTA detachment successfully occupied the residence in Lima of the Japanese ambassador, taking hostage a 'who's who' of diplomats, ministers, top-level military officers, politicians, businessmen and academics – had the effect of temporarily ending the infighting between Hermoza on the one hand and Fujimori and Montesinos on the other. The way in which the crisis was eventually resolved provided clues to the state of these relationships. A military commando group stormed the diplomatic compound in a well-planned and executed raid and liberated the hostages. Fujimori made it clear that the chief author of the successful raid on the Japanese ambassador's residence was Montesinos. The commandos used in the raid came primarily from the navy and the airforce, not the army. Hermoza's share of the glory was thus diminished.

However, other forces were at play complicating things. The opposition within the army continued to work to embarrass both Hermoza and Montesinos. In November 1996, information was leaked to the press about the so-called 'Bermuda Plan' against a well-known journalist, critical of the government. Information also leaked out about the 'Narval Plan' to silence a television channel which had also adopted a critical posture, and the 'El Pino' operation against a lawyer connected with the La Cantuta case. As a consequence of these, Leonor La Rosa, an operative in the army's intelligence service (SIE) was interrogated under torture for her presumed role in revealing this information. She subsequently escaped, and denounced the treatment she had received. Some months previously, the dismembered corpse of another army intelligence operative, Mariela Barreto, had been discovered. That these facts are known is testimony to the continued current of opposition at work within the army. Indicative of this was the fact that the tortured agent asked to be sent to a clinic whose managing director was Robles's brother. For his pains, the government ordered the tax authorities (SUNAT) to investigate supposed tax evasion by the clinic.

Within this context of tension between Hermoza and Montesinos, Fujimori was making plans to ensure his ability to stand as presidential candidate for a third term in 2000. The 1993 Constitution stipulates that a president can only succeed himself once. However, Fujimori's lawyers sought to argue that if he were to stand again in 2000, it would be only the first re-election under the 1993 constitution. Amid strident criticisms from his political opponents concerning the legality of such a move, the authorities took steps to silence and browbeat known opponents. Early in 1997, those members of the Constitutional Tribunal who had declared against the constitutionality of Fujimori's candidacy in 2000 were accused of exceeding their functions. Congressman Javier Díez Canseco, a tireless critic of the government and its human rights record, had his car stolen and then set on fire. The editor of La República, the centre-left opposition daily, was briefly kidnapped. Ricardo Nugent, the head of the Constitutional Tribunal, found himself in the middle of a shoot-out between police and 'criminals' and two of his bodyguards were killed. In April, the government passed a new press statute which envisaged severe penalties for stories not corroborated by adequate evidence. The attorney-general, Miguel Ajovín, found his powers whittled away and then placed in the hands of a Fujimori stalwart appointed to head the executive commission in the Ministerio Público. The director of Channel 2, who had offended military sensibilities in uncovering a number of human rights scandals, found himself deprived of his Peruvian citizenship and therefore his ability to own the channel. This move was triggered by a televised programme on the extent of phone tapping by the security services, which revealed that even the foreign minister had had his phone tapped.

The panorama was complicated by the fact that several struggles seemed to be taking place concurrently: Fujimori and Montesinos against Hermoza; the military opposition against both Montesinos and Hermoza; the political opposition against all three; and Montesinos against the political opposition in laying the plans for Fujimori's re-election in 2000. The fact that both Montesinos and Hermoza found themselves under attack from the same sources appeared to cement their relationship in common defence. Nevertheless, they remained rivals. This became clear when, in July 1997, Fujimori named General César Saucedo as defence minister on Montesinos's advice. Saucedo, close to Hermoza, had been commander of the key second military region, and his removal to an administrative function deprived him of direct control over troops. Similarly, Hermoza recommended General José Villanueva as interior minister. Villanueva, supposedly close to Montesinos, had previously commanded the fifth military region.

Conclusions

Under Alan García, but much more so under Alberto Fujimori, time-honoured methods for distributing power within the armed forces were abandoned in favour of a system of cooptation. This had the effect of a single and quasi-permanent ring being established within the armed forces. Whilst this gave the impression of government control over the military, it destroyed the lines of subordination and created a permanent source of discontent within the institution and among retired officers. Since this new structure was not accompanied by the erection of a parallel structure to limit military power, it meant that those generals coopted by the government achieved a great deal of autonomy in their relations with the president. Faced with this problem, Fujimori sought to use the intelligence service (SIN) as a counterpoint to the power of army commander General Nicolás Hermoza.

In spite of the power amassed by Hermoza, Fujimori retained the upper hand, since Hermoza did not appear to have political ambitions of his own or an alternative policy agenda. Although affected by oscillations in his popularity, Fujimori was not objectionable to the armed forces, either on ideological grounds or because of ineptitude. Meanwhile, Hermoza's main concern was to protect himself and members of his ring from future accusations in relation either to human rights violations or drug-related corruption. Even if Fujimori may not have needed Hermoza, Hermoza needed Fujimori.

What is the likely course that civil-military relations will take in Peru? As of late 1997, some facts stood out clearly. Firstly, there was a body of opinion within the armed forces, responsible for a succession of leaks, which was opposed to Hermoza, Montesinos and the Fujimori government. Secondly, the infighting between Montesinos and Hermoza continued, with Fujimori generally supporting Montesinos.[19] The number of active participants involved in this

---

[19]   In December 1997, frictions between Hermoza and Fujimori once again resurfaced. In an interview on the anniversary of the MRTA assault on the Japanese ambassador's residence in Lima, Fujimori downplayed the role played by Hermoza in the eventual release of the embassy hostages. Hermoza responded by summoning the six regional military chiefs and heads of other detachments to a meeting in Lima. Following an impromptu ceremony in which the military leaders expressed

conflict was relatively small; most senior officers preferred to pursue their own careers in what were difficult circumstances. Thirdly, the majority of the officer corps supported Fujimori and his government's policies, whilst wishing for less political intervention in the affairs of the armed forces. Opposition accusations that Fujimori was manipulating border tensions with Ecuador for his personal political benefit probably cemented pro-Fujimori elements, since such views were considered little short of treasonable. Indeed, Fujimori seemed little inclined to allow the increased military expenditure that such a conflict would imply. Fourthly, Fujimori appeared ill-disposed towards ridding himself of Montesinos and Hermoza: Hermoza opposed his removal, whilst Montesinos was a necessary counterpoint to Hermoza. The best chances to remove the two appeared either an opposition victory in 2000 or an institutional coup directed not against Fujimori but Hermoza. A full-blown military coup to replace Fujimori seemed improbable. An opposition victory in 2000 would remove the man on whom both Hermoza and Montesinos ultimately depended.

As Fujimori's second government entered its second half and as debate over the issue of re-election seemed unlikely to subside, political opposition to the regime appeared likely to focus increasingly on the role played by the armed forces and intelligence community in perpetuating the regime. In this context, it therefore seemed likely that opposition groups, both within the military and outside, would continue to find common cause in their bid to oust both Hermoza and Montesinos.

---

loyalty to Hermoza, Fujimori issued a stern order that the regional commanders should return to their garrisons. Coming shortly before Christmas, this was intended to test the allegiance of these commanders to Fujimori and reassert his constitutional authority over the armed forces. Montesinos emerged strengthened from this trial of strength.

CHAPTER 11

Tax Reform: The SUNAT Experience

Francisco Durand and Rosemary Thorp

A key question concerning the legacy of the Fujimori administration is whether his government weakened or strengthened institutions. There is no simple answer to this. To begin with, the concept of institutions has a number of different meanings. Institutions can be defined as internalised habits of economic and political agents, as established norms or rules that regulate behaviour, or as private and public organisations (Katz and Kosacoff, 1997). Another factor that makes the task of analysing institutions under President Alberto Fujimori difficult is that he polarised public opinion. Peruvian opposition forces have often argued that the Fujimori administration has 'weakened institutions', an argument that in part arises from the closure of Congress in the wake of the 1992 *autogolpe* (Rochabrun, 1996, p. 18). Another critique focuses on the rearrangement of state agencies and ministries that strengthened the power of the presidency, especially through the Ministry of the Presidency, at the expense of the line ministries in social areas (education, health, housing). The changing role of state agencies in line with the neoliberal orientation of the government is seen by some observers as a dangerous 'privatisation' of the state (Quijano, 1995).

To Fujimori, drastic reform was needed both to overcome a situation of institutional paralysis, caused by corruption and a legacy of excessive bureaucracy, and to implement new policies. Arguably, authority had to be emphasised to cope with the crisis and political gridlock, and to gain much-needed stability (*Newsweek*, 10 May 1993, Latin American edition). Government officials pointed out that some state institutions benefited from positive institutional change. A government plan in 1996 to 'modernise the state' seemed to indicate that Fujimori had developed an overall strategy of institutional change (*La Moneda*, 1996, pp. 52-8). If implemented, such changes would not be partial and limited just to certain parts of the state apparatus, as had been the case in the early years of his administration.

In order to contribute to the understanding of political-institutional change in the Fujimori era, it seems advisable to take one step at a time, to focus on concrete cases, and then refer more objectively to the larger question of institutionality. Study of the tax administration reform is particularly suited for this purpose. It was unquestionably the most successful reform of the Fujimori administration; it has even been acclaimed as a 'success story' for Latin America (Thorp, 1996, p. 34).

In order to study changes in state capacity,[1] this chapter focuses first on the prior evolution of the Peruvian state and the tax administration in order to establish its condition before the reform started. Second, it focuses on top policy elites as key agents of change, and their complex, changing relationship with the rest of the state apparatus and civil society as they pushed reform ahead. To discover these relationships, the SUNAT (National Superintendency of Tax Administration) reform must be seen in a longer-term perspective (1991-97). We identify several stages of institutional evolution and establish how key variables changed over time, both in favour of and against reform efforts. The conclusion is somewhat puzzling: Fujimori was responsible for helping provoke institutional change in tax administration, enhancing state capacity, but also for blocking the process when political conditions changed.

Institutional crisis

Before the Fujimori reforms, Peru had a typical developmentalist state, a large and unwieldy apparatus designed to provide a wide range of social services, and to stimulate industrial development through policy incentives and direct intervention in the economy. In 1989 it employed just over 1 million people (28% of the formal labour force), and owned 120 companies (Arias, 1991, pp. 201-2).

Within the state, we find a 'segmented' apparatus with different standards of bureaucratic capacity (Evans, 1989). 'Modern' branches, 'islands of efficiency' (recruited on merit, efficient and well funded) coexisted with traditional branches (recruited on clientelistic lines, overstaffed and underfunded). Further, inside the traditional branches, an upper level of professional officials predominated over a mass of traditional bureaucrats. This dual segmentation blocked institutional development by preventing the state from effectively designing, implementing and evaluating public policy. The 'traditional' bureaucratic culture was an arbitrary one, accustomed to the use of public resources for private purposes and to hiring personnel amongst relatives, friends or party supporters. The 'modern' bureaucratic culture involved professional recruitment and promotion, much greater efficiency and a stronger sense of the national interest. Both bureaucratic segments, however, shared a common approach, one of concentrating power in the hands of top administrators, and insulating them from other organisations. This autocratic, 'feudalistic' logic was so embedded that it also manifested itself in the modern sector.

Three circumstantial factors further debilitated the capacity of the Peruvian state in the 1980s: a deep recession; dramatic policy oscillations; and high levels of political violence. A fiscal crisis was already evident as early as 1976, a problem that continued to plague the country until the early 1990s. Constant policy shifts reflected a political stalemate between competing forces. A pro-

---

[1]   On the issue of state capacity in contemporary Latin America, see Geddes (1994).

market administration, elected in 1980 and led by Fernando Belaúnde, was replaced in 1985 by a more developmentalist one led by Alan García. For more than a decade, the state could not move ahead in any consistent way, causing confusion and preventing coherent policy planning (Gonzales de Olarte and Samamé, 1991, p. 15). Labour strikes and mass demonstrations became common during the ongoing economic crisis. In addition, the activities of Sendero Luminoso and the MRTA (Movimiento Revolucionario Túpac Amaro) not only resulted in up to 23,000 deaths, but also widespread acts of sabotage on power lines, bridges, police stations and other state agencies (Mauceri, 1992).

These three factors generated the conditions for a continuing deterioration in state capacities. Institutional degradation was particularly evident in the tax administration: it lost the ability to identify taxpayers, conduct basic auditing operations and even update archives. In 1991, the average monthly wage for the 3,025 tax administrators was 50 dollars (US dollars), two thirds less in real terms than in 1970. Most employees were organised in labour unions, which in turn resorted to continual strikes that achieved only short-term wage increases since hyperinflation soon eroded the gains. Continuing paralysis and low wages in the public sector forced employees to search for alternative sources of income; about one quarter of public employees had a second job in the private sector (Arias, 1991, p. 202).

In this context of continual dislocation, the developmentalist state rapidly degenerated into a predatory state. The most important taxpayers became used to making under-the-table agreements with 'friendly' employees, often ending up victims of extortion. Tax officials worked part time as private consultants. Smaller taxpayers paid bribes to avoid law enforcement against open tax evasion and fraud. The deterioration of state capacities was accelerated by trends in civil society, especially when taxpayers were hit by the recession and resorted to generalised evasion.

The resulting loss of tax revenue forced the government to introduce emergency measures. From 1980 on, taxes on gasoline became the main source of budget revenues. In 1988, in the midst of the crisis, the sales tax rate was raised from 10 to 15%. When this source of revenue declined, excise taxes were once again given priority (Arias, 1991, p. 210; Thorp, 1996, p. 36).

This situation generated complaints by trade associations, whose leaders became used to the extension of deadlines to pay income tax obligations. When the crisis reached an intolerable pitch, tax amnesties were granted. All told, about 6 million people had a *libreta tributaria*, a card which served as an ID and tax identification number. In 1985, 498,000 forms were submitted, but only 80,000 filers were required to pay taxes. In 1990, only 13,482 businesses paid the sales tax (Arias, 1991, p. 211). Existing tax legislation became a 'legal jungle', a chaotic body of legal requirements, with more than 180 different taxes and hundreds of regulatory measures, making tax administration and legal interpretation particularly difficult. Tax collection was centralised in the Banco de la Nación, a large, state-run bank, known for its corruption and inefficiency, where taxpayers had to wait long hours to buy tax forms before ever paying their taxes.

The authority of the state apparatus, given such organisational weakness, rapidly diminished. Indeed, arguably, guerrilla organisations like Sendero Luminoso became more efficient than the state in collecting 'revolutionary' taxes in some places, penalising those who sought to evade their responsibilities. Tax revenues as a percentage of GDP decreased from 15.6% in 1980 to 13.2% in 1985 and 5.8% 1989. At the moment of the initiation of the reform, in the first half of 1991, they reached a mere 4.9% (Estela, 1992, p. 1).

Origins of the reform

Only once the perception of a serious crisis sank in at the highest levels of government did the stakes become high enough to force the executive to react (Grindle and Thomas, 1991, p. 6; Bird and Casanegra, 1992, p. 60).

The origins of the reform (changes in the administration and tax laws) are to be found within the state apparatus, the central space for policy formulation, debate, adoption and implementation, a fact that suggests relative state autonomy.[2] Congress played a lesser role, interacting with civil society, and in debating and adopting the policy plans prepared by state elites working in coordination with international experts. Civil society came into play later on, largely in response to government initiatives.

During the crisis of the 1980s, reformers in Latin America targeted tax administration as a key area for policy priority (Pita, 1993; Berenztein, 1996). They developed a partial model for reform, in which tax administration gained priority as a means of coping with the fiscal crisis and contributing to overall state reform. The strategy separated the tax administration out from the finance ministry, transforming it into an autonomous agency or superintendency, linked directly to the presidency. Material resources would increase through the direct assignation of a percentage of tax receipts to the tax administration. Given the fact that tax compliance was low, revenues could immediately increase, and thus generate resources to increase wages, modernise systems and acquire new infrastructure. Tax reforms also formed part of a major effort to lower inflation, since higher tax revenues would help achieve fiscal targets. At the same time, lower inflation would help since the tax yield would automatically increase with greater price stability. However, once prices were stabilised, the only way to keep tax revenues rising was by reforming the tax system as a whole.

---

[2]   In her analysis of developmentalism in Brazil and Argentina, Sikkink (1991, p. 11) argues that a state-centred approach, focused on state capacity and policy elites, instead of state autonomy, is better suited to explaining why policies are adopted. A state autonomy approach, however, helps us understand the conditions under which policy elites enjoy greater room for manoeuvre.

Successive attempts at reform resulted in progress through trial and error, helping to identify problems and grapple towards solutions. The most important, failed, antecedent of the SUNAT reform occurred in mid-1988. The García government issued Law 24829, transforming the tax authority – the Dirección General de Contribuciones, a branch of the finance ministry (MEF) – into SUNAT, granting it 2% of revenues to finance its budget. Nevertheless, the García reform never took off, since the legal preconditions never meshed with other factors. Firstly, the policy team did not have the preparation or training to suggest sound policy or administrative changes.[3] Secondly, the authority granted by the president and MEF was weak and vacillating. Thirdly, the additional resources given to raise wages still required special authorisation. Since SUNAT continued to operate on MEF premises, wage increases immediately generated controversy elsewhere and raised opposition from labour unions. Fourthly, the government was trapped in a severe economic recession, attempting to combat hyperinflation but without a credible or coherent stabilisation plan.

The failure of macroeconomic stabilisation blocked the reform effort, thus further undermining state capacities. Predatory bureaucrats took advantage of increased institutional weakness to organise internal mafias,[4] which only re-emerged with greater force once the reform effort had stalled. Honest bureaucrats became demoralised and many of the leading reformers resigned, further eroding institutional capacities.[5]

The initial phase

Identification of three stages in the reform process helps explain the sequence of institutional change in greater detail. Stage I (1991-92) was defined by the initiation of the reform in a context of general crisis in such a way as to empower policy elites to confront internal challenges successfully. Stage II (1992-94) was characterised by institutional consolidation, with the policy team successfully setting the conditions for institutionalising the reform within the state and creating a new relationship with civil society. In Stage III (1994-97), although the legacy of the reform process prevailed over countervailing tendencies, worrying features emerged that threatened the continuity of institutional development.

The following factors typically condition the course of a successful reform:

---

[3]   For that reason, SUNAT documents distinguish between formal and real autonomy. See SUNAT (1993).

[4]   One of these scams was discovered years later. Taxes paid to the Banco de la Nación were appropriated by bank officials and tax administrators who forged documents. Since the computerised registry system did not work, inefficiency prevented crime prevention. Only when the systems were set up was it possible to identify the mafia and eradicate it.

[5]   The assessment of earlier reform attempts owes much to conversations between F. Durand and Esteban Pavletich, a former director of the Dirección General de Ingresos. He resigned in 1986 after attempting to reform the tax administration.

1.   Continuous political support from the top. This is a critical variable (Bird and Casanegra, 1992, p. 4; Radano, 1994, p. 3; Arias, 1994). If the president or top officials do not sustain change, the reform process will lose its initial impetus. Congressional support is also important if it is in a position to override executive authority.

2.   Upgrading the quality and continuity of top policy elites. These have to possess both the technical skills and the political instincts to face down the forces that oppose reform, in order to take advantage of the state's relative autonomy vis-à-vis civil society, and use wisely the policy space they have at their disposal. Strong leadership and team-work help a policy team make better choices, assisting them to gain credibility amongst the rest of the state apparatus and the business community. The team has to deal with the 'principal agent' problem, whereby the tax collection agency cannot directly control its employees. The reformers must then remove the old team and replace it with a new one not contaminated by the agency's past and with its roots in the 'modern' part of the state. Techniques must be found to encourage new and distinct forms of behaviour. Furthermore, to succeed, the reform package must appear to be 'a home-grown product' and not one imported from outside. Local policy elites have to be able to devise, carry out and evaluate policy plans on their own and efficiently (World Bank, 1991, p. 62).

3.   Ongoing bureaucratic regeneration. A Weberian leap to achieve a higher stage of bureaucratic development can only be accomplished by the creation of a modern civil service. This is a major challenge since very few tax administrations in Latin America have been able to move in this direction. If key decisions in this area are not taken, including the removal of bureaucratic mafias and traditional bureaucrats alongside the recruitment, training and promotion of a new generation of professionals, the reform can easily be reversed.

4.   Improvements in the relationship between the state and civil society. The degree of consensus obtained in favour of reform, and the way people 'play the game' once the reform is under way and the government enforces the law are critical to ensuring the consolidation of the reform process (Bird and Casanegra, 1992, p. 9). Whether or not civil society contributes to the reform process depends on the degree of public support it enjoys and on whether the state opens itself up to societal demands that mesh with the parameters of the reform programme (Sikkink, 1991, p. 2). The agency, at the same time, should become insulated against corrupting influences, and perform its role in a positive manner, providing efficient services and timely information. In the end, the state has to base this relationship with society more on trust and reciprocity than on coercion.

If taxpayers are to pay for reasons other than coercion, then there must be trust and respect for the tax collection system itself and a sense of reciprocity in terms of the benefits of paying taxes. Thus, contributing factors in achieving institutional development include often elusive contextual variables such as sustained economic growth and political stability. Continuous growth will help reassure taxpayers, in particular those prone to resisting sanctions. Political stability will help provide the continuity required to institutionalise change. In this wider context, one of the most difficult aspects is to reassure taxpayers about the quality of state expenditure. If they are not convinced that the quality of expenditure is improving, the tax collection system risks losing its new-found credibility.

The above list indicates how difficult it is to have all the conditions for institutional renovation. SUNAT initially benefited from a very positive situation, but it had to struggle against a less favourable context in the later stages of the reform process. Moreover, it was never able to influence important variables like the quality of spending.

In Stage I (1991-92), the main actors were the state and international organisations. Change came about from within the state apparatus, although induced by external forces. Civil society was in a dormant state, unaware of the process that was about to take place, traumatised by recession, ungovernability and violence. In this context, the different bureaucratic factions played a wait-and-see game, waiting for signals to enable them to define their course of action. At centre stage was the new policy team, politically empowered by the executive.

Fujimori's rise to power in 1990 coincided with a desperate fiscal situation. One of Fujimori's first executive decisions was to embrace free market policies and obtain support from the international financial organisations (Pease, 1990, pp. 9-10). Fujimori and his inner *nisei* circle (in particular his brother Santiago, a lawyer and a key advisor), were convinced of the need to stem corruption, re-establish state authority, and reform some agencies so as to guarantee the successful application of a stabilisation plan.[6] This approach to both administrative and legislative reform was also supported by Carlos Boloña, a firm advocate of liberalisation who became finance minister in 1991.

Manuel Estela, a former head of economic research in the central bank who had familiarised himself with earlier reform attempts while serving at the MEF, was nominated National Superintendent in May 1991. He was asked to prepare a strategy to transform SUNAT into a model institution. Estela and his taskforce relied on three elements of strategy development: trust and team building, goals and planning, and the use of foreign advisors (Thorp, 1996, p. 36).[7]

Most of the team put together by Estela came from the central bank, the only

---

[6] Fujimori considered an increase in tax collection critical to the success of the economic stabilisation plan. When in May 1991 he approached Estela and persuaded him to direct the reform, he told him, 'this is a matter of the utmost importance and I will be personally involved'. Manuel Estela, interview with F. Durand, Lima, 7 April 1997.

[7] Estela was convinced that it was crucial that 'nothing was left to chance'. Interview with R. Thorp, Lima, August 1995.

public sector institution with a strong and relatively undamaged professional tradition. Other key members came from a handful of private universities, notably the Catholic University and the University of Lima. Trust within the team was developed thanks to this common background, and soon extended to other members, including a select and honest group of tax administrators and MEF officials. All brought with them diverse experiences and were committed to the idea of tax reform. This was the main means by which the principal agent problem, the downfall of the previous attempt, was resolved.

The 'master plan', as Estela liked to call it, was prepared by a select group of Peruvian experts from outside the tax administration, in conjunction with a group of international experts who had previous experience of tax reforms elsewhere in Latin America, but were unsullied by the twisted logic of Peruvian politics.[8] The plan advocated wholesale transformation rather than incremental change, an approach known as *comerse el elefante entero*.[9] Special authority was needed to move the premises to a modern building, evaluate all personnel and fire employees unable to pass an exam or known to be corrupt. New penalties were put forward for congressional approval to deter tax evasion. The team also requested financial autonomy from the MEF.[10] With the central bank in mind as a model, the idea was to introduce modern recruitment policies and raise wages to levels similar to those paid by the bank. The plan was risky, but the team feared the consequences of a slow start. In Peru, as Estela put it 'all temporary decisions become permanent'; it was best to set off on a path of institutional development with an initial 'great leap forward' – and hope for the best later on.

The plan was discussed with Fujimori and his brother Santiago, in particular with the latter, who helped by suggesting legal changes and advising on what was politically feasible. The president supported the plan since it seemed consistent and the team sufficiently determined and capable to transform the tax administration. A key element was Estela's argument that the Fujimori government would win credit for having set out to build a successful tax administration. Linking political outcomes with policy reforms in this way was important to obtaining solid presidential backing.

The plan, once approved by the president and the MEF, was presented to Congress. The apparent solidity of the plan, and the team's reputation for

---

[8]   Estela, while working at the MEF in the 1980s, collaborated on a draft a plan to reform the tax administration. This was an important previous experience 'because we already knew what to do'. Alberto Radano and Alberto Conde were experienced tax administrators in their home country, Argentina, and had been international consultants in Bolivia. Interview with F. Durand, Lima, 5 April 1997.

[9]   This decision was taken by the local team, and initially opposed by the international experts, who feared that the reform process could be endangered at an early stage. Estela, interview with R. Thorp, Lima, August 1995.

[10]   Estela was designated Superintendent by the president himself, a decision basically rubber-stamped by Finance Minister Carlos Boloña, appointed at the same time as Estela. The tax reform started without any dependence on any other executive position but the president.

technical expertise, along with concern about the fiscal crisis and the extent of corruption, made for a balanced dialogue with key congressional committees. Although leftist senators objected to the dismissals involved and the new privileges granted to tax administrators, the plan finally obtained broad multi-party support and Congress approved it in May 1991. This was a preliminary step in changing the relationship with civil society.

Once the team obtained solid political backing, the reform started to be implemented. The tactic was to take full advantage of an element of surprise. Changes in the bureaucratic structure had to be implemented against opposition from mafias, labour unions, traditional bureaucrats afraid of change, and even terrorist organisations. As soon as the taskforce announced the reform plan, the unions objected to the staff evaluation process and the physical removal of the tax administration to new premises. During three critical weeks, in April 1991, the future of the reform hung by a thread. Street demonstrations, a wildcat strike, and even a guerrilla rocket attack took place, but the team held its ground.[11] A positive signal came when a small but growing number of employees came round to accepting the proposal.[12] An option was offered of early retirement benefits to those laid off, plus a 50 dollar bonus to those who took the test. Employees knew that honest administrators were collaborating with the team in order to root out those who were corrupt. Following a strict personnel evaluation, the number of employees was eventually reduced from 3,025 to 991. The remainder resigned and were given retirement benefits totalling 2.3 million dollars (Arias, 1994, p. 3). The move to new premises, a modern thirteen-storey building was also important, since previously SUNAT operated from a cramped, dilapidated building, without sufficient computers or vehicles.

Once the opposing vested interests were removed and union resistance broken, Congress approved a law authorising SUNAT to pay private sector wages. The salaries of professional employees suddenly jumped from 50 dollars a month to 890 dollars. From then on, the SUNAT policy team gained cohesion and a strong sense of institutional identity emerged, buttressed by external support. The first obstacles had been surmounted.

Once this phase was completed, SUNAT faced two critical challenges in gaining credibility among taxpayers: (i) to increase tax collection, and (ii) to generate respect for existing legislation. This was the point at which the issue of state power and authority over civil society became critical. Having broken internal opposition, it became important to create a momentum of institutional development. A contributing factor in establishing a positive relationship with taxpayers and convincing them to accept law enforcement was to devise an

---

[11] The team was at one point barricaded in the Superintendent's office, surrounded by demonstrators who threatened to enter by force. A special police unit, sent by the president, had to use tear gas to free them.

[12] This period required extraordinary commitment from the team in all senses. Luis Alberto Arias, second-in-command, recalled that he personally talked to more than 300 employees to help persuade them. Interview with R. Thorp, Lima, 29 August 1995.

effective advertising campaign. Coercion had to be balanced with effective communication.

Since SUNAT started from scratch, it was important to 'make sufficient noise' to let taxpayers of all categories feel the presence of the new tax administration and to perceive the risk of evasion, whilst winning the time needed to install new, modern administrative systems. Institutional development required the building up of an information base. Selective auditing programmes were introduced for this purpose, with Congress approving a system to monitor commercial firms. Young, well-mannered university recruits were chosen to visit commercial establishments and search for tax evasion. If evasion was spotted, these were closed for a week, a sign that the administration 'meant business'. Tax evasion proved to be so evident and generalised, the army of 'fedatarios' so educated and convincing, that soon hundreds of stores were penalised without much reaction. The business sector, caught by surprise, reacted defensively: inept and corrupt accountants were fired and replaced by professional tax experts; instructions were issued to establish business practices in accordance with the law. The goal became one of 'putting the house in order' before penalties could be applied or made more severe. The relationship with civil society thus changed: both state authorities and taxpayers moved towards restoring a social pact.

Since tax reform impinged on powerful interest groups, full support from the top was needed and was forthcoming. Fujimori was able to provide strong leadership in this direction, partly because he had so few political debts to repay: his surprising electoral victory in 1990 was achieved without large campaign contributions from private donors.[13] Another factor was the support of the press and public opinion for those whose job it was to audit firms. This helped isolate the critics and neutralise angry taxpayers. Good communication also helped. A well-designed advertising campaign, and an intelligent public relations strategy (conducted by media expert Oscar Dufour), helped legitimise the reform efforts. Finally, private meetings between Estela's team and top business people, including representatives from the main business association (led at that time by Jorge Camet, who later became finance minister), helped to communicate the significance of the reform to individual businessmen, as well as the nature of the auditing process and the overall goals of the reform.

Consolidation

Stage II (1992-94) was one of institutional consolidation. The policy space generated in Stage I was sufficient for conditions to develop to institutionalise the reform over the medium-term. Given the fact that increased tax revenues automatically translated into a larger budget, lack of resources was not an

---

[13]   When Estela asked if the executive would support auditing measures that impinged on powerful interests, Fujimori was quoted as replying 'I do not have any prior commitments with anyone. How about you?' Manuel Estela, interview with F. Durand, 7 Lima, April, 1997.

obstacle. The policy team had the chance to introduce widespread administrative changes, implement a merit-based human resources policy and modernise its infrastructure. On this basis, institutional change could become soundly based.

Administrative changes were developed by joint teams of Peruvian and foreign experts, who presented proposals to the managing committee (Comité de Alta Dirección), in which heads of department and top advisors participated in weekly day-long meetings to evaluate implementation of the 'master plan'. The committee discussed the feasibility of technical change and the possible consequences of the reforms, both within the state and civil society. The idea was collectively to discuss the best possible course of action, since in most cases SUNAT was moving into uncharted territory. Three sequential plans were developed. The first was a new system to recruit, train, and promote personnel. The second involved administrative modernisation to gather and process data on taxpayers more efficiently, and to improve tax collection and auditing operations. On the basis of this, it became easier to elaborate annual plans and set monthly targets for tax collection. The third plan was directed at the establishment of a positive state/taxpayer relationship, based on efficient services, legal compliance and mutual respect.

Improvements in training and management, another crucial aspect of the reform and the key to the principal agent problem, were achieved through close coordination and teamwork between the personnel manager and the training centre, the Institute for Tax Administration (IAT). SUNAT attracted thousands of applicants from the best universities to replace those who had been retired. The selection process included newspaper advertisements inviting applicants to sit several multiple choice exams and take part in extensive interviews. Between 1992 and 1995, 647 applicants were recruited out of 15,410, a less than 3% success rate. To avoid influence over admissions, IAT insulated itself and created strict standards of information and admission. Once recruited, applicants were trained in tax reform, legal matters, auditing, tax collection, computerised systems and ethics. From 1992 to 1996, IAT offered 32 basic training courses to 1,114 professionals, new and old. It provided 281 seminars on ethics to almost all employees. Special auditing courses and middle-management courses were also taught on a regular basis.[14]

Administrative modernisation was based on three 'basic systems', implemented with international expert advice. The Inter-American Development Bank (IDB) and the Inter-American Center of Tax Administrators provided both funds and expertise to institute in Peru systems already adopted elsewhere in Latin America.[15] The first system was a new computerised registry of taxpayers (*Registro Unico de Contribuyentes*). The second was a differentiated auditing system inside each department. Major taxpayers were monitored by a special

---

[14]   Information on training comes from the IAT library.
[15]   External support helped in cancelling a pre-existing contract for US$8-10 million of inappropriate computer equipment! Arias. Interview with R. Thorp, Lima, 29 August 1995.

unit, to ensure a continuing increase in tax revenues. The rest was monitored by ordinary units. Tax collection was also modernised. Major taxpayers paid taxes directly at SUNAT premises, whilst small and medium-sized taxpayers used a private banking network, established to break the monopoly of the Banco de la Nación. In 1994, 72% of all tax payments were received at 1,100 bank branches (Arias, 1994, p. 7). On the basis of these two systems and the new banking network, data analysis greatly improved. It also became possible to follow collection trends and plan auditing operations with precision.

The third system was the reorganisation of the system of sales receipts. Sales tax (VAT) became the most important single tax, representing 44% of total tax collection in 1994. The sales tax made it possible to reduce dependence on excise taxes. A strategy to simplify the tax structure reduced the number of taxes to five (value added tax, income tax, assets tax, excise duties, and a housing and urban planning tax known as Fonavi). The control and reorganisation of the sales receipt system, coupled with tax simplification, was crucial to sustaining increased tax revenues and improving levels of respect for the tax administration. Cross-checking of sales receipts from both buyers and sellers, and using all three systems, was a leap forward in terms of facilitating auditing operations and monitoring tax compliance. Most of these decisions, it should be noted, were designed by SUNAT and approved by the executive when Congress had been closed down.

Institutional administrative renovation was complemented by better infrastructure. This was made possible by increased resources. The budget increased from 2.5 million dollars in 1991 to 10.9 million in 1992, indicating the extent of resource availability (SUNAT, 1993, p. 12). New purpose-built offices were established throughout the country, with computerised systems, modern communication facilities and a new fleet of vehicles.

The state/taxpayer relationship was, without question, the hardest aspect to establish. The basis of the new philosophy was 'clear rules and strict law enforcement, combined with good relations with taxpayers', guaranteeing effective communication and the neutral application of technical procedures (Estela, 1996, p. 3). Clear rules were introduced at the outset. However, once the systems were set up and the tax administration realised the extent of tax debts owed by taxpayers of all categories, a special amnesty was granted. If a taxpayer complied with the law from the time the reform began, all past debts were to be erased. If taxpayers had not cooperated, tax auditing would consider all accumulated debts. If they were unable to pay their debts, and depending on their financial situation, the amount owed was made payable in instalments. If, finally, taxpayers resisted compliance, enforcement included the embargo of assets. To avoid the possibility of regenerating clientelistic/corrupt practices, auditors were instructed not to accept any gifts from taxpayers. If caught receiving bribes, they were prosecuted and fired. SUNAT issued a regulation whereby all gifts sent at Christmas were to be returned. These measures helped create a new image that became SUNAT's trademark.

The consolidation phase in Stage II was greatly assisted by the enlarged policy space and innovative planning amongst the policy team. By this stage, most of the obstacles to continuing institutional development had become surmountable. A number of indicators showed that the state had regained a capacity to implement policy and win over public support. The most obvious sign of success was that tax revenues as a percentage of GDP rose from less than 5% in 1991 to 11% in 1993 to 14% in 1995 (Thorp, 1996; *Gestión*, 22 February 1996, p. 10). The increase in tax collection was initially accomplished thanks to extraordinary measures (a sharp increase in gasoline tax) and lower inflation rates (the 'Olivera-Tanzi' effect). By 1992, higher revenues were basically sustained by the systematic expansion of the tax base, and strict application of sanctions against tax evasion and fraud.

The number of registered taxpayers rose from 80,000 in 1991 to approximately 300,000 'active' taxpayers in 1994, plus a further 200,000 'irregular' taxpayers. The number of large taxpayers rose from 700 (representing 90% of all tax collection in 1991, an indication of an extreme income gap) to 2,916 in 1993 (representing 85.5% of tax collection). The number of income tax returns filed rose from less than 200,000 in 1991 to 227,519 in 1993 and 423,444 in 1994. The ratio of income tax returns filed per inhabitant grew from 0.72% in 1983 to 18.64% in 1994, indicating that the tax reform had been a great deal more efficient than those of the early 1980s, when tax revenues had yet to decline so dramatically (Arias, 1994, p. 2 and *passim.*). With regard to penalties, the number of premises closed by SUNAT for non-compliance with the sales tax rose from 620 in 1991, to 5,319 in 1992, 7,910 in 1993 and 7,268 in 1994 (SUNAT, 1994). In 1995, a Tax Targeting Plan prepared by SUNAT divided the country geographically into tax priority areas and ordered audits in each one. With new infrastructure, and the general application of auditing policies, SUNAT became one of the few public organisations able to act efficiently throughout the country.

The tax reform won widespread public recognition. Originally centred on Lima, its scope was soon extended to almost all social strata in every part of Peru, with the exception of isolated rural areas. According to opinion surveys in 1993, 73.8% of taxpayers in ten cities thought SUNAT was 'improving as an institution', while only 8.1% thought it was deteriorating.[16] In 1994, the SUNAT reform was considered as the third 'most positive aspect of the Fujimori administration' by a leading polling firm, the first two being the fight against terrorism and hyperinflation (*Apoyo*, 1994, p. 23). Another poll on corruption in public institutions indicated strong public recognition. Only 1.3% of those interviewed (in Lima) considered SUNAT 'corrupt', while 52.9% considered the police the 'most corrupt institution', followed by the judicial system (40.2%) (*La República*, 2 March 1995, p. 20). Such positive responses were sustained over the years: a 1997 poll ranked SUNAT as the 'most efficient' of all private and public institutions (*Debate*, July-August 1997, p. 21).

---

[16]   Data from the Institute of Tax Administration, SUNAT.

Loss of momentum

Stage III (1994-97) saw the emergence of factors that slowed down the reform process. SUNAT had to battle internally against problems of corporate leadership and excessive bureaucracy. Furthermore, it found itself less well positioned in the power struggle within the state and its relationship with civil society became more problematic. However, SUNAT still managed to survive as a modernised institution, surrounded by less efficient state agencies.

The first factor that slowed down the reform process was the constant change in the policy teams which impeded institutional continuity (Sikkink, 1991, p. 24). Changing leadership opened the door to power centralisation and 'feudalisation' at a point at which the institution still lacked the traditions and conventions of a modern civil service. In six years, SUNAT had four directors. Given its broad powers and autonomy, SUNAT's leaders had the power to take the institution in the direction they pleased. The first two directors shared the view that the tax reform needed to be institutionalised and to that end maintained the policy team intact. After Estela was replaced in December 1992 by Sandro Fuentes less emphasis was placed on team work and more on concentrating decision-making in the Superintendent's hands.[17] The third director, Adrián Revilla, appointed in March 1994, continued this trend. Revilla decided to experiment with Total Quality Management theories rather than keeping the focus on the original reform plan. Other problems also emerged. Under Revilla, some top policy makers were arbitrarily removed (*El Comercio*, 16 July 1995, section E 2) and the various intendencies struggled to concentrate power in their own hands. Revilla was forced to resign in late 1996 and the fourth director, Jorge Baca, tried to restore the original policy team. He jettisoned the Total Quality approach in favour of renewed team work. However, these changes were less effective, partly because the external situation was less favourable to ongoing reform. Constant changes and the resurgence of old bureaucratic habits provoked a gradual loss of institutional cohesion and sense of *esprit de corps*.

Second, presidential priorities shifted from fiscal austerity to more populist politics. Internal changes within SUNAT coincided with a fall-off in presidential backing and increased subordination to the MEF. Sensing that SUNAT was more vulnerable when Estela left, Jorge Camet, the new finance minister and a business leader, sought to increase the MEF's influence over SUNAT. Top administrators in the MEF appear to have felt that SUNAT had accumulated too much power and too many privileges. When Fuentes became Superintendent, the delicate balance of forces within the state was still kept, thanks to his close ties with Santiago Fujimori, who managed to contain the increasing influence of the MEF on presidential politics. When Revilla replaced Fuentes in 1994, the balance of forces shifted more decisively in favour of the MEF. After the 1995 elections, the MEF became a key link between Fujimori and the business sector.

---

[17]   Fuentes followed a more cautious approach than Estela. When he voluntarily resigned, he advised Revilla 'to be very careful, because SUNAT has made significant progress and each step has to be carefully taken' (*Solo Negocios*, 29 August 1996, p. 14).

In part because of the MEF's pressure, Santiago Fujimori withdrew as the president's main advisor; SUNAT thus lost its privileged access to the presidency.

This was reinforced by a third factor, a tax revolt. The loss of momentum described above was not necessarily visible to the public. However, important taxpayers sought to ease the tax burden by seeking to restore their influence over the government, especially through the new Congress elected in 1993, after the *autogolpe*. Whilst street vendors organised demonstrations, big business demands were channelled towards the MEF, now led by a businessman. This took place at a moment of infighting when SUNAT lost its ability to exert influence over business leaders and trade associations. Complaints about SUNAT were orchestrated through the Confederación Inter-sectorial de las Empresas Privadas (Confiep), the main business lobby organisation.[18] Some of these demands were perfectly rational, since tax rates were high and many aspects of tax legislation needed to be adjusted. However, others were aimed at obtaining selective exoneration by political means, which posed a danger to the reform process. During Fujimori's second administration, after 1995, several decisions indicated that he was more open to social demands and less concerned with the coherence of macroeconomic policies (Zolezzi, 1996). In 1996, the rate of the assets tax was reduced from 2 to 1.5%, and tax exonerations were granted to publications, the construction sector, agribusiness and tourism. In late 1996 a wide amnesty was approved (DL 848), despite SUNAT's opposition, and without referring to its technical expertise. The amnesty created a serious administrative burden: 75,421 firms were registered to lower or reschedule debts, estimated at 750 million dollars, on a case-by-case basis (*Perú Económico*, February 1997, p. 3). Finally, in July 1997, at a moment when Fujimori's popularity was at a low ebb, the president surprisingly announced in his state of the union address a reduction of the Fonavi tax from 7 to 5% and lower excise taxes on fuel (*Expreso*, 28 July 1997, p. 1).

The limits to SUNAT's actions were also put to the test by the criminal justice system, one of the more corrupt branches of the state apparatus (see Chapter 9). Law enforcement against tax fraud often encountered resistance and lack of collaboration from the police. Judges also often sided with taxpayers. All legal tax fraud cases brought by SUNAT between 1991 and 1996 were lost in the courts. The relatively low efficiency of the spending ministries also made problems for SUNAT. In 1997, less than a year after Fujimori announced a major transformation of the whole state apparatus, the plan for state reform was abandoned.

Stage III represented less of an abandonment of the tax reform than a fall-off in the impetus behind reform and a loss of efficacy. Tax collection targets, as a consequence, became harder to accomplish. In early 1996, an IMF report revealed growing concern about the government's ability to maintain tax

---

[18]   Interview by F. Durand with Eduardo de Voto, manager of Confiep, Lima, August 1995.

collection on an upward path (*Gestión*, 22 February 1996, p. 10). SUNAT's decreasing contribution to tax revenues was already visible by mid 1996 (*Nota Tributaria*, February 1997). Top policy-makers in government circles expressed concern that tax compliance was lower than expected, and that the government would have a hard time meeting the goals agreed with the IMF on tax collection. Between 1995 and 1996, tax collection as a percentage of GDP increased only marginally, from 14.0 to 14.1% of GDP. For 1997, the government achieved 14.1% again, whereas the original goal when SUNAT began setting targets in 1991, was to pass the 16% percent mark by 1997.[19]

Conclusions

Serious, committed reform efforts to improve state capacities took place during the early period of the Fujimori administration, and in the midst of crisis. In these circumstances, the executive considered it feasible to empower a task force that would attempt to transform a branch of the state apparatus targeted for reform.

Given the high degree of political backing, successful reform was largely dependent on the commitment, experience, quality, and continuity of top policy elites. As a rule, the weaker the institution, the more critical it is to have a strong policy team. Once empowered, the team had to prove itself capable of defeating internal resistance to reform, win the confidence of both the executive and the legislative powers, and establish a more positive relationship with civil society. On this basis, the team could hope to expand the policy space available to it and set out on a path of institutional development to improve state capacities.

Internally, the authorities used their budgetary advantage and institutional autonomy to clean up the old administration, set up the basis of a modern civil service, establish new administrative systems and develop the infrastructure necessary to operate efficiently. Modern, adequately recruited, well-trained bureaucracies need to operate with private sector wages, and count on adequate facilities to implement policies effectively. This is particularly important in the case of tax administration, since this is the agency that collects revenues and therefore funds the rest of the state. Fortunately, SUNAT made significant progress in human resource policies during Stage II, when conditions to achieve a Weberian 'leap' were still present. In Stage III, constant leadership changes, and the resurgence of old bureaucratic habits, slowed down the reform process.

In terms of the relationship with the rest of the state, Congress played an important role in Stage I of the reform effort. Later on, after it had been closed down by Fujimori after the 1992 *autogolpe*, policy decisions were basically taken by the executive, either through top-down decisions, or through a

---

[19]   As of mid 1998, it seemed that the tax yield for that year will be no more than 14.1% of GDP again.

Congress controlled by Fujimori supporters. Political support for the reform efforts shifted in Stage III. Tax legislation was approved on the basis of a political agenda designed to appease taxpayers rather than deepen the tax reforms. In 1994/95, in a context of growth and political stability, the initial fiscal policy rationale was supplanted by a more populist one. The resumption of the MEF's control of fiscal policy, and its pro-business orientation, together with the effects of corruption in the judiciary, frustrated further reform. The government's abandonment of the state reform proposals in 1997 further reduced the chances of continuing institutional development. The inability of the rest of the state to provide better services contributed to a slow-down in the momentum of reform. The tax system lost some of its credibility amongst the general public, since taxpayers broadly speaking complied with the law so long as higher taxation translated into better services.

In terms of the relationship between the tax authorities and civil society, changes also took place in Stage III as the alignment of the planets became less auspicious for the SUNAT reformers. In Stage I, taxpayers reacted in a positive manner and compliance with the law improved. They welcomed a reform effort that eradicated corruption and inefficiencies in the tax collecting agency. The policy team was skilful enough to combine heightened fear about the possible consequences of evasion with increased respect for the institution. It evolved an effective communications strategy. However, once the tax base was significantly expanded, and the new auditing systems installed, SUNAT lost its initial element of surprise, and the margin of state autonomy shrunk as taxpayers started to retaliate. All these factors limited the continuity of the reform effort, and this resulted in a gradual loss of policy efficacy. SUNAT was still an 'island of efficiency', but one surrounded by a sea of less developed branches of the state apparatus.

PART V

SOCIETY

CHAPTER 12

From *Movimientismo* to Media Politics: The Changing Boundaries between Society and Politics in Fujimori's Peru

Martín Tanaka

This chapter seeks to assess the changes that have taken place in recent decades between the state and the political arena on the one hand and popular sectors and popular organisations in the urban sphere on the other. Under President Alberto Fujimori, there has been a striking process of demobilisation, following a period of active social movement (*movimientismo*)[1] in the late 1970s and for most of the 1980s. In this chapter, I suggest that there was also an important change in the characteristics of political participation and a redefinition of the frontiers separating the social and political spheres. Political participation thus moved on from the *movimientismo* of the previous period to what I loosely characterise as 'media politics'. What we therefore see is the eclipse of a particular type of relationship between the popular sectors and the state, and its replacement by a new one in which public opinion plays a key role.

Popular sectors and social movements: the founders of a new order?

In the second half of the 1970s and throughout most of the 1980s, popular sectors in Peru demonstrated impressive and unprecedented degrees of political protagonism. In part, this reflected a cycle of popular mobilisation which affected other Latin American countries, notably Argentina, Brazil, Chile and Mexico. In Peru in the late 1970s, labour unions and other popular organisations spearheaded a series of national strikes and protests which played a crucial part in paving the way towards democratic transition. In the 1980s, the strength of popular organisation proved a major obstacle to the Belaúnde government's attempts at neoliberal reform. These movements were not just comprised of industrial labour unions, but of peasants' organisations in rural areas, regional movements throughout the country and an array of grass-roots organisations in the major cities, especially Lima. These movements were sustained by strong support groups, such as NGOs and church base communities and, perhaps most importantly, they enjoyed the backing of influential and broadly-based left-wing parties which gave them political expression.

Popular sectors and their organisations showed high degrees of political

---

[1] I borrow the term *movimientismo* from Giorgio Alberti (1991), who conceives this as an 'exacerbated populism', a political dynamic situated at a macro-political level. I locate *movimientismo* here at the micro-level (where the collective action is produced) and the meso-level (the space that relates the social and political arenas).

consciousness, reflecting the influence of radical and left-wing ideologies. They also revealed democratic and participatory values and practices. This led some authors to consider them to be 'the founders of a new order' (Ballón, 1986) in which society and the state would become closer and more democratic, thanks to greater political participation and a more active civil society which interacted with and nurtured the political sphere.

Since the end of the 1980s and throughout the Fujimori years, dramatic changes have taken place which have produced a very different political landscape. Political activism among the labour unions has all but disappeared, whilst political participation in popular organisations has weakened and such organisations have been marginalised. This is equally the case for different regions of the country, rural as well as urban areas, and for large national organisations as well as small local ones. These organisations have been unable to block the neoliberal reforms enacted by the Fujimori government, which whilst successfully ending hyperinflation, did so on the back of policies which had high social costs and which have greatly increased the proportion of the population living below the poverty level. The reforms themselves have also had a strong impact on the capacity for mobilisation and collective action on the part of these popular sectors.

In response to these changes, Peruvian social scientists have reacted in two main ways. One reaction is perplexity: how to understand these changes which eroded the social protagonism of popular sectors in such a dramatic way. The answers to this question tended to stress the effects of specific government policies in weakening popular organisation, as well as pointing to the corrosive effects on organisational capabilities of economic crisis and political violence. The second reaction is one of regret: this sort of demobilisation weakened the chances of democratic consolidation, since this relied on the vitality of civil society, whilst the changes helped buttress Fujimori's authoritarianism. The conclusion that follows from such lines of analysis was that a key task lay ahead in the rebuilding of the popular organisation that had preceded Fujimori's *tsunami* (tidal wave).

Although this portrayal of the situation is correct in many respects, it is inadequate for the following reasons: (i) the extent of disappointment and regret vis-à-vis popular demobilisation stems from the exaggerated and often unjustified expectations about what popular organisations were and what they were likely to achieve; (ii) the attention paid to the destructive effects of economic crisis and political violence obscured a significant parallel process of restructuring, with an important reconfiguration of political and social identities at the popular level; and (iii) although it is important to reconstitute the old social and political identities in order to consolidate Peruvian democracy, it is also important to create new social and political leadership and organisation, and to develop new practices capable of expressing the new social and political identities that have emerged during the Fujimori years.

Mobilisation and demobilisation: popular identities, support groups and incorporation

Much of the literature on the relationship between popular sectors and popular organisations, on the one hand, and the state and the political arena on the other, has been developed using the theory of 'new social movements', and specifically the 'identity paradigm'.[2] The emphasis placed on collective identities in popular sectors led to the neglect of the context in which these identities developed and changed. As a consequence, much of the literature has tended to rely on unjustified assumptions, taking for granted aspects which need to be understood in relation to other variables. Two common assumptions were, first, that popular sectors should somehow follow collective forms of action in order to express themselves politically and that if political participation through collective action diminishes it is symptomatic of depoliticisation. The second assumption was that the existing popular organisations somehow represented the interests and demands of the popular sectors. Rarely was there any discussion about the continuities and discontinuities between popular sectors and popular organisations, or between rank-and-file members and their leaders.

Whilst such assumptions may have been generally valid in the late 1970s and for much of the 1980s, this was not the case in the 1990s. The earlier period was characterised by the centrality of the state in political, social and economic terms.[3] Social conflict therefore implied a public and political conflict, given the extensive role played by the state. There were strong incentives for political participation through collective action. When able to mobilise successfully, popular organisations could provide state resources to the popular sectors. Success legitimated their existence.

This sort of dynamic was a consequence of that particular form of state. However, the relationship between the social and political arenas, whose boundaries are movable, is determined according to historical circumstances. For this reason, a more dynamic model is required to analyse political participation, capable of explaining the outcome of changing circumstances. The model used here is very simple and open to further elaboration, and it needs to be tested in particular cases. It uses as one variable the strength of collective identities among popular sectors, but also includes consideration of changes in the political opportunity structures. This helps us surmount some of the limitations in the existing literature.[4]

---

[2]   I follow here the classical distinction established by Cohen between the 'identity paradigm' and 'resource mobilization theory' (Cohen, 1988). For a recent review of these paradigms and the current tendencies in the literature, see Gerardo Munck (Munck, 1997).

[3]   This centrality of the state was a common characteristic of most Latin American countries from the 1930s and 1940s until the 1980s. For general views of the characteristics of this state, see Douglas Chalmers (1997), and Marcelo Cavarozzi (1996) who wrote about the 'state-centred matrix'. Alain Touraine (1989) wrote about the lack of autonomy between the social and political spheres under the 'national-popular state'. For the Peruvian state and some of its economic and political aspects, see Carol Wise (1994).

[4]   For the theoretical foundations of this kind of approach, see McAdam, McCarthy and Zald

This model helps explain the logic behind political participation by popular sectors in different periods of Peruvian politics, from the mid-1970s up to the present. We will focus on political participation through collective action, recognising that there are other important forms of public involvement that do not involve collective action (e.g. voting or expressing political opinions). There are also other forms of collective action that do not imply political participation – for instance social action to improve conditions in urban neighbourhoods. As we shall see, these distinctions are crucial to understanding changes in the frontiers that separate the political and social spheres. However, at this stage, we will focus on collective action addressed to the state and carried out in the political arena, in pursuit of non-excludable public goods.

We will use the concept of political opportunity structure to provide a context, since the starting point for the analysis of collective action is the structure of costs and benefits. For the popular sectors, the rationale for participation depends on the anticipated benefits that the acquisition of public and collective goods can bring, taking into consideration the scarce resources expended and the probabilities of success.

The literature on political opportunity structures mentions a number of variables that affect these calculations. Two variables are particularly relevant. The first is the capacity of the state to distribute collective goods. The existence of available resources, obtainable through mobilisation, creates incentives for political participation through collective action. However, if the state is repressive, or facing severe fiscal constraints, collective action may seem a waste of time and resources. The second variable is the extent to which popular sectors themselves have the resources required to mount collective action. One of the main sources for such action comes from support groups which can provide backing, varying from cash to the provision of ideology. The main support groups for popular organisations in Peru have been left-wing parties, non-governmental organisations (NGOs) and the base communities of the Catholic Church.

Finally, a third variable needs to be considered, one highlighted by the 'identity paradigm': the strength of popular collective identities. This depends on a number of factors, including the size of the groups involved, the degree of consolidation of the urban environment (in the case of urban shantytowns) and other broader elements such as the extent of economic crisis and/or political violence. There can be strong incentives for collective action within a distributive state where there are strong support groups, but without strong collective identities the free-rider problem cannot be surmounted. Indeed, with strong identities, collective action can still take place, even though the political environment may not be favourable.

(1996) and Kriesi, Koopmas, Duyvendak and Giugni (1995). For a recent review article about this literature, see Tarrow (1996).

The model is summarised in Table 1. The combination of the strength of collective identities, the presence of support groups and the distributive capacities of the state defines a pattern of incentives that makes it rational to embark on certain kinds of political participation. It also influences the relationships between the state, the political arena and popular sectors.[5]

Table 1. Political Participation among Popular Sectors

	Greater state distribution capacities	Lesser state distribution capacities
Strong support groups	Strong collective identities: *participatory democracy* Weak collective popular identities: *elite democracy*	Strong collective identities: *movimientismo* Weak collective identities: *negotiation*
Weak support groups	Strong collective identities: *corporatism* Weak collective identities: *(neo)clientelism*	Strong collective identities: *social movements* Weak collective identities: *pragmatism*

I propose to analyse the political participation of the popular sectors in Peru in recent decades on the basis of these categories. During the second half of the 1970s, I believe that political participation in Peru can be modelled within a *social movement* dynamic that combines weak support groups, lesser state distribution capacities and strong collective identities. During most of the 1980s, on the other hand, when there was intervention by important support groups, participation was best modelled as a *movimientista* dynamic. During the first half of the 1990s, the economic and political crisis debilitated the support groups and popular collective identities, and the dynamic became more pragmatic. With the consolidation of economic adjustment and neoliberal reform, the distributive capacities of the state improved, whilst support groups and collective identities remained weak. Thus, in the early 1990s we can observe a 'neo-clientelistic' type of participation amongst the popular sectors.

This model helps us understand and compare different forms of political participation among popular sectors and helps clarify their dynamic and capacity for change. First, we start by analysing the mobilisation cycle that covered the period of democratic transition in the second half of the 1970s. This period was marked by the beginning of the crisis in the state-led development model and therefore in state capacities for distribution. This period coincides with the 'second phase' of the military regime under General Francisco Morales Bermúdez (1975-80). The crisis and the shift to orthodox economic policies had only just begun, so it appeared rational that mobilisation in favour of distribution policies would help block that policy shift.

Under an authoritarian military regime, popular sectors could not count on

---

[5]   Elsewhere I have proposed similar ideas, within a more detailed theoretical framework (Tanaka, 1994).

backing from support groups, although there were organisations which assumed some of the costs and provided some resources for mobilisation. This was the case, for instance, of the leftist parties that had successfully challenged APRA's traditional domination of the popular movement. Finally, these generally had strong collective identities, stimulated by the Velasco (1968-75) reforms. Under Velasco, through Sinamos (Sistema Nacional de Movilización Social), the government's social mobilisation agency, popular sectors had gained access to state resources for mobilisation purposes.

Thus, a social movement came into being during the period of the military government: a collective expression of popular sectors in the political arena, autonomous from other actors and in conflict with the state. This was the combination of variables behind the successful national strikes and protests which opened up the way to democratic transition. However, these conditions did not last very long. Peru followed a path similar to that of other South American countries in its transition from authoritarianism. The strength of social movements was sapped by the economic situation that ensued. Also, and perhaps more importantly, social movements tended to be eclipsed by party political activity in the transition to a new sort of regime.

The 1980s brought a different phase in the relationship between popular sectors and the state, one where this was conducted mainly in a competitive political arena opened up after twelve years of military rule. In this setting, popular sectors could count on strong support groups. These included the same left-wing parties present in the previous phase but which had become a more consolidated force with the foundation of the Izquierda Unida (IU) in September 1980. The Peruvian left managed to overcome some of its ideological divisions, and IU enjoyed impressive electoral success. In the November 1983 municipal elections, it became the second national political force after APRA, its vote very much class-rooted among popular sectors. IU won control of many municipal governments, whilst in Lima, its president, Alfonso Barrantes, became the capital's first marxist mayor. IU provided an efficient administration in many municipalities, using this to support popular organisations, primarily through a neighbourhood participation organisation, the Oficinas de Participación Vecinal. Popular sectors could count not only on support from the political left, but also from a large number of NGOs and Church-based groups in low-income districts.

Under the second Belaúnde government (1980-85) and in the early years of the García government (1985-90), the capacity of the state to distribute resources went into decline, as the state found itself in ever-deeper fiscal difficulties. Meanwhile, collective identities remained fairly strong, although these tended to become weaker as the decade progressed. This configuration led to what can be called *movimientismo*, a type of collective expression of popular sectors in the political arena, involving the maximisation of demands through collective action, taking advantage of the support groups already mentioned. This *movimientismo* expressed itself in national labour strikes and protests, regional movements, strikes by individual urban or rural labour unions, squatters' movements and a wide array of popular organisations (including women's and youth movements) in the shantytowns.

A third period covers the last years of the García government and the first years of the Fujimori government, up until 1992. This period was characterised by extreme crisis, which had very adverse effects on popular sectors, thereby weakening collective identities. The economy entered into hyperinflation, and political violence peaked. Sendero Luminoso took up a strategy at this time of developing its own popular organisations, which meant destroying those organisations that it could not control, often by assassinating their leaders. In response, the armed forces used repression, often indiscriminately, which had similar effects on autonomous organisations to Sendero's actions. In such circumstances, collective action became extremely difficult to mount, and at the same time popular sector organisations lost the support of groups that had helped them before. The left found itself in crisis, and finally split in 1989. Foreign NGOs began to reduce their programmes in Peru, discouraged by the scale of the economic crisis, the problem of violence and the perception that their efforts were probably useless in this sort of context.

Popular collective identities were also debilitated by the crisis, as the available resources became very scarce. The growth of the highly fragmented informal economy made it more difficult to express collective identities. In such conditions, the distance and divergences between popular organisations and popular sectors became wider. Within such organisations, the breach also became wider between the leaders (who could obtain selective benefits from collective action), and the rank and file which usually lost out.

Thus, in these circumstances – weak collective popular identities, weak support groups and a state without resources to distribute – it is hardly surprising that political participation through collective action was not an attractive proposition. The key-note of this phase was a strong dose of pragmatism in the relations between popular sectors and the state, based on strict cost-benefit criteria. Such pragmatism helps explain how the left lost electoral appeal amongst the poor, who responded to everyday problems of survival by practical calculations, not ideological or partisan considerations. In terms of voting patterns, they opted for independents like Fujimori. Furthermore, their capacity to resist neoliberal reforms was much reduced.

Summarising the argument so far, variations in the level of public involvement and political participation by collective action depend on changes in the political opportunity structures and mobilisation capacities. As yet, this is an unexplored area in which further research would help us better to understand the changing relationships between popular sectors, popular organisations and the state in the political arena. The relationship between popular sectors and the state under Fujimori was characterised by a strong pragmatism, arising from the weakness of collective identities, a crisis of the state and of the various support groups, in a context of high levels of violence and a crisis of governability. This would suggest a process of demobilisation and social *anomie* amongst popular sectors. In the next section, I argue that this view is simplistic, and fails to take account of the complexities of the situation. The situation reflects changes in the boundaries between the social and the political spheres, leading to new forms of political expression and new types of public involvement.

New boundaries between the social and political spheres

Under Fujimori, it is often argued, popular sectors faced the worst possible situation, as a consequence of economic crisis and political violence, and low levels of public involvement and political participation. Whilst there are strong grounds for such a conclusion, we argue here that there is significant evidence that points in a different direction and which gives grounds for a more 'optimistic' assessment of future possibilities. The aggregate data on poverty and underemployment has obscured an important and remarkable process of consolidation among the poor and popular sectors. Indeed, demobilisation may not be an expression of weakness and retreat; rather, the profound structural changes that have arisen as a consequence of neoliberal reform have redefined the frontiers between the social and political arenas. In this new context, political participation and public involvement ought not to be as intense as during the preceding state-centred order, in which both the state and social life became highly politicised. However, within these new confines, novel forms of public involvement began to appear, a new dynamic in which public opinion became increasingly important.

Political protagonism on the part of popular sectors has been a response to such long-term, structural processes as rural-urban migration and modernisation, which led to the eruption of the mass into politics. In Peru, such processes became notable features in the 1940s and 1950s, giving an important role to the poor in urban conflicts. The demands for property rights and access to basic urban services (like electricity or running water) became, for popular sectors, as important as traditional class demands related to wages and working conditions.

This made the question of how to integrate these mobilised masses a central issue in political life. The relatively successful 'formula' that worked for Peru and other Latin American countries for some decades was what Cavarozzi called the 'state-centred matrix' (Cavarozzi, 1996), a model of economic development and of state-society relationships in which legitimacy was derived from distributional capacities. As we have already seen, this dynamic implied the politicisation of social conflicts.

Popular demands thus entered the political arena, as the urban poor fought for public and collective goods such as basic services and property rights. During the 1970s and most of the 1980s, such demands were intense, given the strength of support groups and of collective identities. Here it is important to note that these identities tended to be particularly strong in unconsolidated urban environments, owing to the centrality of the public goods required and the reduced problem posed by 'free-riders', since property rights had yet to be defined and depended mainly on neighbourhood associations being able to prevent such non-cooperative behaviour.

During the 1970s and 1980s, despite a protracted economic crisis, the urban poor had attained many of their original demands. Anyone who walks through low-income neighbourhoods in Lima now and compares them with what they were like in the 1970s, will appreciate the development of these settlements and accompanying urban infrastructure. Rudimentary building materials were replaced by bricks and cement. Intense commercial activity developed everywhere, with the appearance of modern shopping centres and neon-lit discos. Such changes are all the more remarkable when we recall that they were made during years of great economic and political hardship.

The point I want to stress is that, in this new more consolidated urban environment, the need for collective public goods was less pressing than it was in the early years of settlement. State agencies existed to provide these goods. The demands of popular sectors could not be ignored, and nor could their votes. Data provided by Henry Dietz (Dietz, 1997) show this clearly. Dietz conducted surveys in five poor neighbourhoods in 1970, 1982, 1985 and 1990, in the districts of Comas (Primero de Mayo), San Juan de Miraflores (Pampa de Arena), Cercado (Santiago), El Agustino (28 de Julio) and Surquillo (Sendas Frutales). In tracing degrees of participation since 1970, Dietz was able to show that political participation was higher in 'newer' neighbourhoods and declined in accordance with the trend towards urban consolidation, a point confirmed over time in the same neighbourhoods.

We have already referred to the redefinition of the boundaries between the social and political spheres. Dietz's data show that although political participation through collective action declined with urban consolidation, other forms of collective action – participation in social and local activities – did not decrease. On the contrary, they even increased during the crisis years. Thus, whilst collective action to demand specific responses from the state diminished, participation in local associations grew. In response to the crisis, popular sectors were forced to rely more on their own efforts and invested less time and resources in political mobilisation, the outcome of which was very far from certain. This reflected not just the decline in the distributional capacities of the state, but also the degree of urban consolidation achieved. The basic public goods needed, which had motivated political participation through collective action, had already been obtained in most low-income urban districts. Increasingly, the inhabitants of such areas looked primarily for private (non-public) goods; sometimes these objectives required collective action to attain, but often not.[6]

---

[6]   In recent years, for example, most opinion polls show employment to be the main demand of the popular sectors. Although people may insist that the state should do something to promote employment, this is typically a private good, provided by the private sector and market

Analysis of generational responses confirms this view. Youth in popular sectors revealed different patterns of political socialisation from the preceding generations, which grew up in a more politicised context amid strong support groups, radical ideologies, a more active and interventionist state and in less consolidated urban neigbourhoods. Today's youth is growing up in a more consolidated (albeit still precarious) modern urban landscape, with cinemas, shopping centres and discos. Their behaviour tends to be more individualistic than that of their parents and grandparents (Tanaka, 1995).

Nevertheless, such consolidation coexists with widespread poverty and underemployment. The difficulty here is that, conventionally, poverty is measured by income levels or housing conditions. Such indicators do not tell us what kinds of goods have been acquired and what are still needed. It is therefore unclear to what extent the poor still require public goods – leading to political participation through collective action – or, on the other hand, private goods for which different strategies are demanded.

Thus, whilst it seems that one area of political socialisation and public involvement is being eclipsed, others are appearing. Society has undergone a process of restructuring, but not along old class lines. The type of socialisation that gave rise to *movimientismo* is being replaced by new types of social aggregation. These are better analysed from a social network point of view; although more loosely constituted, such informal networks (based on family, friendships and neighbourhood ties) are not necessarily less effective. Such networks function for a wide range of purposes, varying from childcare to forms of collective action to deal with such neighbourhood problems as urban violence, delinquency and prostitution. The networks can also act as employment agencies or even banking systems (Panfichi and Twanama, 1997). This is an area open for further research.

Neo-Clientelism, '*Delegación Vigilada*' and media politics

To ascertain the depth and extent of the changes that have come about in the Fujimori years, the analysis of the post-coup relationship between the state and the political arena on the one hand and the popular sectors on the other is revealing.

Following the April 1992 *autogolpe*, pro-government candidates won a majority in the new Congress (CCD).[7] However, in October 1993, in the referendum called to approve the new constitution, the government won only a

---

mechanisms, especially in a situation of state retreat and neoliberal reform. Of course, state policies have a strong influence over employment levels, but this relationship is not evident. Employment is a private and excludable good that acts as a disincentive to collective action.

[7]   Fujimori's candidates for Congress obtained 49.2% of the vote, followed by the opposition PPC list which won only 9.8% of the vote.

slim majority.[8] Especially worrying for Fujimori was that the 'no' vote correlated strongly with high poverty levels, especially in rural areas, often far from Lima, where income levels were lowest. Price stabilisation had primarily benefited the urban poor, particularly in Lima where a high proportion of consumption is concentrated in final goods. In rural areas on the other hand, where producers and their families still consumed a fairly high proportion of output and where stabilisation may have depressed agricultural prices further, Fujimori's policies had less obviously beneficial effects.

Following these poor results in the referendum, Fujimori developed a strategy to build up popular backing for himself and his government, prior to the April 1995 presidential and congressional elections. This consisted of social spending, targeted at the poor, especially in rural areas. A key instrument of this programme was the Fondo de Compensación para el Desarrollo (Foncodes). Helped by the recovery in state revenues and the resources from privatisation, Fujimori could afford to carry out an ambitious spending programme.

Thus, in the 1992-95 period, the state recovered some of its distributional capacities. At the same time, both popular organisations and the collective identities of the popular sectors were debilitated. This configuration gave rise to a relationship between popular sectors and the state definable as 'neo-clientelism'. This distinguishes itself from traditional clientelism, because in this instance there was a more politically conscious citizenry. State resources were used and accepted simply because they were needed. Besides, since such forms of state expenditure were a response to the verdict of the voters in the referendum, they were more a response to popular discontent than political manipulation.

Fujimori's political support cannot be explained in terms of manipulation. Public opinion was critical and the citizenry was aware. Support for him was conditional and selective. In elections, voters supported Fujimori's candidates in the CCD elections of November 1992, but were noticeably less enthusiastic in the referendum on the constitution ten months later. In the November 1993 municipal elections, Fujimori's candidates were also defeated. Helped by government social spending, Fujimori won the April 1995 presidential elections with more than 60% of the vote; but again in November 1995 his candidates fared poorly in municipal elections.

The 'critical' nature of this support for Fujimori also became clear from the results of opinion polls. These showed selective support for the government, and at times a strong rejection of specific policies and actions. Between 1992 and 1995, human rights violations perpetrated by the government and the armed forces met with overwhelming disapproval. Balbi (Balbi, 1996) acutely called this relationship '*delegación vigilada*', borrowing and adapting O'Donnell's

---

[8]   The 'yes' vote for the new constitution was 52.3%; the 'no' 47.7%. Opposition groups alleged that the results were marred by fraud.

movements in public opinion.

Public involvement and political participation among popular sectors appeared to approximate to what we could call 'media politics'. This was not just a conjunctural and temporary phenomenon, but one that reflected the new social environment in which popular sectors found themselves. If popular sectors no longer needed public goods, and if their demands and interests were increasingly geared to acquiring private and individual goods, this implied profound changes with respect to the way they involved themselves politically. Popular interests had become more complex and dispersed, and were no longer catered for by traditional types of social organisation. Demands became more particularistic, with the maintenance of overall stability becoming a key requirement at the macro level. In the sphere of media politics, public opinion played a key role; indeed, the media became an all-important form of political mediation.

The centrality of the media and public opinion poses important questions about the performance of democratic institutions and their accountability (Conaghan, 1995). However, these are traditional problems, not just a consequence of the new social and political context or the increased importance of the media. We can at least anticipate that, if the government systematically ignores public opinion, especially that of popular sectors, it can expect to be punished at the polls and this may cause changes in coalitions and alignments. Here lies the importance of the opposition parties and their capacity to provide viable alternatives. The media also became the way in which popular sectors themselves began to express their own preferences, complementing the older forms of exerting pressure through collective action. With the exhaustion of the old state-centred order and the implementation of neoliberal structural reforms, with the shift from the politics of *movimientismo* to media politics, political success became less related to the capacity to mobilise strategic sectors and more a matter of winning the battle for consensus in public opinion.

The failed attempts by popular organisations and opposition parties to block neoliberal reforms came about, at least in part, because these had not properly understood the nature of these changes. The weakness of popular organisations after years of economic crisis and political violence was not the only cause; it was also the fact that they could no longer constitute a viable alternative for society as a whole. Such demands seemed to defend only the short-term and particular interests of a minority. To prevail, popular interests and demands would have to be able to present themselves as defending general interests. An example of this was the opposition campaign against the privatisation of Petroperú in 1994 and 1995. In this instance, the interests of workers appeared to tie in with national concerns, and the fight by the oilworkers was supported by the majority in the battle to control public opinion. Although the workers were unable to prevent the advance of privatisation, the campaign proved politically costly for the government.

In the new context, popular interests and demands had to compete with other issues of debate in gaining political prominence, making it easier to implement neoliberal reforms. During the 1980s, the need to incorporate the popular sectors, mobilised in the 1970s, had been a widely accepted priority. This concern was implicit in the 1979 Constitution, with all its emphasis on social rights. The problem of incorporation, the legacy inherited from the Velasco years, permeated politics in the 1980s. Under Fujimori, however, with the exhaustion of the old state-centred order and the implementation of the neoliberal agenda, incorporation was no longer the key issue. Instead policies of 'social compensation', which gave less importance to issues of incorporation, prevailed. Social policy came to be regarded as a transitory problem to mitigate the negative effects of structural adjustment. The future 'incorporation' of popular sectors was left to private initiatives and market mechanisms.

In the years since 1995, however, Peru may have entered a new phase, with popular interests playing a rather more important role. Between 1990 and 1992, as well as counterinsurgency, the main points on the agenda were the design of stabilisation measures, the control of inflation and the development of social compensatory policies. In the post-*autogolpe* period (from April 1992 to July 1995 when Fujimori began his second term of office), the main points on the economic agenda were privatisation and state reform. Meanwhile, in the political sphere the main debate was over the need to consolidate democratic institutions, whilst the popular sectors benefited from Fujimori's concern with re-election. After 1995, attention turned more to ensuring the longer-run sustainability of the reform process and the need for a viable political coalition to sustain it politically. The extension of the gains of the new model to the popular sectors thus appeared as a more central issue (Naím, 1994). As Naím suggests for Latin America, I would argue that Peru entered a 'second stage of reform' after 1995, with renewed state activity to improve social conditions taking on greater importance. This implied the restructuring of the ministries involved in providing welfare services in order to improve delivery of health care, education and other public services. In this process, the role of popular organisation was considered important. The challenge facing the popular sectors and popular organisations with their support groups was how to place such interests and demands on this agenda, without taking refuge in particularistic demands or limiting itself simply to the politics of *denuncia*.

Conclusions

It is hard to reach any definitive conclusions about sustainability when analysing the relationship between the state and the popular sectors under Fujimori. We cannot talk about the existence of a well-established dynamic between the political and the social spheres. Nevertheless, even if Fujimori's appeal declines, it seems unlikely that history will undo itself or that there will be a return to the *movimientista* past. Fujimori's success in executing deep structural reforms has dramatically and definitively altered the rationality of political participation and public involvement. Moreover, in response to their remarkable efforts, popular sectors have had some success in improving living conditions, irrespective of periods of economic crisis and widespread political violence. This success reinforces rather than undermines the changes in the boundaries between the social and political spheres.

This situation demands that social scientists revise old assumptions, many of which patently are no longer valid (if they ever were). One of the most important lessons is to appreciate the discontinuities between popular sectors and popular organisations, especially at the national level. Popular organisations were reduced to the short-sighted defence of particularistic demands, thereby showing up the difficulties in aggregating and representing new popular interests. This was something that political actors were slow to recognise.

In the new context, where media politics and public opinion are increasingly influential, the aggregation and articulation of popular demands emphasises rather than minimises the role of political parties. The exhaustion of the *movimientista* dynamic does not imply the weakening of popular interests, rather that their influence depends on new approaches to politics. The new context is not better nor worse than the preceding ones; it is simply different. This increases the importance of trying to understand how the new social and political configurations function and to operate within the new rules of the game rather than to hark back to an ever more distant past.

CHAPTER 13

Government, Citizenship and Democracy: A Regional Perspective

Carlos Iván Degregori, José Coronel and Ponciano del Pino

Decentralisation and local government

For most of the twentieth century, the Peruvian state has shown little vocation for decentralisation. With one or two brief exceptions, there have been no strong social movements oriented by demands for regionalisation or decentralisation. As a consequence of the 1933 constitution, the country was divided up into departments, provinces and districts. However, even though the constitution envisaged the creation of departmental councils, elected directly on a secret ballot, no democratically-elected body ever came into being at the departmental level. At the provincial and district levels, from 1920 onwards – with the sole exception of the period between 1963 and 1969 – local mayors were appointed by the executive.

It could be argued that departments and provinces were represented in Congress since deputies were elected for each province and senators for each department. However, according to Adrianzén,[1] what seems a fairly decentralised system of representation was in fact an oligarchic system with three main characteristics: (i) congressmen were local notables; (ii) through the system of regional spending powers ('*iniciativa del gasto*') they operated a system of patronage and clientelism within their constituencies which supplanted local democracy; and (iii) since central government controlled the purse strings, deputies were highly dependent on the executive.

As well as obstructing the separation of powers between the executive and the legislature, Adrianzén argues that this system prevented the emergence of local government, since municipalities were prevented from resolving almost all the problems faced by citizens. Particularly in the highland areas of the country, the low value placed on local democracy had to do with what Andrés Guerrero (looking at Ecuador) called 'ethnic administration'. He argues that, because of the suppression of the system of indigenous taxation in the mid-19th century, the supporting structure of the 'Indian Republic' was dismantled, and administration fell into the hands of local potentates. What emerged was 'a multifaceted and hierarchical political configuration, a conglomerate of institutions and social linkages, at the apex of which was always the local *patrón*' (Guerrero, 1993).

---

[1]   We would like to thank Alberto Adrianzén for allowing us to read an unpublished article of his, written in 1996. He also helped us with other information and data used in this section.

Peruvian readers will recognise in this description a clear definition of the *gamonalismo* which expanded and consolidated itself in Peru during the latter half of the 19th and the beginning of the 20th centuries. Reflecting the demise of 'ethnic administration', Decree Law 14250 of 1962 brought to an end the system whereby deputies were elected for provinces, replacing it with the election of both deputies and senators on a departmental basis. Thereafter, the 1979 Constitution abolished the system of *iniciativa del gasto*, thereby ending one of the main mechanisms propagating local clientelism. The constitution also contemplated the establishment of a system of regions, with a view to the Senate eventually being elected on this basis. In the meantime, until the new system of regions was up and running, elections for the Senate would be conducted on the basis of a single nationwide electoral district; this was the case in the elections of 1980 and 1985, and again in 1990, even though by then the new system of regionalisation had been introduced. President Alberto Fujimori's *autogolpe* in 1992 put an end to the process of regionalisation. The 1993 Constitution ratified a unicameral legislative system, in which representatives were elected on the basis of a nationwide electoral district. Although this was considered a provisional step towards an eventual revision of the process of regionalisation that took place in the late 1980s, this system appeared unlikely to change, at least so far as the elections in 2000 were concerned.

Thus, the country moved from one extreme to another: from a system of clientelism and local *caudillos* to a parliament composed of members elected without any direct regional, departmental or provincial representation. Congressmen were thus far removed from those who elected them – and only too close to influences emanating from the government palace.

Nevertheless, it would be overly simplistic to argue that this represented a return to the old system in which the interests of the provinces were ignored and forgotten. In practice, the situation was a good deal more complex than this. Even though municipal spending in the 1990s remained at or around an historic low of 4% of total government spending – in 1996 it fell to 3.6% – there were new elements in play that need to be taken into account. One was the introduction of Decree Law 776 in 1994, which established the Municipal Compensation Fund (Fondo de Compensación Municipal), allocated to the municipalities on the basis of population and indicators of relative poverty (Adrianzén, 1996). The Fund gave priority to rural areas, which received roughly twice the resources allocated to urban ones, and to district over provincial governments (the latter probably receiving no more than 20% of the total).

Thus, there was an attempt under Fujimori to redistribute still relatively small amounts of spending – 379.4 million dollars in the 1996 budget – towards the most needy areas. However, one effect of this was a further atomisation of spending, particularly since not only did provincial authorities find their resources cut, but also their spheres of responsibility. Even prior to DL 776, an article by Hildebrando Castro-Pozo Díaz provided a 'Summary chronological listing of the main centralising attacks affecting local and regional governments under the government of the head of state, Alberto Fujimori Fujimori (1990-94)' (Castro-Pozo Díaz, 1994). Following DL 776, the diminution of the role of local government reached such levels that in Lima central authority took over responsibility even for traffic management, the siting of street markets and protection of parks.

This ties in with a second development: the concentration of public spending in the hands of the Ministry of the Presidency, whose resources multiplied five times in three years to reach 22.6% of total government spending in 1996. Many of the various offices which came under the Ministry of the Presidency – most notably Foncodes and Pronaa[2] – were involved in activities which could and had been carried out by local government. Together, the combined resources of these two agencies, totalling 1.2 billion soles in 1996, were well in excess of the 870 million soles channelled through the Municipal Compensation Fund. If we add together the resources of both of these, local spending – focused on the most depressed areas of the country – rose to 8% of total spending. The increase was particularly impressive in areas of the country previously hit by the war with Sendero Luminoso, where in addition to Foncodes and Pronaa, the Programa de Apoyo al Repoblamiento (PAR) and the armed forces themselves were actively involved in development spending of one kind or another. Whilst the increase in spending in many places was dramatic, the methods used for distributing resources did nothing to revitalise local government.

What we are seeing therefore was a decentralisation of spending, combined with a further atomisation of local government and a sharp increase in centralised political control. Many districts therefore oriented themselves not only towards the Ministry of the Presidency, but to Fujimori himself, who travelled the country tirelessly, involving himself directly in the projects concerned. This formed part of what could be defined as a sort of 'techno-populism' in which the *iniciativa del gasto*, once in the hands of local *caudillos*, was appropriated by the president himself.[3]

Such spending is insufficient on its own to explain the electoral support afforded to Fujimori in the 1995 elections, which he won with 64% of the vote, and by an even larger margin in the poorest provinces of the country. Explaining this simply in terms of resource flows would make it seem that the inhabitants were just passive and manipulable clients. This was not the case. Or at least, it was not wholly the case, since they were above all political actors with the capacity to shape the future of their own regions and the country as a whole.

---

[2]   Foncodes is the National Fund for Compensation and Social Development. Pronaa is the National Food Assistance Programme.

[3]   Techno-populism means that presidential hand-outs consisted of computers and television dishes rather than more traditional fare like pisco and food. The government bears a great resemblance to what O'Donnell called 'delegative democracy'. Applying this concept to Peru, Carmen Rosa Balbi talks of *delegación vigilada*, in view of the prerogatives of the armed forces and the intelligence services (Balbi, 1996).

It is thus necessary to know what '*fujimorismo*' meant in the provinces, many of them far removed from the capital. In order to investigate this, we have initiated research in ten municipalities in the department of Ayacucho: four districts of the province of Huamanga – Socos, Vinchos, Quinua and Acocro – and six in the province of Huanta – Iguaín, Luricocha, Huamanguilla, Santillana, Ayahuanco and the provincial capital of Huanta itself. On account of its distance from central authority, a point often stressed during the years when Sendero Luminoso was advancing, Ayacucho represents a useful prism through which to observe the relationship between the 'centre' and the 'periphery' in contemporary Peru. Furthermore, since it was the area worst affected by the internal war of the 1980s, it helps demonstrate the way in which political violence affected this relationship.

Our story begins in the 1960s when Ayacucho was still a land of *gamonales*, lords and serfs, of *mistis* and *indios*. It carries through to the present (the late 1990s). The main actors are the mayors of the ten municipalities concerned, especially those in charge at three key moments: in 1966, following the establishment of municipal elections, but prior to the agrarian reform; in 1980, after the agrarian reform, but prior to the outbreak of guerrilla violence; and in 1996, after the worst of the violence was over, but when there was nevertheless a period of great uncertainty. The accounts of the mayors concerned help us outline the changes and continuities in the management of local power in Ayacucho. They give us a glimpse of the extent to which the differences between *mistis* and *indios* had remained, those between the city and rural areas, the valleys and the highland *puna*, the young and the old, men and women, the educated and the non-educated. They help us to see whether these were things of the past, or, alternatively, if the old hierarchies persisted, albeit with different actors involved. Finally, it is interesting to note the socio-cultural profile of those elected in 1995 and how they exercised authority.

As will have become clear, our main concern in this study has to do with the processes of social and political democratisation, the reformulation of ethnic, local and citizenship identities.[4] With the help of a wide historical framework, we believe it is possible to reach a better understanding of what '*fujimorismo*' meant at the periphery.[5] In what follows, we summarise some of the initial and tentative conclusions of a study which is still at a fairly incipient stage.

---

[4]   David Sulmont provides an interesting definition of citizenship (Sulmont, 1997). He sees it as a form of social integration that operates within the political system and which permits the existence of rules by which individuals belong to a society. These define their rights and obligations. Historically, in modern society, these rules have been institutionalised as citizens' duties and rights that are universal and equal. Here, we share Sulmont's interest in seeing how these rules work (in this case in rural Peru), starting with social practices, and specifically the development of political strategies by social actors.

[5]   When we refer to *fujimorismo* we mean adhesion to the Fujimori government, principally as expressed in successive elections.

Landowners and *varayocc*: 'ethnic administration'

A striking feature of 'ethnic administration', which still existed in the 1960s in some of the areas under study, was the extent of the privatisation of power alongside the legitimacy of the traditional system. The legitimacy of this system of power was derived from multiple ties of unequal reciprocity, similar to those described by Platt (in relation to Bolivia) as a 'colonial pact' (*pacto colonial*) between the *ayllus* and the state (Platt, 1981). Power relations were legitimate so long as they were conducted within the overall framework of this pact. Thus in 1966, the mayor of Santillana was treated with considerable respect because 'he was not abusive'. He and those who came before him were remembered as benevolent *patrones* 'because they did not indulge in physically punishing the members of the community'.

Of the eight mayors in office in 1966 on whom we have information,[6] three were landowners (*hacendados*): the provincial mayor of Huanta and the mayors of Ayahuanco and Santillana, districts which included the high *puna* areas of Huanta province, furthest away physically and least connected to the market economy.[7] However, the influence of the landowners went beyond these areas. In Iguaín, for example, a district in the valley of Huanta close to the provincial capital, the landowners were too powerful to concern themselves with local administration. They preferred to exercise their influence in Huanta, where some lived, and even in Lima, where some had occupied influential positions in government. Two institutions in particular underscored the legitimacy of the system: the *cabildos* (assemblies) through which adult males from urban areas could express themselves, and the system of traditional authorities (the *varas, envarados* and *varayocc*).[8]

The *varayocc* had a dual role. On the one hand, within the communities they organised the rotation of crops, communal labour (*faenas*), the calendar of communal festivities and dealt with conflicts either within or between families. On the other hand, they provided a degree of mediation between the *misti* district authorities and the Quechua *comuneros* on such matters as road repairs, the construction of communal buildings and the organisation of festivals. Those interviewed expressed nostalgia for the system of indigenous authorities which had helped provide a bridge between these two worlds.

---

[6] At this time, Socos and Vinchos were in the same district. It was not possible to interview the person who was mayor of Quinua in 1966.

[7] For example, Uchuraccay comes under Santillana, the community which became famous in 1983 because of the assassination of eight journalists there. In the extreme north of Ayahuanco is Viscatán, an impenetrable area said to be the refuge of 'Feliciano', the leader of the dissident fraction of Sendero Luminoso ('Sendero Rojo') which continued the armed struggle after the capture of Abimael Guzmán in 1992.

[8] *Cabildos* have been held in communities since colonial times, but they generally have been used to deal with internal problems and have had little to do with municipal affairs as such. Unless specified to the contrary, here we are speaking of *cabildos* held in district capitals. *Varas, envarados* and *varayocc* are synonyms and refer to traditional authorities.

However, in 1966, both traditional landowners and *varayocc* were already in retreat. The system of ethnic administration had begun to break down, although at different speeds – in the valleys more so than in the highlands, in the communities more so than on the landed estates. In districts like Huamanguilla, Quinua and Acocro, for example, small-scale property-owners prevailed to a greater or lesser extent, producing potato and maize for the local market with relatively high levels of technification. Even further ahead in this respect was Luricocha where, well before 1966, the mayoralty was occupied by those classified in the literature as 'rich peasants', 'farmers' or *kulaks* – in other words by prosperous small landowners involved directly in the production process, paying daily wages to their workers and sowing sugar cane and vines to make *aguardiente* and wine. The Acción Popular mayor elected in 1966 had a 26 hectare property dedicated to this sort of cultivation, a distillery and a truck. These property owners became paradigms for small and medium-sized producers in the valleys. However, these mayors did not have much influence at the provincial level, where power was still in the hands of the landowners from Huanta and Iguaín.

The pattern of local government was upset by the 1968 military coup and the twelve years of military government (1968-80) to which it gave rise, which whilst emphasising 'democratisation' in the social sense was wholly averse to the institutionalisation of democratic practices. Although Ayacucho was not one of the departments most affected by the agrarian reform, this law and the institutions and programmes to which it gave rise further eroded the old system of 'ethnic administration', opening up new horizons for the peasant population. Politically, participation suffered a blow, and all the mayors during this time were appointed by the executive. Socially, however, the process of democratisation continued; this was not a return to the times prior to 1963 when it was only the notables of a district (or a *cabildo* in the district capital) who decided who the mayor should be.

'Social democratisation with full participation'[9]

Víctor Ramos, who was mayor of Quinua in these years, demonstrates these tendencies – social, political and cultural – which (despite a number of difficulties) became increasingly pronounced. Between 1970 and 1973, and again between 1976 and 1977, Ramos held office. As he himself admitted, the appointment of mayor at that time was fairly arbitrary, 'practically *a dedo*'. Born in the community of Yanahuillca, the son of a hacienda *peón*, he was the first ever mayor from a surrounding community (*anexo*) and one of the first of our interviewees who defined himself along ethnic lines. Referring to cultural differences, he stated that 'now there is no Indian blood, we are all *cholos*'. Like many of his generation, Ramos had migrated to the coast to work on the cotton plantations. There he had been elected general secretary of a cotton pickers'

---

[9]   This was the slogan used by the Velasco government (1968-75).

union. Thereafter he had done his military service in Lima before returning to his community and subsequently moving to the district capital.

Ramos was a self-taught intellectual and proud to be so: 'I have no further education, only first grade in primary school, but because of my own efforts I am as good as any professional'. Like other intellectuals in his area, Ramos inclined towards the study of history.[10] Quinua, known as the 'birthplace of freedom in the Americas', has a special place in local history, since on the plains nearby the battle of Ayacucho took place in 1824 which sealed the fate of the Spanish armies in South America. Ramos came across the original document of surrender,[11] was the prime mover in the establishment of a local museum, and during his first period as mayor (with help from local scholars) initiated a dramatisation of the battle. However, he was not just an intellectual, but a social leader, an activist who became a political figurehead. As well as a union leader, he became sub-governor (*teniente gobernador*) of his community, and when he moved to Quinua he was treasurer of the local church for seven years. A product of his times, Ramos had sympathy for the ideology of the more radical sectors within the government.

Víctor Ramos was a new type of social leader, different from the *varayocc*. However, he could work with them, perhaps because – despite all the changes – the language of power remained the same: 'to be a mayor is to be the father of the community, whose job it is to protect all its members... There people address you "good afternoon *Señor Alcalde*, good morning". More than anything else it is (a question of) concern, respect and affection, a level of confidence which no longer exists, which has changed totally'. Respect arose because the mayor became immersed in the intricate patterns of Andean reciprocity: 'Previously, we would go to any place and they would invite us in; we, in turn, would have to take a gift, a small-scale project, a solution to some problem...'. But it was not all a question of consensus; despite a favourable national context, Ramos confronted the debilitated landowners from the outset, for instance taking advantage of a new law on water which ended the monopoly control they had previously wielded over this resource.

Violence, obstruction and regrouping

Towards the end of the twelve-year military government, the mystique of the first few years had all but disappeared and municipal governments in the area appeared more isolated from society. For example, in Huamanguilla, the mayor at the time was remembered as a shyster lawyer (*tinterillo*) who personally profited from the resources of the municipality. In Luricocha, the mayor was remembered as being 'a loner'.

---

[10] On the role of local intellectuals (also in the case of Mexico), see Mallon (1995).

[11] 'I found it amongst the possessions of a gentleman who died ... He was from an *anexo*. His father had stolen it thinking it was a title deed to a piece of land, since he couldn't read. This gentleman had learnt to read; he had studied to do so.'

However, when in 1980 Sendero Luminoso launched its 'popular war', the picture was perhaps not quite so bleak as this would suggest. In order to explain the apparent ease with which Sendero Luminoso advanced in the few years after 1980, previous studies have tended to emphasise the lack of social organisation beyond that of the community and the fragility of civil society in Ayacucho.[12] This is true, but resorting to the old metaphor of the half-full glass, it is worth looking at the half that is full, and even if it is not quite half full it is still worth taking into account.

The period of democratic transition (1978-80) and the restoration of municipal elections in November 1980 helped revive local political life. In the municipal elections, Acción Popular – which had won the presidential elections six months earlier – triumphed in six of the ten districts under study. A new actor, Izquierda Unida (IU) won in the provincial elections in Huanta and in the district elections in Huamanguilla.

Political leaders from both Acción Popular and the left helped accentuate some traits which had already been observable previously. Indeed, the 1980 municipal elections represented the political institutionalisation of the wave of social democratisation that had taken place during the 1970s. As a consequence of the 1979 Constitution, illiterates had been given the vote for the first time. The result was the success at the polls of new political identities of the sort represented by Víctor Ramos a decade earlier. Thus it was that those elected included peasants from outlying communities who had received the benefits of education and who had had experience as leaders of social movements. The mayor of Vinchos, for instance, had previously been vice-president of his community and sub-governor of the district. The mayor of Socos had been president of his community and a district governor.

Even in those places where traditional landowners had retained control up until the 1960s, relations between the municipality and the rural population became more democratic. Although a *misti*, the Acción Popular mayor of Ayahuanco's relationship with the communities was more one of equals since 'he was young and worked in the fields'.

These mayors worked with meagre budgets, but they sought to undertake public works projects, and to a certain extent tried to redistribute power by using the old *cabildos* which by this time incorporated not just district capitals but outlying *anexos*. The relationship between municipal councillors and various state agencies – which had been intense at the beginning of the military period but less so subsequently – once again picked up. The mayor of Quinua recorded having been four times to the government palace in Lima and once to the transport ministry to look for support. Also, at this time, the first contacts were established with foreign aid agencies.

---

[12]   See Degregori (1985) and Degregori, Coronel and del Pino (1996).

Whilst Ramos was a good example of the self-taught intellectual, Enrique Sánchez, the provincial mayor of Huanta from 1981 to 1983 was a typical regional intellectual. He was a member of a landowning family which had come down in the world.[13] Sánchez took up the old liberal tradition of the Huantino elite[14] until he found his path blocked by Sendero Luminoso and the subsequent repression unleashed by the marines. In 1983, he was arrested and tortured by the Sinchis.[15] He was finally forced to resign before his period in office ended because of illness. However, memories of his period as mayor were positive, partly on account of his cultural activities, his willingness to take on established power groups, the honesty with which he administered resources and the way in which he opened up the provincial municipality to the rural population.

This reactivation in local political life was interrupted by the war. However, the proof that Sendero Luminoso did not enter into an institutional desert was the number of local leaders and municipal authorities it had to assassinate.[16] It is therefore important to qualify the usual view that there was a power vacuum in Ayacucho. In other studies (Degregori, 1985), we have pointed to the recomposition of social movements in the area at the end of the 1970s, stressing that this was limited largely to the capital of the department and the economically more dynamic rural areas, especially in the Apurimac valley. From our recent research, the extent to which this was such a hard-and-fast distinction seems questionable. Whilst it is important not to exaggerate the municipal revival, it does appear to be the case that the reactivation of municipal activity we have mentioned was a serious attempt at closer articulation with the state, and that this formed part of the slow and intermittent transition from 'ethnic administration' to citizenship.

Sendero Luminoso thus challenged this fairly well-established trend. This may explain not only why it had to assassinate so many authorities but also why it failed in its strategic quest to win over the support of the peasantry which, in large part, ended up in alliance with the armed forces. It has been argued that amongst the reasons why the peasantry reacted against Sendero Luminoso was the insistence that it withdraw from the market economy, produce solely for subsistence and accept the replacement of communal authorities by its own

---

[13]   His father had been a governor, his grandfather a provincial mayor. Several of his forebears had been congressmen for Huanta province in the 19th century.

[14]   On this tradition, see Coronel (1983).

[15]   The Sinchis were the specialist counter-insurgency arm of the police force, the Guardia Civil.

[16]   The price paid by authorities elected in Ayacucho during these years was very high. Just limiting ourselves to the mayors of these ten districts in the period between 1981 and 1983, three were assassinated and four more either resigned or fled. Enrique Sánchez was tortured by the Sinchis and his period ended asphyxiated by violence. The mayors of Socos and Acocro fled to Lima in 1981, persecuted by Sendero Luminoso. The mayor of Ayahuanco resigned in 1982. In Iguaín, the mayor, Víctor Cordero, abandoned the office because of threats from Sendero, but ended up 'disappearing' at the hands of the navy in 1984. Alberto La Rosa, mayor of Santillana, was assassinated by Sendero Luminoso on 28 July 1984, along with a former governor and former mayor, Juan Contreras. The mayor of Huamanguilla (1981-83) was lynched by Sendero in April 1984 in the main square of the town, along with the justice of the peace.

'commissars'. However, as well as these explanations, we need to take into account the way in which Sendero's intrusion challenged the march from serf to citizen by seeking to convert the peasantry into a 'mass' that could be administered by the party.[17]

But how can we explain the rapid and apparently easy advance of Sendero Luminoso during these years? The strength of the nexus between teachers and students, Sendero's solid nucleus which became devastating given the organisation's tight Leninist structure, remains a valid explanation. The organisation had an explosive effect operating in the part of the glass that was 'half empty', exploiting poverty, isolation, ethnic and generational divides. However, the situation did not become explosive just because of this isolation, but because of the slow, halting process towards citizenship. Furthermore, it is essential to take into account the counter-insurgency response of the state, especially in 1983 and 1984. A fragile civil society needed to link up with a state that was sensitive to its demands. This did not happen. One indication of this is the number of authorities and leaders of grass-roots movements who were assassinated by the armed forces or who simply 'disappeared'.

In sum, the first few years of the 1980s were a period of aborted change. The restoration of municipal elections could have injected a new dynamic into a faltering process of democratisation in society, carried over from the previous decade. Instead, the embryonic experiment in municipal democracy collapsed. In November 1983, when municipal elections were held elsewhere in Peru, they were not held in any of the districts of Huanta, or even in the provincial capital. Nor were they held in the ten districts of Huamanga, including three of the four included in this study.[18]

However, as the 1980s proceeded, for those who were neither killed nor forced to flee, life in the department went on. In various places, a recomposition of local authorities began to become discernible. Everywhere, concern for public works became less important, replaced by concern for security. In many places, mayors coordinated their activities with those of the so-called 'self defence committees' (CDCs) and the armed forces, whilst other district authorities rotated for short periods to avoid Senderista reprisals.

It was in the areas closest to the *puna* in Huanta that these changes were most notable. In Ayahuanco, for example, from 1982 onwards, there was a succession of interim mayors who replaced the landowners and others who had monopolised municipal office previously and who, with the onset of violence, had fled to Huanta or Lima. The new mayors were peasants from the outlying communities. One of the most representative was Nemesio Reyes Saime, who came from the community of Parobamba, was Quechua-speaking and whose interrupted primary schooling gave him the status of being 'educated'. He had

[17]   On the extremes to which the oppression of the 'masa' could go, see del Pino (1997).
[18]   Acocro, Socos and Quinua. On the 1993 elections, see Tapia (1996).

less than a hectare of land in his community and worked small parcels of land in a neighbouring community which his wife (who spoke only Quechua and was illiterate) had inherited. In order to supplement this meagre income, he migrated for periods to the valley of the River Apurímac. Like other mayors at the time, Reyes had occupied other positions previously. He had been president of his wife's community and then a councillor in Ayahuanco. Then, when no-one else would take on the job, he became mayor. The communities remember him as the mayor who led the CDC in opposing Sendero. He was wounded when on patrol in 1991. In 1997, he was a member of the Reconstruction Committee in Ayahuanco, having become something of a symbol of resistance to terrorism.

'Now we have the opportunity':[19] the new mayors

The CDCs, otherwise known as *rondas campesinas*, inflicted the first strategic defeat on Sendero Luminoso, creating the conditions for life in the region to begin to return to normal, especially following the capture of Abimael Guzmán in 1992 and the consequent division and weakening of Sendero. In November 1995, for the first time in 15 years, municipal elections were held without major problems. As elsewhere, in Ayacucho the political parties practically vanished from the scene. Only one of the ten mayors elected was a party militant (from Acción Popular). Another two had had ties with APRA, but stood as independents. Of the remainder, five were classifiable as *'Fujimoristas'*, although one – the provincial mayor of Huanta – insisted on being seen as an 'independent' supported by Fujimori's party, Cambio 90.

The profile of those elected for the 1996-98 period casts considerable light on both the changes and continuities in regional society and the local power structure. In the first instance, we notice a continued improvement in the level of education. In 1966, none of the ten mayors (not even the landowners) had studied at university. Thirty years on, three mayors had professional qualifications and another three had pursued courses in higher education without having finished them. In spite of the crisis of the 1980s, they had benefited from the struggle for education that their parents had waged. They were also beneficiaries of the access to education provided by the reopening of the Universidad San Cristóbal de Huamanga in 1959.[20] Three of the mayors were teachers, a profession which earlier mayors had pursued, but two were economists working for NGOs, a profession which barely existed in the area prior to the period of violence. Two were small-scale tradesmen, one an employee of the provincial council of Huamanga, and only two declared

---

[19]   The slogan adopted by Fujimori in the 1995 elections.

[20]   There were no women mayors in our survey, but the improvement in educational levels was also evident among their wives. Three were professionals, of whom one had undertaken university studies. However, as is the case nationally, the differences between these women were greater. Whilst only one of the mayors had not finished primary education (and in spite of this had become an agricultural businessman), two of the wives were illiterate and one had not completed primary education.

themselves to be farmers.[21] All, however, possessed small landholdings. Another characteristic was the multiplicity of occupations of some of the mayors. For example, the mayor of Vinchos, an evangelical, as well as cultivating small plots of land, was a clothes trader in Ayacucho and ran a restaurant in his community on the main 'Los Libertadores' highway.

The evangelicals were also a novelty. One evangelical, the mayor of Acocro, was one of the most dynamic and prosperous farmers in the district. He rented 30 hectares to cultivate potatoes, had a tractor, a Toyota truck, a mill and a house in Ayacucho. According to him, his luck had changed when he converted to being an evangelical, since at that point he had been able to purchase all the things he required. He said that the people had elected him mayor because they respected his hardworking spirit. However, he also gained respect as a social leader: he had been president of his community, sub-governor and had also been in charge of the CDC. This was another characteristic which became more general over the previous ten years; many mayors had gained experience as community leaders.

Since the landowners had departed prior to the agrarian reform, it might seem likely that the new mayors would have been the sons of the former *vecinos* of the urban centres. However, this was not so. The 1995 elections confirmed the advance of the outlying *anexos* in gaining control over the district capitals, a process helped by the withdrawal of urban *vecinos* to cities like Huanta, Ayacucho and Lima in response to the violence. Six of the ten mayors were born in outlying communities, as opposed to only one in 1966.

In an area where the numbers who spoke quechua had dwindled and where bilingual, pluricultural education tended to be of little interest to those who still did, it is perhaps remarkable that all ten mayors were bilingual and that for seven of them quechua was their mother tongue. In 1966, this was the case of only one. Five of the ten had a quechua surname and one had two quechua surnames. However, whilst in Bolivia and Ecuador the majority would define themselves as 'quechua', 'aymara' or *indio*, most in Ayacucho preferred to identify themselves by their occupation or some other more 'neutral' categorisation.[22] If people did accept an 'ethnic' identity, it tended to be the new status of *cholo*. Only the mayors of Vinchos and Quinua defined themselves as *cholos*.

---

[21]   The professional profile of the provincial mayor of Huanta and the 14 members of the council is also revealing: three were school teachers, three engineers (one with a university degree in engineering), two were doctors, one a dentist, one a social worker, one an economist (with a degree), one with a degree in fisheries and one a technician. Three members of the council were women: two of them school teachers and one a social worker.

[22]   Even when defining themselves occupationally, they preferred terms that were more neutral or prestigious. For instance, they preferred the term 'farmer' (*agricultor*) to peasant (*campesino*) which is synonymous in many places with *indio* or poor person (*pobre*). Indeed, one of the mayors who in our account appears as a small-scale trader (*pequeño comerciante*) appeared in the list of those participating in a provincial meeting as 'marketing technician' (*técnico de marketing*). On the reasons for the hiding of ethnic origin, see Degregori (1993). On changes in ethnic and regional identities in Peru and Guatemala, see Bourque and Kay (1976).

According to Susano Mendoza, mayor of Quinua, 'I feel happy, content with what I have. I live with my *cancha* and my *mote*'.

This renewal and transformation of the local elites went hand-in-hand with a redefinition of the relationship between urban centres and rural peripheries. Whilst previously the *varayocc* used to mobilise the peasants for public works in the district capital, now the mayors seek to legitimise themselves by undertaking projects not just in the more populous centres but in the outlying communities as well. A good example was Juan Quispe Flores, one of the two who defined himself as a *cholo* and who had studied four years of economics at the University of Huamanga and had worked as an employee for the municipality of Huamanga for 14 years. Quispe showed us 27 sets of documents for irrigation and drinking water schemes in the communities of his district, presented to Foncodes, foreign embassies and international aid agencies. He told us that in 1997, eleven *anexos* would receive electricity, and that all the resources available in 1996 had been devoted to public works schemes in these outlying communities. Public works notwithstanding, the municipality in Socos organised three open *cabildos* in 1996. Whereas previously, only the *vecinos* of the urban centre would convene such an assembly, the *cabildos* of the 1990s had involved rural communities. This is a change which, amongst other things, has to do with the fact that peasants vote. However, as elsewhere in Peru, public works tended to predominate as a priority over the consolidation of democratic institutions.

If there is an axis of continuity linking the various decades, perhaps it was the importance of infrastructural work, which in the 1990s became more explicitly a demand for urbanisation. Whereas previously peasant communities would look for engineers to lay out plans for their communal terrain with a view to gaining official recognition, their priorities shifted to gaining for their villages such urban features as street lighting and electricity. As well as providing services, urbanisation involved improving their ability to defend themselves and gaining improved access to information. It also presupposed a certain degree of social mobility since such new services improved the quality of life, as well as opening up the potential for new sorts of economic activity.[23]

To what extent do services and infrastructure constitute citizen demands? Sinesio López has pointed out that the construction of citizenship in Peru, the struggle for social rights, preceded the struggle for political rights and individual freedoms (López, 1996). For David Sulmont, the demand for services forms but part of the struggle for a 'decent life' (Sulmont, 1997). He maintains that traditionally in Western societies, such demands have been a product of the acquisition of certain social rights. In Peru, on the other hand, they arise from a situation of social exclusion, and this clashes with the acquisition of certain political rights.

---

[23]   On the demand for urban planning and services, as well as for information (especially from the displaced returning to their communities, see Degregori, Coronel, del Pino and Starn (1996). On urbanisation and social mobility, see Sulmont (1997).

Other demands take on a more explicitly political hue, such as allowing youngsters to undertake compulsory military service within the community as part of the *ronda campesina*, or fighting for district status. In many places, communities and *anexos* fight to become districts in their own right, or at least part of more locally-based smaller administrative jurisdictions. This was seen as the best way to achieve greater self-government, to be recognised by the state, and to be able to negotiate for funds (for instance within the framework of DL 776 which distributed cash to the municipalities). The promulgation of the new land law (Law 26505) made this even more important, since it further eroded the prerogatives of the peasant community.

In some cases, the demarcation between districts made little sense. Ayahuanco, for example, was a district which had poor communications with the provincial capital. The mayor sought to bypass the provincial authorities and enter into agreements with NGOs and government departments. Even within the district, communication was far from fluid. Ayahuanco, the former district capital, was destroyed by Sendero, and in 1990 this status was transferred to Viracochán. However, a number of communities, far from Viracochán, pushed in 1997 for the creation of a new district, Ayahuanco Norte. In other instances, it was the authoritarian conduct of local authorities that led to pressure for new districts. Often, even the new local elites found it difficult to act as equals with the *ronderos* of the CDCs. In Huanta, the problem became more difficult because the farmers of the valley did not wish to be identified with the *chutos* from the highlands.[24] It was not surprising, then, that the highlanders sought to become separate or smaller districts (*concejos menores*). In so doing, they challenged the role of the elites as 'mediators' between the 'ignorant *indios*' and the state.

The frequent use of the adjective 'ignorant' made us aware of the ambiguous role of education; it democratises, but at the same time creates new distinctions. It is therefore unsurprising that school teachers and those working with NGOs sometimes reveal themselves as authoritarian. The mayor of Iguaín was a school teacher and his counterpart in Huamanguilla an extension worker (*promotor*) with an NGO. Both adopted a vertical style in their dealings with the authorities from the communities and *anexos*. This was typically the attitude of a 'professional' who 'knows' towards the 'ignorant' *comunero*. For this reason, a number of mayors gave little importance to dialogue with communal assemblies or *cabildos*: 'why waste time with those who do not know (what they are talking about)?'

Such attitudes were by no means the rule. The mayors of Santillana and Ayahuanco, for example, operated in a very different way to the old *gamonales*. They lived in their districts and were involved in the life of the communities. The mayor of Santillana was a young school teacher who visited the

---

[24]   *Chuto* is a rather disrespectful term used to describe quechua-speaking peasants from the highlands who, until the 1960s, lived within the *haciendas*.

communities fairly frequently. The mayor of Ayahuanco, as well as being a small-scale trader, was a *comunero* and dealt with the communal leaders on an equal basis.

However, amongst the everyday bustle of public works and the creation of new districts, there were evident limits to the regeneration of the municipality and the advance of citizenship. Public works did not form part of any overall development plan which went beyond the locality. And added to this lack of a wider picture, often the absence of linkages between *anexos*, districts, provinces and department made each seek their own direct relationship with the centralised state (and specifically with the Ministry of the Presidency or one of its component organisations) or with NGOs and international aid agencies. In some cases, as we have seen, the rejection of these linkages represented the rejection of authoritarian powers at the local level and formed part of a wider democratising tendency. The province of Huamanga was a case in point, where ignoring the provincial mayor was but a consequence of his widely acknowledged inefficiency. As the hard-working mayor of Acocro put it: 'there is no relation with the mayor of Huamanga because he doesn't care (*es un alcalde dejado*)'.[25]

To some extent, a similar situation arose in Huanta, where the mayor went to the other extreme in his levels of activity. Milton Córdova had done postgraduate studies at ESAN and was head of an NGO. Under him, the provincial government had a reputation for dynamism and achieving results. It also opened itself up to rural organisations like mothers' clubs, the association of farmers with irrigated land, and the Association of the Displaced which represented the highland *chutos*. In Huanta, the problem was one of disorganisation in the way in which projects were carried out. The inadequate linkages were symptomatic not just of the crisis affecting provincial and regional elites, displaced by the violence and replaced by local elites which tended to reproduce old patterns of discrimination and proved themselves unable to aggregate demands. The disorder also reflected the desire of the government to impose itself on a region that was in any case atomised and to build new types of clientelism, rather than respect existing institutions and channels.

This desire on the part of the government expressed itself, first and foremost, through the style of Fujimori, who would appear by helicopter out of the blue with almost no warning, either on his own or with such diverse travelling companions as Chabeli Iglesias[26] or the UN High Commissioner for Refugees. The relationship established by Fujimori with local authorities tended to be highly personalised. The mayor of Santillana had been visited by Fujimori twice. Susano Mendoza, the mayor of Quinua, said he had an excellent rapport with

---

[25] The failings of the council in Huamanga were part of a wider crisis of the regional elite, which had been incubating from before the period of violence. Indicative of the fragmentation of interests and the lack of strong local leadership was the participation of twelve lists in the 1995 municipal elections. The winning list obtained a mere 20% of valid votes.

[26] Chabeli Iglesias is the daughter of the singer, Julio Iglesias.

Fujimori and that, with help from the World Bank, had been sent to recount his experiences as mayor and CDC leader in the United States, Nicaragua and Bolivia. According to Juan Quispe, it was thanks to Fujimori that Socos had achieved a television dish, an ambulance, 42 sewing machines, orthodontic equipment and had a Foncodes-financed civic centre under construction. If not directly with the president, the mayors sought to maintain a special relationship with the various organisations that came under the Ministry of the Presidency: PAR, Pronaa and Foncodes. Furthermore, the atomising tendency was underscored by DL 776 in prioritising the district over the provincial authorities.

It is worth asking whether the style of the president had the effect of reproducing at a local level a passion for infrastructure projects, or whether this was in fact an amplified version of a local, community-based style. The answer is probably that the two tendencies mutually reinforced one another; that between them they highlighted a 'techno-populism' which sought to reverse social exclusion through public works, whilst blocking or impeding the aggregation of demands and denying a mediating role to the departmental and regional elites.

It was a style which frequently combined – as in the 1970s – inclusion and social democratisation with political authoritarianism. Susano Mendoza was representative of this tendency. He maintained that his relationship with the communities was very close, both through the projects executed and through the CDC in the district of which he was coordinator. He related how every Sunday he met with the CDCs, the communal authorities, the livestock rearers, to discuss their problems and look for solutions. He claimed to be on equal terms with everyone, whether 'the president of the republic or just any peasant'. However, Mendoza warned of the need to 'discipline' the peasants: 'you have to use force so that they advance, so that they move; if not, they do nothing'. He proposed that the CDCs should fulfil a development function: 'You have to use the discipline of the *Comités de Autodefensa* for self-development (*autodesarrollo*).' As at the national level, 'techno-populism' acquired a military connotation.

However, in other cases 'techno-populism' privileged the technical side, with mayors concerning themselves with enhancing management capabilities, thereby taking steps to redress one of the key weaknesses of municipal government in Peru. The mayor of Acocro pointed out that he had taken part in courses for the training of mayors in ESAN. This training was also reflected in some of the new activities taken up by the municipalities. In Luricocha, the projects undertaken by the mayor, Amador Barboza, were not many, but he organised a district fruitgrowing fair and encouraged tourism by promoting such traditional festivals as Las Cruces. He also distributed to mothers' clubs small animals like guinea pigs and hens 'so that they work, rather than hang around waiting for donations'.

An important attempt to check short-termism and atomisation (not just in our area but throughout the department) was an agreement between the municipality of Huanta and a grouping of NGOs to work together, as of December 1996, to organise meetings in each district, culminating in a meeting at the provincial level in March 1997.[27] Following this, in May 1997, a *Mesa de Concertación Provincial* was established to 'move from the administration of services to the planning of development' (Tavara, 1997). At the time of writing, it was still not possible to evaluate the results of this initiative. According to some of those involved, the scheme depended more on external support agencies than on the efforts of the people of Huanta. Nevertheless, it is worth pointing out that organisations like the Ministry of the Presidency and their officials began to talk more enthusiastically about the virtues of strategic planning, and the need to move from a policy of handouts to one of more carefully elaborated projects, calibrated at the regional level. Also, there was greater apparent disposition to collaborate with NGOs. However, short-termism remained a central problem: the electoral timetable remaining a constant and pressing consideration.[28]

Fujimorismos and *Fujimoristas*

After he became president in 1990, Fujimori had the possibility of converting his own grouping, Cambio 90-Nueva Mayoría, into a movement which would renew politics, one different from the traditional parties against which it had been a reaction. He did not do so. Faithful to his role as 'anti-politician', and distrustful of institutions, he preferred Cambio 90-Nueva Mayoría to remain just an acronym, useful for electoral purposes but wholly dependent on his own personal wishes.

From the institutional point of view, *fujimorismo* was the most amorphous force to emerge in Peru in the second half of the 20th century. Yet viewed from the angle of social actors, especially in rural parts of the country, it was a polymorphic entity. In the absence of an official identity, everyone could imagine and internalise *fujimorismo* as they saw fit. This became clear when Fujimori decided against supporting official candidates in the November 1995 municipal elections. Different lists of groupings appeared, each purporting to represent the government line, some with such explicit labels as 'Fujimori-95'. However, the president's own inner circle retained the last word as to which list represented most faithfully the 'orange' Cambio-90 ticket, rendering each dependent on the leader's grace and favour. In some instances, that official blessing was just momentary, as official favouritism was liable to change.

---

[27]   137 delegates took part (118 men and 19 women). There were 42 local authorities present: mayors, *regidores*, governors, sub-governors and justices of the peace; 53 leaders from peasant communities, mothers' clubs, development committees, neighbourhoods, properties (*pagos*), groups with irrigated land, *rondas* and student groups; 20 local officials; 18 delegates from NGOs; two from foreign aid agencies and one from a tourist concern (Municipalidad Provincial de Huanta, 1997).

[28]   It remained to be seen the extent to which the presidential desire to run for re-election in 2000 would distort the focus of government organisations.

In general terms, *fujimorismo* in the regions of Peru represented a broad collection of social interests, many of them frequently counterposed, as revealed by the continuous splits and divisions between those claiming to be its supporters. *Fujimorismo* was a channel for participation for those sectors of the population previously at the margins of politics or represented by forces that had collapsed, like the Izquierda Unida or even *Velasquismo*. The switch by IU voters to Cambio 90 in 1990 was evident in Ayacucho. Milton Córdova was nominated director of the Huanta microregional office in 1991 by the then IU-led regional government. Not even IU made possible the election of the Ayacuchan congressman Miguel Quicana, who came from a peasant community in Huamanga, despite his lack of qualifications for the post or representativeness of the sector from which he came. Nevertheless, as if to stress the ambiguities of *fujimorismo*, Monsignor Juan Luis Cipriani, the archbishop of Ayacucho, at the same time was able to slot into such offices as the prefecture or the regional government (appointed by the executive after 1992) members of traditional families who had come down in the world.

However, when dealing with what we might call 'popular *fujimorismo*', those who predominated were not just valid but privileged interlocutors of the government. Comparing three personalities from these pages and their relationship with the government helps us understand what *fujimorismo* meant in this area. One is Víctor Ramos, the mayor of Quinua in the 1970s, a one-time sympathiser on the left-wing *Velasquista* party, the PSR. In the context of the 1990s, he became an admirer of the government. Another is Susano Mendoza, mayor of Quinua, the head of the *rondas* both in the district and the whole province of Huamanga. The third is Milton Córdova, the provincial mayor of Huanta.

Ramos and Mendoza were on either side of a strident debate in the district. Ramos was an activist in the field of human rights, and worked with the Instituto para la Paz (IPAZ), an institution in Ayacucho, and nationally with the Coordinadora Nacional de Derechos Humanos. In Quinua, the *rondas campesinas* had been organised late in the day and for somewhat confused objectives. Rather than respond to attacks by Sendero Luminoso, the *rondas* effectively existed to defend territory from the community's neighbours in Acos-Vinchos, with whom there was a long-standing boundary dispute. Quickly, the *rondas* in Quinua became one of the most dynamic in the province; they also acquired one of the worst reputations for arbitrariness and killing. Despite this (or perhaps because of it), Mendoza was chosen as the coordinator for the *rondas* throughout the province.

For Ramos, Fujimori was synonymous with public works projects, his government literally 'coming from the people'. He perceived him as almost 'one of us'. He goes on to say 'I was an independent up until the moment that *el chino* became president. I liked him. We all struggled for him. But those of us who backed him, unfortunately, have received nothing up to now'. Ramos was referring to the 1995 municipal elections, which Mendoza won by only 15 votes.

According to him, they switched four ballot boxes. 'Not himself, but the army captain who came with the young girls from ONPE.... .'[29] He adds 'What can we do when the army intervenes in such cases? It's disgraceful.' According to Ramos, 'Susano never takes advice from those who are older, from the authorities'. Yet, on the other hand, 'with the help of the general (head of the political-military command in Ayacucho) and the bishop (Cipriani) he represses those who oppose his administration. He is authoritarian'.

Listening to Ramos, it seems that in some cases *fujimorismo* had a more local and personal meaning than at the regional political level. For Susano Mendoza, *fujimorismo* was the political expression of the people organised, as represented by his administration. Whether in the guise of the CDCs in the province of Huamanga or in that of the district mayors as represented in the Asociación Municipal Regional (Amre), he and his friends felt themselves to be the representatives of the peasants. After all, all of them, Susano included, were the sons of peasants.

However, when he stood for the presidency of Amre, Mendoza was defeated by another 'orange' mayor, Milton Córdova. Amongst many other things this signified that the memory of the war and the role played by the *rondas* had faded, and that the peasantry in the new liberal scheme of things was only a secondary ally for the government. Córdova, for his part, distanced himself, proclaiming his independence. It was, he says, Cambio 90 which took the decision to support him in the elections and maintains that he had 'good friends in the government, especially in the Ministry of the Presidency'. This is but one of the many faces of *fujimorismo*, which for Córdoba was linked more with market economics than as a response to the war: it was a government that placed emphasis on individual effort, and this had allowed him to rise socially through his professional activities and his executive capacities.

Authoritarianism and clientelism, but also feelings of inclusion, recognition and meritocracy, were part of the weft which held together support for the government in places such as Ayacucho.

---

[29]   ONPE was the Oficina Nacional de Procesos Electorales.

CONCLUSIONS

CONCLUSIONS

Neoliberalism, Democracy and Exclusion

John Crabtree and Jim Thomas

In this collective work, we have set out to provide an evaluation of Peruvian politics and economics in the 1990s – at least on the evidence available up until the end of 1997. Our purpose was two-fold: to detect continuities and discontinuities between this period and the past, and to offer an answer – albeit preliminary – to the question of whether or not the Fujimori governments had laid the basis for a greater degree of economic and political stability. The answers to these questions have been mixed. There appear to have been more continuities than some would suppose, although clearly 1990 still represents in a real sense a break with the past. And, while a degree of political and economic stability was achieved, it was by no means clear that the changes introduced would prove sustainable over the longer term. Time, of course, will tell whether the apparent fragilities in the 'new order' prove its undoing, or whether they turn out to be minor problems which can be effectively overcome. Our conclusions are tentative. Nevertheless, we hope that those who have contributed to this book have helped you, the reader, to understand the nature of the Fujimori regime, its achievements and its limitations.

In terms of economic performance, there can be little doubt that the outcome has been in many respects an improvement on what went before. The stabilisation policies of 1990-91 successfully brought to an end a period of hyperinflation in which the previous government had lost all control over macroeconomic aggregates. Inflation continued to fall over the whole of our period, to reach single digits in 1997 for the first time since 1972. Economic growth, too, picked up after a period of unprecedented contraction in the 1988-90 period, and as demographic growth declined, GDP per capita increased proportionately. However, the pattern of GDP expansion was erratic, and as the downturn in 1996 showed, still subject to balance of payments constraints. For the first time since the late 1970s, Peruvian exports began to increase quite substantially, based primarily on increases in investment and output in the mining industry. Foreign investment also increased rapidly, spurred on both by changes in investment legislation and by the government's privatisation programme.

However, the 'miracle' was not achieved without costs, especially with regard to human welfare. Real incomes for the majority of the population were squeezed further in the 1990s, having already fallen rapidly during the 1980s. Under-employment remained at one of the highest levels of any country in Latin America. Distribution of income in Peru, long one of the Latin America's most unequal countries, became even more skewed than before. Fiscal austerity caused further deterioration in publicly-provided education and health services, reducing their accessibility to much of the population. On the external front, imports rose faster than exports, whilst increased debt service payments helped push the current account deficit up into the 5-7% of GDP range in the 1995-97 period, not much less than Mexico's on the eve of the December 1994 peso crash. Meanwhile, an overvalued currency, whilst helping to underpin price stability, exacerbated the trade deficit.

The extent of the reorientation in economic policy-making is beyond dispute. In many ways, the García government had represented the 'last gasp' of old-style 'developmentalism', with its emphasis on import-substituting industrialisation (ISI), reliance on the domestic market, public enterprise and state intervention in the workings of the market economy. The first two years of the Fujimori administration saw Latin America's most abrupt and dramatic 'about-turn' in policy orientation, made possible in large part by the scale of the economic collapse that had preceded it. Trade was suddenly liberalised, with non-tariff barriers being abolished and tariffs reduced to a lower, more uniform rate; the government set out to sell almost all public companies; state subsidies were abruptly wound up and other forms of market intervention abolished; the rules for foreign investment were rewritten to court foreign capital, and an accommodation sought with the international banks and other creditors which the previous government had vilified. In historical terms, the neoliberal agenda implied a return to the sort of 'open' economy which had prevailed up until the early 1960s, with the emphasis placed squarely on reinsertion into the global economy, export-led growth and the attraction of foreign capital largely to develop the country's resource base. This was, of course, in step with the policy orientation of the 'Washington consensus', followed by other Latin American countries. Peru was not one of the countries to pioneer liberalisation. However, under Fujimori, neoliberalism was pursued with a conviction and a consistency which was probably unmatched elsewhere in the region. There was no pretence of 'gradualism' here.

In analysing the effects of this economic reorientation, it is, of course, important to disaggregate and to distinguish between different sectors or different industries at different times. Here we have sought to enter into rather more detail in looking at two sectors of the economy particularly susceptible to the switch over from ISI to a more export-oriented approach: agriculture and manufacturing. In both of these, it is clear that the severe problems these faced arose prior to the period of the Fujimori reforms, largely as a consequence of the collapse in domestic purchasing power between 1988 and 1990. In the case of manufacturing, trade liberalisation added to the difficulties facing firms selling in the domestic market, forcing some to shift production into export activity. Those which adapted best were those able to do this most easily, those supplying particularly dynamic local markets (like construction) and those with best access to capital. In the case of agriculture, performance began to pick up after 1993 as the economy stabilised and growth resumed, although it varied greatly from one region to another. In the case of coca, an export crop *par excellence*, the high rents arising from its being an illicit activity made it an important source of wealth for those displaced from other agricultural activities. But, like other commodities, it was subject to sharp variations in price to producers.

In seeking to address the question of whether the economy was placed on a more sustainable growth-path over the longer term, we have been cautiously optimistic. Peru appears to have natural resources in sufficient quantities to supply the world market for years to come; moreover, those natural resources are fairly varied, including not just minerals but hydrocarbons (including natural gas), agricultural products and marine products, not forgetting the country's potential in such service sectors as tourism. So long as the government guarantees attractive investment conditions, the increase in exportable surpluses should be forthcoming. Although primary products are often subject to extreme price volatility in world markets (coca included) and also to resource availability constraints (especially in the fishing industry), the indications from known reserves of raw materials (especially minerals and hydrocarbons) suggest that the country has the capacity to increase export revenues over the period 1997-2007. Such projections suggest that the country should be able to avoid renewed bouts of balance of payments difficulty once identified projects come on stream. Although debt servicing may increase up to 2002 or so, it should be accompanied by a commensurate increase in exports, so long as international commodity prices hold up. However, as well as having to cope with price uncertainties, export performance may well continue to depend on the political climate in the country and whether future governments can avoid a return to the uncertainty and violence of the past.

Where the economic model of export-led growth seems less promising is in its ability to generate the employment opportunities to absorb a still rapidly increasing labour force. High rates of population increase in the 1970s are still feeding through into the labour force twenty years later. Eventually, the increase in the number of new entrants will fall off as the demographic 'bulge' passes and the lagged effects of lower birth-rates in the 1980s and 1990s feed through. However, this will not be until the first and second decades of the 21st century. Meanwhile, growth in the economy seems unlikely to be such as to reduce unemployment and underemployment substantially. In part, this is because the most dynamic sectors of the economy, linked to the export sector, are relatively capital-intensive and in themselves will only absorb a small proportion of labour supply. Moreover, many of them – mining, oil and gas, agriculture or fishing – are themselves not located in places, like Lima, where surplus labour is abundant. The informal sector and the black economy – or more appropriately in the case of coca and cocaine, the 'white' economy – remain the chief mechanisms for reconciling this contradiction. As in the past, there is a danger of a pattern of development setting in, which may provide plentiful foreign exchange but which has few backward linkages into society as a whole. In contrast with the period of ISI, there is unlikely to be a rapid increase of industrial and public sector employment to absorb surplus labour in the major cities, although the construction industry may play an important role in this respect.

If this turns out to be the case, there are also worrying implications for wages. The continued existence of a large pool of very low-income earners in (or on the fringes of) the informal sector implies downward pressure on wages, except in those industries where skills are at a premium. While this may help keep firms' costs low, it is unlikely to assist in improving the quality of human capital. One of the challenges facing Peru and countries like it in improving their position in the world division of labour is the lack of workforce skills. We have argued that the change in the labour market took place prior to Fujimori coming to office, but that the reforms his government enacted helped encourage further flexibility in the workings of that market, as did policies of deregulation and privatisation. Whilst this may have helped improve industrial productivity, it had the effect of increasing the pool of long-term unemployed. It seems unlikely that there will be a return to the sort of labour legislation that came into being under the Velasco government in the early 1970s. Workers will, as a whole, find it difficult to raise either their living standards or their skills; their share of national income may well fall further as a result.

The shift in the dominant economic model has brought with it – as one would expect – both beneficiaries and casualties. Indeed, the shift itself only became politically possible because of the prior weakening of those sectors in society which earlier on had resolutely opposed moves towards economic liberalisation, privatisation and deregulation. The coalition of interests that had supported the ISI model – industrialists at one end of the spectrum through to trade unions at the other – was badly undermined by the economic crisis of the late 1980s and the evident inability of the state, in a context of fiscal crisis, to shore up the old system. The late 1980s also saw the emergence in the political arena of new protagonists supporting the neoliberal model in a way that had not happened previously. In this context, it became politically possible to embark on a liberalising reform project in a way that had proved fruitless at the beginning of the 1980s under Fernando Belaúnde.

Similarly, stabilisation and then structural adjustment had different effects on different sectors of society. Although it was achieved at considerable social cost in the short-term (especially in 1990-91), stabilisation provided some respite for the poorest sections of the population, in ways that were not fully perceived at the time. The successful Peruvian experience in stabilisation – like that of Argentina, Brazil, Bolivia and other countries which underwent very high inflation rates or hyperinflation – helped those who had been least able to protect themselves during times of high inflation by means of indexation, dollarisation or other survival strategies. Like other Latin American presidents who 'banished' inflation, Fujimori reaped the political dividends. Policies of structural adjustment, most of them imposed after the period of initial stabilisation, created winners and losers. As well as many of the poorest in society, the winners included the business and financial elite – at least those interests capable of surviving the transition to a more internationally competitive environment – which benefited from policies of deregulation and privatisation. Amongst those who benefited least were workers in formerly protected industries and public sector employees, many of whom lost their jobs and found it impossible to find new ones.

Although data on income distribution provide only an approximate view of the distributive effects of policy over time, it is clear that the pursuit of greater equity was not one of the government's priorities. At the outset, the government deliberately avoided establishing the sort of 'safety nets' erected in other countries to cushion the negative effects of macroeconomic adjustment on the poor. Thereafter, although social spending increased, it was oriented more towards establishing nuclei of political support for the government amongst the poor than pursuing any long-term policy of poverty alleviation through redistribution. Frequently, policy was conducted in such a way as to create clientelistic relationships at the local level rather than citizens' rights. There was little by way of 'empowerment' in the social sphere. That this was so is hardly surprising; to empower the poor would have intensified the demands made on government, adding to problems of governability. Peru has long been a country with a high degree of social exclusion, a situation underpinned by ethnic and cultural discrimination. Although the emergence of organisations like Sendero Luminoso cannot be linked to exclusion in any mechanistic way, there is little doubt that social deprivation and exclusion played a part in the complex of factors that gave rise to such insurgent movements. This has not changed in any notable way. In spite of the macroeconomic recovery achieved under Fujimori after 1992, the effects on reducing levels of poverty were marginal. In 1996, for instance, 51.3% of the population was still classified as 'poor'. As in the past, the mechanisms of 'trickle down' showed themselves to be weak and ineffectual; indeed the return to the paradigm of export-led growth threatened further to attenuate the linkages between the more dynamic areas of the economy and the most indigent sectors of society.

In looking at the effects of government policy on a specific area like Ayacucho, where poverty is particularly widespread and social exclusion the norm, we sought to see how government policy – and in particular social policy – affected ordinary people. The conclusions we came to underline the distinction between the strengthening of citizen rights (which implies a certain equality – at least before the law) and the reproduction of old forms of clientelism with their top-down, authoritarian connotations and limited scope for participation. 'Fujimorismo' at the local level meant different things to different people, but the 'Fujimoristas' were those with pull in the government and those through whom the government sought to impose its will at the local level. Although the situation in Ayacucho may not necessarily be typical of that of other parts of the country – it attracted rather more attention because of the counter-insurgency implications of social policy – it provides a useful prism through which to evaluate the ways in which relations between the 'centre' and the 'periphery' were conducted.

This vision complements that which emerges at the urban level, where the autonomous capacity of popular movements to set their own political agenda was weakened by both the decline in the distributional capacities of the state as well as in the ability of 'support groups' (including but not limited to political parties) to mobilise on their behalf. At the level of grass-roots politics, the more pragmatic nature of popular organisations in the 1990s stands in contrast with the strident positions taken by similar organisations only ten years earlier. Although this was partly a consequence of the relatively sudden collapse of Peru's left-wing marxist parties, it was also a result of changing conditions within low-income communities and shifts in the type of demands they made on governments. The ways in which the economic and political crisis of the late 1980s affected grass-roots politics represent a striking change in the overall political atmosphere in the country, one which Fujimori was able skilfully to turn to his advantage. No longer did the central government need to respond to mobilisation; it was able to distribute resources on its own terms using its own channels, creating new clientelistic networks among a public which saw it to its advantage to proceed in this way.

The collapse of political parties as 'mediators' between the state and society is, of course, one of the most obvious developments in the political sphere during these years. The crisis of the party system, although echoed elsewhere in Latin America, was at its most palpable in Peru. This, of course, raises the question of whether the parties ever really represented the people, or whether they too were top-down clientelistic structures dominated by traditional elites. Some had stronger roots in civil society than others. The reasons for the demise of representative institutions (which had managed to consolidate themselves to a degree during the 1980s) are to be found in the inability of the state to provide for even minimal security for the citizenry during the late 1980s and its growing irrelevance as a means to resolve everyday problems. If the state was inoperative, what use were political parties? In this setting, they became an easy target for accusations of graft and corruption, an image that Fujimori adroitly propagated.

As we have seen, the political system as it has evolved under Fujimori is highly personalist, with political power concentrated in the office of the president. The president on occasions has likened his role to that of the managing director of a firm. Although top-down and vertical forms of government were nothing new, Fujimori took the personalisation of power to new lengths, weakening those representative institutions which sought a deliberative or balancing role. The power of the executive over other branches of the state was thus further enhanced. After the *autogolpe* of 1992 and the subsequent election of a new Congress, Fujimori could count on having an uncritical majority in the new unicameral legislature, prepared to do his bidding. On occasions, when deemed necessary, the new Congress approved measures which openly violated established constitutional norms. Likewise, judicial reorganisation – arguably a much-needed priority in a country where the judiciary had long been seen as inefficient and corrupt – led to the erosion of its autonomy in important respects. Fujimori's system of government involved a strongly 'populist' dimension, in that – like some of his predecessors – he sought to build a direct rapport between himself and the people, bypassing intermediaries. The demise of political parties made this easier to achieve. However, this was both a source of strength and weakness: strength in that it provided his government with a source of visible legitimacy in pursuit of policies which might otherwise have proved unpopular and encountered resistance; weakness in that once dissipated, the government lacked an alternative system of structured political support.

A further characteristic of the Fujimori government was its close relationship with the armed forces. Although criticised for a disregard for human and civil rights in its conduct of counter-insurgency operations, the military emerged enhanced from its successful counter-insurgency war against Sendero Luminoso. It retained its position as a key national institution, providing Fujimori with a valuable institutional structure which compensated for his lack of a strong party. The relationship between the president and the army high command was in, many respects, one of symbiosis. From the 'green book' onwards, the military was interested in establishing a political power that would last well beyond the term of office of a single government and one strong and authoritative enough to push through unpopular but necessary policies. For his part, Fujimori looked for military backing not just to crush the guerrilla challenge which had proved too much for his predecessors, but to provide a back-up for other policies. In order to cement the relationship, Fujimori overturned the traditional system of promotions, maintaining a particular military group in power. He also turned his back on the problem of corruption in the armed forces, a problem made more serious by the army's involvement in the main drug-producing areas of the country. While Fujimori retained the final option of changing the commander-in-chief of the armed forces, the political influence of the army was made manifest at specific points, particularly on issues connected with responsibility for human rights crimes. The military therefore played a key political role in these years, acting as a guarantor of regime stability.

The concentration of political power and the lack of organised political opposition enabled the Fujimori government to pursue areas of reform which otherwise would have been much harder to achieve. The use of decrees greatly facilitated the process of privatisation, for example. The reform of the tax system, as we have seen, was aided by the creation of an institution with a great deal of autonomy which was effectively isolated from countervailing political influences. In SUNAT, the government created an institution which was much needed if the state apparatus was to become more efficient. However, in building institutions which encouraged public participation and debate – at any level of government – the government was very deficient. Participation clashed with the 'managerial' approach to public administration.

The political system that evolved after 1990 bore strongly authoritarian characteristics, with the Fujimori government presiding over the burial of one economic system and its replacement by another. Although respecting democratic forms (to a certain extent), it undermined the democratic content of political institutions in such a way as to maximise the discretionality of government and minimise its responsiveness to external political pressure. The peculiarities of the 1990 elections made Fujimori unusually autonomous in terms of the debts otherwise repayable to specific groups in society. The popularity of the Fujimori government, especially in its early years when the social costs of adjustment were highest, is explicable partly by the severity of the economic and political crisis that preceded it, but partly by Fujimori's own ability to achieve a direct rapport with the people and marginalise possible rivals. His political autonomy was a considerable asset in this respect.

How enduring will the regime prove to be? In terms of economic policy, the model seems reasonably sustainable and unlikely to run into the sort of external constraints that have bedevilled successive Peruvian governments since the 1960s or before. Its weakness seems to lie more in its failure to provide for the material needs of a large part of the population. In 1997, when the papers that constitute this book were written, there was no obvious alternative set of policies emerging to challenge the neoliberal scheme of things. Although debate about economic management seemed likely to return to distributional issues, the accent seemed likely to fall on a 'technocratic' solution to finding ways to make the neoliberal paradigm work better for more people. On the political side, the future seemed much less certain. The concentration of power in the hands of one man brought with it obvious dangers, particularly with regard to succession. Although the debate over whether Fujimori could stand for a third term in 2000 had yet to be finally resolved, his difficulties in sustaining his popularity undermined the legitimacy of his government. New actors and coalitions seemed likely to appear, with agendas different to those which had made Fujimori popular. The perpetuation of deep social, ethnic and regional inequalities, combined with the lack of representative institutions, provided an unfavourable context for the resolution of potential political conflict. Therefore, a key question for the future was whether, as the memory of the economic and political dislocation of the 1980s fades, the consensus of the Fujimori years will dissipate as new issues come to dominate political debate. If historical precedent is anything to go by, the longer the period of *continuismo* the more destabilising its eventual *dénouement*.

Bibliography

Abugattas, Luis (1996) 'Estabilización, reforma estructural e industria en el Perú, 1990-1995: lineamientos para una política de desarrollo industrial', *Socialismo y Participación*, vol. 74, no. 1, pp. 9-40.

Adrianzén, Alberto (1996) 'La descentralización y los espacios locales: un nuevo sentido de la reforma política' (manuscript).

Alberti, Giorgio (1991) 'Democracy by Default: Economic Crisis, Movimientismo and Social Anomie', Paper delivered to the XV Congress of the International Political Science Association, Buenos Aires.

Altamirano, Teófilo (1992) *Exodo: Peruanos en el exterior* (Lima: Pontificia Universidad Católica del Perú).

Altimir, O. (1994) 'Income Distribution and Poverty through Crisis and Adjustment', in G. Bird and A. Helwege (eds.) *Latin America's Economic Future* (London: Academic Press), pp. 265-302.

Alvarado, Javier (1995) 'Innovación en las tecnologías crediticias', *Debate Agrario*, no. 21, pp. 1-13.

Alvarez Rodrich, Augusto (1991) *Empresas estatales y privatización* (Lima: Apoyo).

Alvarez, Elena (1983) *Política Económica y Agricultura en el Perú, 1969-1979* (Lima: Instituto de Estudios Peruanos).

Alvarez, Elena (1991) *La economía ilegal de la coca en el Perú* (Lima: Fundación Friedrich Ebert).

Alvarez, Elena (1992) 'Coca Production in Peru', in P. Smith (ed.), *Drug Policy in the Americas* (Boulder: Westview Press).

Alvarez, Elena (1993a) 'The Political Economy of Coca Production in Bolivia and Peru: Economic Importance and Political Implications', Report prepared for the North-South Center, University of Miami, in collaboration with Instituto Cuanto (Lima) and Centro de Estudios Bolivianos Multidisciplinarios (La Paz).

Alvarez, Elena (1993b) 'Illegal Export-led Growth in the Andes: A Preliminary Economic and Soci-political Assessment', Report prepared for UNRISD.

Alvarez, Elena (1995) 'Economic Development, Restructuring and the Illicit Drug Sector in Bolivia and Peru: Current Policies', *Journal of Inter-American Studies and World Affairs*, vol. 37, no. 3, pp.125-49.

Alvarez, Elena (1996) 'Economic Structure, Size and the Economic Impact of the Illicit Drug Sector in Peru', Report prepared with Cuanto S.A. for the Office of Project Services of the United Nations Development Programme (UNDP).

Alvarez, Elena and Cervantes, F. (1996) 'The Economic Consequences of the Peruvian Disease', in E. Gonzales de Olarte (ed.), *The Peruvian Economy and Structural Adjustment: Past, Present and Future* (Coral Gables: North-South Center Press).

Arenas de Mesa, A. and Bertranou, F. (1997) 'Learning from Social Security Reforms: Two Different Cases, Chile and Argentina', *World Development*, vol. 25 (March), pp. 329-48.

Arías, Luis Alberto (1991) 'Politica fiscal', in C. Paredes and J. Sachs (eds.), *Estabilización y crecimiento en el Perú* (Lima: GRADE).

Arías, Luis Alberto (1994) 'El fortalecimiento institucional de la administración tributaria peruana', Instituto de Administración Tributaria-SUNAT, Documentos de Trabajo, no. 2.

Avant, Deborah (1994) *Political Institutions and Military Change* (Ithaca: Cornell University Press).

Baca, Epifanio (1996) 'La Agricultura del Cusco en Tiempos del Ajuste: 1989-93', *Debate Agrario*, no. 24, pp. 1-37.

Baer, W. and Maloney, W. (1997) 'Neoliberalism and income distribution in Latin America', *World Development*, vol. 25 (March), pp. 311-27.

Balbi, Carmen Rosa (1996) 'El Fujimorismo: delegación vigilada y ciudadanía', *Pretextos*, no 9.

Ballon, Eduardo (1986) *Movimientos sociales y democracia: la fundación de un nuevo orden* (Lima: Desco).

Banco Central de Reserva del Perú (1989) *Compendio Estadístico del Sector Público no financiero* (Lima: Banco Central de Reserva del Perú).

Banco Central de Reserva del Perú (1995) 'Tipo de cambio real', Departamento de Análisis del Sector Externo' (Lima: Banco Central de Reserva del Perú).

Banco Central de Reserva del Perú (various years) *Memorias* (Lima: Banco Central de Reserva del Perú).

Barro, Robert (1990) *Macroeconomics* (New York: Wiley).

Bartov, Omar (1992) *Hitler's Army* (Oxford: Oxford University Press).

Bedoya, E. (1990) 'Las causas de la deforestación en la Amazonia Peruana: un problema estructural', Clark University Institute for Development Anthropology.

Berenztein, Sergio (1996) 'Rebuilding State Capacity in Contemporary Latin America: The Politics of Taxation in Argentina and Mexico', in Roberto Patricio Korzeniewicz and William C. Smith (eds.), *Latin America in the World Economy* (Westport, CT: Greenwood Press).

Berry, A. (1997) 'The Income Distribution Threat in Latin America', *Latin American Research Review*, vol. 32, no. 2, pp. 3-40.

Binder, Alberto (1993) *Justicia penal y estado de derecho* (Buenos Aires: Editorial Ad-Hoc S.R.L).

BINM (Bureau for International Narcotics and Law Enforcement Affairs – US State Department) (1996) *International Narcotics Control Strategy Report* (Washington, D.C.: US Government Printing Office)

Bird, G. and Helwege, A. (eds.) (1996) *Can Neoliberalism Survive in Latin America?*, University of Surrey Centre for International Economic Studies Working Paper No. 96/3.

Bird, Richard M. and Casanegra, Milka (eds.) (1992) *Improving Tax Administration in Developing Countries* (Washington D.C.: International Monetary Fund).

Boloña, Carlos (1996) 'The Viability of Alberto Fujimori's Economic Strategy', in Efraín Gonzales de Olarte (ed.), *The Peruvian Economy and Structural Adjustment: Past, Present and Future* (Coral Gables: North-South Center Press), pp. 183-264.

Bourque, Susan and Key, Warren (1976) *Denial and Reaffirmation of Ethnic Identities: A Comparative Examination of Guatemalan and Peruvian Communities* (Amherst: University of Massachusetts at Amherst, occasional papers).

Bowles, Samuel (1985) 'The Production Process in a Competitive Economy: Walrasian, Neo-Hobbesian, and Marxian Models', *American Economic Review*, vol. 75, no. 1.

Boza, Beatriz (ed.) (1994) *Invirtiendo en el Perú: guía legal de negocios* (Lima: Pacific Press).

Bulmer-Thomas, Victor (ed.) (1996) *The New Economic Model in Latin America and its Impact on Income Distribution and Poverty* (Basingstoke: Macmillan).
Bustamante, Alberto (1993) *Justicia alternativa* (Lima: Instituto de Economía de Libre Mercado).
Calderón, F. (1993) 'The trade union system: its background and future prospects', *CEPAL Review*, vol. 49 (April), pp. 103-115.
Campodónico, Humberto et.al (1993) *De poder a poder* (Lima: DESCO).
Castro-Pozo Díaz, Hildebrando (1994) *Somera relación cronológica de las principales agresiones y normas legales centralistas que afectan a los gobiernos locales y regionales, producidas durante el gobierno del Jefe del Estado, Sr. Ing, Alberto Fujimori Fujimori (1990-1994)* (Lima: manuscript).
Cavarozzi, Marcelo (1996) *El capitalismo tardío y su crisis en América Latina* (Rosario: Homo Sapiens).
Cervantes, F. (1996) 'The Economic Impact of the Illicit Drug Industry in Peru', Report prepared for Cuanto (Albany N.Y.)
Chalmers, Douglas (1977) 'The Politicized State in Latin America', in James Malloy (ed.), *Authoritarianism and Corporatism in Latin America* (Pittsburgh: University of Pittsburgh Press).
Clogg, Richard and Yannopoulos, George (1972) *Greece under Military Rule* (New York: Basic Books).
Coase, Ronald (1960) 'The Problem of Social Cost', *Journal of Law and Economics*, no. 3 (October), pp. 1-44.
Cobián Vidal, Ana María (1993) *Los decretos de la guerra: Dos años de políticas antisubversivas y una propuesta de paz* (Lima: IDS).
Cohen, Jean (1988) 'Estrategia o identidad: paradigmas teóricos nuevos y movimientos sociales contemporáneos', in *Teoría de los movimientos sociales* (San Jose: FLACSO; previously published as 'Strategy or Identity: New Theoretical paradigms and Contemporary Social Movements', *Social Research*, no. 52 (Winter 1985), pp. 663-716).
Collier, David (1976) *Squatters and Oligarchs: Authoritarian Rule and Policy Change in Peru* (Baltimore: Johns Hopkins University Press).
Colton, Timothy J. and Gustafson, Thane (eds.) (1990) *Soldiers and the Soviet State: civil-military relations from Brezhnev to Gorbachev* (Princeton: Princeton University Press).
Conaghan, Catherine (1995) 'Polls, Political Discourse and the Public Sphere: the Spin on Peru's Fujigolpe', in Peter Smith (ed.), *Latin America in Comparative Perspective: New Approaches to Methods and Analysis* (Boulder: Westview Press).
Conniff, L. (ed.) (1982) *Latin American Populism in Comparative Perspective* (Albuquerque: University of New Mexico).
Conovan, Margaret (1981) *Populism* (London: Junction Books).
Consejo de Coordinación Judicial (1997) *Plan Integral de Reforma del Poder Judicial* (Lima: Consejo de Coordinación Judicial).
Consorcio de Investigación Económica (1996) *Boletín de Opinión*, no. 23.
Corden, W.M. (1981) *Inflation, Exchange Rates and the World Economy* (Chicago: University of Chicago Press).
Coronel, José (1983) 'Pugnas por el poder local: Don Manuel J. Urbina y la creación del colegio González Vigil', in *González Vigil. Libro Jubilar 1933-83* (Huanta: Colegio González Vigil/UNSCH).
Cotler, Julio (1978) *Clases, estado y nación* (Lima: Instituto de Estudios Peruanos)

Cotler, Julio (1993) 'Political and Institutional Conditions of the Fight against Drugs in Peru', in E. Alvarez (ed.), *The Political Economy of Coca Production* (Albany: University of Miami).

Cotler, Julio (1994) *Política y sociedad en el Perú: cambios y continuidades* (Lima: Instituto de Estudios Peruanos).

Cotler, Julio (1996) 'Coca, sociedad y estado en el Perú', Report prepared for UNDP.

Cotler, Julio (ed.) (1995) *Peru, 1964-1994 : economía, sociedad y política* (Lima: Instituto de Estudios Peruanos).

Crabtree, John (1992) *Peru under Garcia: An Opportunity Lost* (Basingstoke: Macmillan).

Crabtree, John (1995a) *The 1995 Elections in Peru: End of the Road for the Party System?* (London: Institute of Latin American Studies, Occasional Papers, No. 12).

Crabtree, John (1995b) 'Impunity in Peru', in Rachel Sieder (ed.), *Impunity in Latin America* (London: Institute of Latin American Studies).

Cuanto (1991) *Ajuste y economía familiar: 1985-1990* (Lima: Instituto Cuanto).

Cuanto (varios years) *Perú en números* (Lima: Instituto Cuanto).

International Commission of Jurists (1994) *Informe sobre la administración de justicia en el Perú* (Lima: Instituto de Defensa Legal).

Cuba, Elmer (1995) 'Estimación del PBI potencial y la brecha del PBI: 1970-95', *Revista Economía*.

Dancourt, Oscar (1997) 'Reformas estructurales y política macroeconómica en el Perú 1990-1996' (Lima: PUCP).

Dancourt, Oscar and Mendoza, Waldo (1997) 'Informe de coyuntura 1996' (Lima: PUCP).

De Janvry, A. (1987) 'Dilemmas and Options in the Formulation of Agricultural Policies in Africa', in J. Gettinger and L. Hoisington (eds.), *Food Policy: Integrating Supply, Distribution and Consumption* (Baltimore: Johns Hopkins University Press).

De Soto, Hernando (1986) *El otro sendero* (Lima: Instituto Libertad y Democracia). Published in English as *The Other Path: The Invisible Revolution in the Third World* (London: I.B. Tauris).

Degregori, Carlos Iván (1985) *Sendero Luminoso I. Los hondos y mortales desencuentros. II. Lucha armada y utopía autoritaria* (Lima: Instituto de Estudios Peruanos Documentos de Trabajo).

Degregori, Carlos Iván (1993) 'Identidad étnica, movimientos sociales y participación política en el Perú', in Alberto Adrianzén (ed.), *Democracia, etnicidad y violencia política en los países andinos* (Lima: IFEA/Instituto de Estudios Peruanos).

Degregori, Carlos Iván and Grompone, Romeo (1991) *Elecciones 1990: Demonios y redentores en el Nuevo Perú* (Lima: Instituto de Estudios Peruanos).

Degregori, Carlos Iván, Coronel, José, del Pino, Ponciano and Starn, Orin (1996) *Las rondas campesinas y la derrota de Sendero Luminoso* (Lima: Instituto de Estudios Peruanos).

Deininger, Klaus and Squire, Lyn (1996), 'A New Data Set Measuring Income Inequality', *The World Bank Economic Review*, vol. 30, no. 3.

Del Pino, Ponciano (1995) 'Familia, cultura y "revolución": vida cotidiana en Sendero Luminoso', Paper presented at the seminar 'Shining and Other Paths', University of Wisconsin-Madison, May.

Dellepiani Massa, José (1997) *La reforma judicial en el Perú* (Lima: mimeo)
Devlin, R. (1996) 'Privatization and social welfare in Latin America', in G. Bird and A. Helwege (eds.) *Can Neoliberalism Survive in Latin America?*, University of Surrey Centre for International Economic Studies Working Paper No. 96/3, pp. 185-228.
Di Tella, Torcuato (1965) 'Populism and Reform in Latin America', in Claudio Véliz (ed.), *Obstacles to Change in Latin America* (Oxford: Oxford University Press).
Dietz, Henry (forthcoming) *Pobreza urbana, participación política y el estado 1970-1990* (Lima: Universidad Católica del Perú).
Diwan, I. and Walton, M. (1997) 'How international exchange, technology and institutions affect workers: an introduction', *World Bank Economic Review*, no. 11 (January), pp. 1-15.
Dornbusch, Rudiger. and Edwards, Sebastian (eds.) (1991) *The Macroeconomics of Populism in Latin America* (Chicago: University of Chicago Press).
Dourojeanni, M. (1989) 'Impactos ambientales del cultivo de coca y la producción de cocaína en la Amazonia Peruana', in F. León and R. Castro de la Mata (eds.), *Pasta básica de cocaína* (Lima: CEDRO)
Drake, Paul (1991) Comment on a chapter by Kauffman and Stallings in Rudiger Dornbusch and Sebastian Edwards (eds.), *The Macroeconomics of Populism* (Chicago: University of Chicago Press).
Dupuy, Trevor N. (1977) *A Genius for War: The German Army and General Staff (1807-1945)* (London: Macdonald and James).
Durand, Francisco (1996). *Incertidumbre y soledad. Reflexiones sobre los grandes empresarios de América Latina* (Lima: Fundación Friedrich Ebert).
Eguiguren Praeli, Francisco (1989) 'El estado de emergencia y su aplicación en la experiencia constitucional peruana (1980-88)', in Enrique Bernales et al, *La Constitución diez años después* (Lima: Fundación Friedrich Naumann).
Eguiguren Praeli, Francisco (1991) 'El Tribunal de Garantías Constitucionales: las limitaciones del modelo y las decepciones de la realidad', in *Lecturas sobre temas constitucionales No. 7* (Lima: Comisión Andina de Juristas).
Escobal, Javier (1994) 'Impacto de las políticas de ajuste sobre la pequeña agricultura', *Debate Agrario*, no. 20, pp. 51-78.
Escobal, Javier and Agüero, Jorge (1996) 'Ajuste macroeconómico y distribución del ingreso en el Perú, 1985-94', in Guillermo Moncada and Richard Webb (eds.) *¿Cómo Estamos? Análisis de la Encuesta de Niveles de Vida* (Lima: Instituto Cuanto and UNICEF).
Escobal, Javier and Castillo, M. (1994) 'Sesgos en la medición de la inflación en contextos inflacionarios: el caso peruano', GRADE. Documento de Trabajo No. 21.
Espinoza-Saldana Barrera, Eloy (1995) 'Aplicación jurisprudencial de los criterios de razonabilidad, temporalidad, proporcionalidad y necesidad para la resolución de Habeas Corpus durante la vigencia de Estado de Excepción: el caso peruano', *Derecho y Sociedad*, nos. 10 and 11.
Estela, Manuel (1992) 'La tributación frente a la economía mundial: Cambios en la organización. El caso del Perú', Paper presented at the 26th General Assembly of the Inter-American Center for Tax Administration, CIAT, Montego Bay, Jamaica, 15-19 June.
Estela, Manuel (1996) 'Consideraciones en torno a la problemática tributaria', Paper presented at the Primer Curso Avanzado de Administración Tributaria, Managua, Nicaragua.

Evans, Peter B. (1989) 'Predatory, Developmental and Other Apparatuses: A Comparative Political Perspective on the Third World State', Paper presented at the XV International Congress of the Latin American Studies Association, Miami, Florida.

Figueroa, A. (1995) 'Peru: Social Policies and Economic Adjustment in the 1980s', in N. Lustig (ed.), *Coping with Austerity: Poverty and Inequality in Latin America* (Washington, D.C.: The Brookings Institution), pp. 375-99.

Figueroa, A., Altamirano, T. and Sulmont, D. (1996) *Social Exclusion and Inequality in Peru* (Geneva: International Institute for Labour Studies).

Figueroa, Adolfo (1984) *Capitalist Development and the Peasant Economy in Peru* (Cambridge: Cambridge University Press).

Figueroa, Adolfo (1984a) 'The Distribution Problem in Different Sociopolitical and Economic Contexts: Peru, 1950-1980', in S. Sudman and M. Spaeth (eds.), *The Collection and Analysis of Economic and Consumer Behavior Data. In Memory of Robert Ferber* (Champaign, ILL: University of Illinois).

Figueroa, Adolfo (1993) *Crisis distributiva en el Perú* (Lima: Fondo Editorial, Pontificia Universidad Católica del Perú).

Figueroa, Adolfo, Altamirano, Teófilo and Sulmont, Denis (1996) *Social Exclusion and Inequality in Peru* (Geneva: International Institute for Labour Studies).

Fitzgerald, E.V.K. (1983) 'State Capitalism in Peru: A Model of Economic Development and its Limitations', in Cynthia McClintock and Abraham Lowenthal (eds.), *The Peruvian Experiment Reconsidered* (Princeton: Princeton University Press).

Gallo, M., Tello, L. and Rivera, L. (1994) *El impacto económico del cultivo de la coca* (Lima: CEDRO).

García Belaúnde, Diego and Planas, Pedro (1993) *La constitución traicionada: páginas de historia reciente* (Lima: Seglusa Editores).

Garvito, Cecilia (1996) 'Intervención del estado en el mercado de trabajo' (Lima: PUCP).

Gavin, Michael, Haussman, Ricardo, Perotti, Roberto and Talvi, Ernesto (1996) 'Managing fiscal policy in Latin America and the Caribbean: Volatility, Procyclicality, and Limited Creditworthiness' (Washington, D.C.: Inter-American Development Bank; and New York: Columbia University).

Geddes, Barbara (1994) *Politician's Dilemma: Building State Capacity in Latin America* (Berkeley: University of California Press).

Gómez, Rosario, Urrunaga, Roberto and Bel, Roberto (1997) *Evaluación de la estructura tributaria nacional 1990-94* (Lima: Universidad del Pacífico (CIUP)).

Gonzales de Olarte, Efraín (1996) *El Ajuste Estructural y los Campesinos* (Lima: Instituto de Estudios Peruanos).

Gonzales de Olarte, Efraín and Samamé, Liliana (1991) *El péndulo peruano* (Lima: Instituto de Estudios Peruanos).

Gonzales, J. (1989) 'Perú: Sendero Luminoso en el Valle de la Coca', in D. García-Sayan (ed.), *Coca, cocaina y narcotráfico* (Lima: Comisión Andina de Juristas).

Gorriti, G. (1988) 'Democracia, Narcotráfico y la Insurrección de Sendero Luminoso', in L. Pasara and J. Parodi (eds.), *Democracia, sociedad y gobierno en el Perú* (Lima: CEDYS).

Gorriti, G. (1990) *Sendero: Historia de la Guerra Milenaria en el Perú* (Lima: Apoyo).

Graham, C. (1993) 'From Emergency Employment to Social Investment: Changing Approaches to Poverty Alleviation in Chile', in A. Angell and B. Pollock (eds.), *The Legacy of Dictatorship: Political, Economic and Social Change in Pinochet's Chile* (Liverpool: University of Liverpool, Institute of Latin American Studies, Monograph Series No. 17), pp. 27-74.

Grindle, Merilee S. and Thomas, John W. (1991) *Public Choices and Policy Change* (Baltimore: Johns Hopkins University Press).

Grinspoon, L. and Bakalar, J. (1976) *Cocaine: A Drug and its Social Evolution* (New York: Basic Books).

Guerrero, Andrés (1993) 'De sujetos indios a ciudadanos-étnicos: de la manifestación de 1961 al levantamiento indígena de 1990', in Alberto Adrianzén (ed.), *Democracia, etnicidad y violencia política en los países andinos* (Lima: IFEA/Instituto de Estudios Peruanos).

Hachette, D., Lüders, R. and Tagle, G. (1993) 'Five Cases of Privatisation in Chile', in M. Sánchez and R. Corona (eds.), *Privatization in Latin America* (Washington, D.C.: Inter-American Development Bank), pp. 41-100.

Held, Gunther and Szalachman, Raquel (1996) 'Flujos de capital externo en América Latina y el Caribe: experiencias y políticas en los 1990' (Santiago: ECLA).

Hidalgo, E. (1985) 'Estudio de algunos aspectos sociales del ámbito del Proyecto Especial Alto Huallaga', Report for USAID No. FN-144-85.

Hirschman, Alberto O. (1958) *The Strategy of Economic Development* (New Haven: Yale University Press).

Hollist, W. and Tullis, L. (eds.) (1987) *Pursuing Food Security* (Boulder: Reinner).

Hopkins, Raúl (1993) 'Exchange Rates and Agricultural Prices in a Developing Economy: the Case of Peru', *Oxford Agrarian Studies,* vol. 21, no. 2.

Hopkins, Raúl (1995) 'Agricultural Performance and Macroeconomic Policies in Peru, 1950-1990', PhD Thesis, University of London.

Hopkins, Raúl and Grenier, Philippe (1996) 'Joint Evaluation of Programme Food Aid of the European Union. Peru: A Rapid Evaluation' (London: Overseas Development Institute).

Horton, S., Kanbur, R. and Mazumdar, D. (eds.) (1994) *Labor Markets in an Era of Adjustment, Volume 1: Issues Papers; Volume 2: Case Studies* (Washington, D.C.: The World Bank).

Howard, Michael (1976) *War in European History* (Oxford: Oxford University Press).

Hunt, Shane (1995) 'Crecimiento económico a largo plazo: Perú y América Latina en el contexto mundial' (Lima: Instituto de Estudios Peruanos; also published in Consorcio de Investigación Económica, *Boletín de Opinión*, no 29, November 1996).

Huntington, Samuel (1964) *The Soldier and the State* (New York: Vintage Books).

IDL (Instituto de Defensa Legal) (1994) *177 casos de injusticia y error judicial en el Perú* (Lima: IDL).

IFAD (1991), 'Strategic proposal for rural development in Peru' (Rome: International Fund for Agricultural Development).

Iguíñiz, Javier (1996) 'Para crear empleo productivo', *El Dominical* (supplement of *El Comercio*), 22 December.

Iguíñiz, Javier (1997) '¿Banca central: autonomía contra libertad?' *Expectativas*, año 2, no. 2.

IILS (1993) *Reestructuración y regulación institucional del mercado de trabajo en*

América Latina (Geneva: International Institute for Labour Studies).

ILO (1972) *Employment, Incomes and Equality: A Strategy for Increasing Productive Employment in Kenya* (Geneva: International Labour Office).

ILO (1990) *Surveys of Economically Active Population, Employment, Unemployment and Underemployment: An ILO Manual on Concepts and Methods* (Geneva: International Labour Office).

ILO (1994) *El Desafío del Empleo en América Latina y el Caribe* (Santiago, Chile: International Labour Office Regional Office Working Paper No. 7).

ILO (1995) *1995 Labour Overview: Latin America and the Caribbean* (Geneva: International Labour Office).

ILO (1996) *1996 Labour Overview: Latin America and the Caribbean* (Geneva: International Labour Office).

INEI (1992) *Perú: Compendio Estadístico 1991-92* (Lima: Instituto Nacional de Información y Estadísticas).

INEI (1993) *Compendio Estadístico 1992-93* (Lima: Instituto Nacional de Información y Estadísticas).

INEI (1996) *Compendio Estadístico 1995-96* (Lima: Instituto Nacional de Información y Estadísticas).

Infante, R. (1995) *Perú. Adjuste del mercado laboral urbano y sus efectos sociales: evolución y políticas* (Lima: Organización Internacional de Trabajo).

Instituto Cuanto (see Cuanto).

Jiménez, Félix (1996) 'Notas sobre la desindustrialización reciente y la necesidad de una nueva política industrial', *Socialismo y Participación*, no. 74.

Jiménez, Félix (1997) 'Ciclos y determinantes del crecimiento económico: Perú 1950-1996' (Lima: PUCP).

Katz, Jorge and Kosacoff, Bernardo (1997) 'Aprendizaje tecnológico, desarrollo institucional y la macroeconomía de la sustitución de importaciones', Paper presented to the conference 'Economic History of Latin America in the 20th Century', organised by St. Antony's College, Oxford University, at Paipa, Colombia.

Kay, Bruce H. (1996) '"Fujipopulism" and the Liberal State in Peru, 1990-1995', *Journal of Inter-American Studies and World Affairs*, vol. 38, no. 4, pp. 55-98.

Kohn, Richard (1994) 'Out of Control: The Crisis in Civil Military Relations', *The National Interest*, no 36.

Kriesi, Hanspeter, Koopmas, Ruud, Duyvendak, Jan W. and Giugni, Marco (1995) *New Social Movements in Western Europe: A Comparative Analysis* (London: University College London Press).

La Moneda (1996) 'La modernización del estado', año VIII, no. 99.

Lago, R. (1991) 'The Illusion of Pursuing Redistribution through Macropolicy: Peru's Heterodox Experience, 1985-1990', in R. Dornbusch. and S. Edwards (eds.), *The Macroeconomics of Populism in Latin America* (Chicago: University of Chicago Press), pp. 263-330.

Lagos, R.A. (1994) 'Labour Market Flexibility: What Does It Really Mean?', *CEPAL Review*, vol. 54 (December), pp. 81-94.

Lagos, R.A. (1995) *Effects of Extreme De-regulation of the Labour Market: Chile 1974-1990* (Santiago: OIT Equipo Técnico Multidisciplinario, Working Paper No. 17).

Laity, J. (1989) 'The Coca Economy in the upper Huallaga' (Lima: mimeo).

Landa Arroyo, César (1996) 'Límites constitucionales de la ley de amnestía peruana', *Pensamiento Constitucional*, año 3, no 3.

Leach, Barry (1973) *The German General Staff* (New York: Ballantine Books).

Londoño, J.L. (1995) 'Poverty, Inequality and Human Capital Development in Latin America, 1950-2025', in S.J. Burki, S-R. Aiyer and S. Edwards (eds.), *Annual Bank Conference on Development in Latin America 1995* (Washington, D.C.: World Bank Latin American and Caribbean Studies), pp. 129-54.

López, Sinesio (1996) 'Estado y ciudadanía: vuelcos y revuelcos de una relación tormentosa', *Cuestión del Estado*, no. 17.

Lustig, N. (ed.) (1995) *Coping with Austerity: Poverty and Inequality in Latin America* (Washington, D.C.: The Brookings Institution).

MacIsaac, D.J. and Patrinos, H.A. (1995) 'Labour Market Discrimination Against Indigenous People in Peru', *Journal of Development Studies*, vol. 32 (December), pp. 218-33.

Macroconsult S.A (1991) 'La reforma comercial en el Perú después de 1990' (Lima: Macroconsult).

Macroconsult S.A (1992) 'El sector privado: obstáculos a la inversión' (Lima: Macroconsult).

Macroconsult S.A. (1997) 'La política tributaria en los proyectos mineros' (Lima: Macroconsult).

Macroconsult S.A. (various years) *Reporte Económico Mensual.*

Mallon, Florencia (1995) *Peasants and Nation: The Making of Post-Colonial Mexico and Peru* (Berkeley: University of California Press).

Malpica, Carlos (1989) *El poder económico en el Perú,* 2 vols. (Lima: Mosca Azul).

Marcelo, B. (1987) 'Víctimas del Narcotráfico', *Medio Ambiente,* no. 23.

Marshall, A. (1991) *The Impact of Labour Law on Employment Practices: Temporary and Part-Time Employment in Argentina and Peru* (Geneva: International Institute for Labour Studies Discussion Paper DP/38/1991).

Matos Mar, José (1984) *Desborde popular y crisis del estado* (Lima: Instituto de Estudios Peruanos).

Mauceri, P. (1995) 'State Reform, Coalitions and the Neoliberal *Autogolpe* in Peru', *Latin American Research Review,* vol. 30, no. 1, pp. 7-37.

Mauceri, Philip (1996) *State under Siege: Development and Policy Making in Peru* (Boulder: Westview Press).

McAdam, Doug, McCarthy, John and Zald, Mayer (eds.) (1996) *Comparative Perspectives on Social Movements. Political Opportunities, Mobilizing Structures and Cultural Framings* (Cambridge: Cambridge University Press).

Meller, Patricio (1992) *La apertura comercial chilena,* Working Paper No. 189 (Washington, D.C.: Inter-American Development Bank).

Mesa-Lago, C. (1992) 'Protection for the Informal Sector in Latin America and the Caribbean by Social Security or Alternative Means', in V.E. Tokman (ed.), *Beyond Regulation: The Informal Sector in Latin America* (London: Lynne Reinner), pp. 169-206.

Mesa-Lago, C. (1994) *Changing Social Security in Latin America: Towards Alleviating the Social Costs of Economic Reform* (London: Lynne Reinner).

Mesa-Lago, C. (1997) 'Social Welfare Reform in the Context of Economic-Political Liberalization: Latin American Cases', *World Development* (April), pp. 497-517.

Ministerio de Agricultura (1993) *Primer Compendio Estadístico Agrario, 1950-1991* (Lima: Ministerio de Agricultura).

Ministerio de Agricultura (1996) *Segundo Compendio Estadístico Agrario, 1950-1991* (Lima: Ministerio de Agricultura).

282 FUJIMORI'S PERU: THE POLITICAL ECONOMY

Ministerio de Economía y Finanzas (1993) *Programa de Apoyo Social al Perú,* Document presented to Peru's Consultative Group, Paris, 21-22 June.

Moncada, Guillermo and Webb, Richard (eds.) (1996) *¿Cómo Estamos? Análisis de la Encuesta de Niveles de Vida* (Lima: Instituto Cuanto and UNICEF).

Morales, E. (1989) *Cocaine: White Gold Rush in Peru* (Tucson: University of Arizona Press).

Morande, Felipe (1996) 'El Ahorro en Chile: ¿Donde estuvo el acierto?' (Washington, D.C.: Inter-American Development Bank).

Morley, S.A. (1995) *Poverty and Inequality in Latin America: The Impact of Adjustment and Recovery in the 1980s* (Baltimore: Johns Hopkins University Press).

Mujica, Francisco (1994) 'Agricultura y agroindustria', in Beatriz Boza (ed.), *Invirtiendo en el Perú: guía legal de negocios* (Lima: Pacific Press).

Munck, Gerardo (1997) 'Social Movements and Latin America: Conceptual Issues and Empirical Applications', Paper presented to 1997 Latin American Studies Association conference, Guadalajara, Mexico.

Municipalidad Provincial de Huanta y Servicios Educativos Rurales (1997) *Primer Encuentro de Concertación de la Provincia de Huanta: Memoria* (Huanta: Municipalidad Provincial de Huanta).

NACLA (1996) 'Privilege and Power in Fujimori's Peru', *Report on the Americas,* vol. 30 (July/August), pp. 15-43.

NACLA (1997) 'Latin America in the Age of the Billionaires', *Report on the Americas,* vol. 30 (May/June), pp. 19-44.

Naím, Moisés (1994) 'Latin America: the Second Stage of Reform', *Journal of Democracy,* vol. 5, no. 4.

Norton, Roger (1987) 'Agricultural Issues in Structural Adjustment Programmes', FAO Economic and Social Development Paper No. 66 (Rome: FAO).

Núñez, Javier and Reátegui, Rolando (1990) 'La economía cocalera en el Alto Huallaga: impacto económico', unpublished thesis, Universidad del Pacífico, Lima.

Núñez, Javier and Reátegui, Rolando (1995) 'La economía cocalera 1995', Report prepared for Cuanto S.A., Lima, December.

O'Donnell, Guillermo (1994) 'Delegative Democracy', *Journal of Democracy,* vol. 5, no 1.

Obando, Enrique (1991) 'La burocracia antisubversiva', *¿Qué Hacer?,* no 71.

Obando, Enrique (1993) 'Subversion and Antisubversion in Peru, 1980-92: A View from Lima', *Low Intensity Conflict and Law Enforcement,* vol. 2, no. 2.

Obando, Enrique (1994) 'The Power of Peru's Armed Forces', in Joseph Tulchin and Gary Bland (eds.), *Peru in Crisis* (Washington, D.C.: Woodrow Wilson Center).

Okun, Arthus (1975) *Equity and Efficiency: The Big Trade Off* (Washington, DC: Brookings Institution).

Panfichi, Aldo and Sanborn, Cynthia (1995) '"Vino viejo en odres nuevos": democracia y neopopulismo en el Perú', *Márgenes,* no. 13/14.

Panfichi, Aldo and Twanama, Walter (1997) 'Networks and Identities among Urban Poor in Lima', Paper presented to the 1997 Latin American Studies Association conference, Guadalajara, Mexico.

Paredes, C.E. and Sachs, J.D. (eds.) (1991) *Peru's Path to Recovery: A Plan for Economic Stabilization and Growth* (Washington, D.C.: Brookings Institution).

Pasco, Mario (1994) 'Contratos de trabajo', in Beatriz Boza (ed.), *Invirtiendo en el Perú: Guía Legal de Negocios* (Lima: Pacific Press).

Pease, Henry (1990) 'Los primeros pasos del presidente', *Nueva Sociedad*, no. 110.

Peru Reporting (1997) *Agribusiness in Peru: ¿El Despegue de la Agroindustria?* (Lima: Peru Reporting).

Pinzás, T. (1996) 'Political conditions, economic results and the sustainability of the reform process in Peru', in E. Gonzales de Olarte (ed.), *The Peruvian Economy and Structural Adjustment: Past, Present and Future* (Coral Gables: North-South Center Press), pp. 127-46.

Pita, Claudina (1993) 'La reforma tributaria en América Latina en la década de los años 80', Banco Inter-americano de Desarrollo, Serie Documentos de Trabajo 164.

Platt, Tristan (1981) *Estado boliviano y ayllú andino* (Lima: Instituto de Estudios Peruanos).

Portocarrero, Gonzalo (1993) *Mestizaje en el Perú* (Lima: Sur).

Promperú (1996) 'Invertiendo en el Perú: un país libre en crecimiento' (Lima: Promperú).

Promperú (1997) 'Perú, país en marcha: oportunidades de inversión' (Lima: Promperú).

Psacharopoulos, G., Morley, S., Fiszbein, A., Lee, H. and Wood, B. (1997) *Poverty and Income Distribution in Latin America: The Story of the 1980s* (Washington, D.C.: World Bank Technical Paper No. 351).

Quijano, Aníbal (1995) 'El Fujimorismo y el Perú', *La República*, 13 March.

Radano, Alberto (1994) 'Factores críticos para el éxito de una administración tributaria', Instituto de Administración Tributaria-SUNAT, Documentos de Trabajo No. 1.

Rivera Paz, Carlos (1997) *La reforma del poder judicial en el Perú* (Lima: mimeo).

Roberts, Kenneth (1995) 'Neoliberalism and the Transformation of Populism in Latin America: the Peruvian Case', *World Politics*, vol. 48, no 1.

Rochabrún, Guillermo (1996) 'Deciphering the Enigmas of Alberto Fujimori', *NACLA Report on the Americas*, vol. XXX, no. 1.

Rojas, Jorge (1994) 'La reforma del sistema financiero peruano, 1990-1995', *Economía*, vol. XVII, nos. 33-34.

Rojas, Jorge and Vilcapoma, Leopoldo (1996) 'Algunas características importantes de la nueva banca peruana: un estudio preliminar', Documentos de Trabajo No. 124, PUCP, March.

Rojas-Suárez, Liliana and Weisbrod, Steven (1995) 'Achieving Stability in Latin American Financial Markets in the Presence of Volatile Capital Flows', IDB Working Papers, Series 304 (Washington, D.C.: Inter-American Development Bank).

Rospigliosi, Fernando (1988) 'Perú: entre el acuerdo y la libanización', *Pensamiento Iberoamericano*, no. 14.

Sagasti, Francisco and Guerra-García, Gustavo (1997) 'La modernización del poder ejecutivo: problemas y posibilidades', Paper delivered at a round table entitled 'La reforma del poder ejecutivo' in CEDEP, Lima, 7 May.

Sagasti, Francisco and others (1994) *Democracia y buen gobierno: informe final del proyecto Agenda Perú* (Lima: Apoyo S.A.).

Salazar, A. (1990) 'Análisis económico de cultivos alternativos a la coca en la región Alto Huallaga', Report for UNDP Project AD/PER/86/459, Lima.

Schemo, D. (1997) 'Peru's Stark Poverty Dulls Fujimori's Gleam', *New York Times*, 10 June 1997, p. A12.

Schuldt, Jurgen (1994) 'La enfermedad holandesa y otros virus de la economía peruana', Universidad del Pacífico, Documento de Trabajo No. 20.

Schuldt, Jurgen (1995) *Repensando el desarrollo: hacia una concepción alternativa para los países andinos* (Quito: Centro Andino de Acción Popular (CAAP)).

Schydlowsky, Daniel and Schuldt, Jurgen (1996) *Modelo económico de fin de siglo: alcances y límites* (Lima: Fundación Friedrich Ebert).

Segura, Alonso (1995) 'Efectos de la reforma financiera sobre la banca en el Perú' (Lima: GRADE).

Seminario, Bruno (1995) *Reformas estructurales y política de estabilización* (Lima: CIUP-Consorcio de Investigación Económica).

Seminario, Bruno (1997) *Efectos macroeconómicos de la reforma previsional* (Lima: Superintendencia de AFP).

Shapiro, Carl and Stiglitz, Joseph (1984) 'Equilibrium Unemployment as a Worker Discipline Device', *American Economic Review*, vol. 74, no. 3.

Sikkink, Kathryn (1991) *Ideas and Institutions* (Ithaca: Cornell University Press).

Smethurst, Richard (1974) *A Social Basis for Pre-war Japanese Militarism* (Berkeley: University of California Press).

Sociedad Nacional de Industrias (Comité Textil) (1996) 'Encuesta a empresas textiles' (Lima: SNI).

Sociedad Nacional de Minería y Petroleo (1995) 'Peru: Mining, Oil and Energy 1995' (Lima: SNMP).

Solow, Robert (1990) *The Labour Market as a Social Institution* (Cambridge, Mass: Basil Blackwell).

Stiglitz, Joseph and Weiss, Andrew (1981) 'Credit Rationing in Markets with Imperfect Information', *American Economic Review*, vol. 71, no. 3.

Sulmont, David (1997) 'Ciudadanía y estrategias políticas en la sociedad peruana. Algunas reflexiones', Paper given to the first interdisciplinary seminar on political studies (Lima: PUCP).

SUNAD (1997) *Boletín Estadístico de Comercio Exterior*, March.

SUNAT – National Superintendency of Tax Administration (1993) 'La gestión de una administración tributaria con mayor autonomía', Document presented to the 27 Asamblea del Centro Interamericano de Administradores Tributarios, 19-23 April, Santiago de Chile.

SUNAT– National Superintendency of Tax Administration (1994) *Memoria 1994 de la Unidad de Clausura y Sanción* (Lima: SUNAT)

Superintendencia de Banca y Seguros (various years) *Memorias* (Lima).

Tamayo León, Giulia and Vásquez, Roxana (1989) *Violencia y legalidad* (Lima: no publisher stated).

Tamkog, Metin (1976) *The Warrior Diplomats, Guardians of the National Security and Modernization of Turkey* (Salt Lake City: University of Utah Press).

Tanaka, Martín (1994) 'Individuo y racionalidad en el análisis de los movimientos sociales y la participación política en América Latina', *Estudios Sociológicos*, vol. XII, no 36.

Tanaka, Martín (1995) 'Jóvenes, actores sociales y cambio generacional: de la acción colectiva al protagonismo individual', in Julio Cotler (ed.), *Perú 1964-1994: economía, sociedad y política* (Lima: Instituto de Estudios Peruanos).

Tandon, P. (1994) 'Mexico', in A. Galal. and M. Shirley (eds.), *Does Privatization Deliver? Highlights from a World Bank Conference* (Washington, D.C.: The World Bank), pp. 59-74.

Tapía, Carlos (1996) *Las fuerzas armadas y Sendero Luminoso. Dos estrategias y un final* (Lima: Instituto de Estudios Peruanos).

Tarrow, Sidney (1996) 'Social Movements in Contentious Politics: A Review Article', *American Political Science Review*, vol. 90, no 4.

Tavara, Gerardo (1997) 'Abriendo puertas. Concertación or el desarrollo de Huanta', *Andenes*, no. 97.

Tavara, José (1994) 'La política industrial 1990-93: diagnóstico y opciones', *Pretextos*, no 1, April.

Taylor, Lance and Ganuza, Enrique (eds.) (forthcoming) *Políticas macroeconómicas y pobreza en América latina* (Mexico: Fondo de Cultura Económica).

Thomas, Hugh (1961) *The Spanish Civil War* (New York: Harper).

Thomas, J.J. (1995) *Surviving in the City: The Urban Informal Sector in Latin America* (London: Pluto Press).

Thomas, J.J. (1996) 'The New Economic Model and Labour Markets in Latin America', in V. Bulmer-Thomas (ed.), *The New Economic Model in Latin America and its Impact on Income Distribution and Poverty* (Basingstoke: Macmillan), pp. 79-102.

Thorndike, Guillermo (1969) *El año de la barbarie: Perú 1932* (Lima: Mosca Azul).

Thorp, Rosemary (1996) 'The Reform of the Tax Administration in Peru', in Antonia Silva (ed.), *Implementing Policy Innovations in Latin America* (Washington D.C.: Social Agenda Policy Group, Inter-American Development Bank) , pp. 34-51.

Thorp, Rosemary and Bertram, Geoffrey (1978) *Perú 1890-1977: Growth and Policy in an Open Economy* (London: Macmillan).

Thoumi, Francisco (ed.) (1997) *Drogas ilegales y sociedad en Colombia* (Bogotá: El Planeta).

Tokman, V.E. (ed.) (1992) *Beyond Regulation: The Informal Sector in Latin America* (London: Lynne Reinner).

Tokman, V.E. and Klein, E. (1996) *Regulation and the Informal Economy: Microenterprises in Chile, Ecuador and Jamaica* (London: Lynne Rienner).

Touraine, Alain (1989) *América Latina: política y sociedad* (Madrid: Espasa-Calpe).

Trazegnies Granda, Fernando de (1996) 'Reformando el poder judicial: balance de situación', in Fernando de Trazegnies Granda, *Reflexiones sobre la sociedad civil y el poder judicial* (Lima: ARA editores), pp. 81-94.

Tuesta Soldevilla, Fernando (1994) *Perú Político en Cifras* (Lima: Fundación Friedrich Ebert).

Tulchin, J.S. and Bland, G. (eds.) (1994) *Peru in Crisis: Dictatorship or Democracy?* (Boulder: Lynne Rienner).

UN (1995) *The World's Women 1995: Trends and Statistics* (New York: United Nations).

UN (1996) *Economic Survey of Latin America and the Caribbean, 1995-1996* (New York: United Nations).

UNDCP/PNUFID (1994) *Actividades en el Perú* (Lima: UNDCP).

Uribe, S. and Mestre, S. (1997) 'Los cultivos ilícitos en Colombia: Evaluación, extensión, técnica y tecnologías para la producción y rendimientos y magnitud de la industria', in F. Thoumi (ed.), *Drogas ilegales y sociedad en Colombia* (Bogotá: El Planeta).

Urrutia, Jaime (1996) 'Relaciones laborales, empleo agrícola y sociedad rural en Cajamarca', *Debate Agrario*, no. 24, pp. 93-114.

US Department of Labor (1992) *The Informal Sector and Worker Rights* (Washington, D.C.: US Department of Labor, Bureau of International Labor Affairs).

USAID (US Agency for International Development) (1995a) *Alternative Development Project 527-0348 (30 June)* (Lima: USAID).

USAID (US Agency for International Development) (1995b) *Alternative Development Project 527-0348 (10 April)* (Lima: USAID).

Valverde, L. (1997) 'Los límites del método', *Coyuntura Laboral* (July), pp. 2-4.

Van der Hoeven, R. and Stewart, F. (1993) *Social Development during Periods of Structural Adjustment in Latin America* (Geneva: International Labour Organisation Interdepartmental Project on Structural Adjustment Occasional Paper No. 18).

Van der Hoeven, R. and Sziraczki, G. (1997) *Lessons from Privatization: Labour Issues in Developing and Transitional Countries* (Geneva: International Labour Organisation).

Varillas, Alberto (1994) 'Legislación laboral', in Beatriz Boza (ed.), *Invirtiendo en el Perú: guía legal de negocios.* (Lima: Pacific Press).

Vázquez Villanueva, Absalon (1993) *Los desafíos del agro en la década del noventa* (Lima: Ministerio de Agricultura).

Verdera, F. (1993) 'Empleo asalariado temporal y a tiempo parcial en Lima Metropolitana entre 1984 y 1989', in IILS, *Reestructuración y regulación institucional del mercado de trabajo en América Latina* (Geneva: International Institute for Labour Studies), pp. 232-74.

Verdera, F. (1996), 'Evaluación de la reforma laboral Peruana, 1990-1995', Consorcio de Investigación Económica, *Boletín de Opinión* (June), pp. 3-10.

Villanueva, Víctor (1977) *Así cayó Leguía* (Lima: Retama Editorial).

Webb, Richard (1977) *Government Policy and the Distribution of Income in Peru* (Cambridge Mass: Harvard University Press).

Webb, Richard and Fernández Baca, G. (1991) *Perú en Números 1991: Anuario Estadístico* (Lima: Cuanto).

Webb, Richard and Fernández Baca, G. (1992) *Perú en Números 1992: Anuario Estadístico* (Lima: Cuanto).

Webb, Richard and Fernández Baca, G. (1996) *Perú en Números 1996: Anuario Estadístico* (Lima: Cuanto).

Webb, Richard and Figueroa, Adolfo (1975) *Distribución del ingreso en el Perú* (Lima: Instituto de Estudios Peruanos).

Wise, Carol (1994) 'The Politics of Peruvian Economic Reform: Overcoming the Legacies of State-led Development', *Journal of Interamerican Studies and World Affairs*, vol. 36, no. 1.

Woodhouse, C.M. and Montague, Christopher (1985) *The Rise and Fall of the Greek Colonels* (London: Granada).

World Bank (1991) 'Lessons of Tax Reform' (Washington D.C.: World Bank).

World Bank (1993) *Latin America and the Caribbean: A Decade after the Debt Crisis* (Washington, D.C.: World Bank).

World Bank (1995) *World Tables* (Baltimore and London: Johns Hopkins University Press).

World Bank (1995a) *World Development Report 1995: Workers in an Integrating*

World (Washington, D.C.: World Bank).

World Bank (1995b) *Regional Perspectives on World Development Report 1995: Labor and Economic Reforms in Latin America and the Caribbean* (Washington, D.C.: World Bank)

Yépez de Castillo, I. (1993) 'Sindicalismo y precarización del empleo en el Perú', in IILS, *Reestructuración y regulación institucional del mercado de trabajo en América Latina* (Geneva: International Institute for Labour Studies), pp. 275-301.

Zolezzi, Armando (1996) 'Política tributaria: de tumbo en tumbo', *La Moneda*, vol. VIII, no. 98 (Aug.), p. 48.

Zuvekas Jr., C. (1997) 'Latin America's struggle for equitable economic adjustment', *Latin American Research Review*, vol. 32, no. 2, pp. 152-69.

Index